Mathematical Foundations
of Computer Networking

The Addison-Wesley
Professional Computing Series

♦ Addison-Wesley

Visit informit.com/series/professionalcomputing
for a complete list of available publications.

The Addison-Wesley Professional Computing Series was created in 1990 to provide serious programmers and networking professionals with well-written and practical reference books. There are few places to turn for accurate and authoritative books on current and cutting-edge technology. We hope that our books will help you understand the state of the art in programming languages, operating systems, and networks.

Consulting Editor Brian W. Kernighan

Make sure to connect with us!
informit.com/socialconnect

Mathematical Foundations of Computer Networking

Srinivasan Keshav

♦♦ Addison-Wesley

Upper Saddle River, NJ • Boston • Indianapolis • San Francisco
New York • Toronto • Montreal • London • Munich • Paris • Madrid
Capetown • Sydney • Tokyo • Singapore • Mexico City

Many of the designations used by manufacturers and sellers to distinguish their products are claimed as trademarks. Where those designations appear in this book, and the publisher was aware of a trademark claim, the designations have been printed with initial capital letters or in all capitals.

The author and publisher have taken care in the preparation of this book, but make no expressed or implied warranty of any kind and assume no responsibility for errors or omissions. No liability is assumed for incidental or consequential damages in connection with or arising out of the use of the information or programs contained herein.

The publisher offers excellent discounts on this book when ordered in quantity for bulk purchases or special sales, which may include electronic versions and/or custom covers and content particular to your business, training goals, marketing focus, and branding interests. For more information, please contact:

U.S. Corporate and Government Sales
(800) 382-3419
corpsales@pearsontechgroup.com

For sales outside the United States, please contact:

International Sales
international@pearson.com

Visit us on the Web: informit.com/aw

Library of Congress Cataloging-in-Publication Data
Keshav, Srinivasan.
    Mathematical foundations of computer networking / Srinivasan Keshav.
        p. cm.
    Includes index.
    ISBN 978-0-321-79210-5 (pbk. : alk. paper)—ISBN 0-321-79210-6 (pbk. :
alk. paper) 1. Computer networks—Mathematics—Textbooks. I. Title.
    TK5105.5.K484 2012
    004.601'519—dc23
                                                    2011052203

ISBN-13: 978-0-321-79210-5
ISBN-10:   0-321-79210-6
This product is printed digitally on demand.

First printing, April 2012

Editor-in-Chief
Mark L. Taub

Senior Acquisitions Editor
Trina MacDonald

Managing Editor
John Fuller

Full-Service Production Manager
Julie B. Nahil

Copy Editor
Evelyn Pyle

Indexer
Ted Laux

Proofreader
Linda Begley

Technical Reviewers
Alan Kaplan
Abraham Matta
Johnny Wong

Publishing Coordinator
Olivia Basegio

Compositor
Rob Mauhar

Contents

Preface

Motivation

Graduate students, researchers, and professionals in the field of computer networking often require a firm conceptual understanding of its theoretical foundations. Knowledge of optimization, information theory, game theory, control theory, and queueing theory is assumed by research papers in the field. Yet these subjects are not taught in a typical computer science undergraduate curriculum. This leaves only two alternatives: to either study these topics on one's own from standard texts or take a remedial course. Neither alternative is attractive. Standard texts pay little attention to computer networking in their choice of problem areas, making it a challenge to map from the text to the problem at hand, and it is inefficient to require students to take an entire course when all that is needed is an introduction to the topic.

This book addresses these problems by providing a single source to learn about the mathematical foundations of computer networking. Assuming only a rudimentary grasp of calculus, the book provides an intuitive yet rigorous introduction to a wide range of mathematical topics. The topics are covered in sufficient detail so that the book will usually serve as both the first and ultimate reference. Note that the topics are selected to be *complementary* to those found in a typical undergraduate computer science curriculum. The book, therefore, does not cover network foundations, such as discrete mathematics, combinatorics, or graph theory.

Each concept in the book is described in four ways: intuitively, using precise mathematical notation, providing a carefully chosen numerical example, and offering a numerical exercise to be done by the reader. This progression is designed to gradually deepen understanding. Nevertheless, the depth of coverage provided here is not a substitute for that found in standard textbooks. Rather, I hope to provide enough intuition to allow a student to grasp the essence of a research paper that uses these theoretical foundations.

Organization

The chapters in this book fall into two broad categories: foundations and theories. The first five chapters are foundational, covering probability, statistics, linear algebra, optimization, and signals, systems, and transforms. These chapters provide the basis for the four theories covered in the latter half of the book: queueing theory, game theory, control theory, and information theory. Each chapter is written to be as self-contained as possible. Nevertheless, some dependencies do exist, as shown in Figure P.1, where dashed arrows show weak dependencies and solid arrows show strong dependencies.

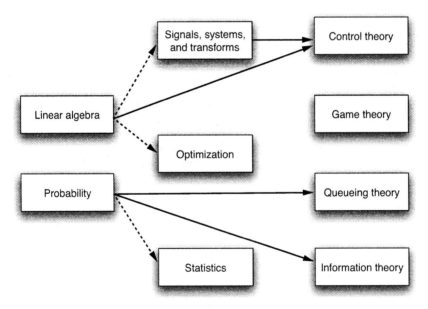

Figure P.1 Chapter organization

Using This Book

The material in this book can be completely covered in a sequence of two graduate courses, with the first course focusing on the first five chapters and the second course on the latter four. For a single-semester course, some possible alternatives are to cover

- Probability, statistics, queueing theory, and information theory
- Linear algebra; signals, systems, and transforms; control theory; and game theory
- Linear algebra; signals, systems, and transforms; control theory; selected portions of probability; and information theory
- Linear algebra; optimization, probability, queueing theory, and information theory

This book is designed for self-study. Each chapter has numerous solved examples and exercises to reinforce concepts. My aim is to ensure that every topic in the book is accessible to the perservering reader.

Acknowledgments

I have benefited immensely from the comments of dedicated reviewers on drafts of this book. Two reviewers in particular who stand out are Alan Kaplan, whose careful and copious comments improved every aspect of the book, and Johnny Wong, who not only reviewed multiple drafts of the chapters on probability and statistics but also used a draft to teach two graduate courses at the University of Waterloo.

I would also like to acknowledge the support I received from experts who reviewed individual chapters: Augustin Chaintreau, Columbia (probability and queueing theory); Tom Coleman, Waterloo (optimization); George Labahn, Waterloo (linear algebra); Kate Larson, Waterloo (game theory); Abraham Matta, Boston University (statistics; signals, systems, and transforms; and control theory); Sriram Narasimhan, Waterloo (control theory); and David Tse, UC Berkeley (information theory).

I received many corrections from my University of Waterloo students who took two courses based on book drafts in Fall 2008 and Fall 2011: Andrew Arnold, Nasser Barjesteh, Omar Beg, Abhirup Chakraborty, Betty Chang, Leila Chenaei, Francisco Claude, Andy Curtis, Hossein Falaki, Leong Fong, Bo Hu, Tian Jiang, Milad Khalki, Robin Kothari, Alexander Laplante, Constantine Murenin, Earl Oliver, Sukanta Pramanik, Ali Rajabi, Aaditeshwar Seth, Jakub Schmidtke, Kanwaljit Singh, Kellen Steffen, Chan Tang, Alan Tsang, Navid Vafaei, and Yuke Yang.

I would like to thank the staff of Addison-Wesley responsible for publishing this book, especially my editor, Trina MacDonald, and production editor, Julie Nahil.

Last but not the least, I would never have completed this book were it not for the unstinting support and encouragement from every member of my family—in particular, my wife, Nicole, and my daughters, Maya and Leela—for the last five years. Thank you.

—S. Keshav
Waterloo, February 2012

1

Probability

1.1 Introduction

The concept of probability pervades every aspect of our lives. Weather forecasts are couched in probabilistic terms, as are economic predictions and even outcomes of our own personal decisions. Designers and operators of computer networks need to often think probabilistically, for instance, when anticipating future traffic workloads or computing cache hit rates. From a mathematical standpoint, a good grasp of probability is a necessary foundation to understanding statistics, game theory, and information theory. For these reasons, the first step in our excursion into the mathematical foundations of computer networking is to study the concepts and theorems of probability.

This chapter is a self-contained introduction to the theory of probability. We begin by introducing the elementary concepts of outcomes, events, and sample spaces, which allows us to precisely define the conjunctions and disjunctions of events. We then discuss concepts of conditional probability and Bayes's rule. This is followed by a description of discrete and continuous random variables, expectations and other moments of a random variable, and the moment generating function. We discuss some standard discrete and continuous distributions and conclude with some useful theorems of probability and a description of Bayesian networks.

Note that in this chapter, as in the rest of the book, the solved examples are an essential part of the text. They provide a concrete grounding for otherwise abstract concepts and are necessary to understand the material that follows.

1.1.1 Outcomes

The mathematical theory of probability uses terms such as *outcome* and *event* with meanings that differ from those in common practice. Therefore, we first introduce a standard set of terms to precisely discuss probabilistic processes. These terms are shown in boldface. We will use the same convention to introduce other mathematical terms in the rest of the book.

Probability measures the degree of uncertainty about the potential **outcomes** of a **process**. Given a set of **distinct** and **mutually exclusive** outcomes of a process, denoted $\{o_1, o_2, \ldots\}$, called the **sample space S**, the probability of any outcome, denoted $P(o_i)$, is a real number between 0 and 1, where 1 means that the outcome will surely occur, 0 means that it surely will not occur, and intermediate values reflect the degree to which one is confident that the outcome will or will not occur.[1] We assume that it is certain that *some* element in S occurs. Hence, the elements of S describe all possible outcomes, and the sum of probability of all the elements of S is always 1.

EXAMPLE 1.1: SAMPLE SPACE AND OUTCOMES

Imagine rolling a six-faced die numbered 1 through 6. The process is that of rolling a die, and an outcome is the number shown on the upper horizontal face when the die comes to rest. Note that the outcomes are distinct and mutually exclusive because there can be only one upper horizontal face corresponding to each throw.

The sample space is $S = \{1, 2, 3, 4, 5, 6\}$, which has a size $|S| = 6$. If the die is fair, each outcome is equally likely, and the probability of each outcome is $\frac{1}{|S|} = \frac{1}{6}$.

EXAMPLE 1.2: INFINITE SAMPLE SPACE AND ZERO PROBABILITY

Imagine throwing a dart at random onto a dartboard of unit radius. The process is that of throwing a dart, and the outcome is the point where the dart penetrates the dartboard. We will assume that this point is vanishingly small, so that it can be thought of as a point on a two-dimensional real plane. Then, the outcomes are distinct and mutually exclusive.

The sample space S is the infinite set of points that lie within a unit circle in the real plane. If the dart is thrown truly randomly, every outcome is equally likely; because the outcomes are infinite, every outcome has a **probability of zero**. We need special care in dealing with such outcomes. It turns

---

1. Strictly speaking, S must be a measurable σ field.

out that, in some cases, it is necessary to interpret the probability of the occurrence of such an event as being vanishingly small rather than exactly zero. We consider this situation in greater detail in Section 1.1.5. Note that although the probability of any particular outcome is zero, the probability associated with any *subset* of the unit circle with area a is given by $\frac{a}{\pi}$, which tends to zero as a tends to zero.

1.1.2 Events

The definition of probability naturally extends to any subset of elements of S, which we call an **event**, denoted E. If the sample space is discrete, every event E is an element of the power set of S, which is the set of all possible subsets of S. The probability associated with an event, denoted $P(E)$, is a real number $0 \leq P(E) \leq 1$ and is the sum of the probabilities associated with the outcomes in the event.

EXAMPLE 1.3: EVENTS

Continuing with Example 1.1, we can define the event "the roll of a die results in an odd-numbered outcome." This corresponds to the set of outcomes $\{1,3,5\}$, which has a probability of $\frac{1}{6} + \frac{1}{6} + \frac{1}{6} = \frac{1}{2}$. We write $P(\{1,3,5\}) = 0.5$.

1.1.3 Disjunctions and Conjunctions of Events

Consider an event E that is considered to have occurred if either or both of two other events E_1 or E_2 occur, where both events are defined in the same sample space. Then, E is said to be the **disjunction**, or logical OR, of the two events denoted $E = E_1 \vee E_2$ and read "E_1 or E_2."

EXAMPLE 1.4: DISJUNCTION OF EVENTS

Continuing with Example 1.1, we define the events E_1 = "the roll of a die results in an odd-numbered outcome" and E_2 = "the roll of a die results in an outcome numbered less than 3." Then, $E_1 = \{1, 3, 5\}$ and $E_2 = \{1, 2\}$ and $E = E_1 \vee E_2 = \{1, 2, 3, 5\}$.

In contrast, consider event E that is considered to have occurred only if *both* of two other events E_1 or E_2 occur, where both are in the same sample space. Then, E

is said to be the **conjunction**, or logical AND, of the two events denoted $E = E_1 \wedge E_2$ and read "E_1 and E_2." When the context is clear, we abbreviate this to $E = E_1 E_2$.

EXAMPLE 1.5: CONJUNCTION OF EVENTS

Continuing with Example 1.4, $E = E_1 \wedge E_2 = E_1 E_2 = \{1\}$.

Two events E_i and E_j in S are **mutually exclusive** if only one of the two may occur simultaneously. Because the events have no outcomes in common, $P(E_i \wedge E_j) = P(\{\ \}) = 0$. Note that outcomes are *always* mutually exclusive, but events need not be so.

1.1.4 Axioms of Probability

One of the breakthroughs in modern mathematics was the realization that the theory of probability can be derived from just a handful of intuitively obvious axioms. Several variants of the axioms of probability are known. We present the three axioms as stated by Kolmogorov to emphasize the simplicity and elegance that lie at the heart of probability theory.

1. $0 \leq P(E) \leq 1$; that is, the probability of an event lies between 0 and 1.
2. $P(S) = 1$, that is, it is certain that at least some event in S will occur.
3. Given a potentially infinite set of *mutually exclusive* events $E_1, E_2,...$

$$P\left(\bigcup_{i=1}^{\infty} E_i\right) = \sum_{i=1}^{\infty} P(E_i) \tag{EQ 1.1}$$

That is, the probability that any *one* of the events in the set of mutually exclusive events occurs is the sum of their individual probabilities. For any finite set of n mutually exclusive events, we can state the axiom equivalently as

$$P\left(\bigcup_{i=1}^{n} E_i\right) = \sum_{i=1}^{n} P(E_i) \tag{EQ 1.2}$$

An alternative form of axiom 3 is:

$$P(E_1 \vee E_2) = P(E_1) + P(E_2) - P(E_1 \wedge E_2) \tag{EQ 1.3}$$

This alternative form applies to non–mutually exclusive events.

EXAMPLE 1.6: PROBABILITY OF UNION OF MUTUALLY EXCLUSIVE EVENTS

Continuing with Example 1.1, we define the mutually exclusive events {1, 2} and {3, 4}, which both have a probability of 1/3. Then, $P(\{1, 2\} \cup \{3, 4\}) = P(\{1, 2\}) + P(\{3, 4\}) = \frac{1}{3} + \frac{1}{3} = \frac{2}{3}$.

EXAMPLE 1.7: PROBABILITY OF UNION OF NON–MUTUALLY EXCLUSIVE EVENTS

Continuing with Example 1.1, we define the non–mutually exclusive events {1, 2} and {2, 3}, which both have a probability of 1/3. Then, $P(\{1, 2\} \cup \{2, 3\}) = P(\{1, 2\}) + P(\{2, 3\}) - P(\{1, 2\} \wedge \{2, 3\}) = \frac{1}{3} + \frac{1}{3} - P(\{2\}) = \frac{2}{3} - \frac{1}{6} = \frac{1}{2}$.

1.1.5 Subjective and Objective Probability

The axiomatic approach is indifferent as to *how* the probability of an event is determined. It turns out that there are two distinct ways in which to determine the probability of an event. In some cases, the probability of an event can be derived from counting arguments. For instance, given the roll of a fair die, we know that only six outcomes are possible and that all outcomes are equally likely, so that the probability of rolling, say, a 1, is 1/6. This is called its **objective** probability. Another way of computing objective probabilities is to define the probability of an event as being the limit of a counting process, as the next example shows.

EXAMPLE 1.8: PROBABILITY AS A LIMIT

Consider a measurement device that measures the packet header types of every packet that crosses a link. Suppose that during the course of a day, the device samples 1,000,000 packets, of which 450,000 are UDP packets, 500,000 are TCP packets, and the rest are from other transport protocols. Given the large number of underlying observations, to a first approximation, we can consider the probability that a randomly selected packet uses the UDP protocol to be 450,000/1,000,000 = 0.45. More precisely, we state

$$P(UDP) = \lim_{t \to \infty} (UDPCount(t))/(TotalPacketCoun(t)),$$

where *UDPCount(t)* is the number of UDP packets seen during a measurement interval of duration t, and *TotalPacketCount(t)* is the total number of packets seen during the same measurement interval. Similarly, $P(TCP) = 0.5$.

Note that in reality, the mathematical limit cannot be achieved, because no packet trace is infinite. Worse, over the course of a week or a month, the underlying workload could change, so that the limit may not even exist. Therefore, in practice, we are forced to choose "sufficiently large" packet counts and hope that the ratio thus computed corresponds to a probability. This approach is also called the **frequentist** approach to probability.

In contrast to an objective assessment of probability, we can also use probabilities to characterize events **subjectively**.

EXAMPLE 1.9: SUBJECTIVE PROBABILITY AND ITS MEASUREMENT

Consider a horse race in which a favored horse is likely to win, but this is by no means assured. We can associate a subjective probability with the event, say, 0.8. Similarly, a doctor may look at a patient's symptoms and associate them with a 0.25 probability of a particular disease. Intuitively, this measures the degree of confidence that an event will occur, based on expert knowledge of the situation that is not (or cannot be) formally stated.

How is subjective probability to be determined? A common approach is to measure the odds that a knowledgeable person would bet on that event. Continuing with the example, a bettor who really thought that the favorite would win with a probability of 0.8, should be willing to bet $1 under the terms: If the horse wins, the bettor gets $1.25; if the horse loses, the bettor gets $0. With this bet, the bettor expects to not lose money; if the reward is greater than $1.25, the bettor will expect to make money. We can elicit the implicit subjective probability by offering a high reward and then lowering it until the bettor is just about to walk away, which would be at the $1.25 mark.

The subjective and frequentist approaches interpret zero-probability events differently. Consider an infinite sequence of successive events. Any event that occurs only a finite number of times in this infinite sequence will have a frequency that can be made arbitrarily small. In number theory, we do not and cannot differentiate between a number that can be made arbitrarily small and zero. So, from this perspective, such an event can be considered to have a probability of occurrence of zero *even though it may occur a finite number of times* in the sequence.

From a subjective perspective, a zero-probability event is defined as an event E such that a rational person would be willing to bet an arbitrarily large but finite amount that E will not occur. More concretely, suppose that this person were to receive a reward of $1 if E did not occur but would have to forfeit a sum of F if E occurred. Then, the bet would be taken for any finite value of F.

1.2 Joint and Conditional Probability

Thus far, we have defined the terms used in studying probability and considered single events in isolation. Having set this foundation, we now turn our attention to the interesting issues that arise when studying **sequences of events**. In doing so, it is very important to keep track of the sample space in which the events are defined: A common mistake is to ignore the fact that two events in a sequence may be defined on different sample spaces.

1.2.1 Joint Probability

Consider two processes with sample spaces S_1 and S_2 that occur one after the other. The two processes can be viewed as a single **joint process** whose outcomes are the tuples chosen from the **product space** $S_1 \times S_2$. We refer to the subsets of the product space as **joint events**. Just as before, we can associate probabilities with outcomes and events in the product space. To keep things straight, in this section, we denote the sample space associated with a probability as a subscript, so that $P_{S_1}(E)$ denotes the probability of event E defined over sample space S_1, and $P_{S_1 \times S_2}(E)$ is an event defined over the product space $S_1 \times S_2$.

EXAMPLE 1.10: JOINT PROCESS AND JOINT EVENTS

Consider sample space $S_1 = \{1, 2, 3\}$ and sample space $S_2 = \{a, b, c\}$. Then, the product space is given by $\{(1, a), (1, b), (1, c), (2, a), (2, b), (2, c), (3, a), (3, b), (3, c)\}$. If these events are equiprobable, the probability of each tuple is $\frac{1}{9}$. Let $E = \{1, 2\}$ be an event in S_1 and $F = \{b\}$ be an event in S_2. Then, the event EF is given by the tuples $\{(1, b), (2, b)\}$ and has probability $\frac{1}{9} + \frac{1}{9} = \frac{2}{9}$.

We will return to the topic of joint processes in Section 1.8. We now turn our attention to the concept of conditional probability.

1.2.2 Conditional Probability

Common experience tells us that if a sky is sunny, there is no chance of rain in the immediate future but that if the sky is cloudy, it may or may not rain soon. Knowing that the sky is cloudy, therefore, increases the chance that it may rain soon, compared to the situation when it is sunny. How can we formalize this intuition?

To keep things simple, first consider the case when two events E and F share a common sample space S and occur one after the other. Suppose that the probability of E is $P_S(E)$ and the probability of F is $P_S(F)$. Now, suppose that we are informed that event E actually occurred. By definition, the **conditional probability** of the event F conditioned on the occurrence of event E is denoted $P_{S \times S}(F|E)$ (read "the probability of F given E") and computed as

$$P_{S \times S}(F|E) = \frac{P_{S \times S}(E \wedge F)}{P_S(E)} = \frac{P_{S \times S}(EF)}{P_S(E)} \qquad \text{(EQ 1.4)}$$

If knowing that E occurred does not affect the probability of F, E and F are said to be **independent** and

$$P_{S \times S}(EF) = P_S(E)P_S(F)$$

EXAMPLE 1.11: CONDITIONAL PROBABILITY OF EVENTS DRAWN FROM THE SAME SAMPLE SPACE

Consider sample space $S = \{1, 2, 3\}$ and events $E = \{1\}$ and $F = \{3\}$. Let $P_S(E) = 0.5$ and $P_S(F) = 0.25$. Clearly, the space $S \times S = \{(1, 1), (1, 2), ..., (3, 2), (3, 3)\}$. The joint event $EF = \{(1, 3)\}$. Suppose that $P_{S \times S}(EF) = 0.3$. Then,

$$P_{S \times S}(F|E) = \frac{P_{S \times S}(EF)}{P_S(E)} = \frac{0.3}{0.5} = 0.6$$

We interpret this to mean that if event E occurred, the probability that event F occurs is 0.6. This is higher than the probability of F occurring on its own (which is 0.25). Hence, the fact the E occurred improves the chances of F occurring, so the two events are not independent. This is also clear from the fact that $P_{S \times S}(EF) = 0.3 \neq P_S(E)P_S(F) = 0.125$.

The notion of conditional probability generalizes to the case in which events are defined on more than one sample space. Consider a sequence of two processes with sample spaces S_1 and S_2 that occur one after the other. (This could be the condition of the sky now, for instance, and whether it rains after 2 hours.) Let event E be a subset of S_1 and event F a subset of S_2. Suppose that the probability of E is $P_{S_1}(E)$ and the probability of F is $P_{S_2}(F)$. Now, suppose that we are informed that event E occurred. We define the probability $P_{S_1 \times S_2}(F|E)$ as the **conditional probability** of the event F conditional on the occurrence of E as

$$P_{S_1 \times S_2}(F|E) = \frac{P_{S_1 \times S_2}(EF)}{P_{S_1}(E)} \qquad \text{(EQ 1.5)}$$

If knowing that E occurred does not affect the probability of F, E and F are said to be **independent** and

$$P_{S_1 \times S_2}(EF) = P_{S_1}(E) \times P_{S_2}(F) \qquad\qquad \text{(EQ 1.6)}$$

EXAMPLE 1.12: CONDITIONAL PROBABILITY OF EVENTS DRAWN FROM DIFFERENT SAMPLE SPACES

Consider sample space $S_1 = \{1, 2, 3\}$ and sample space $S_2 = \{a, b, c\}$ with product space $\{(1, a), (1, b), (1, c), (2, a), (2, b), (2, c), (3, a), (3, b), (3, c)\}$. Let $E = \{1, 2\}$ be an event in S_1 and $F = \{b\}$ be an event in S_2. Also, let $P_{S_1}(E) = 0.5$, and let $P_{S_1 \times S_2}(EF) = P_{S_1 \times S_2}(\{(1, b), (2, b)\}) = 0.05$.
    If E and F are independent,

$$P_{S_1 \times S_2}(EF) = P_{S_1 \times S_2}(\{(1, b), (2, b)\}) = P_{S_1}(\{1, 2\}) \times P_{S_2}(\{b\})$$

$$0.05 = 0.5 \times P_{S_2}(\{b\})$$

$$P_{S_2}(\{b\}) = 0.1$$

Otherwise,

$$P_{S_1 \times S_2}(F|E) = \frac{P_{S_1 \times S_2}(EF)}{P_{S_1}(E)} = \frac{0.05}{0.5} = 0.1$$

It is important not to confuse $P(F|E)$ and $P(F)$. The conditional probability is defined in the product space $S_1 \times S_2$ and the unconditional probability in the space S_2. Explicitly keeping track of the underlying sample space can help avoid apparent contradictions such as the one discussed in Example 1.14.

EXAMPLE 1.13: USING CONDITIONAL PROBABILITY

Consider a device that samples packets on a link, as in Example 1.8. Suppose that measurements show that 20% of the UDP packets have a packet size of 52 bytes. Let $P(UDP)$ denote the probability that the packet is of type UDP, and let $P(52)$ denote the probability that the packet is of length 52 bytes. Then, $P(52|UDP) = 0.2$. In Example 1.8, we computed that $P(UDP) = 0.45$. Therefore, $P(UDP \text{ AND } 52) = P(52|UDP) * P(UDP) = 0.2 * 0.45 = 0.09$. That is, if we were to pick a packet at random from the sample, there is a 9% chance that it is a UDP packet of length 52 bytes, but it has a 20% chance of being of length 52 bytes if we know already that it is a UDP packet.

EXAMPLE 1.14: THE MONTY HALL PROBLEM

Consider a television show (loosely modeled on a similar show hosted by Monty Hall) in which three identical doors hide two goats and a luxury car. You, the contestant, can pick any door and obtain the prize behind it. Assume that you prefer the car to the goat. If you did not have any further information, your chance of picking the winning door is clearly 1/3. Now, suppose that after you pick one of the doors—say, Door 1—the host opens one of the other doors—say, Door 2—and reveals a goat behind it. Should you switch your choice to Door 3 or stay with Door 1?

Solution:

We can view the Monty Hall problem as a sequence of three processes: (1) the placement of a car behind one of the doors, (2) the selection of a door by the contestant, and (3) the revelation of what lies behind one of the other doors. The sample space for the first process is {Door 1, Door 2, Door 3}, abbreviated {1, 2, 3}, as are the sample spaces for the second and third processes. So, the product space is {(1, 1, 1), (1, 1, 2), (1, 1, 3), (1, 2, 1),..., (3, 3, 3)}.

Without loss of generality, assume that you pick Door 1. The game show host is now forced to pick either Door 2 or Door 3. Without loss of generality, suppose that the host picks Door 2, so that the set of possible outcomes that constitutes the reduced sample space is {(1, 1, 2), (2, 1, 2), (3, 1, 2)}. However, we know that the game show host will never open a door with a car behind it. Therefore, the outcome (2, 1, 2) is not possible. So, the reduced sample space is just the set {(1, 1, 2), (3, 1, 2)}. What are the associated probabilities?

To determine this, note that the initial probability space is {1, 2, 3} with equiprobable outcomes. Therefore, the outcomes {(1, 1, 2), (2, 1, 2), (3, 1, 2)} are also equiprobable. When moving to open Door 2, the game show host reveals private information that the outcome (2, 1, 2) is impossible, so the probability associated with this outcome is 0. The show host's forced move cannot affect the probability of the outcome (1, 1, 2), because the host never had the choice of opening Door 1 once you selected it. Therefore, its probability in the reduced sample space continues to be 1/3. This means that $P(\{(3, 1, 2)\}) = 2/3$, so it doubles your chances for you to switch doors.

One way to understand this somewhat counterintuitive result is to realize that the game show host's actions reveal private information, that is, the location of the car. Two-thirds of the time, the prize is behind the door you did not choose. The host always opens a door that does not have a prize behind it.

Therefore, the residual probability (2/3) must all be assigned to Door 3. Another way to think of it is that if you repeat a large number of experiments with two contestants—one who never switches doors and the other who always switches doors—the latter would win twice as often.

1.2.3 Bayes's Rule

One of the most widely used rules in the theory of probability is due to an English country minister: Thomas Bayes. Its significance is that it allows us to infer "backwards" from effects to causes rather than from causes to effects. The derivation of his rule is straightforward, though its implications are profound.

We begin with the definition of conditional probability (Equation 1.4):

$$P_{S \times S}(F|E) = \frac{P_{S \times S}(EF)}{P_S(E)}$$

If the underlying sample spaces can be assumed to be implicitly known, we can rewrite this as

$$P(EF) = P(F|E)P(E) \qquad \textbf{(EQ 1.7)}$$

We interpret this to mean that the probability that both E and F occur is the product of the probabilities of two events: first, that E occurs; second, that conditional on E, F occurs.

Recall that $P(F|E)$ is defined in terms of the event F following event E. Now, consider the converse: F is known to have occurred. What is the probability that E occurred? This is similar to the problem: If there is fire, there is smoke, but if we see smoke, what is the probability that it was due to a fire? The probability we want is $P(E|F)$. Using the definition of conditional probability, it is given by

$$P(E|F) = \frac{P(EF)}{P(F)} \qquad \textbf{(EQ 1.8)}$$

Substituting for $P(F)$ from Equation 1.7, we get

$$P(E|F) = \frac{P(F|E)}{P(F)}P(E) \qquad \textbf{(EQ 1.9)}$$

which is **Bayes's rule**. One way of interpreting this is that it allows us to compute the degree to which some effect, or **posterior** F, can be attributed to some cause, or **prior** E.

EXAMPLE 1.15: BAYES'S RULE

Continuing with Example 1.13, we want to compute the following quantity: Given that a packet is 52 bytes long, what is the probability that it is a UDP packet?

Solution:

From Bayes's rule:

$$P(UDP|52) = \frac{P(52|UDP)P(UDP)}{P(52)} = \frac{0.2(0.45)}{0.54} = 0.167$$

We can generalize Bayes's rule when a posterior can be attributed to more than one prior. Consider a posterior F that is due to some set of n priors E_i such that the priors are mutually exclusive and exhaustive: That is, at least one of them occurs, and only one of them can occur. This implies that $\sum_{i=1}^{n} P(E_i) = 1$. Then,

$$P(F) = \sum_{i=1}^{n} P(FE_i) = \sum_{i=1}^{n} P(F|E_i)P(E_i) \qquad \text{(EQ 1.10)}$$

This is also called the **law of total probability**.

EXAMPLE 1.16: LAW OF TOTAL PROBABILITY

Continuing with Example 1.13, let us compute $P(52)$, that is, the probability that a packet sampled at random has a length of 52 bytes. To compute this, we need to know the packet sizes for all other traffic types. For instance, if $P(52|TCP) = 0.9$ and all other packets were known to be of length other than 52 bytes, then $P(52) = P(52|UDP) * P(UDP) + P(52|TCP) * P(TCP) + P(52|other) * P(other) = 0.2 * 0.45 + 0.9 * 0.5 + 0 = 0.54$.

The law of total probability allows one further generalization of Bayes's rule to obtain **Bayes's theorem**. From the definition of conditional probability, we have

$$P(E_i|F) = \frac{P(E_iF)}{P(F)}$$

From Equation 1.7, we have

$$P(E_i|F) = \frac{P(F|E_i)P(E_i)}{P(F)}$$

Substituting Equation 1.10, we get

$$P(E_i|F) = \frac{P(F|E_i)P(E_i)}{\left(\sum_{i=1}^{n} P(F|E_i)P(E_i)\right)} \qquad \text{(EQ 1.11)}$$

This is called the **generalized Bayes's rule**, or Bayes's theorem. It allows us to compute the probability of any one of the priors E_i, conditional on the occurrence of the posterior F. This is often interpreted as follows: We have some set of mutually exclusive and exhaustive hypotheses E_i. We conduct an experiment, whose outcome is F. We can then use Bayes's formula to compute the revised estimate for each hypothesis.

EXAMPLE 1.17: BAYES'S THEOREM

Continuing with Example 1.15, consider the following situation: We pick a packet at random from the set of sampled packets and find that its length is *not* 52 bytes. What is the probability that it is a UDP packet?

Solution:

As in Example 1.6, let *UDP* refer to the event that a packet is of type UDP and *52* refer to the event that the packet is of length 52 bytes. Denote the complement of the latter event, that is, that the packet is not of length 52 bytes by 52^c.
From Bayes's rule:

$$P(UDP|52^c) = \frac{P(52^c|UDP)P(UDP)}{P(52^c|UDP)P(UDP) + P(52^c|TCP)P(TCP) + P(52^c|other)P(other)}$$

$$= \frac{0.8(0.45)}{0.8(0.45) + 0.1(0.5) + 1(0.05)}$$

$$= 0.78$$

Thus, if we see a packet that is *not* 52 bytes long, it is quite likely a UDP packet. Intuitively, this must be true because most TCP packets are 52 bytes long, and there aren't very many non-UDP and non-TCP packets.

1.3 Random Variables

So far, we have restricted ourselves to studying events, which are collections of out-comes of experiments or observations. However, we are often interested in abstract quantities or outcomes of experiments that are derived from events and observations but are not themselves events or observations. For example, if we throw a fair die, we may want to compute the probability that the square of the face value is smaller than 10. This is random and can be associated with a probability and, moreover, depends on some underlying random events. Yet, it is neither an event nor an observation: It is a **random variable**. Intuitively, a random variable is a quantity that can assume any one of a set of values, called its **domain D**, and whose value can be stated only probabilistically. In this section, we will study random variables and their distributions.

More formally, a **real random variable**—the one most commonly encountered in applications having to do with computer networking—is a mapping from events in a sample space S to the domain of real numbers. The probability associated with each value assumed by a real random variable[2] is the probability of the underlying event in the sample space, as illustrated in Figure 1.1.

A random variable is **discrete** if the set of values it can assume is finite and countable. The elements of D should be *mutually exclusive*—that is, the random variable cannot simultaneously take on more than one value—and *exhaustive*—the random variable cannot assume a value that is not an element of D.

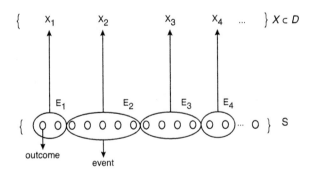

Figure 1.1 The random variable X takes on values from the domain D. Each value taken on by the random variable is associated with a probability corresponding to an event E, which is a subset of outcomes in the sample space S.

---

2. We deal with only real random variables in this text, so at this point will drop the qualifier "real."

EXAMPLE 1.18: A DISCRETE RANDOM VARIABLE

Consider a random variable I defined as the size of an IP packet rounded up to closest kilobyte. Then, I assumes values from the domain $D = \{1,2,3,..., 64\}$. This set is both mutually exclusive and exhaustive. The underlying sample space S is the set of potential packet sizes and is therefore identical to D. The probability associated with each value of I is the probability of seeing an IP packet of that size in some collection of IP packets, such as a measurement trace.

A random variable is **continuous** if the values it can take on are a subset of the real line.

EXAMPLE 1.19: A CONTINUOUS RANDOM VARIABLE

Consider a random variable T defined as the time between consecutive packet arrivals at a port of a switch, also called the packet interarrival time. Although each packet's arrival time is quantized by the receiver's clock, so that the set of interarrival times are finite and countable, given the high clock speeds of modern systems, modeling T as a continuous random variable is a good approximation of reality. The underlying sample space S is the subset of the real line that spans the smallest and largest possible packet interarrival times. As in the previous example, the sample space is identical to the domain of T.

1.3.1 Distribution

In many cases, we are not interested in the actual value taken by a random variable but in the probabilities associated with each such value that it can assume. To make this more precise, consider a discrete random variable X_d that assumes distinct values $D = \{x_1, x_2,..., x_n\}$. We define the value $p(x_i)$ to be the probability of the event that results in X_d assuming the value x_i. The function $p(X_d)$, which characterizes the probability that X_d will take on each value in its domain, is called the **probability mass function** of X_d.[3] It is also sometimes called the **distribution** of X_d.

---

3. Note the subtlety in this standard notation. Recall that $P(E)$ is the probability of an event E. In contrast, $p(X)$ refers to the distribution of a random variable X, and $p(X = x_i) = p(x_i)$ refers to the probability that random variable X takes on the value x_i.

EXAMPLE 1.20: PROBABILITY MASS FUNCTION

Consider a random variable H defined as 0 if fewer than 100 packets are received at a router's port in a particular time interval T and 1 otherwise. The sample space of outcomes consists of all possible numbers of packets that could arrive at the router's port during T, which is simply the set $S = \{1, 2, ..., M\}$, where M is the maximum number of packets that can be received in time T. Assuming that $M > 99$, we define two events $E_0 = \{0, 1, 2, ..., 99\}$ and $E_1 = \{100, 101, ..., M\}$. Given the probability of each outcome in S, we can compute the probability of each event, $P(E_0)$ and $P(E_1)$. By definition, $p(H = 0) = p(0) = P(E_0)$ and $p(H = 1) = p(1) = P(E_1)$. The set $\{p(0), p(1)\}$ is the probability mass function of H. Notice how the probability mass function is closely tied to events in the underlying sample space.

Unlike a discrete random variable, which has nonzero probability of taking on any particular value in its domain, the probability that a continuous real random variable X_c will take on any specific value in its domain is 0. Nevertheless, in nearly all cases of interest in the field of computer networking, we will be able to assume that we can define the **density** function $f(x)$ of X_c as follows: The probability that X_c takes on a value between two reals, x_1 and x_2, $p(x_1 \leq x \leq x_2)$, is given by the integral $\int_{x_1}^{x_2} f(x)dx$. Of course, we need to ensure that $\int_{-\infty}^{\infty} f(x)dx = 1$. Alternatively, we can think of $f(x)$ being implicitly defined by the statement that a variable x chosen randomly in the domain of X_c has probability $f(a)\Delta$ of lying in the range $\left[a - \frac{\Delta}{2}, a + \frac{\Delta}{2}\right]$ when Δ is very small.

EXAMPLE 1.21: DENSITY FUNCTION

Suppose that we know that packet interarrival times are distributed *uniformly* in the range [0.5s, 2.5s]. The corresponding density function is a constant c over the domain. It is easy to see that $c = 0.5$ because we require $\int_{-\infty}^{\infty} f(x)dx = \int_{0.5}^{2.5} cdx = 2c = 1$. The probability that the interarrival time is in the interval $\left[1 - \frac{\Delta}{2}, 1 + \frac{\Delta}{2}\right]$ is therefore 0.5Δ.

1.3.2 Cumulative Density Function

The domain of a discrete real random variable X_d is totally ordered; that is, for any two values x_1 and x_2 in the domain, either $x_1 > x_2$ or $x_2 > x_1$. We define the **cumulative density function** $F(X_d)$ by

$$F(x) = \sum_{i|x_i \leq x} p(x_i) = p(X_d \leq x) \qquad \text{(EQ 1.12)}$$

Note the difference between $F(X_d)$, which denotes the cumulative distribution of random variable X_d, and $F(x)$, which is the value of the cumulative distribution for the value $X_d = x$.

Similarly, the cumulative density function of a continuous random variable X_c, denoted $F(X_c)$, is given by

$$F(x) = \int_{-\infty}^{x} f(y)dy = p(X_c \leq x) \qquad \text{(EQ 1.13)}$$

By definition of probability, in both cases, $0 \leq F(X_d) \leq 1$, $0 \leq F(X_c) \leq 1$.

EXAMPLE 1.22: CUMULATIVE DENSITY FUNCTIONS

Consider a discrete random variable D that can take on values {1, 2, 3, 4, 5} with probabilities {0.2, 0.1, 0.2, 0.2, 0.3}, respectively. The latter set is also the probability mass function of D. Because the domain of D is totally ordered, we compute the cumulative density function $F(D)$ as $F(1) = 0.2$, $F(2) = 0.3$, $F(3) = 0.5$, $F(4) = 0.7$, $F(5) = 1.0$.

Now, consider a continuous random variable C defined by the density function $f(x) = 1$ in the range [0,1]. The cumulative density function $F(C) = \int_{-\infty}^{x} f(y)dy = \int_{-\infty}^{x} dy = y|_0^x = x$. We see that, although, for example, $f(0.1) = 1$, this does not mean that the value 0.1 is certain!

Note that, by definition of cumulative density function, it is necessary that it achieve a value of 1 at right extreme value of the domain.

1.3.3 Generating Values from an Arbitrary Distribution

The cumulative density function $F(X)$, where X is either discrete or continuous, can be used to generate values drawn from the underlying discrete or continuous distribution $p(X_d)$ or $f(X_c)$, as illustrated in Figure 1.2. Consider a discrete random

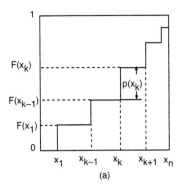
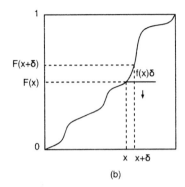

Figure 1.2 Generating values from an arbitrary (a) discrete or (b) continuous distribution

variable X_d that takes on values $x_1, x_2, ..., x_n$ with probabilities $p(x_i)$. By definition, $F(x_k) = F(x_{k-1}) + p(x_k)$. Moreover, $F(X_d)$ always lies in the range [0,1].
Therefore, if we were to generate a random number u with uniform probability in
the range [0,1], the probability that u lies in the range $[F(x_{k-1}), F(x_k)]$ is $p(x_k)$.
Moreover, $x_k = F^{-1}(u)$. Therefore, the procedure to generate values from the discrete distribution $p(X_d)$ is as follows: First, generate a random variable u uniformly
in the range [0,1]; second, compute $x_k = F^{-1}(u)$.

We can use a similar approach to generate values from a continuous random
variable X_c with associated density function $f(X_c)$. By definition, $F(x + \delta) = F(x) +
f(x)\delta$ for very small values of δ. Moreover, $F(X_c)$ always lies in the range [0,1].
Therefore, if we were to generate a random number u with uniform probability in
the range [0,1], the probability that u lies in the range $[F(x), F(x+\delta)]$ is $f(x)\delta$,
which means that $x = F^{-1}(u)$ is distributed according to the desired density function $f(X_c)$. Therefore, the procedure to generate values from the continuous distribution $f(X_c)$ is as follows: First, generate a random variable u uniformly in the range
[0,1]; second, compute $x = F^{-1}(u)$.

1.3.4 Expectation of a Random Variable

The **expectation, mean,** or **expected value** $E[X_d]$ of a discrete random variable
X_d that can take on n values x_i with probability $p(x_i)$ is given by

$$E[X_d] = \sum_{i=1}^{n} x_i p(x_i) \qquad \text{(EQ 1.14)}$$

Similarly, the expectation $E[X_c]$ of a continuous random variable X_c with density
function $f(x)$ is given by

$$E[X_c] = \int_{-\infty}^{\infty} xf(x)dx \qquad \text{(EQ 1.15)}$$

Intuitively, the expected value of a random variable is the value we expect it to take, knowing nothing else about it. For instance, if you knew the distribution of the random variable corresponding to the time it takes for you to travel from your home to work, you expect your commute time on a typical day to be the expected value of this random variable.

EXAMPLE 1.23: EXPECTATION OF A DISCRETE AND A CONTINUOUS RANDOM VARIABLE

Continuing with the random variables C and D defined in Example 1.22, we find

$E[D] = 1*0.2 + 2*0.1 + 3*0.2 + 4*0.2 + 5*0.3 = 0.2 + 0.2 + 0.6 + 0.8 + 1.5 = 3.3$.

Note that the expected value of D is in fact a value it cannot assume! This is often true of discrete random variables. One way to interpret this is that D will take on values close to its expected value: in this case, 3 or 4.
Similarly,

$$E[C] = \int_{-\infty}^{\infty} xf(x)dx = \int_{0}^{1} x dx = \left.\frac{x^2}{2}\right|_{0}^{1} = \frac{1}{2}$$

C is the *uniform* distribution, and its expected value is the midpoint of the domain: 0.5.

The expectation of a random variable gives us a reasonable idea of how it behaves in the long run. It is important to remember, however, that two random variables with the same expectation can have rather different behaviors.
We now state, without proof, four useful properties of expectations.

1. For constants a and b:

$$E[aX + b] = aE[X] + b \qquad \text{(EQ 1.16)}$$

2. $E[X+Y] = E[X] + E[Y]$, or, more generally, for any set of random variables X_i:

$$E\left[\sum_{i=1}^{n} X_i\right] = \sum_{i=1}^{n} E[X_i] \qquad \text{(EQ 1.17)}$$

3. For a discrete random variable X_d with probability mass function $p(x_i)$ and any function $g(.)$:

$$E[g(X_d)] = \sum_i g(x_i)p(x_i) \qquad \text{(EQ 1.18)}$$

4. For a continuous random variable X_c with density function $f(x)$ and any function $g(.)$:

$$E[g(X_c)] = \int_{-\infty}^{\infty} g(x)f(x)dx \qquad \text{(EQ 1.19)}$$

Note that, in general, $E[g(X)]$ is not the same as $g(E[X])$; that is, a function cannot be taken out of the expectation.

EXAMPLE 1.24: EXPECTED VALUE OF A FUNCTION OF A DISCRETE RANDOM VARIABLE

Consider a discrete random variable D that can take on values $\{1, 2, 3, 4, 5\}$ with probabilities $\{0.2, 0.1, 0.2, 0.2, 0.3\}$, respectively. Then, $E[e^D] = 0.2e^1 + 0.1e^2 + 0.2e^3 + 0.2e^4 + 0.3e^5 = 60.74$.

EXAMPLE 1.25: EXPECTED VALUE OF A FUNCTION OF A CONTINUOUS RANDOM VARIABLE

Let X be a random variable that has equal probability of lying anywhere in the interval [0,1]. Then, $f(x) = 1; 0 \leq x \leq 1$. $E[X^2] = \int_0^1 x^2 f(x)dx = \frac{1}{3}x^3\Big|_0^1 = \frac{1}{3}$.

1.3.5 Variance of a Random Variable

The **variance** of a random variable is defined by $V(X) = E[(X - E[X])^2]$. Intuitively, it shows how far away the values taken on by a random variable would be from its expected value. We can express the variance of a random variable in terms of two expectations as $V(X) = E[X^2] - E[X]^2$. For

$$
\begin{aligned}
V[X] &= E[(X - E[X])^2] \\
&= E[X^2 - 2XE[X] + E[X]^2] \\
&= E[X^2] - 2E[XE[X]] + E[X]^2 \\
&= E[X^2] - 2E[X]E[X] + E[X]^2 \\
&= E[X^2] - E[X]^2
\end{aligned}
$$

In practical terms, the distribution of a random variable over its domain D—this domain is also called the **population**—is not usually known. Instead, the best we can do is to sample the values it takes on by observing its behavior over some period of time. We can estimate the variance of the random variable by keeping running counters for $\sum x_i$ and $\sum x_i^2$. Then,

$$V[X] \approx \left(\frac{\sum_i x_i^2 - (\sum x_i)^2}{n} \right),$$

where this approximation improves with n, the size of the sample, as a consequence of the law of large numbers, discussed in Section 1.7.4.

The following properties of the variance of a random variable can be easily shown for both discrete and continuous random variables.

1. For constant a:

$$V[X + a] = V[X] \qquad \text{(EQ 1.20)}$$

2. For constant a:

$$V[aX] = a^2 V[X] \qquad \text{(EQ 1.21)}$$

3. If X and Y are independent random variables:

$$V[X + Y] = V[X] + V[Y] \qquad \text{(EQ 1.22)}$$

1.4 Moments and Moment Generating Functions

Thus far, we have focused on elementary concepts of probability. To get to the next level of understanding, it is necessary to dive into the somewhat complex topic of moment generating functions. The *moments* of a distribution generalize its mean and variance. In this section, we will see how we can use a moment generating function (MGF) to compactly represent *all* the moments of a distribution. The moment generating function is interesting not only because it allows us to prove some useful results, such as the central limit theorem but also because it is similar in form to the Fourier and Laplace transforms, discussed in Chapter 5.

1.4.1 Moments

The **moments** of a distribution are a set of parameters that summarize it. Given a random variable X, its first **moment about the origin**, denoted M_0^1, is defined to be $E[X]$. Its **second moment about the origin**, denoted M_0^2, is defined as the expected value of the random variable X^2, or $E[X^2]$. In general, the rth moment of X about the *origin*, denoted M_0^r, is defined as $M_0^r = E[X^r]$.

We can similarly define the **rth moment about the *mean***, denoted M_μ^r, by $E[(X - \mu)^r]$. Note that the **variance** of the distribution, denoted by σ^2, or $V[X]$, is the same as M_μ^2. The third moment about the mean, M_μ^3, is used to construct a measure of **skewness**, which describes whether the probability mass is more to the left or the right of the mean, compared to a normal distribution. The fourth moment about the mean, M_μ^4, is used to construct a measure of peakedness, or **kurtosis**, which measures the "width" of a distribution.

The two definitions of a moment are related. For example, we have already seen that the variance of X, denoted $V[X]$, can be computed as $V[X] = E[X^2] - (E[X])^2$. Therefore, $M_\mu^2 = M_0^2 - (M_0^1)^2$. Similar relationships can be found between the higher moments by writing out the terms of the binomial expansion of $(X - \mu)^r$.

1.4.2 Moment Generating Functions

Except under some pathological conditions, a distribution can be thought to be uniquely represented by its moments. That is, if two distributions have the same moments, they will be identical except under some rather unusual circumstances. Therefore, it is convenient to have an expression, or "fingerprint," that compactly represents all the moments of a distribution. Such an expression should have terms corresponding to M_0^r for all values of r.

We can get a hint regarding a suitable representation from the expansion of e^x:

$$e^x = 1 + x + \frac{x^2}{2!} + \frac{x^3}{3!} + \dots \qquad \text{(EQ 1.23)}$$

We see that there is one term for each power of x. This suggests the definition of the **moment generating function** of a random variable X as the expected value of e^{tX}, where t is an auxiliary variable:

$$M(t) = E[e^{tX}]. \qquad \text{(EQ 1.24)}$$

To see how this represents the moments of a distribution, we expand $M(t)$ as

$$M(t) = E[e^{tX}] = E\left[1 + (tX) + \left(\frac{t^2 X^2}{2!}\right) + \left(\frac{t^3 X^3}{3!}\right) + \dots\right]$$

$$= 1 + E[tX] + E\left[\frac{t^2 X^2}{2!}\right] + E\left[\frac{t^3 X^3}{3!}\right] + \dots$$

$$\text{(EQ 1.25)}$$

$$= 1 + tE[X] + \frac{t^2}{2!}E[X^2] + \frac{t^3}{3!}E[X^3] + \dots$$

$$= 1 + tM_0^1 + \frac{t^2}{2!}M_0^2 + \frac{t^3}{3!}M_0^3 + \dots$$

Thus, the MGF represents all the moments of the random variable X in a single compact expression. Note that the MGF of a distribution is undefined if one or more of its moments are infinite.

We can extract all the moments of the distribution from the MGF as follows: If we differentiate $M(t)$ once, the only term that is not multiplied by t or a power of t is M_0^1. So, $\dfrac{dM(t)}{dt}\bigg|_{t=0} = M_0^1$. Similarly, $\dfrac{d^2M(t)}{dt^2}\bigg|_{t=0} = M_0^2$. Generalizing, it is easy to show that to get the rth moment of a random variable X about the origin, we need to differentiate only its MGF r times with respect to t and then set t to 0.

It is important to remember that the "true" form of the MGF is the series expansion in Equation 1.25. The exponential is merely a convenient representation that has the property that operations on the series (as a whole) result in corresponding operations being carried out in the compact form. For example, it can be shown that the series resulting from the product of

$$e^x = 1 + x + \frac{x^2}{2!} + \frac{x^3}{3!} + \dots \quad \text{and} \quad e^y = 1 + y + \frac{y^2}{2!} + \frac{y^3}{3!} + \dots \quad \text{is}$$

$$1 + (x+y) + \frac{(x+y)^2}{2!} + \frac{(x+y)^3}{3!} + \dots = e^{x+y}.$$

This simplifies the computation of operations on the series. However, it is sometimes necessary to revert to the series representation for certain operations. In particular, if the compact notation of $M(t)$ is not differentiable at $t = 0$, we must revert to the series to evaluate $M(0)$, as shown next.

EXAMPLE 1.26: MGF OF A STANDARD UNIFORM DISTRIBUTION

Let X be a uniform random variable defined in the interval $[0,1]$. This is also called a **standard uniform distribution**. We would like to find all its moments. We find that $M(t) = E[e^{tX}] = \int_0^1 e^{tx}dx = \frac{1}{t}e^{tx}\bigg|_0^1 = \frac{1}{t}[e^t - 1]$. However, this function is not defined—and therefore not differentiable—at $t = 0$. Instead, we revert to the series:

$$\frac{1}{t}[e^t - 1] = \frac{1}{t}\left[t + \frac{t^2}{2!} + \frac{t^3}{3!} + \dots\right] = 1 + \frac{t}{2!} + \frac{t^2}{3!} + \dots$$

which *is* differentiable term by term. Differentiating r times and setting t to 0, we find that $M_0^r = 1/(r+1)$. So, $M_0^1 = \mu = 1/(1+1) = 1/2$ is the mean, and $M_0^2 = 1/(1+2) = 1/3 = E[X^2]$. Note that we found the expression for $M(t)$ by using the compact notation, but reverted to the series for differentiating it. The justification is that the integral of the compact form is identical to the summation of the integrals of the individual terms.

1.4.3 Properties of Moment Generating Functions

We now prove two useful properties of MGFs.

First, if X and Y are two independent random variables, the MGF of their sum is the product of their MGFs. If their individual MGFs are $M_1(t)$ and $M_2(t)$, respectively, the MGF of their sum is

$$M(t) = E[e^{t(X+Y)}] = E[e^{tX}e^{tY}] = E[e^{tX}]E[e^{tY}] \text{ (from independence)}$$
$$= M_1(t).M_2(t) \qquad \text{(EQ 1.26)}$$

EXAMPLE 1.27: MGF OF THE SUM

Find the MGF of the sum of two independent $[0,1]$ uniform random variables.

Solution:

From Example 1.26, the MGF of a standard uniform random variable is $\frac{1}{t}[e^t - 1]$, so the MGF of random variable X defined as the sum of two independent uniform variables is $\frac{1}{t^2}[e^t - 1]^2$.

Second, if random variable X has MGF $M(t)$, the MGF of random variable $Y = a+bX$ is $e^{at}M(bt)$ because

$$E[e^{tY}] = E[e^{t(a+bX)}] = E[e^{at}e^{bXt}] = e^{at}E[e^{btX}] = e^{at}M(bt) \qquad \text{(EQ 1.27)}$$

As a corollary, if $M(t)$ is the MGF of a random variable X, the MGF of $(X - \mu)$ is given by $e^{-\mu t}M(t)$. The moments about the origin of $(X - \mu)$ are the moments about the mean of X. So, to compute the rth moment about the mean for a random variable X, we can differentiate $e^{-\mu t}M(t)$ r times with respect to t and set t to 0.

EXAMPLE 1.28: VARIANCE OF A STANDARD UNIFORM RANDOM VARIABLE

The MGF of a standard uniform random variable X is $\frac{1}{t}[e^t - 1]$. So, the MGF of $(X - \mu)$ is given by $\frac{e^{-\mu t}}{t}[e^t - 1]$. To find the variance of a standard uniform random variable, we need to differentiate twice with respect to t and then set t

to 0. Given the t in the denominator, it is convenient to rewrite the expression as $\left(1 - \mu t + \frac{\mu^2 t^2}{2!} - ...\right)\left(1 + \frac{t}{2!} + \frac{t^2}{3!} + ...\right)$, where the ellipses refer to terms with third and higher powers of t, which will reduce to 0 when t is set to 0. In this product, we need consider only the coefficient of t^2, which is $\frac{1}{3!} - \frac{\mu}{2!} + \frac{\mu^2}{2!}$. Differentiating the expression twice results in multiplying the coefficient by 2, and when we set t to zero, we obtain $E[(X - \mu)^2] = V[X] = 1/12$.

These two properties allow us to compute the MGF of a complex random variable that can be decomposed into the linear combination of simpler variables. In particular, it allows us to compute the MGF of independent, identically distributed (i.i.d.) random variables, a situation that arises frequently in practice.

1.5 Standard Discrete Distributions

We now present some discrete distributions that frequently arise when studying networking problems.

1.5.1 Bernoulli Distribution

A discrete random variable X is called a **Bernoulli** random variable if it can take only two values, 0 or 1, and its probability mass function is defined as $p(0) = 1 - a$ and $p(1) = a$. We can think of X as representing the result of some experiment, with $X=1$ being success, with probability a. The expected value of a Bernoulli random variable is a and variance is $p(1 - a)$.

1.5.2 Binomial Distribution

Consider a series of n Bernoulli experiments where the result of each experiment is *independent* of the others. We would naturally like to know the number of successes in these n trials. This can be represented by a discrete random variable X with parameters (n,a) and is called a **binomial** random variable. The probability mass function of a binomial random variable with parameters (n,a) is given by

$$p(i) = \binom{n}{i} a^i (1 - a)^{n - i}$$

(EQ 1.28)

If we set $b = 1 - a$, then these are just the terms of the expansion $(a+b)^n$. The expected value of a variable that is binomially distributed with parameters (n,a) is na.

EXAMPLE 1.29: BINOMIAL RANDOM VARIABLE

Consider a local area network with ten stations. Assume that, at a given moment, each node can be active with probability $p = 0.1$. What is the probability that (a) one station is active, (b) five stations are active, (c) all ten stations are active?

Solution:

Assuming that the stations are independent, the number of active stations can be modeled by a binomial distribution with parameters (10, 0.1). From the formula for $p(i)$, we get

a. $p(1) = \binom{10}{1} 0.1^1 0.9^9 = 0.38$

b. $p(5) = \binom{10}{5} 0.1^5 0.9^5 = 1.49 \times 10^{-3}$

c. $p(10) = \binom{10}{10} 0.1^{10} 0.9^0 = 1 \times 10^{-10}$

This is shown in Figure 1.3. Note how the probability of one station being active is 0.38, which is *greater* than the probability of any single station being active. Note also how rapidly the probability of multiple active stations drops. This is what drives **spatial statistical multiplexing**: the provisioning of a link with a capacity smaller than the sum of the demands of the stations.

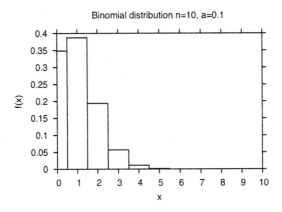

Binomial distribution n=10, a=0.1

Figure 1.3 Example binomial distribution

1.5.3 Geometric Distribution

Consider a sequence of independent Bernoulli experiments, each of which succeeds with probability a. In section 1.5.2, we wanted to count the number of successes; now, we want to compute the probability mass function of a random variable X that represents the number of trials before the first success. Such a variable is called a **geometric** random variable and has a probability mass function

$$p(i) = (1-a)^{i-1}a \qquad \text{(EQ 1.29)}$$

The expected value of a geometrically distributed variable with parameter a is $1/a$.

EXAMPLE 1.30: GEOMETRIC RANDOM VARIABLE

Assume that a link has a loss probability of 10% and that *packet losses are independent*, although this is rarely true in practice. Suppose that when a packet gets lost, this is detected and the packet is retransmitted until it is correctly received. What is the probability that it would be transmitted exactly one, two, and three times?

Solution:

Assuming that the packet transmissions are independent events, we note that the probability of success = p = 0.9. Therefore, $p(1)$ = 0.1^0 * 0.9 = 0.9; $p(2)$ = 0.1^1 * 0.9 = 0.09; $p(3)$ = 0.1^2 * 0.9 = 0.009. Note the rapid decrease in the probability of more than two transmissions, even with a fairly high packet loss rate of 10%. Indeed, the expected number of transmissions is only 1/0.9 = $1.\bar{1}$.

1.5.4 Poisson Distribution

The **Poisson** distribution is widely encountered in networking situations, usually to model the arrival of packets or new end-to-end connections to a switch or a router. A discrete random variable X with the domain {0, 1, 2, 3,...} is said to be a Poisson random variable with parameter λ if, for some $\lambda > 0$:

$$P(X = i) = e^{-\lambda}\left(\frac{\lambda^i}{i!}\right) \qquad \text{(EQ 1.30)}$$

Poisson variables are often used to model the number of events that happen in a fixed time interval. If the events are reasonably rare, the probability that multiple events occur in a fixed time interval drops off rapidly, due to the $i!$ term in the denominator. The first use of Poisson variables, indeed, was to investigate the number of soldier deaths due to being kicked by a horse in Napoleon's army!

The Poisson distribution, which has only a single parameter λ, can be used to model a binomial distribution with two parameters (n and a) when n is "large" and a is "small." In this case, the Poisson variable's parameter λ corresponds to the product of the two binomial parameters (i.e., $\lambda = n_{Binomial} * a_{Binomial}$). Recall that a binomial distribution arises naturally when we conduct independent trials. The Poisson distribution, therefore, arises when the number of such independent trials is large, and the probability of success of each trial is small. The expected value of a Poisson distributed random variable with parameter λ is also λ.

Consider an endpoint sending a packet on a link. We can model the transmission of a packet by the endpoint in a given time interval as a trial as follows: If the source sends a packet in a particular interval, we will call the trial a success; if the source does not send a packet, we will call the trial a failure. When the load generated by each source is light, the probability of success of a trial defined in this manner, which is just the packet transmission probability, is small. Therefore, as the number of endpoints grows, and if we can assume the endpoints to be independent, the sum of their loads will be well modeled by a Poisson random variable. This is heartening because systems subjected to a Poisson load are mathematically tractable, as we will see in our discussion of queueing theory. Unfortunately, over the last two decades, numerous measurements have shown that actual traffic can be far from Poisson. Therefore, this modeling assumption should be used with care and only as a rough approximation to reality.

EXAMPLE 1.31: POISSON RANDOM VARIABLE

Consider a link that can receive traffic from one of 1,000 independent endpoints. Suppose that each node transmits at a uniform rate of 0.001 packets/second. What is the probability that we see at least one packet on the link during an arbitrary 1-second interval?

Solution:

Given that each node transmits packets at the rate of 0.001 packets/second, the probability that a node transmits a packet in any 1-second interval is $p_{Binomial} = 0.001$. Thus, the Poisson parameter $\lambda = 1000*0.001 = 1$. The probability that we see at least one packet on the link during any 1-second interval is therefore

$$1 - p(0)$$
$$= 1 - e^{-1}1^0/0!$$
$$= 1 - 1/e$$
$$= 0.64$$

That is, there is a 64% chance that, during an arbitrary 1-second interval, we will see one or more packets on the link.

It turns out that a Poisson random variable is a good approximation to a binomial random variable even if the trials are weakly dependent. Indeed, we do not even require the trials to have equal probabilities, as long as the probability of success of each individual trial is "small." This is another reason why the Poisson random variable is frequently used to model the behavior of aggregates.

1.6 Standard Continuous Distributions

This section presents some standard continuous distributions. Recall from Section 1.3 that, unlike discrete random variables, the domain of a continuous random variable is a subset of the real line.

1.6.1 Uniform Distribution

A random variable X is said to be uniformly randomly distributed in the domain $[a,b]$ if its density function $f(x) = 1/(b-a)$ when x lies in $[a,b]$ and is 0 otherwise. The expected value of a uniform random variable with parameters a,b is $(a+b)/2$.

1.6.2 Gaussian, or Normal, Distribution

A random variable is **Gaussian**, or **normally** distributed, with parameters μ and σ^2 if its density is given by

$$f(x) = \frac{1}{\sigma\sqrt{2\pi}} e^{-\frac{1}{2}\left(\frac{x-\mu}{\sigma}\right)^2}$$

(EQ 1.31)

We denote a Gaussian random variable X with parameters μ and σ^2 as $X \sim N(\mu,\sigma^2)$, where we read the "$\sim$" as "is distributed as."

The Gaussian distribution can be obtained as the limiting case of the binomial distribution as n tends to infinity and p is kept constant. That is, if we have a very large number of independent trials, such that the random variable measures the number of trials that succeed, the random variable is Gaussian. Thus, Gaussian random variables naturally occur when we want to study the statistical properties of aggregates.

The Gaussian distribution is called *normal* because many quantities, such as the heights of people, the slight variations in the size of a manufactured item, and the time taken to complete an activity approximately follow the well-known bell-shaped curve.[4]

---

4. With the caveat that many variables in real life are never negative, but the Gaussian distribution extends from $-\infty$ to ∞.

When performing experiments or simulations, it is often the case that the same quantity assumes different values during different trials. For instance, if five students were each measuring the pH of a reagent, it is likely that they would get five slightly different values. In such situations, it is common to assume that these quantities, which are supposed to be the same, are in fact normally distributed about some mean. Generally speaking, if you know that a quantity is supposed to have a certain standard value but you also know that there can be small variations in this value due to many small and independent random effects, it is reasonable to assume that the quantity is a Gaussian random variable with its mean centered on the expected value.

The expected value of a Gaussian random variable with parameters μ and σ^2 is μ and its variance is σ^2. In practice, it is often convenient to work with a **standard Gaussian distribution**, which has a zero mean and a variance of 1. It is possible to convert a Gaussian random variable X with parameters μ and σ^2 to a Gaussian random variable Y with parameters 0,1 by choosing $Y = (X - \mu)/\sigma$.

The Gaussian distribution is symmetric about the mean and asymptotes to 0 at $+\infty$ and $-\infty$. The σ^2 parameter controls the width of the central "bell": The larger this parameter, the wider the bell, and the lower the maximum value of the density function as shown in Figure 1.4. The probability that a Gaussian random variable X lies between $\mu - \sigma$ and $\mu + \sigma$ is approximately 68.26%; between $\mu - 2\sigma$ and $\mu + 2\sigma$ is approximately 95.44%; and between $\mu - 3\sigma$ and $\mu + 3\sigma$ is approximately 99.73%.

It is often convenient to use a Gaussian continuous random variable to approximately model a discrete random variable. For example, the number of packets arriving on a link to a router in a given fixed time interval will follow a discrete distribution. Nevertheless, by modeling it using a continuous Gaussian random variable, we can get quick estimates of its expected extremal values.

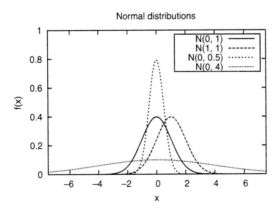

Figure 1.4 Gaussian distributions for different values of the mean and variance

---

EXAMPLE 1.32: GAUSSIAN APPROXIMATION OF A DISCRETE RANDOM VARIABLE

Suppose that the number of packets arriving on a link to a router in a 1-second interval can be modeled accurately by a normal distribution with parameters (20, 4). How many packets can we expect to see with at least 99% confidence?

Solution:

The number of packets are distributed (20, 4), so that $\mu = 20$ and $\sigma = 2$. We have more than 99% confidence that the number of packets seen will be $\mu \pm 3\sigma$, or between 14 and 26. That is, if we were to measure packets' arrivals over a long period of time, fewer than 1% of the 1-second intervals would have packet counts fewer than 14 or more than 26.

The MGF of the normal distribution is given by

$$M(t) = \frac{1}{\sigma\sqrt{2\pi}} \int_{-\infty}^{\infty} e^{tx - \frac{1}{2}\frac{(x-\mu)^2}{\sigma^2}} \, dx$$

$$= \frac{e^{\mu t + \frac{1}{2}\sigma^2 t^2}}{\sigma\sqrt{2\pi}} \int_{-\infty}^{\infty} e^{-\frac{1}{2}\frac{(x-\mu-\sigma^2 t)^2}{\sigma^2}} \, dx$$

$$= e^{\mu t + \frac{1}{2}\sigma^2 t^2}$$

where in the last step, we recognize that the integral is the area under a normal curve, which evaluates to $\sigma\sqrt{2\pi}$. Note that the MGF of a normal variable with zero mean and a variance of 1 is therefore

$$M(t) = e^{\frac{1}{2}t^2} \tag{EQ 1.32}$$

We can use the MGF of a normal distribution to prove some elementary facts about it.

a. If $X \sim N(\mu,\sigma^2)$, then $a+bX \sim N(a+b\mu, b^2\sigma^2)$, because the MGF of $a+bX$ is

$$e^{at}M(bt) = e^{at}e^{\mu bt + \frac{1}{2}\sigma^2(bt)^2}$$

$$= e^{(a+\mu b)t + \frac{1}{2}(\sigma^2 b^2)t^2}$$

which can be seen to be a normally distributed random variable with mean $a+b\mu$ and variance $b^2\sigma^2$.

b. If $X \sim N(\mu,\sigma^2)$, then $Z = (X - \mu)/\sigma \sim N(0,1)$. This is obtained trivially by substituting for a and b in expression (a). Z is called the **standard normal variable**.

c. If $X \sim N(\mu_1,\sigma_1^{\,2})$ and $Y \sim N(\mu_2,\sigma_2^{\,2})$ and X and Y are independent, $X+Y \sim N(\mu_{1+}\mu_2,$ $\sigma_1^{\,2}+\sigma_2^{\,2})$, because the MGF of their sum is the product of their individual

MGFs $= e^{\mu_1 t + \frac{1}{2}\sigma_1^2 t^2} e^{\mu_2 t + \frac{1}{2}\sigma_2^2 t^2} = e^{(\mu_1 + \mu_2)t + \frac{1}{2}(\sigma_1^2 + \sigma_2^2)t^2}$. As a generalization, the sum of any number of independent normal variables is also normally distributed with the mean as the sum of the individual means and the variance as the sum of the individual variances.

1.6.3 Exponential Distribution

A random variable X is exponentially distributed with parameter λ, where $\lambda > 0$, if its density function is given by

$$f(x) = \begin{cases} \lambda e^{-\lambda x} & \text{if } x \geq 0 \\ 0 & \text{if } x < 0 \end{cases}$$ (EQ 1.33)

Note than when $x = 0$, $f(x) = \lambda$ (see Figure 1.5). The expected value of such a random variable is $\dfrac{1}{\lambda}$ and its variance is $\dfrac{1}{\lambda^2}$. The exponential distribution is the continuous analog of the geometric distribution. Recall that the geometric distribution measures the number of trials until the first success. Correspondingly, the exponential distribu-

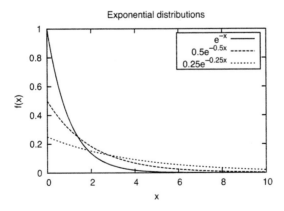

Figure 1.5 Exponentially distributed random variables with $\lambda = \{1, 0.5, 0.25\}$

tion arises when we are trying to measure the duration of time before some event happens (i.e., achieves success). For instance, it is used to model the time between two consecutive packet arrivals on a link.

The cumulative density function of the exponential distribution, $F(X)$, is given by

$$F(X) = p(X \le x) = 1 - e^{-\lambda x} \qquad \text{(EQ 1.34)}$$

EXAMPLE 1.33: EXPONENTIAL RANDOM VARIABLE

Suppose that measurements show that the average length of a phone call is 3 minutes. Assuming that the length of a call is an exponential random variable, what is the probability that a call lasts more than 6 minutes?

Solution:

Clearly, the λ parameter for this distribution is 1/3. Therefore, the probability that a call lasts more than six minutes is $1 - F(6) = 1 - e^{-6/3} = 1 - e^{-2} = 13.5\%$.

An important property of the exponential distribution is that, like the geometric distribution, it is **memoryless** and, in fact, is the *only* memoryless continuous distribution. Intuitively, this means that the expected remaining time until the occurrence of an event with an exponentially distributed waiting time is *independent* of the time at which the observation is made. More precisely, $P(X > s+t \mid X>s) = P(X>t)$ for all s, t. From a geometric perspective, if we truncate the distribution to the left of any point on the positive X axis and then rescale the remaining distribution so that the area under the curve is 1, we will obtain the original distribution. The following examples illustrate this useful property.

EXAMPLE 1.34: MEMORYLESSNESS 1

Suppose that the time a bank teller takes is an exponentially distributed random variable with an expected value of 1 minute. When you arrive at the bank, the teller is already serving a customer. If you join the queue now, you can expect to wait 1 minute before being served. However, suppose that you decide to run an errand and return to the bank. If the same customer is still being served (i.e., the condition $X>s$), and if you join the queue now, the expected waiting time for you to be served would *still* be 1 minute!

EXAMPLE 1.35: MEMORYLESSNESS 2

Suppose that a switch has two parallel links to another switch and that packets can be routed on either link. Consider a packet A that arrives when both links are already in service. Therefore, the packet will be sent on the first link that becomes free. Suppose that this is link 1. Now, assuming that link service times are exponentially distributed, which packet is likely to finish transmission first: packet A on link 1 or the packet continuing service on link 2?

Solution:

Because of the memorylessness of the exponential distribution, the expected remaining service time on link 2 at the time that A starts transmission on link 1 is exactly the same as the expected service time for A, so we expect both to finish transmission at the same time. Of course, we are assuming that we don't know the service time for A. If a packet's service time is proportional to its length, and if we know A's length, we no longer have an expectation for its service time: We know it precisely, and this equality no longer holds.

1.6.4 Power-Law Distribution

A random variable described by its minimum value x_{min} and a scale parameter $\alpha > 1$ is said to obey the power-law distribution if its density function is given by

$$f(x) = \frac{(\alpha - 1)}{x_{min}}\left(\frac{x}{x_{min}}\right)^{-\alpha} \qquad \textbf{(EQ 1.35)}$$

Typically, this function needs to be normalized for a given set of parameters to ensure that $\int_{-\infty}^{\infty} f(x)dx = 1$.

Note that $f(x)$ decreases rapidly with x. However, the decline is not as rapid as with an exponential distribution (see Figure 1.6). This is why a power-law distribution is also called a **heavy-tailed distribution**. When plotted on a log-log scale, the graph of $f(x)$ versus x shows a linear relationship with a slope of $-\alpha$, which is often used to quickly identify a potential power-law distribution in a data set.

Intuitively, if we have objects distributed according to an exponential or power law, a few "elephants" occur frequently and are common, and many "mice" are relatively uncommon. The elephants are responsible for most of the probability mass. From an engineering perspective, whenever we see such a distribution, it makes sense to build a system that deals well with the elephants, even at the expense of

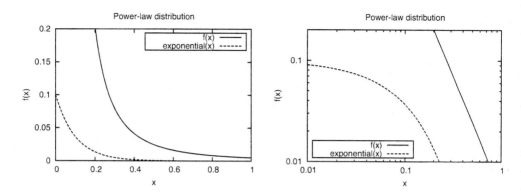

Figure 1.6 A typical power-law distribution with parameters $x_{min} = 0.1$ and $\alpha = 2.3$ compared to an exponential distribution using a linear-linear (left) and a log-log (right) scale

ignoring the mice. Two rules of thumb that reflect this are the *90/10 rule*—90% of the output is derived from 10% of the input—and the dictum *optimize for the common case*.

When $\alpha < 2$, the expected value of the random variable is infinite. A system described by such a random variable is unstable (i.e., its value is unbounded). On the other hand, when $\alpha > 2$, the tail probabilities fall rapidly enough that a power-law random variable can usually be well approximated by an exponential random variable.

A widely studied example of power-law distribution is the random variable that describes the number of users who visit one of a collection of Web sites on the Internet on any given day. Traces of Web site accesses almost always show that all but a microscopic fraction of Web sites get fewer than one visitor a day: Traffic is garnered mostly by a handful of well-known Web sites.

1.7 Useful Theorems

This section discusses some useful theorems: Markov's and Chebyshev's inequality theorems allow us to bound the amount of mass in the tail of a distribution, knowing nothing more than its expected value (Markov) and variance (Chebyshev). Chernoff's bound allows us to bound both the lower and upper tails of distributions arising from independent trials. The law of large numbers allows us to relate real-world measurements with the expectation of a random variable. Finally, the central limit theorem shows why so many real-world random variables are normally distributed.

1.7.1 Markov's Inequality

If X is a *non-negative* random variable with mean μ, then for any constant $a > 0$,

$$p(X \geq a) \leq \frac{\mu}{a} \qquad\qquad \text{(EQ 1.36)}$$

Thus, we can bound the probability mass to the right of any constant a by a value proportional to the expected value of X and inversely proportional to a (Figure 1.7). Markov's inequality requires knowledge only of the mean of the distribution. Note that this inequality is trivial if $a < \mu$ (why?). Note also that the Markov inequality does not apply to some standard distributions, such as the normal distribution, because they are not always non-negative.

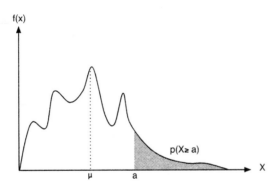

Figure 1.7 Markov's inequality

EXAMPLE 1.36: MARKOV INEQUALITY

Use the Markov inequality to bound the probability mass to the right of the value 0.75 of a uniform (0,1) distribution.

Solution:

The mean of this distribution is 0.5, so $p(X \geq 0.75) \leq \dfrac{0.5}{0.75} = 0.66$. The actual probability mass is only 0.25, so the Markov bound is quite loose. This is typical of a Markov bound.

1.7.2 Chebyshev's Inequality

If X is a random variable with a finite mean μ and variance σ^2, then for any constant $a > 0$,

$$p(|X - \mu| \geq a) \leq \frac{\sigma^2}{a^2} \qquad \text{(EQ 1.37)}$$

Chebyshev's inequality bounds the "tails" of a distribution on both sides of the mean, given the variance. Roughly, the farther away we get from the mean (the larger a is), the less mass there is in the tail (because the right-hand size decreases by a factor quadratic in a), as shown in Figure 1.8.

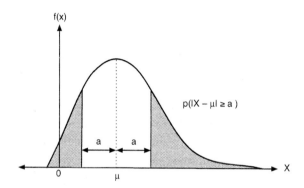

Figure 1.8 Chebyshev's inequality

EXAMPLE 1.37: CHEBYSHEV BOUND

Use the Chebyshev bound to compute the probability that a standard normal random variable has a value greater than 3.

Solution:

For a standard normal variable, $\mu = 0$ and $\sigma = 1$. We have $a = 3$. So, $p(|X| \geq 3) \leq \frac{1}{9}$, so that $p(X > 3) \leq \frac{1}{18}$, or about 5.5%. Compare this to the tight bound of 0.135% (Section 1.6.2).

1.7.3 Chernoff Bound

Let the random variable X_i denote the outcome of the ith iteration of a process, with $X_i = 1$ denoting success and $X_i = 0$ denoting failure. Assume that the probability of success of each iteration is independent of the others (this is critical!). Denote the probability of success of the ith trial by $p(X_i = 1) = p_i$. Let X be the number of successful trials in a run of n trials. Clearly,

$$X = \sum_{i=1}^{n} X_i = \sum_{i=1}^{n} p_i.$$

Let $E[X] = \mu$ be the expected value of X (the expected number of successes). Then, we can state two Chernoff bounds that tell us the probability that there are too few or too many successes.

The **lower bound** is given by

$$p(X < (1-\delta)\mu) < \left(\frac{e^{-\delta}}{(1-\delta)^{1-\delta}}\right)^{\mu}, \qquad 0 < \delta \leq 1 \qquad \text{(EQ 1.38)}$$

This is somewhat hard to compute. A weaker but more tractable bound is

$$p(X < (1-\delta)\mu) < e^{\frac{-\mu\delta^2}{2}}, \qquad 0 < \delta \leq 1 \qquad \text{(EQ 1.39)}$$

Note that both equations bound the area under the density distribution of X between $-\infty$ and $(1-\delta)\mu$. The second form makes it clear that the probability of too few successes declines quadratically with δ.

The **upper bound** is given by

$$p(X > (1+\delta)\mu) < \left(\frac{e^{\delta}}{(1+\delta)^{1+\delta}}\right)^{\mu}, \qquad \delta > 0 \qquad \text{(EQ 1.40)}$$

A weaker but more tractable bound is

$$p(X > (1+\delta)\mu) < e^{\frac{-\mu\delta^2}{4}} \qquad \text{if } \delta < 2e - 1 \qquad \text{(EQ 1.41)}$$
$$p(X > (1+\delta)\mu) < 2^{-\delta\mu} \qquad \text{if } \delta > 2e - 1$$

EXAMPLE 1.38: CHERNOFF BOUND

Use the Chernoff bound to compute the probability that a packet source that suffers from independent packet losses, where the probability of each loss is 0.1, suffers from more than four packet losses when transmitting ten packets.

Solution:

We define a successful event to be a packet loss, with the probability of success being $p_i = 0.1 \; \forall i$. We have $E[X] = (10)(0.1) = 1 = \mu$. Also, we want to compute $p(X > 4) = p(X > (1+3)\mu)$ so that $\delta = 3$. So,

$$p(X > 4) < \left(\frac{e^3}{(1+3)^{1+3}}\right)^1 = \frac{e^3}{256} = 0.078$$

As with all bounds, this is looser than the exact value computed from the binomial theorem, given by

$$(1 - p(X = 0) + p(X = 1) + p(X = 2) + p(X = 3) + p(X = 4))$$

$$= 1 - \binom{10}{0}(0.9)^{10} - \binom{10}{1}(0.1)(0.9)^9 - \binom{10}{2}(0.1)^2(0.9)^8 - \binom{10}{3}(0.1)^3(0.9)^7$$

$$= 0.0033$$

1.7.4 Strong Law of Large Numbers

The law of large numbers relates the **sample mean**—the average of a set of observations of a random variable—with the **population**, or **true mean**, which is its expected value. The **strong** law of large numbers, the better-known variant, states that if $X_1, X_2,..., X_n$ are n independent, identically distributed random variables with the same expected value μ, then

$$P\left(\lim_{n \to \infty} (X_1 + X_2 + ... + X_n)/n = \mu\right) = 1 \qquad \text{(EQ 1.42)}$$

No matter how X is distributed, by computing an average over a sufficiently large number of observations, this average can be made to be as close to the true mean as we wish. This is the basis of a variety of statistical techniques for hypothesis testing, as described in Chapter 2.

We illustrate this law in Figure 1.9, which shows the average of 1,2,3,..., 500 successive values of a random variable drawn from a uniform distribution in the range

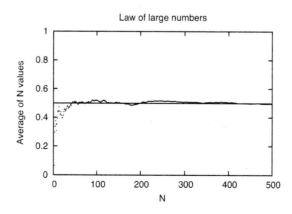

Figure 1.9 Strong law of large numbers: As N increases, the average value of sample of N random values converges to the expected value of the distribution.

[0, 1]. The expected value of this random variable is 0.5, and the average converges to this expected value as the sample size increases.

1.7.5 Central Limit Theorem

The central limit theorem deals with the sum of a *large* number of *independent* random variables that are arbitrarily distributed. The theorem states that no matter how each random variable is distributed, as long as its contribution to the total is small, the sum is well described by a Gaussian random variable.

More precisely, let $X_1, X_2,..., X_n$ be n independent, identically distributed random variables, each with a finite mean μ and variance σ^2. Then, the distribution of the normalized sum given by $\dfrac{X_1 + ... + X_n - n\mu}{\sigma\sqrt{n}}$ tends to the standard (0,1) normal as $n \to \infty$. The central limit theorem is the reason why the Gaussian distribution is the limit of the binomial distribution.

In practice, the central limit theorem allows us to model aggregates by a Gaussian random variable if the size of the aggregate is large and the elements of the aggregate are independent.

The Gaussian distribution plays an important role in statistics because of the central limit theorem. Consider a set of measurements of a physical system. Each measurement can be modeled as an independent random variable whose mean and variance are those of the population. From the central limit theorem, their sum, and therefore their mean, which is just the normalized sum, is approximately normally distributed. As we will study in Chapter 2, this allows us to infer the population mean from the sample mean, which forms the foundation of statistical confidence. We now prove the central limit theorem by using MGFs.

The proof proceeds in three stages. First, we compute the MGF of the sum of n random variables in terms of the MGFs of each of the random variables. Second, we find a simple expression for the MGF of a random variable when the variance is large: a situation we expect when adding together many independent random variables. Finally, we plug this simple expression back into the MGF of the sum to obtain the desired result.

Consider a random variable $Y = X_1 + X_2 + ... + X_n$, the sum of n *independent* random variables X_i. Let μ_i and σ_i denote the mean and standard deviation of X_i, and let μ and σ denote the mean and standard deviation of Y. Because all the X_i s are independent,

$$\mu = \sum \mu_i \; ; \; \sigma^2 = \sum \sigma_i^2 \qquad \text{(EQ 1.43)}$$

Define the random variable W_i to be $(X_i - \mu_i)$: It represents the distance of an instance of the random variable X_i from its mean. By definition, the rth moment of W_i about the origin is the rth moment of X_i about its mean. Also, because the X_i are independent, so are the W_i. Denote the MGF of X_i by $M_i(t)$ and the MGF of W_i by $N_i(t)$.

Note that $Y - \mu = X_1 + X_2 + \dots + X_n - \sum \mu_i = \sum (X_i - \mu_i) = \sum W_i$. So, the MGF of $Y - \mu$ is the product of the MGFs of the $W_i = \prod_{i=1}^{n} N_i(t)$. Therefore, the MGF of $(Y - \mu)/\sigma$ denoted $N^*(t)$ is given by

$$N^*(t) = \prod_{i=1}^{n} N_i\left(\frac{t}{\sigma}\right) \tag{EQ 1.44}$$

Consider the MGF $N_i(t/\sigma)$, which is given by $E\left(e^{\frac{W_i t}{\sigma}}\right)$. Expanding the exponential, we find that

$$N_i\left(\frac{t}{\sigma}\right) = E\left(e^{\frac{W_i t}{\sigma}}\right) = 1 + E(W_i)\frac{t}{\sigma} + \frac{E(W_i^2)}{2!}\left(\frac{t}{\sigma}\right)^2 + \frac{E(W_i^3)}{3!}\left(\frac{t}{\sigma}\right)^3 + \dots \tag{EQ 1.45}$$

Now, $E(W_i) = E(X_i - \mu_i) = E(X_i) - \mu_i = \mu_i - \mu_i = 0$, so we can ignore the second term in the expansion. Recall that σ is the standard deviation of the sum of n random variables. When n is large, so too is σ, which means that, to first order, we can ignore terms that have σ^3 and higher powers of σ in the denominator in Equation 1.45. Therefore, for large n, we can write

$$N^i\left(\frac{t}{\sigma}\right) \approx \left(1 + \frac{E(W_i^2)}{2!}\left(\frac{t}{\sigma}\right)^2\right) = 1 + \frac{\sigma_i^2}{2}\left(\frac{t}{\sigma}\right)^2 \tag{EQ 1.46}$$

where we have used the fact that $E(W_i^2) = E(X_i - \mu)^2$ which is the variance of $X_i = \sigma_i^2$.

Returning to the expression in Equation 1.44, we find that

$$\log N^*(t) = \log\left(\prod_{i=1}^{n} N_i\left(\frac{t}{\sigma}\right)\right) = \sum_{i=1}^{n} \log\left(N_i\left(\frac{t}{\sigma}\right)\right) \approx \sum_{i=1}^{n} \log\left(1 + \frac{\sigma_i^2}{2}\left(\frac{t}{\sigma}\right)^2\right) \tag{EQ 1.47}$$

It is easily shown by the Taylor series expansion that when h is small—so that h^2 and higher powers of h can be ignored—$\log(1+h)$ can be approximated by h. So, when n is large and σ is large, we can further approximate

$$\sum_{i=1}^{n} \log\left(1 + \frac{\sigma_i^2}{2}\left(\frac{t}{\sigma}\right)^2\right) \approx \sum_{i=1}^{n} \frac{\sigma_i^2}{2}\left(\frac{t}{\sigma}\right)^2 = \frac{1}{2}\left(\frac{t}{\sigma}\right)^2 \sum_{i=1}^{n} \sigma_i^2 = \frac{1}{2}t^2 \qquad \text{(EQ 1.48)}$$

where, for the last simplification, we used Equation 1.43. Thus, $\log N^*(t)$ is approximately $1/2\, t^2$, which means that

$$N^*(t) \approx e^{\frac{t^2}{2}} \qquad \text{(EQ 1.49)}$$

But this is just the MGF of a standard normal variable with 0 mean and a variance of 1 (Equation 1.32). Therefore, $(Y - \mu)/\sigma$ is a standard normal variable, which means that $Y \sim N(\mu, \sigma^2)$. We have therefore shown that the sum of a large number of independent random variables is distributed as a normal variable whose mean is the sum of the individual means and whose variance is the sum of the individual variances (Equation 1.43), as desired.

1.8 Jointly Distributed Random Variables

So far, we have considered distributions of one random variable. We now consider the distribution of two random variables simultaneously.

EXAMPLE 1.39: JOINT PROBABILITY DISTRIBUTION

Consider the two events: "rain today" and "rain tomorrow." Let the random variable X be 0 if it does not rain today and 1 if it does. Similarly, let the random variable Y be 0 if it does not rain tomorrow and 1 if it does. The four possible values for the random variables X and Y considered together are 00, 01, 10, and 11, corresponding to four joint events. We can associate probabilities with these events with the usual restrictions that these probabilities lie in [0,1] and that their sum be 1. For instance, consider the following distribution:

$$p(00) = 0.2,$$
$$p(01) = 0.4,$$
$$p(10) = 0.3,$$
$$p(11) = 0.1,$$

where the 00 is now interpreted as shorthand for $X = 0$ AND $Y = 0$, and so on. This defines the **joint probability** distribution of X and Y, which is denoted $p_{XY}(xy)$ or sometimes $p(X,Y)$. Given this joint distribution, we can extract the distribution of X alone, which is the probability of $X = 0$ and of $X = 1$, as follows: $p(X = 0) = p(00) + p(01) = 0.2 + 0.4 = 0.6$. Similarly, $p(X = 1) = 0.3 + 0.1 = 0.4$. As expected, $p(X = 0) + p(X = 1) = 1$. Similarly, note that $p(Y = 0) = 0.5$ and $p(Y = 1) = 0.5$.

We call the distribution of X alone as the **marginal** distribution of X and denote it p_X. Similarly, the marginal distribution of Y is denoted p_Y. Generalizing from the preceding example, we see that to obtain the marginal distribution of X, we should set X to each value in its domain and then sum over *all possible values of Y*. Similarly, to obtain the marginal distribution of Y, we set Y to each value in its domain and sum over all possible values of X.

An important special case of a joint distribution is when the two variables X and Y are **independent**. Then, $p_{XY}(xy) = p(X = x \ AND \ Y = y) = p(X = x \ ) * p(Y = y) = p_X(x)p_Y(y)$. That is, each entry in the joint distribution is obtained simply as the product of the marginal distributions corresponding to that value. We sometimes denote this as $= p_X(x)p_Y(y)$.

EXAMPLE 1.40: INDEPENDENCE

In Example 1.39, $p_{XY}(00) = 0.2$, $p_X(0) = 0.6$, and $p_Y(0) = 0.5$, so X and Y are *not* independent: We *cannot* decompose the joint distribution into the product of the marginal distributions.

Given the joint distribution, we define the **conditional probability mass function of X**, denoted by $p_{X|Y}(x|y)$ by $p(X = x \mid Y = y) = p(X = x \ AND \ Y = y)/p(Y = y) = \dfrac{p_{XY(xy)}}{p_Y(y)}$.

EXAMPLE 1.41: CONDITIONAL PROBABILITY MASS FUNCTION

Continuing with Example 1.39, suppose that we want to compute the probability that it will rain tomorrow, given that it rained today: $p_{Y|X}(1|1) = p_{XY}(11)/p_X(1) = 0.1/0.4 = 0.25$. Thus, knowing that it rained today makes it less probable that it will rain tomorrow because $p_{(Y=1)} = 0.5$ and $p_{(Y=1|X=1)} = 0.25$.

We can generalize the notion of joint probability in three ways. We outline these generalizations next. Note that the concepts we have developed for the simple preceding case continue to hold for these generalizations.

1. Instead of having only two values, 0 and 1, X and Y could assume any number of finite discrete values. In this case, if there are n values of X and m values of Y, we would need to specify, for the joint distribution, a total of nm values. If X and Y are independent, however, we need to specify only $n+m$ values to completely specify the joint distribution.

2. We can generalize this further and allow X and Y to be continuous random variables. Then, the joint probability distribution $p_{XY}(xy)$ is implicitly defined by

$$p(a \leq X \leq a + \alpha, b \leq Y \leq b + \beta) = \int_b^{(b+\beta)} \int_a^{(a+\alpha)} p_{XY}(xy)dxdy \qquad \text{(EQ 1.50)}$$

Intuitively, this is the probability that a randomly chosen two-dimensional vector will be in the vicinity of (a,b).

3. As a further generalization, consider the joint distribution of n random variables, $X_1, X_2,..., X_n$, where each variable is either discrete or continuous. If they are all discrete, we need to define the probability of each possible choice of each value of X_i. This grows exponentially with the number of random variables and with the size of each domain of each random variable. Thus, it is impractical to completely specify the joint probability distribution for a large number of variables. Instead, we exploit pairwise independence between the variables, using the construct of a Bayesian network, which is described next.

1.8.1 Bayesian Networks

Bayes's rule allows us to compute the degree to which one of a set of mutually exclusive prior events contributes to a posterior condition. Suppose that the posterior condition was itself a prior to yet another posterior, and so on. We could then imagine tracing this chain of conditional causation back from the final condition to the initial causes. This, in essence, is a Bayesian network. We will study one of the simplest forms of a Bayesian network next.

A Bayesian network with n nodes is a directed acyclic graph whose vertices represent random variables and whose edges represent conditional causation between these random variables: There is an edge from a random variable E_i, called the *parent*, or *cause*, to every random variable E_j whose outcome depends on it, called its *children*, or *effects*. If there is no edge between E_i and E_j, they are independent.

Each node in the Bayesian network stores the conditional probability distribution $p(E_j | \text{parents}(E_j))$, also called its **local distribution**. Note that if the node has no parents, its distribution is unconditionally known. The network allows us to compute the joint probability $p(E_1 E_2...E_n)$ as

$$p(E_1 E_2 ... E_n) = \prod_i p(E_i | parents(E_i)) \qquad \text{(EQ 1.51)}$$

That is, the joint distribution is simply the product of the local distributions. This greatly reduces the amount of information required to describe the joint probability distribution of the random variables. Choosing the Bayesian graph is a nontrivial problem and one that we will not discuss further. An overview can be found in the text by Russell and Norvig cited in Section 1.9.

Note that, because the Bayesian network encodes the full joint distribution, we can in principle extract any probability we want from it. Usually, we want to compute something much simpler. A Bayesian network allows us to compute probabilities of interest without having to compute the entire joint distribution, as the next example demonstrates.

EXAMPLE 1.42: BAYESIAN NETWORK

Consider the Bayesian network in Figure 1.10. Each circle shows a discrete random variable that can assume only two values: true or false. Each random variable is associated with an underlying event in the appropriate sample space, as shown in the figure. The network shows that if L, the random variable

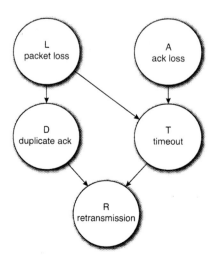

Figure 1.10 A Bayesian network to represent TCP retransmissions

representing packet loss event, has the value true (the cause), this may lead to a timeout event at the TCP transmitter (effect), so that the random variable representing this T, has a higher probability of having the value true. Similarly, the random variable denoting the loss of an acknowledgment packet may also increase the probability that T assumes the value true. The node marked T, therefore, stores the probabilty that it assumes the value true conditional on the parents, assuming the set of values {(true, true), (true, false), (false, true), (false, false)}.

The network also represents the fact that a packet loss event affects the likelihood of a duplicate acknowledgment event. However, packet and ack loss events are mutually exclusive, as are duplicate acks and timeouts. Finally, if there is either a duplicate ack or a timeout at the transmitter, it will surely retransmit a packet.

The joint distribution of the random variables (L, A, D, T, R) would assign a probability to every possible combination of the variables, such as $p(packet\ loss\ AND\ no\ ack\ loss\ AND\ no\ duplicate\ ack\ AND\ timeout\ AND\ no\ retransmission)$. In practice, we rarely need the joint distribution. Instead, we may be interested only in computing the following probability: $p(packet\ loss\ |\ retransmission)$ = $p(L|R)$. That is, we observe the event that the transmitter has retransmitted a packet. What is the probability that the event packet loss occurred: What is $p(L|R)$?

For notational simplicity, let $p(R = true) = p(R) = r$, $p(L = true) = p(L) = l$, $p(T = true) = p(T) = t$, $p(A = true) = p(A) = a$ and $p(D = true) = p(D) = d$. From the network, it is clear that we can write $p(R)$ as $p(R|T)t + p(R|D)d$. Similarly, $t = p(T|L)l + p(T|A)a$ and $d = p(D|L)l$. Therefore,

$$p(R) = r = p(R|T)(p(T|L)l + p(T|A)a) + p(R|D)p(D|L)l$$

If we know a and l and the conditional probabilities stored at each node, we can therefore compute r.

From the definition of conditional probabilities:

$$p(L|R) = \frac{p(LR)}{r} \tag{EQ 1.52}$$

We have already seen how to compute the denominator. To compute the numerator, we sum across all possibilities for L and R as follows:

$$p(LR) = p(LRTD) + p(LRT\bar{D}) + p(LR\bar{T}D) + p(LR\bar{T}\bar{D})$$

where the overbar represents the probability that the random variable assumes the value false. However, note that T and D are mutually exclusive, so

$$p(TD) = 0$$
$$p(T\,\overline{D}\,) = p(T)$$
$$p(\overline{T}\,D) = p(D)$$

Thus,

$$p(LR) = p(LRT) + p(LRD) + p(LR\,\overline{T}\overline{D}\,)$$

The last term is 0 because we do not have a retransmission unless there is either a timeout or a duplicate ack. Thus, $p(LR) = P(LRT) + P(LRD)$.

Replacing this in Equation 1.52, we get

$$p(PLR) = \frac{p(LRT) + p(LRD)}{p(R|T)(p(T|L)l + p(T|A)a) + p(R|D)p(D|L)l}$$

All these variables can be computed by observations over sufficiently long durations of time. For instance, to compute $p(LRT)$, we can compute the ratio of all retransmissions where there was both a packet loss and timeout event to the number of transmissions. Similarly, to compute $p(R\,|\,T)$, we can compute the ratio of the number of times a retransmission happens due to a timeout to the number of times a timeout happens. This allows us to compute $p(L\,|\,R)$ in practice.

1.9 Further Reading

A number of excellent introductory texts on probability treat this subject in more detail, such as S. Ross, *A First Course in Probability*, 7th ed., Prentice Hall, 2006. A more sophisticated treatment is the classic text by W. Feller, *An Introduction to Probability Theory and Its Applications*, 3rd ed., Wiley, 1968. Bayesian analysis is described in the standard textbook on artificial intelligence: S. Russell and P. Norvig, *Artificial Intelligence: A Modern Approach*, 3rd ed., Prentice Hall, 2010.

1.10 Exercises

1. **Sample space**

   In the IEEE 802.11 protocol, the congestion window (CW) parameter is used as follows: Initially, a terminal waits for a random time period, or *backoff*, chosen in the range $[1, 2^{\text{CW}}]$ before sending a packet. If an acknowledgment for the packet is not received in time, CW is doubled, and the process is repeated until

CW reaches the value CWMAX. The initial value of CW is CWMIN. What are the sample spaces for the value of CW and the value of the backoff?

2. Interpretations of probability

Consider the statement: Given the conditions right now, the probability of a snowstorm tomorrow morning is 25%. How would you interpret this statement from the perspective of an objective, frequentist, and subjective interpretation of probability, assuming that these are possible?

3. Conditional probability

Consider a device that samples packets on a link.

a. Suppose that measurements show that 20% of packets are UDP and that 10% of all packets are UDP packets with a packet size of 100 bytes. What is the conditional probability that a UDP packet has size 100 bytes?

b. Suppose that 50% of packets were UDP, and 50% of UDP packets were 100 bytes long. What fraction of all packets are 100-byte UDP packets?

4. Conditional probability again

Continuing with Exercise 3: How does the knowledge of the protocol type change the sample space of possible packet lengths? In other words, what is the sample space before and after you know the protocol type of a packet?

5. Bayes's rule

For Exercise 3(a), what additional information do you need to compute $P(UDP | 100)$? Setting that value to x, express $P(UDP | 100)$ in terms of x.

6. Cumulative distribution function (CDF)

a. Suppose that *discrete* random variable D take values $\{1, 2, 3,...,i,...\}$ with probability $1/2^i$. What is its CDF?

b. Suppose continuous random variable C is uniform in the range $[x_1, x_2]$. What is its CDF?

7. Expectations

Compute the expectations of the D and C in Exercise 6.

8. Variance

Prove that $V[aX] = a^2 V[X]$.

9. **Moments**

   Prove that $M_\mu^3 = M_0^3 - 3M_0^2 M_0^1 + 2(M_0^1)^3$.

10. **MGFs**

    Prove that the MGF of a uniform random variable, expressed in terms of its series expansion, is $E(e^{tx}) = \int_0^1 \left(1 + tx + \frac{(tx)^2}{2!} + \frac{(tx)^3}{3!} + \ldots\right) dx = \frac{1}{t}[e^t - 1]$.

11. **MGFs**

    Prove that the rth moment of the uniform distribution about the origin is $1/(r+1)$.

12. **MGF of a sum of two variables**

    Use MGFs to find the variance of the sum of two independent uniform standard random variables.

13. **MGF of a normal distribution**

    Prove that if $X \sim N(\mu, \sigma^2)$, then $(X - \mu)/\sigma \sim N(0,1)$.

14. **Bernoulli distribution**

    A hotel has 20 guest rooms. Assuming that outgoing calls are independent and that a guest room makes 10 minutes worth of outgoing calls during the busiest hour of the day, what is the probability that 5 calls are simultaneously active during the busiest hour? What is the probability of 15 simultaneous calls?

15. **Geometric distribution**

    Consider a link that has a packet loss rate of 10%. Suppose that every packet transmission has to be acknowledged. Compute the expected number of data transmissions for a successful packet+ack transfer.

16. **Poisson distribution**

    Consider a binomially distributed random variable X with parameters $n = 10$, $p = 0.1$.

    a. Compute the value of $P(X = 8)$, using both the binomial distribution and the Poisson approximation.

    b. Repeat for $n = 100, p = 0.1$.

17. Gaussian distribution

Prove that if X is Gaussian with parameters (μ, σ^2), the random variable $Y = aX + b$, where a and b are constants, is also Gaussian, with parameters $(a\mu + b, (a\sigma)^2)$.

18. Exponential distribution

Suppose that customers arrive at a bank with an exponentially distributed interarrival time with mean 5 minutes. A customer walks into the bank at 3 p.m. What is the probability that the next customer arrives no sooner than 3:15?

19. Exponential distribution

It is late August and you are watching the Perseid meteor shower. You are told that the time between meteors is exponentially distributed with a mean of 200 seconds. At 10:05 p.m., you see a meteor, after which you head to the kitchen for a bowl of ice cream, returning outside at 10:08 p.m. How long do you expect to wait to see the next meteor?

20. Power law

Consider a power-law distribution with $x_{min} = 1$ and $\alpha = 2$ and an exponential distribution with $\lambda = 2$. Fill in the following table:

x	$f_{power\_law}(x)$	$f_{exponential}(x)$
1		
5		
10		
50		
100		

It should now be obvious why a power-law distribution is called heavy-tailed!

21. Markov's inequality

Consider a random variable X that exponentially distributed with parameter $\lambda = 2$. What is the probability that $X > 10$ using (a) the exponential distribution and (b) Markov's inequality?

22. Joint probability distribution

Consider the following probability mass function defined jointly over the random variables X, Y, and Z:

$$p(000) = 0.05; p(001) = 0.05; p(010) = 0.1; p(011) = 0.3;$$
$$p(100) = 0.05; p(101) = 0.05; p(110) = 0.1; p(111) = 0.3.$$

a. Write down $p_X, p_Y, p_Z, p_{XY}, p_{XZ}, p_{YZ}$.

b. Are X and Y, X and Z, or Y and Z independent?

c. What is the probability that $X = 0$ given that $Z = 1$.

2

Statistics

This chapter reviews basic statistical concepts and techniques. We start by considering a critical problem in statistics: choosing a representative sample. We then discuss statistical techniques to deal with some situations that frequently arise in carrying out research in computer networking: describing data parsimoniously, inferring the parameters of a population from a sample, comparing outcomes, and inferring correlation or independence of variables. We conclude with some approaches to dealing with large data sets and a description of common mistakes in statistical analysis and how to avoid them.

2.1 Sampling a Population

The universe of individuals under study constitutes a **population** that can be characterized by its inherent **parameters**, such as its range, minimum, maximum, mean, or variance. In many practical situations, the population is infinite, so we have to estimate its parameters by studying a carefully chosen subset, or **sample**. The parameters of a sample, such as its range, mean, and variance, are called its **statistics**. In standard notation, population parameters are denoted using the Greek alphabet, and sample statistics are represented using the Latin alphabet. For example, the population mean and variance parameters are denoted μ and σ^2, respectively, and the corresponding sample mean and variance statistics are denoted m (or $\bar{x}$) and s^2, respectively.

When choosing a sample, it is important to carefully identify the underlying population, as the next example illustrates.

EXAMPLE 2.1: CHOICE OF POPULATION

Suppose that you capture a trace of all UDP packets sent on a link from your campus router to your university's internet service provider (ISP) from 6 a.m. to 9 p.m. on Monday, November 17, 2008. What is the underlying population? There are many choices:

- The population of UDP packets sent from your campus router to your university's ISP from *12:00:01 a.m. to 11:59:59 p.m.* on November 17, 2008

- The population of UDP packets sent from your campus router to your university's ISP from 12:00:01 a.m. to 11:59:59 p.m. *on Mondays*

- The population of UDP packets sent from your campus router to your university's ISP from 12:00:01 a.m. to 11:59:59 p.m. *on days that are not holidays*

- The population of UDP packets sent from your campus router to your university's ISP from 12:00:01 a.m. to 11:59:59 p.m. *on a typical day*

- The population of UDP packets sent *from a typical university's campus router to a typical university's* ISP from 12:00:01 a.m. to 11:59:59 p.m. on a typical day

- The population of UDP packets sent from a *typical access router to a typical ISP router* from 12:00:01 a.m. to 11:59:59 p.m. on a typical day

- ...

- The population of all UDP packets sent on the Internet in 2008

- The population of all UDP packets sent since 1969 (the year the Internet was created)

Each population in this list is a superset of the previous population. As you go down the list, therefore, conclusions about the population that you draw from your sample are more general. Unfortunately, these conclusions are also less valid. For instance, it is hard to believe that a single day's sample on a single link is representative of all UDP packets sent on the Internet in 2008!

The difficulty when setting up a measurement study is determining a sample that is representative of the population under study. Conversely, given a sample, you are faced with determining the population that the sample represents. This population lies in the spectrum between the most specific population—

which is the sample itself—where your conclusions are certainly true and the most general population, about which usually no valid conclusions can be drawn. Unfortunately, the only guide to making this judgment is experience, and even experts may disagree with any decision you make.

2.1.1 Types of Sampling

As Example 2.1 shows, collecting a sample before identifying the corresponding population puts the metaphorical cart in front of the horse. Instead, one should first identify a population to study and only then choose samples that are **representative** of that population. By representative, we mean a sample chosen such that every member of the population is equally likely to be a member of the sample. In contrast, if the sample is chosen so that some members of the population are more likely to be in the sample than others, the sample is **biased**, and the conclusions drawn from it may be inaccurate. Of course, representativeness is in the eye of the beholder. Nevertheless, explicitly stating the population and then the sampling technique will aid in identifying and removing otherwise hidden biases.

Here are some standard sampling techniques.

- In **random**, or **proportional**, sampling, an unbiased decision rule is used to select elements of the sample from the population. An example of such a rule is: "Choose an element of the population with probability 0.05." For example, in doing Monte Carlo simulations, varying the seed values in random-number generators randomly perturbs simulation trajectories so that one can argue that the results of the simulation are randomly selected from the space of all possible simulation trajectories.

- In the **stratified random** approach, the population is first categorized into groups of elements that are expected to differ in some significant way. Then, each group is randomly sampled to create an overall sample of the population. For example, one could first categorize packets on a link according to their transport protocol (TCP, UDP, or other), then sample each category separately in proportion to their ratio in the population.

- The **systematic** approach is similar to random sampling but sometimes simpler to carry out. We assume that the population can be enumerated in some random fashion (i.e., with no discernible pattern). Then, the systematic sampling rule is to select every kth element of this random enumeration. For instance, if we expected packet arrivals to a switch to be in no particular order with respect to their destination port, the destination port of every 100th arriving packet would constitute a systematic sample.

- **Cluster** sampling, like stratified sampling, is appropriate when the population naturally partitions itself into distinct groups. As with stratified sampling, the population is divided into groups, and each group is separately sampled. Grouping may reflect geography or an element type. However, unlike in stratified sampling, with cluster sampling, the identity of the cluster is preserved, and statistics are computed individually for each cluster. In contrast to stratified sampling, where the grouping attempts to increase precision, with cluster sampling, the goal is to reduce the cost of creating the sample. Cluster sampling may be done hierarchically, with each level of the hierarchy, or **stage**, further refining the grouping.

- With **purposive** sampling, the idea is to sample only elements that meet a specific definition of the population. For example, suppose that we wanted to study all IP packets that are 40 bytes long, corresponding to a zero data payload. Then, we could set up a packet filter that captured only these packets, constituting a purposive sample.

- A **convenience** sample involves studying the population elements that happen to be conveniently available. For example, you may examine call traces from a cooperative cell phone operator to estimate mean call durations. Although it may not be possible to claim that call durations on that provider are representative of all cellular calls—because the duration is influenced by pricing policies of each operator—this may be all that is available and, on balance, is probably better than not having any data at all.

2.1.2 Scales

Gathering a sample requires measuring some physical quantity along a scale. Not all quantities correspond to values along a real line. We distinguish four types of scales.

1. A **nominal**, or **categorical**, scale corresponds to categories. Quantities arranged in a nominal scale cannot be mutually compared. For example, the transport-protocol type of a packet (i.e., UDP, TCP, other) constitutes a nominal scale.

2. An **ordinal** scale defines an ordering, but distances along the ordinal scale are meaningless. A typical ordinal scale is the **Likert** scale, where 0 corresponds to "strongly disagree," 1 to "disagree," 2 to "neutral," 3 to "agree," and 4 to "strongly agree." A similar scale, with the scale ranging from "poor" to "excellent," is often used to compute the mean opinion score (MOS) of a set of consumers of audio or video content to rank the quality of the content.

3. An **interval** scale defines an ordering in which distances between index values are meaningful, but there is no absolute zero value. That is, the values are invariant to an affine scaling, or multiplication by a constant, followed by addition of another constant. A good example is von Neumann–Morgenstern utilities, discussed in Chapter 7.

4. A **ratio** scale is an interval scale that also has a well-defined zero element, so that all indices are unique. Such quantities as packet length and interarrival time are measured on ratio scales.

It is important to keep track of the type of scale corresponding to each measured quantity. A typical mistake is to assume that an ordinal scale can be treated as an interval or ratio scale.

2.1.3 Outliers

A common problem when collecting data is to find that some data elements are significantly out of line compared with the rest. These outliers can arise from extreme variations in normal operating conditions or from errors, such as a failure in the measuring instrument, buggy software test harness, or overflowing measurement counters.

Although ignoring outliers is common practice, there are two reasons for treating them with care. First, the presence of an outlier often indicates poor data-collection practices. Examining the root cause of an outlier often reveals problems with the underlying measurement setup. Fixing these problems usually not only eliminates outliers but also results in the collection of statistically valid data. Second, outliers indicate the presence of unusual or unsuspected complexity in the operation of a system. Explaining outliers can result in deeper appreciation of the underlying system. Therefore, when collecting samples, it is imperative to pay special attention to outliers, making certain that they are truly statistical aberrations before dismissing them or removing them from the data set.

2.2 Describing a Sample Parsimoniously

After gathering a sample, the next step is to describe it parsimoniously, that is, with a few well-chosen statistics. These statistics can be thought to constitute a **model** of the sample: Each data item in the sample can be viewed as arising partly from this model and partly from an unmodeled error term, that is:

$$Data = Model + Error$$

A good model accounts for each element of the sample while minimizing the error. Naturally, the greater the number of parameters in a model, the better it fits the sample: The best model of a sample is the sample itself. However, a model with a hundred or a hundred million parameters provides no insight. Our goal is to describe as much of the data as possible with the *fewest* number of parameters. We now consider some standard descriptors of sample data.

2.2.1 Tables

The simplest way to represent data is by tabulation. Let the ith sample value be denoted x_i, and let $n(x)$ denote the number of occurrences of the value x in a sample. Then, a table is defined as the set of tuples $(x, n(x))$.

2.2.2 Bar Graphs, Histograms, and Cumulative Histograms

Bar graphs and histograms graphically represent the number of occurrences of sample values (i.e., $n(x)$) as a function of x. When x is measured on a nominal or ordinal scale, histograms and bar graphs both consist of a set of bars or rectangles of height proportional to $n(x)$ for each value of x. When x is measured on an interval or a ratio scale, the scale is first divided into contiguous ranges called **bins**. Bins may differ in width, or **bin size**. If all bins are the same size, histograms and bar graphs are identical. However, if bin sizes differ, the height of the bar in a histogram is inversely proportional to the bin size; in a bar graph, however, the height is unchanged. In a bar graph, only the height of the bar (rectangle) is significant, whereas for a histogram, the area of the rectangle is significant. A histogram is, therefore, a quantized, or approximate, probability density function[1] of the underlying population, becoming identical to it in the limit as the number of bins goes to infinity.

EXAMPLE 2.2: BAR GRAPHS AND HISTOGRAMS

Table 2.1 shows a set of observations in a sample. Note that the number of samples is quite sparse after the value 3. We have many choices of representation. For example, we can treat the data value as being measured on an ordinal scale and show the frequency of each data value found in the sample. This results in the bar graph/histogram shown in Figure 2.1.

We could also treat the data values as being on an interval scale, with bins [0.5,1.5), [1.5, 2.5), [2.5,4.5), [4.5,10.5), where the bin limits are chosen so that there can be no ambiguity as to which bin a value falls into. Note that the bins are not equally sized. This results in the bar graph and histogram shown in Figure 2.2.

---

1. Probability density functions are described in more detail in Section 1.3.1.

Table 2.1 Sample Data for Example 2.2

Data Value	Frequency
1	5
2	7
3	2
7	2
10	1

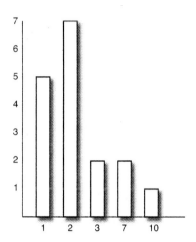

Figure 2.1 Bar graph of the sample with data values on an ordinal scale

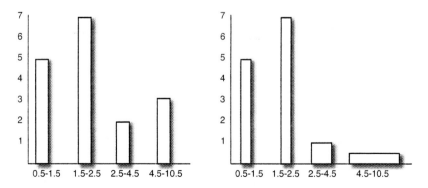

Figure 2.2 Bar graph (left) and histogram (right) for the sample with data values on an interval scale

Choosing a bin size for variables measured on interval or ratio scales requires choosing appropriate bin sizes. Unfortunately, this can usually be accomplished only by trial and error. If the bin sizes are too small, many bins are likely to be empty, and the histogram is visually too wide. In contrast, if the bin sizes are too large, all the data values may cluster into a handful of bins, hiding finer-scale structure. Several heuristics for bin sizing are known for the case of equally sized bins. For example, **Scott's choice** of bin width is $width = \dfrac{3.5s}{\sqrt[3]{n}}$, where s is the standard deviation of the sample (i.e., the square root of its variance; see Section 2.2.5).

The cumulative histogram of a sample is a histogram in which the value represented by the mth bin is the count of sample data values up to and including those in the mth bin: $\sum_{i=1}^{m} n(x_i)$. This can be viewed as the quantized version, or approximation, of the cumulative density function[2] of the underlying population.

2.2.3 The Sample Mean

The sample mean $\bar{x}$ of a sample with n elements is defined as

$$\bar{x} = \frac{1}{n}\sum_{i=1}^{n} x_i = \frac{1}{n}\sum_{i} x_i \qquad \text{(EQ 2.1)}$$

Alternatively, given a sample in tabular form, we can sum over the different possible values of x:

$$\bar{x} = \frac{1}{n}\sum_{x} n(x)x \qquad \text{(EQ 2.2)}$$

Adopting a frequentist approach to probability, where $P(x)$, the probability of a value x, is defined as the limiting value of $n(x)/n$, we see that

$$\lim_{n \to \infty} \bar{x} = \lim_{n \to \infty} \frac{1}{n}\sum_{x} n(x)x = \sum_{x} xP(x) = \mu \qquad \text{(EQ 2.3)}$$

This shows that as the sample size becomes very large, its mean is the expected value of a data item, which is the strong law of large numbers described in Section 1.7.4.

---

2. Cumulative density functions are described in Section 1.3.2.

The sample mean $\bar{x}$ is a random variable whose value depends on the values taken on by the elements in the sample. It turns out that the expected value of this random variable, that is, $E(\bar{x})$, is also μ. (This is not the same as the limiting value of the sample mean.) To see this, we start with the definition of the sample mean: $\bar{x} = \frac{1}{n}(x_1 + x_2 + \ldots + x_n)$, so that $n\bar{x} = (x_1 + x_2 + \ldots + x_n)$. Taking expectations of both sides gives us

$$E(n\bar{x}) = E(x_1 + x_2 + \ldots + x_n) \qquad \text{(EQ 2.4)}$$

From the sum rule of expectations, we can rewrite this as

$$E(n\bar{x}) = E(x_1) + E(x_2) + \ldots + E(x_n) = n\mu \qquad \text{(EQ 2.5)}$$

Therefore,

$$E(\bar{x}) = E\left(\frac{n\bar{x}}{n}\right) = \frac{E(n\bar{x})}{n} = \mu \qquad \text{(EQ 2.6)}$$

as stated.

The mean of a sample is a good representative of the sample for two reasons. First, for a finite sample size, the sample mean is an **estimator** of the population mean. An estimator is **unbiased** if its expected value is the corresponding population parameter. From Equation 2.6, the sample mean is an unbiased estimator of the population mean. If a population is normally distributed, the sample mean is also the most **efficient unbiased estimator** of the population mean, in that it has the least variance of all unbiased estimators of the population mean. Second, it can be easily shown that the mean value of a sample is the value of x^* that minimizes

$\sum_{i=1}^{n} (x_i - x^*)^2$ (i.e., the sum of squared deviations from x^*, which can be interpreted

as errors in choosing x^* as a representative of the sample). In this sense, the mean is the "central" value of a sample.

The mean is therefore the most widely used first-order descriptor of a population. Nevertheless, when using the mean of a sample as its representative, the following issues must be kept in mind.

- The mean of a sample may significantly differ from the true population mean. Consider the means of m samples, where the ith sample mean is derived from a sample with m_i data items (Figure 2.3). These means are likely to differ in value and can be thought of as themselves being data items in a sample with m elements, drawn from a population of sample means. The distribution of this population of sample means is called the **sampling distribution of the**

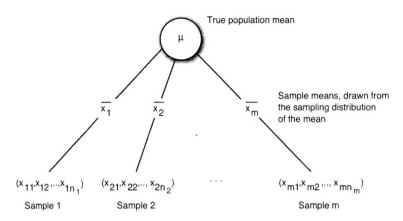

Figure 2.3 Sampling distribution of the mean

mean. If this distribution has a large variance, the mean of any particular sample may be far from representative of the population mean. Therefore, the mean of a sample, especially when the sample size is small, should be treated only as an approximation to the truth. We will examine the topic of statistical significance of the mean of a sample in Section 2.3.

▪ The mean of a sample can be greatly influenced by outliers. Imagine a system in which most packet interarrival times are small but there is one very large gap between packet bursts, corresponding to a very large interarrival time. Unless this outlier is excluded, this single value can bias the mean interarrival time.

EXAMPLE 2.3: EFFECT OF OUTLIERS ON THE MEAN

Table 2.2 shows the effect of an outlier on the sample mean. The sample mean excluding the last value is $(1 * 5 + 2 * 7 + 3 * 2 + 7 * 2)/(5 + 7 + 2 + 2) = 2.43$. The sample mean including the last value is 61.1. It is hard to argue that the mean is representative of this sample, due to the influence of the outlier.

Table 2.2 A Sample with an Outlier

Data Value	Frequency
1	5
2	7
3	2
· 7	2
1,000	1

- The mean of a multimodal distribution usually does not represent a sample very well. Consider a link in which interarrival times are either small (< 1 ms) or large (> 10 s). This will result in a bimodal distribution of sample values. The mean of any sample is therefore not a good representative of a given sample. In such cases, it is best to cluster the sample and compute the means for each cluster separately.

The variance of the sample mean—that is, the variance of the sampling distribution of the mean—can be computed as follows. Recall that

$$n\bar{x} = (x_1 + x_2 + \ldots + x_n)$$

Taking the variance of both sides:

$$V(n\bar{x}) = V(x_1 + x_2 + \ldots + x_n) \qquad \text{(EQ 2.7)}$$

Now, the variance of a sum of a set of independent random variables is the sum of their variances. If we assume that each data value in a sample is independent, an assumption that may not always hold true, then

$$V(n\bar{x}) = V(x_1) + V(x_2) + \ldots + V(x_n) = n\sigma^2 \qquad \text{(EQ 2.8)}$$

Therefore,

$$V(\bar{x}) = V\left(\frac{n\bar{x}}{n}\right) = \frac{V(n\bar{x})}{n^2} = \frac{\sigma^2}{n} \qquad \text{(EQ 2.9)}$$

Therefore, the variance of the sample mean is $1/n$ of the variance of the population variance. As the size of a sample increases, the sample mean, whose expected value is μ, has a smaller and smaller variance, and the mean of each sample is tightly clustered around μ.

2.2.4 The Sample Median

The median value of a sample is the value such that 50% of the elements are larger than this value. For a sample with an odd number of elements, it is the middle element after sorting. For a sample with an even number of elements, it is the mean of the two middle elements after sorting.

For samples that contain outliers, the median is a better representative than the mean because it is relatively insensitive to outliers. The median is also an unbiased estimator of the population mean. However, it can be shown that if the underlying distribution is normal, the asymptotic variance of the median of a sample is 1.57 times larger than the asymptotic variance of the sample mean. Hence, if the underlying distribution is normal, the same accuracy in estimating the population parameter can be obtained by collecting 100 observations and computing their mean or by collecting 157 samples and computing their median. However, if the underlying distribution is unimodal and sharper-peaked than normal (also called **leptokurtic**), the median is a more efficient estimator than the mean because, in such situations, the variance of the mean is higher than the variance of the median due to the presence of outliers.

2.2.5 Measures of Variability

Unlike the mean or the median, which seek to represent the *central tendency* of a sample, we now consider ways of representing the degree to which the elements in a sample differ from each other. These are also called *measures of variability*.

The simplest measure of variability is the **range**, which is the difference between the largest and smallest elements. The range is susceptible to outliers and therefore not reliable. A better measure is to sort the data values and then determine the data values that lie at $q\%$ and $1-q\%$. The difference between the two values is the range of values in which the central $1-2q\%$ of the sample lies. This conveys nearly the same information as the range but with less sensitivity to outliers. A typical value of q is 25, in which case this measure is also called the **interquartile range**. In the context of delay bounds and service-level agreements, a typical value of q is 5 (so that the span is 5%–95%).

EXAMPLE 2.4: INTERQUARTILE RANGE

Consider the sample in Table 2.2. There are 17 data values, so the 25th percentile index is the fourth one, and the 75th percentile index is the thirteenth one. The fourth value in sorted order is 1 and the thirteenth value is 3. Hence, the interquartile range is 2.

Although ranges convey some information, they do not tell us what fraction of the data values are clustered around the sample mean. This information can be represented by the sample variance m_2, which is defined as

$$m_2 = \frac{1}{n} \sum_{i=1}^{n} (x_i - \bar{x})^2 = \frac{1}{n} \sum_{x} (x - \bar{x})^2 n(x) \qquad \text{(EQ 2.10)}$$

Clearly, the variance increases if the sample values are distant from the mean—so that the mean is a poor representative of the sample—and is zero if all the data values are exactly clustered at the mean, in which case the mean perfectly represents the sample. The positive square root of the variance is called the **standard deviation**. Unlike the variance, the standard deviation has the same units as the data values in the sample.

A simple technique to compute the variance of a sample is to maintain a running total of three quantities n, $\sum_i x_i$, and $\sum_i x_i^2$. Then, the variance can be computed as

$$m_2 = \frac{1}{n}\left(\sum_i x_i^2 - \frac{\left(\sum_i x_i\right)^2}{n}\right) \qquad \text{(EQ 2.11)}$$

In the same way that the sample mean estimates the population mean, the sample variance is an estimator for the population variance: σ^2. However, the sample variance is *not* an unbiased estimator of the population variance—it is slightly smaller—with $E(m_2) = (n-1)\sigma^2/n$.

To prove this, recall that each element x_i in a sample can be thought of as being a random variable whose distribution is identical to that of the population, with an expected value of μ and a variance of σ^2. That is, $E(x_i) = \mu$ and $V(x_i) = E((x_i - \mu)^2) = \sigma^2$. Now, by definition of m_2:

$$m_2 = \frac{1}{n}\sum_{i=1}^{n}(x_i - \bar{x})^2 = \frac{1}{n}\left(\sum_{i=1}^{n}(x_i - \mu)^2 - n(\bar{x} - \mu)^2\right) \qquad \text{(EQ 2.12)}$$

where the second step can be verified by expansion. Taking expectations on both sides, we find that

$$E(m_2) = \frac{1}{n}E\left(\sum_{i=1}^{n}(x_i - \mu)^2 - n(\bar{x} - \mu)^2\right)$$

$$= \frac{1}{n}\left(E\left(\sum_{i=1}^{n}(x_i - \mu)^2\right) - nE((\bar{x} - \mu)^2)\right). \qquad \text{(EQ 2.13)}$$

Now, $E\left(\sum_{i=1}^{n}(x_i - \mu)^2\right) = \sum_{i=1}^{n}E(x_i - \mu)^2 = \sum_{i=1}^{n}\sigma^2 = n\sigma^2$. Also, $E(\bar{x}) = \mu$, so $E((\bar{x} - \mu)^2) =$

$V(\bar{x}) = \frac{\sigma^2}{n}$ from Equation 2.9. Substituting these into Equation 2.13, we find that

$$E(m_2) = \frac{1}{n}(n\sigma^2 - \sigma^2) = \frac{(n-1)}{n}\sigma^2, \qquad \text{(EQ 2.14)}$$

as stated. Therefore, to obtain an unbiased estimate of the population variance σ^2, we should multiply m_2 by $n/(n-1)$, so that the unbiased estimator of the population variance is given by

$$E[\sigma^2] = \frac{1}{n-1}\left(\sum_{i=1}^{n}(x_i - \bar{x})^2\right)$$

(EQ 2.15)

2.3 Inferring Population Parameters from Sample Parameters

Thus far, we have focused on statistics that describe a sample in various ways. A sample, however, is usually only a subset of the population. Given the statistics of a sample, what can we infer about the corresponding population parameters? If the sample is small or if the population is intrinsically highly variable, there is not much we can say about the population. However, if the sample is large, there is reason to hope that the sample statistics are a good approximation to the population parameters. We now quantify this intuition.

Our point of departure is the central limit theorem, which states that the sum of n independent random variables, for large n, is approximately normally distributed (see Section 1.7.5). Suppose that we collect a set of m samples, each with n elements, from some population. (In the rest of the discussion, we will assume that n is large enough that the central limit theorem applies.) If the elements of each sample are independently and randomly selected from the population, we can treat the sum of the elements of each sample as the sum of n independent and identically distributed random variables $X_1, X_2,..., X_n$. That is, the first element of the sample is the value assumed by the random variable X_1, the second element is the value assumed by the random variable X_2, and so on. From the central limit theorem, the sum of these random variables is normally distributed. The mean of each sample is the sum divided by a constant, so the mean of each sample is also normally distributed. This fact allows us to determine a range of values where, with high confidence, the population mean can be expected to lie.

To make this more concrete, refer to Figure 2.3 and consider sample 1. The mean of this sample is $\bar{x}_1 = \frac{1}{n}\sum_i x_{1i}$. Similarly, $\bar{x}_2 = \frac{1}{n}\sum_i x_{2i}$, and, in general, $\bar{x}_k = \frac{1}{n}\sum_i x_{ki}$.

Define the random variable $\bar{X}$ as taking on the values $\bar{x}_1, \bar{x}_2, ..., \bar{x}_n$. The distribution of $\bar{X}$ is called the **sampling distribution of the mean**. From the central limit theorem, $\bar{X}$ is approximately normally distributed. Moreover, if the elements are drawn from a population with mean μ and variance σ^2, we have already seen that $E(\bar{X}) = \mu$ (Equation 2.6) and $V(\bar{X}) = \sigma^2/n$ (Equation 2.9). These are, therefore, the parameters of the corresponding normal distribution, or $\overline{X} \sim N(\mu, \sigma^2/n)$. Of course, we do not know the *true* values of μ and σ^2.

If we know σ^2, we can estimate a range of values in which μ will lie, with high probability, as follows. For any normally distributed random variable $Y \sim (\mu_Y, \sigma_Y^2)$, we know that 95% of the probability mass lies within 1.96 standard deviations of its mean and that 99% of the probability mass lies within 2.576 standard deviations of its mean. So, for any value y:

$$P(\mu_Y - 1.96\ \sigma_Y < y < \mu_Y + 1.96\ \sigma_Y) = 0.95 \qquad \text{(EQ 2.16)}$$

The left and right endpoints of this range are called the **critical values** at the 95% confidence level: An observation will lie beyond the critical value, assuming that the true mean is μ_Y, in less than 5% (or 1%) of observed samples. This can be rewritten as

$$P(|\mu_Y - y| < 1.96\ \sigma_Y) = 0.95 \qquad \text{(EQ 2.17)}$$

Therefore, from symmetry of the absolute value:

$$P(y - 1.96\ \sigma_Y < \mu_Y < y + 1.96\ \sigma_Y) = 0.95 \qquad \text{(EQ 2.18)}$$

In other words, given any value y drawn from a normal distribution whose mean is μ_Y, we can estimate a range of values where μ_Y must lie with high probability (i.e., 95% or 99%). This is called the **confidence interval** for μ_Y.

We just saw that $\overline{X} \sim N(\mu, \sigma^2/n)$. Therefore, given the sample mean $\overline{x}$:

$$P(\overline{x} - 1.96\ \frac{\sigma}{\sqrt{n}} < \mu < \overline{x} + 1.96\ \frac{\sigma}{\sqrt{n}}) = 0.95 \qquad \text{(EQ 2.19)}$$

and

$$P(\overline{x} - 2.576\ \frac{\sigma}{\sqrt{n}} < \mu < \overline{x} + 2.576\ \frac{\sigma}{\sqrt{n}}) = 0.99 \qquad \text{(EQ 2.20)}$$

Assuming that we knew the sample mean and σ^2, this allows us to compute the range of values where the population mean will lie with 95% or 99% confidence.

Note that a confidence interval is constructed from the observations in such a way that there is a known probability, such as 95% or 99%, of it containing the population parameter of interest. It is not the population parameter that is the random variable; the interval itself is the random variable.

The situation is graphically illustrated in Figure 2.4. Here, we assume that the population is normally distributed with mean 1. The variance of the sampling distribution (i.e., of $\overline{X}$) is σ^2/n, so it has a narrower spread than the population, with the spread decreasing as we increase the number of elements in the sample. A randomly chosen sample happens to have a mean of 2.0. This mean is the value assumed by a

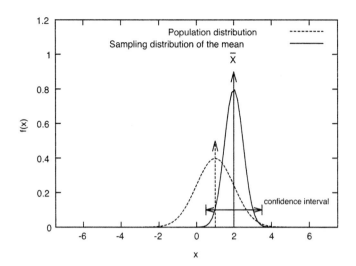

Figure 2.4 Population and sample mean distributions

random variable $\overline{X}$ whose distribution is the sampling distribution of the mean and whose expected value from this single sample is centered at 2. (If we were to take more samples, their means would converge toward the true mean of the sampling distribution.) The double-headed arrow around $\overline{X}$ in the figure indicates a confidence interval in which the population mean μ must lie with high probability.

In almost all practical situations, we do not know σ^2. All is not lost, however. Recall that an unbiased estimator for σ^2 is $\dfrac{1}{n-1}\left(\displaystyle\sum_{i=1}^{n}(x_i-\bar{x})^2\right)$ (Equation 2.15).

Assuming that this estimator is of good quality (in practice, this is true when $n >$ ~20), $\overline{X} \sim N\!\left(\mu, \dfrac{1}{n(n-1)}\left(\displaystyle\sum_{i=1}^{n}(x_i-\bar{x})^2\right)\right)$, therefore, when n is sufficiently large, we can still compute the confidence interval in which the population mean lies with high probability.

EXAMPLE 2.5: CONFIDENCE INTERVALS

Consider the data values in Table 2.1. What are the 95% and 99% confidence intervals in which the population mean lies?

Solution:

We will ignore the fact that $n = 17 < 20$, so that the central limit theorem is not likely to apply. Pressing on, we find that the sample mean is 2.88. We compute $\sum_{i=1}^{n}(x_i - \bar{x})^2$ as 107.76. Therefore, the variance of the sampling distribution of the mean is estimated as 107.76/(17 * 16) = 0.396, and the standard deviation of this distribution is estimated as its square root: 0.63. Using the value of $\pm 1.96\sigma$ for the 95% confidence interval and $\pm 2.576\sigma$ for the 99% confidence interval, the 95% confidence interval is [2.88 − 1.96 * 0.63, 2.88 + 1.96 * 0.63] = [1.65, 4.11], and the 99% confidence interval is [1.26, 4.5].

Because $\bar{X}$ is normally distributed with mean μ and variance σ^2/n, $\dfrac{(\bar{x} - \mu)}{\left(\dfrac{\sigma}{\sqrt{n}}\right)}$ is a $N(0,1)$ variable, also called the **standard Z variable**. In practice, when $n > 20$, we can substitute $m_2(n/(n-1))$ as an estimate for σ^2 when computing the standard Z variable.

In the preceding, we have assumed that n is large, so that the central limit theorem applies. In particular, we have made the simplifying assumption that the estimated variance of the sampling distribution of the mean is identical to the actual variance of the sampling distribution. When n is small, this can lead to underestimating the variance of this distribution. To correct for this, we have to reexamine the distribution of the normally distributed standard random variable $\dfrac{(\bar{x} - \mu)}{\left(\dfrac{\sigma}{\sqrt{n}}\right)}$,

which we actually estimate as the random variable $\dfrac{(\bar{x} - \mu)}{\sqrt{\dfrac{\sum_i (x_i - \bar{x})^2}{n(n-1)}}}$. The latter variable

is *not* normally distributed. Instead, it is called the **standard t variable** that is distributed according to the *t* distribution with $n - 1$ **degrees of freedom** (a parameter of the distribution). The salient feature of the *t* distribution is that, unlike the normal distribution, its shape varies with the degrees of freedom, with its shape for $n > 20$ becoming nearly identical to the normal distribution.

How does this affect the computation of confidence intervals? Given a sample, we proceed to compute the estimate of the mean as $\bar{x}$ as before. However, to compute the, say, 95% confidence interval, we need to change our procedure slightly. We have to find the range of values such that the probability mass under the *t* distribution (not the normal distribution) centered at that mean and with variance

$$\frac{\sum_i (x_i - \bar{x})^2}{n(n-1)}$$ is 0.95. Given the degrees of freedom, which is simply $n - 1$, we can look

this up in a standard t table. Then, we can state with 95% confidence that the population mean lies in this range.

EXAMPLE 2.6: CONFIDENCE INTERVALS FOR SMALL SAMPLES

Continuing with the sample in Table 2.1, we will now use the t distribution to compute confidence intervals. The unbiased estimate of the population standard deviation is 0.63. Since $n = 17$, this corresponds to a t distribution with 16 degrees of freedom. We find from the standard t table that a $(0,1)$ t variable reaches the 0.025 probability level at 2.12, so that there is 0.05 probability mass beyond 2.12 times the standard deviation on both sides of the mean. Therefore, the 95% confidence interval is $[2.88 - (2.12 * 0.63), 2.88 + (2.12 * 0.63)] = [1.54,$ 4.22]. Compare this to the 95% confidence interval of $[1.65, 4.11]$ obtained using the normal distribution in Example 2.5. Similarly, the t distribution reaches the 0.005 probability level at 2.921, leading to the 99% confidence interval of $[2.88 - (2.921 * 0.63), 2.88+(2.921 * 0.63)] = [1.03, 4.72]$ compared to $[1.26, 4.5]$.

So far, we have focused on estimating the population mean and variance and have computed the range of values in which the population mean is expected to lie with high probability, obtained by studying the sampling distribution of the mean. We can obtain corresponding confidence intervals for the population variance by studying the **sampling distribution of the variance**. It can be shown that if the population is normally distributed, this sampling distribution is the χ^2 distribution (discussed in Section 2.4.7). However, this confidence interval is rarely derived in practice, and so we will omit the details of this result.

2.4 Testing Hypotheses about Outcomes of Experiments

We often need to study the outcomes of experiments conducted to measure the performance of computer systems. We typically would like to assert either that a metric associated with the system has a certain value, such as having a mean value of 1.5 units, or that a new heuristic or algorithm improves the performance of the system. Here, we study techniques for making statistically valid assertions about the outcomes of experiments in which we compare at most two values. We study outcomes involving more than two experiments in Section 2.6.

2.4.1 Hypothesis Testing

Assertions about outcomes of an experiment can usually be reformulated in terms of testing a **hypothesis**: a speculative claim about the outcome of an experiment. The goal of an experiment is to show that either the hypothesis is unlikely to be true (i.e., we can reject the hypothesis), or the experiment is consistent with the hypothesis (i.e., the hypothesis need not be rejected).

This last statement bears some analysis. Suppose that we are asked to check whether a coin is biased. We will start with the tentative hypothesis that the coin is unbiased: P(heads) = P(tails) = 0.5. Then, suppose we toss the coin three times and that we get three heads in a row. What does this say about our hypothesis? Conditional on the hypothesis being true, we have a probability of 0.5 * 0.5 * 0.5 = 12.5% that we obtain the observed outcome. This is not too unlikely, so perhaps the three heads in a row were simply due to chance. At this point, all we can state is that the experimental outcome is consistent with the hypothesis.

Now, suppose that we flip the coin ten times and see that it comes up heads nine times. If our hypothesis were true, the probability of getting nine heads in ten coin flips is given by the binomial distribution as $\binom{10}{1}0.5^9 0.5^1 = 10 * 0.5^{10} = 10/1024 <$ 1%. Thus, if the hypothesis were true, this outcome is fairly unlikely: setting the bar for "unlikeliness" at 1%. This is typically stated as: "We reject the hypothesis at the 1% confidence level."

The probability of an outcome assuming that a hypothesis is true is called its **p-value**. If the outcome of an experiment has a p-value less than 1% (or 5%), we would interpret the experiment as grounds for rejecting a hypothesis at the 1% (or 5%) level.

It is important to realize that the nonrejection of a hypothesis does not mean that the hypothesis is valid. For example, instead of starting with the hypothesis that the coin was unbiased, we could have made the hypothesis that the coin was biased, with P(heads) = 0.9. If we toss the coin three times and get three heads, the probability of that event, assuming that the hypothesis were true, would be 0.9 * 0.9 * 0.9 = 0.73. So, we cannot reject the hypothesis that the coin is biased. Indeed, with such a small number of experiments, *we cannot invalidate an infinite number of mutually incompatible hypotheses*!

We are therefore led to two inescapable conclusions. First, even the most careful experiment may lead to an incorrect conclusion due to random errors. Such errors may result in rejection of a hypothesis, even though it ought not be rejected, or in nonrejection, when it should. Second, an experiment cannot result in the acceptance of a hypothesis but only in its rejection or nonrejection, which is not the same as acceptance. We deal with each conclusion in turn.

2.4.2 Errors in Hypothesis Testing

Testing a hypothesis can never be entirely accurate. Random fluctuations in the outcomes of experiments may lead to nonrejection of a hypothesis when it should be rejected and rejecting it when it should not. We now discuss these errors in hypothesis testing.

Consider two universes in each of which a particular hypothesis is either valid or invalid. In each universe, we can expect one of two results from hypothesis testing: "The hypothesis is not rejected" or "The hypothesis is rejected." The four possible outcomes of testing are represented in the following table:

	Outcome of the Experiment	
State of the Universe	**Reject Hypothesis**	**Do Not Reject Hypothesis**
Hypothesis is invalid	Good outcome C_{00}	Bad outcome C_{01} False negative or Type II error
Hypothesis is valid	Bad outcome C_{10} False positive or Type I error	Good outcome C_{11}

- If the hypothesis is invalid and is rejected, we have a good outcome. The probability of this event is denoted C_{00}.
- If the hypothesis is invalid but is not rejected, we have a bad outcome. The probability of this event is denoted C_{01}.
- If the hypothesis is valid and is not rejected, we have a good outcome. The probability of this event is denoted C_{11}.
- If the hypothesis is valid but is rejected, we have a bad outcome. The probability of this event is denoted C_{10}.

We can use the C_{ij} to define the following quantities:

Term	Definition	Meaning
Concordance	$C_{11}+C_{00}$	The probability of an accurate prediction
Error rate	$C_{10}+C_{01}$	The probability of an inaccurate prediction
Sensitivity	$C_{11}/(C_{11}+C_{01})$	Ability to predict correctly conditional on the hypothesis actually being valid
Specificity	$C_{00}/(C_{10}+C_{00})$	Ability to eliminate a false hypothesis conditional on the hypothesis actually being invalid

These quantities apply to all types of hypothesis testing. Our goal is to design experiments that maximize good outcomes while minimizing bad ones. In certain cases, we may trade off a higher sensitivity for a higher error rate, or a higher specificity for a lower concordance. A common rule is to limit Type I errors to 5%. That is, if the hypothesis is valid, we should not mistakenly reject it more than 5% of the time. Note that at the 5% confidence level, we might reject the hypothesis once in 20 times just by chance.

2.4.3 Formulating a Hypothesis

We now return to the problem that an experiment can result only in rejection or nonrejection of a hypothesis. Therefore, we may end up not rejecting an invalid hypothesis. What guidelines should we use in choosing a hypothesis?

The standard technique is to formulate a **null hypothesis** that we believe is sufficient to explain the data unless statistical evidence strongly indicates otherwise. The null hypothesis should be formulated conservatively, that is, preserving the status quo, where this is applicable. A good way to think about this is in terms of a criminal trial. The judicial system starts with the presumption of innocence. It is up to the prosecution to prove that the defendant is guilty. If the prosecution cannot prove beyond reasonable doubt that the defendant is guilty, the defendant is released. No doubt, this will let some guilty parties go unpunished. But it is preferable to the alternative, whereby the defendant is assumed guilty and must prove innocence.

In formulating a null hypothesis, it is necessary to be precise. In the words of Sir R. A. Fisher, the inventor of this approach, the null hypothesis should be "free from vagueness and ambiguity." Otherwise, it may be impossible to reject it, making our effort fruitless. Moreover, a hypothesis should be about a population parameter, not a sample, unless the sample includes the entire population.

EXAMPLE 2.7: FORMULATING A NULL HYPOTHESIS

Consider a router that can execute either scheduling algorithm A or scheduling algorithm B. Suppose that our goal is to show that scheduling algorithm A is superior to scheduling algorithm B for some metric. An acceptable conservative null hypothesis would be "Scheduling algorithm A and scheduling algorithm B have identical performance." Given this assumption, we would expect the performance metrics for both scheduling algorithms to be roughly the same (i.e., our expectation about the state of the world). If our experiments show this to be the case—for example, if the sample means of the performance metrics for both scheduling algorithms were nearly identical—we would conclude that we do not have sufficient evidence to prove that scheduling algorithm B improved the system, a conservative and scientifically valid decision.

In contrast, if the sample mean for algorithm A were much higher than the sample mean for algorithm B, the experiment would be inconsistent with our null hypothesis, and we would reject it, giving credence to the belief that scheduling algorithm A was indeed better.[3]

If we were to invert the null hypothesis, stating it as "Scheduling algorithm A is better than scheduling algorithm B," then we may come to an unwarranted conclusion by being unable to reject the null hypothesis. In any case, this hypothesis is imprecise, in that we did not quantify *how* much better algorithm A is supposed to be better than scheduling algorithm B, so the hypothesis ought to be deprecated on those grounds alone.

We represent the null hypothesis by using the symbol H_0. Alternatives to the null hypothesis are usually labeled H_1, H_2, and so on. The steps in hypothesis testing depend on whether the outcome of an experiment is being compared with a fixed quantity or whether it is being compared with the outcome of another experiment. In the next subsection, we consider outcomes that are compared with a fixed quantity, deferring comparison of outcomes of two experiments to Section 2.4.5.

Hypotheses can be two-tailed or one-tailed. We reject a two-tailed hypothesis if the sample statistic significantly differs from the conjectured corresponding population parameter in absolute value. For example, suppose that we hypothesize that the population mean μ is 0. If observations indicate that $|\bar{x}| > a$, where a is the **critical value**, we reject the hypothesis. In contrast, we reject a one-tailed hypothesis if the sample statistic significantly differs from the corresponding population parameter in a prespecified direction (i.e., is smaller than or larger than the conjectured population parameter), where experimental conditions allow us to rule out deviations in the other direction. An example of a one-tailed hypothesis is $\mu < 0$. If $\bar{x} > a$, where a, again, is the critical value, we can reject this hypothesis. Note that we do not consider the "other tail," that is, the possibility that $\bar{x} < a$.

2.4.4 Comparing an Outcome with a Fixed Quantity

To develop intuition, let us start with a simple example. Suppose that physical considerations lead us to expect that the population mean of a population under study is 0. Assume that there is no particular status quo that we are trying to maintain. Therefore, a reasonable null hypothesis is

$$H_0: \textit{the population mean is } 0$$

---

3. In the Bayesian formulation of hypothesis testing, we view the experiment as updating a prior expectation on the state of the world, thus refining our model for the state of the world. Here, we are presenting the classical statistical view on hypothesis testing.

To test this hypothesis, we need to sample the population multiple times and compute the corresponding sample means. If the number of samples is large, the central limit theorem implies that each sample mean will be drawn from a normal distribution. We can use this fact to compute its confidence interval—say, at the 95% level—using the techniques in Section 2.3. We then check whether 0 lies within this interval. One of two cases arises.

1. If 0 lies in the 95% (99%) confidence interval of the sample mean, we cannot reject the null hypothesis. This is usually *incorrectly* interpreted to mean that with 95% (99%) confidence, the population mean is indeed 0. Of course, all we have shown is that, conditional on the population mean being 0, the outcome of this experiment has a likelihood greater than 95% (99%) (it is consistent with the null hypothesis).

2. If 0 does not lie in the 95% (99%) confidence interval of the sample mean, we reject the null hypothesis. This is usually incorrectly interpreted to mean that, with high confidence, the population mean is not 0. Again, all we have shown is that, conditional on the mean being 0, the outcome we saw was rather unlikely, so we have good reason to be suspicious of the null hypothesis.

This example is easily generalized. Suppose that we want to establish that the population mean is μ_0. We compute the sample mean $\bar{x}$ as before. Then, we test the hypothesis:

$$H_0: (\bar{x} - \mu_0) = 0$$

which can be tested as described earlier, with identical conclusions being drawn about the results.[4]

EXAMPLE 2.8: TESTING FOR A ZERO MEAN

Returning to Example 2.6, note that the 99% confidence interval for the mean of the sample data, using the t test, was [1.03, 4.72]. Therefore, we can state with 99% confidence, with the caveats just stated, that the mean of the underlying population is not 0.

---

4. Advanced readers may note that in this section, we have switched from the Fisher to the Neyman-Pearson approach to hypothesis testing. This hybrid approach is widely used in modern scientific practice.

2.4.5 Comparing Outcomes from Two Experiments

Suppose that we want to test the hypothesis that two samples are drawn from different populations. To fix ideas, consider that we are comparing two systems—a system currently in use and a system that incorporates a new algorithm—on the basis of a particular performance metric. We assume that we can collect performance metrics from each system multiple times to obtain two samples. If the systems do not differ to a statistically significant degree, both samples would be drawn from the same underlying population, with the same population mean, and therefore would have similar statistics, such as the sample mean. However, if the statistics are significantly different, we infer that the two samples are likely to be drawn from different populations and that the new algorithm does indeed affect the performance of the system.

The null hypothesis is the statement

H_0: *the two systems are identical*

We reject H_0 if it is sufficiently unlikely that the two samples are drawn from the same population, because this will result in the conservative position that the new algorithm does not affect the performance of the system.

Suppose that we collect n sets of samples from the first system, labeled A, to get sample means $a_1, a_2,...,a_n$ and collect m sets of samples from the second system, labeled B, to get sample means $b_1, b_2,...,b_m$. Let the means of these means be denoted $\overline{a}$ and $\overline{b}$ with corresponding variances $m_2(a)$ and $m_2(b)$.

If $n=m$, we define an auxiliary random variable C = A – B, which takes values $c_i = a_i - b_i$. Then, we redefine the hypothesis as

H_0: *the population mean of C is zero*

This can be easily tested using the approach described in Section 2.4.4.

EXAMPLE 2.9: COMPARING TWO SAMPLES

Suppose that you are using simulations to study the effect of buffer size at some network queue on packet loss rate. You would like to see whether increasing the buffer size from 5 packets to 100 packets has a significant effect on loss rate. To do so, suppose that you run ten simulations for each buffer size, resulting in loss rates as follows:

Loss rate with 5 Buffers	1.20%	2.30%	1.90%	2.40%	3.00%	1.80%	2.10%	3.20%	4.50%	2.20%
Loss rate with 100 Buffers	0.10%	0.60%	1.10%	0.80%	1.20%	0.30%	0.70%	1.90%	0.20%	1.20%

Does the buffer size have a significant influence on the packet loss rate?

Solution:

Note that each loss rate measurement in each simulation is itself a sample mean. Therefore, these loss rates can be assumed to be distributed approximately normally. Denoting by a_i the loss rate with a buffer of size 5 packets and by b_i the loss rate with a buffer size of 100 packets, we define the auxiliary variable $c_i = a_i - b_i$ that takes values $(1.2 - 0.1), (2.3 - 0.6),..., (2.2 - 1.2)$, so that c is given by

$$c = \{1.1, 1.7, 0.8, 1.6, 1.8, 1.5, 1.4, 1.3, 4.3, 1.0\}$$

We compute the sample mean as 1.65 and sample variance m_2 as 0.87, so that the unbiased estimator for the population variance is given by $(n/n - 1)m_2 = 0.97$. The variance of the sample mean is given by $m_2/n = 0.097$, corresponding to a standard deviation of 0.31. Because the number of values is smaller than 20, we use the t distribution with 9 degrees of freedom to compute the confidence interval at the 95% level as 1.65 ± 0.70. This interval does not include 0. Thus, we conclude that the change in the buffer size does significantly affect the loss rate.

If $n \neq m$, the situation is somewhat more complex. We first use $m_2(a)$ to compute the confidence interval for A's performance metric around its sample mean $\bar{a}$ and similarly use $m_2(b)$ to compute the confidence interval for B's performance metric around its sample mean $\bar{b}$, using the normal, or t, distribution, as appropriate). Now, one of the following two cases holds.

1. *The confidence intervals do not overlap.* Recall that with 95% (or 99%) confidence, A's and B's population means lie within the computed confidence intervals. If the null hypothesis were true and the population means coincided, it must be the case that either A's population mean or B's population mean lies outside its computed confidence interval. However, this has a probability lower than 5% (1%). Therefore, we reject the hypothesis.

2. *The confidence intervals overlap.* In this case, there is some chance that the samples are drawn from the same population. The next steps depend on whether we can make one of two assumptions: (a) the population variances are the same, or (b) n and m are both large.

If the population variances are the same, we define the auxiliary variable s by

$$s^2 = \frac{\displaystyle\sum_{i=1}^{n} (a_i - \bar{a})^2 + \sum_{i=1}^{m} (b_i - \bar{b})^2}{m + n - 2}$$

(EQ 2.21)

Then, it can be shown that if the two samples are drawn from the same population, the variable c defined by

$$c = \frac{\bar{a} - \bar{b}}{s\sqrt{\dfrac{1}{m} + \dfrac{1}{n}}} \qquad \text{(EQ 2.22)}$$

is a standard t variable (i.e., with zero mean and unit variance) with $m + n - 2$ degrees of freedom. Therefore, we can use a t test to determine whether c has a zero mean, using the approach in Section 2.4.4.

EXAMPLE 2.10: COMPARING TWO SAMPLES OF DIFFERENT SAMPLE SIZES

Continuing with Example 2.9, assume that we have additional data points for the simulation runs with five buffers, as follows. Can we still claim that the buffer size plays a role in determining the loss rate?

Loss Rate with 5 Buffers	0.20% 0.30% 0.90% 1.40% 1.00% 0.80% 1.10% 0.20% 1.50% 0.20% 0.50% 1.20% 0.70% 1.30% 0.90%

Loss Rate with 100 Buffers	0.10% 0.60% 1.10% 0.80% 1.20% 0.30% 0.70% 1.90% 0.20% 1.20%

Solution:

Here, $m = 15$ and $n = 10$, so we cannot use the approach of Example 2.9. Instead, we will first compute the mean and confidence intervals of both samples to see whether the intervals overlap. It is easily found that, at the 95% level, using a t distribution with 14 and 9 degrees of freedom, respectively, the confidence intervals are 0.81 ± 0.25 and 0.81 ± 0.40, which overlap. However, the sample variances are not the same, and there is a good chance that the population variances also differ. Nevertheless, for the purpose of this example, we will make the assumption that the population variances are the same. Therefore, we compute s^2 using Equation 2.21 as 2.89, so that $s = 1.7$. We then use Equation 2.22 to compute the standard t variate c as $0.0033/(1.7(1/15 + 1/10)^{1/2})$ $= 0.0048$. Since this has unit variance, it is easy to see using the t test with 23 degrees of freedom that 0 lies in the confidence interval for c, which implies that, with this data set, buffer size has no statistically significant effect on packet loss rate.

If population variances differ, but m *and* n *are both large,* it can be shown that the variable c defined by

$$c = \frac{\bar{a} - \bar{b}}{\sqrt{\left(\dfrac{\displaystyle\sum_{i=1}^{n} (a_i - \bar{a})^2}{m(m-1)} \right) + \left(\dfrac{\displaystyle\sum_{i=1}^{m} (b_i - \bar{b})^2}{n(n-1)} \right)}}$$
(EQ 2.23)

is a standard normal variable (i.e., with a zero mean and unit variance). Therefore, we can use a standard normal test to determine whether c has a zero mean, using the approach discussed in Section 2.4.4.

If neither assumption can be made, it is difficult to draw meaningful comparisons, other than by using **nonparametric tests**, such as the Mann-Whitney U test, which is beyond the scope of this text.

2.4.6 Testing Hypotheses about Quantities Measured on Ordinal Scales

So far, we have tested hypotheses in which a variable takes on real values. We now consider a variable that takes on nominal (categorical) values, such as "UDP" or "TCP," or ordinal values, such as "bad," "satisfactory," and "good." (These terms are defined in Section 2.1.2.) In such cases, hypothesis testing using the techniques described earlier is meaningless because a sample cannot be described by a mean; nor can we define real confidence intervals about the mean. Instead, for such variables, hypotheses are of the form

H_0: *the observed values are drawn from the expected distribution*

Then, we use a statistical test, such as the *Pearson chi-squared test*, to reject or not reject the hypothesis, as described next.

EXAMPLE 2.11: HYPOTHESIS FORMULATION WITH NOMINAL SCALES

Suppose that you want to check whether the distribution of packet types on a link from your campus to the Internet is similar to that reported in the literature. For instance, suppose that 42% of the bytes originating at the University of Waterloo (UW) during the measurement period can be attributed to P2P applications. Suppose that you measure 100 GB of traffic and find that 38 GB can be attributed to P2P applications. Then, a reasonable null hypothesis would be

H_0: *the observed traffic on the campus Internet access link is similar to that at UW*

How should we test hypotheses of this form? A clue comes from the following thought experiment. Suppose that we have a possibly biased coin and that we want to determine whether it is biased. The null hypothesis is

$$H_0\colon P(heads) = P(tails) = 0.5$$

We assume that we can toss the coin as many times as we want and that the outcome of each toss is independent. Let T denote the outcome "Tails" and H denote the outcome "Heads." We will represent a set of outcomes, such as "Nine heads and one tails" by the notation TH^9. As we saw earlier, if a coin is unbiased, this outcome has the probability $\binom{10}{1} 0.5^9 0.5^1$. Any outcome from n coin tosses—such as a Heads, represented by $\text{H}^a \text{T}^{n-a}$—can be viewed as one sample drawn at random from the set of all possible outcomes when tossing a coin n times. A little thought indicates that the probability of this outcome, given that the probability of heads is p and of tails is $q = 1 - p$, is given by the binomial distribution $\binom{n}{a} p^a q^{n-a}$, which is also the ath term of the expansion of the expression $(p + q)^n$. As $n \to \infty$, the binomial distribution tends to the normal distribution, so that the probability of each outcome is approximated by the normal distribution.

Now, consider an experiment in which each individual outcome is independent of the others, and an outcome results in one of k ordinal values, $o_1, o_2,\ldots, o_k$. Let the expected probability of the ith outcome be p_i, so that the expected count for the ith outcome, $e_i = np_i$. Suppose that we run the experiment n times and that the ith outcome occurs n_i times with $\sum_i n_i = n$. We can represent any particular outcome by $o_1^{n_1} o_2^{n_2} \ldots o_k^{n_k}$, and this outcome can be viewed as one sample drawn at random from the set of all possible outcomes. The probability of such an outcome is given by the **multinomial** distribution as

$$P(o_1^{a_1} o_2^{a_2} \ldots o_k^{a_k}) = \binom{n}{n_1}\binom{n-n_1}{n_2}\ldots\binom{n-\sum_i^{k-1} n_i}{n_k} p_1^{n_1} p_2^{n_2} \ldots p_k^{n_k} \qquad \text{(EQ 2.24)}$$

$$= \frac{n!}{n_1! n_2! \ldots n_k!} p_1^{n_1} p_2^{n_2} \ldots p_k^{n_k} \qquad \text{(EQ 2.25)}$$

This outcome is one of the terms from the expansion of $(p_1 + p_2 + \ldots + p_k)^n$. As with the binomial distribution, we can use the multinomial distribution to test whether any particular outcome, conditional on a null hypothesis on the p_is being true, is "too unlikely," indicating that the null hypothesis should be rejected.

In many cases, using the multinomial distribution for testing the validity of a hypothesis can be cumbersome. Instead, we use a standard mathematical result that the variable $X_i = \dfrac{n_i - e_i}{\sqrt{e_i}}$, for values of $e_i > 5$, closely approximates a standard normal variable with zero mean and unit variance. But we immediately run into a snag: The n_i are not independent. For example, if $n_3 = n$, all the other n_i must be zero. Therefore, the X_i are also not independent. However, it can be proved that this set of k *dependent* variables X_i can be mapped to a set of $k - 1$ *independent* standard normal variables while keeping the sums of squares of the variables constant. By definition, the sum of squares of $k - 1$ independent standard normal variables follows the χ^2 (also written chi-squared and pronounced kai-squared) distribution with $k - 1$ degrees of freedom. Therefore, if the null hypothesis is true—that is, the observed quantities are drawn from the distribution specified implicitly by the expected values—the variable

$$X = \sum_{i=1}^{k} \frac{(n_i - e_i)^2}{e_i}$$

(EQ 2.26)

is an χ^2 variable with $k - 1$ degrees of freedom. Standard statistical tables tabulate $P(X > a)$, where X is an χ^2 variable with k degrees of freedom. We can use this table to compute the degree to which a set of observations corresponds to a set of expected values for these observations. This test is the *Pearson* χ^2 *test*.

EXAMPLE 2.12: CHI-SQUARED TEST

We use the Pearson χ^2 test to test whether the observation in Example 2.11 results in rejection of the null hypothesis. Denote P2P traffic by ordinal 1 and non-P2P traffic by ordinal 2. Then, $e_1 = 42$, $e_2 = 58$, $n_1 = 38$, $n_2 = 62$. Therefore, $X = (38 - 42)^2/42 + (62 - 58)^2/58 = 0.65$. From the χ^2 table with 1 degree of freedom, we see that $P(X > 3.84) = 0.05$, so that any value greater than 3.84 occurs with probability less than 95% and is unlikely. Since $0.65 < 3.84$, the observation is not unlikely, which means that we cannot reject the null hypothesis.

In contrast, suppose that the observation was $n_1 = 72$, $n_2 = 28$. Then, $X = (72 - 42)^2/42 + (28 - 58)^2/58 = 36.9$. Since $36.9 > 3.84$, such an observation would suggest that we should reject the null hypothesis at the 5% level.

2.4.7 Fitting a Distribution

When testing a hypothesis using a chi-square test, we need to compute the expected distribution of sample values. These expected values may come from prior studies, as in the preceding example, or from physical considerations. In many cases, however, the expected values can be derived by assuming that the observations arise from a standard distribution, such as the Poisson, exponential, or normal distributions, and then choosing the parameters of the distribution to best match the observed values. This is called *fitting* a distribution to the observations. A general technique for fitting a distribution is called the **method of maximum likelihood**, discussed next.

Suppose that random variables $X_1, X_2,..., X_n$ have a known joint density function $f_\theta(x_1, x_2,..., x_n)$, where θ denotes the unknown parameters of the distribution, such as its mean and variance. Given the observation $X_i = x_i$, where $i = 1, 2,..., n$, we would like to compute the **maximum likelihood estimate** (MLE) of θ, that is, the value of θ that makes the observed data the "most likely." Intuitively, conditional on the observations being what they are, we would like to work backward to find the value of θ that made these observations likely: We then assume that we observed what we did because the parameters were what they were.

Assuming that the X_i values are independent and identically distributed according to $f_\theta(.)$, the joint probability that the observation is $(x_1, x_2,..., x_n)$ is simply the product of the individual probabilities $\prod_{i=1}^{n} f_\theta(X_i)$. Note that the distribution function is parametrized by θ. We make this explicit by defining *likelihood*(θ) as

$$likelihood(\theta|x_1,x_2,...,x_n) = \prod_{i=1}^{n} f_\theta(X_i) \qquad \text{(EQ 2.27)}$$

We find the MLE by maximizing *likelihood*(θ) with respect to θ. In practice, it is more convenient to maximize the natural logarithm of *likelihood*(.) denoted $l(.)$, defined by

$$l(\theta|x_1,x_2,...,x_n) = \sum_{i=1}^{n} \log(f_\theta(X_i)) \qquad \text{(EQ 2.28)}$$

For example, suppose that we want to fit a Poisson distribution with parameter λ to an observation $(x_1, x_2,..., x_n)$. Recall that for a Poisson distribution,

$$P(X = x) = \frac{\lambda^x e^{-\lambda}}{x!}.$$

If the X_i are independent and identically distributed (i.i.d.) Poisson variables, their joint probability is the product of their individual distributions, so that

$$l(\lambda) = \sum_{i=1}^{n} (X_i \log \lambda - \lambda - \log X_i!)$$

$$l(\lambda) = \log \lambda \sum_{i=1}^{n} X_i - n\lambda - \sum_{i=1}^{n} \log X_i!$$

(EQ 2.29)

We maximize $l(.)$ by differentiating it with respect to λ and setting the derivative to 0:

$$\frac{dl}{d\lambda} = \frac{1}{\lambda} \sum_{i=1}^{n} X_i - n = 0$$

(EQ 2.30)

which yields the satisfying result

$$\lambda = \overline{X}$$

(EQ 2.31)

Thus, we have found that the mean of a set of observations is the value that maximizes the probability that we obtain that particular set of observations, conditional on the observations being independent and identically distributed Poisson variables.

Proceeding along similar lines, it is possible to show that the maximum likelihood estimators for a set of i.i.d. normal variables is

$$\mu = \overline{X}$$

$$\sigma = \sqrt{\frac{1}{n} \sum_{i=1}^{n} (X_i - \overline{X})^2}$$

(EQ 2.32)

Note that the MLE for the standard deviation is not a consistent estimator, to get one, we need to divide by $n - 1$, rather than n, as discussed in Section 2.2.5. Maximum likelihood estimators for other distributions can be found in standard texts on mathematical statistics.

It is possible to obtain confidence intervals for maximum likelihood estimators by considering the sampling distribution of the estimated parameters. This is discussed in greater depth in more advanced texts.

Note that if we use the sample itself to estimate p parameter values of the population, we reduce the number of degrees of freedom in the sample by p. Recall that a sample that has n counts (ordinal types), has $n - 1$ degrees of freedom. If, in addition, p parameters are estimated to compute the expected counts, the degree of freedom when conducting a chi-squared test is $n - 1 - p$.

EXAMPLE 2.13: FITTING A POISSON DISTRIBUTION

In an experiment, a researcher counted the number of packets arriving to a switch in each 1 ms time period. The following table shows the count of the number of time periods with a certain number of packet arrivals. For instance, there were 146 time periods that had six arrivals. The researcher expects the packet arrival process to be a Poisson process. Find the best Poisson fit for the sample. Use this to compute the expected count for each number of arrivals. What is the chi-squared variable value for this data set? Determine whether the Poisson distribution adequately describes the data.

Number of Packet Arrivals	1	2	3	4	5	6	7	8	9	10	11	12	13	14	15	16
Count	18	28	56	105	126	146	164	165	120	103	73	54	23	16	9	5

Solution:

The total number of time periods is $18 + 28 + \ldots + 5 = 1{,}211$. The total number of arrivals is $(18 * 1) + (28 * 2) + \ldots + (5 * 16) = 8{,}935$. Therefore, the mean number of packets arriving in 1 ms is $8{,}935/1{,}211 = 7.38$. This is the best estimate for the mean of a fitted Poisson distribution. We use this to generate the probability of a certain number of arrivals in each 1 ms time period. This probability multiplied by the total number of time periods is the expected count for that number of arrivals, and this is shown next. For instance, we compute $P(1) = 0.0046$ and $0.0046 * 1211 = 6$.

Number of Packet Arrivals	1	2	3	4	5	6	7	8	9	10	11	12	13	14	15	16
Count	18	28	56	105	126	146	164	165	120	103	73	54	23	16	9	5
Expected Count	6	21	51	93	138	170	179	165	135	100	67	41	23	12	6	3

Although at first glance the fit appears to be good, it is best to compute the chi-squared value: $((18 - 6)^2/6) + (28 - 21)^2/21 + \ldots + (5 - 3)^2/3 = 48.5$. Since we estimated one parameter from the sample, the degrees of freedom $= 16 - 1 - 1 = 14$. From the chi-squared table, with 14 degrees of freedom, at the 95% confidence level, the critical value is 23.68. Therefore, we reject the hypothesis that the sample is well described by a Poisson distribution at this confidence level. That is, we have 95% confidence that this sample was not drawn from a Poisson population. The critical value at the 99.9% level for 14 degrees of freedom is 36.12. So, we can be even more confident and state that with 99.9% confidence, the sample is not drawn from a Poisson population.

At first glance, this is a surprising result because the fit appears quite good. The reason the test fails is clear when we examine the $((n_i - ei)^2/e_i)$ values. The largest value is 27.6, which is for 1 packet arrival, where we expected a count of 6 but got 18. Because the denominator here is small (6), the contribution of this sample value to the chi-squared variable is disproportionate. If we were to ignore this value as an outlier and computed the fit only for 2–16 packet arrivals, the revised estimate of the distribution mean is 7.47, and the revised chi-squared variable is 19.98 (see Exercise 2.12). This does meet the goodness-of-fit criterion with 13 degrees of freedom even at the 95% confidence level. In cases like these, it is worthwhile looking into why there was a deviation from the Poisson process: a systematic error in the experiment or perhaps a heretofore unknown phenomenon.

2.4.8 Power

Recall that when we test a hypothesis, we determine the probability of obtaining an observed outcome conditional on the null hypothesis being true. If the outcome is less probable than the significance level, such as 5% or 1%, we reject the null hypothesis. Of course, the hypothesis could still be true. Nevertheless, we reduce the Type I error, that of rejecting a hypothesis when it is in fact true, to a value below the significance level.

We now discuss a related concept: the power of a test. The **power** of a statistical test is the probability that the test will reject a null hypothesis when it is in fact false. If the power is low, we may not reject a null hypothesis even when it is false, a Type II error. Thus, the greater the power, the lower the chance of making a Type II error. Usually, the only way to increase the power of a test is to increase its significance level, which makes a Type I error more likely.

The practical difficulty in computing the power of a test is that we don't know the ground truth. So, it becomes impossible to compute the probability that we will reject the null hypothesis conditional on the ground truth being different from the null hypothesis. For instance, suppose that the ground truth differs infinitesimally from the null hypothesis. Then, the probability that we reject the null hypothesis, which is false, is essentially the same as the significance level. In contrast, suppose that the ground truth is far from the null hypothesis. Then, the sample mean is likely to be near the ground truth, and we are likely to reject the null hypothesis, increasing the power of the test. But we have no way of knowing which of these situations holds. Therefore, we can precisely compute the power of a test only in the context of an alternative hypothesis about the state of the world. Unfortunately, in many cases, this is impossible to determine. Therefore, despite its intuitive merit, the power of a test is rarely computed.

2.5 Independence and Dependence: Regression and Correlation

Thus far, we have studied primarily single variables in isolation. In this section, we study data sets with two variables. In this situation, some questions immediately crop up: Are the variables independent? If not, are pairs of variables correlated with each other? Do some of the variables depend linearly or nonlinearly on the others? Can the variability in one of the variables be explained as being due to variability in another variable? These are the types of questions that we will study in this section.

2.5.1 Independence

Consider a data set in which each element can be simultaneously placed into more than one category. For example, we could characterize an IP packet by both its size and its type. Are these variables independent of each other? Given the size, can we say anything about the type and vice versa? If knowing the value of one variable does not give us any additional information about the other, the variables are **independent**. We now describe a test to determine whether we can confidently reject the hypothesis that two variables are independent.

In testing for independence, it is useful to represent the data set in the form of a **contingency table**. For a sample that has two variables that take one of m and n ordinal values, respectively, the contingency table has $m \times n$ cells, with each cell containing the count of the number of sample elements that simultaneously fall into both corresponding categories.

Given the contingency table, we can use the Pearson chi-squared test to determine whether two variables are independent as follows. We use the sample to estimate the population parameters. From these estimates, assuming independence of the variables, we compute the expected numbers of sample values that will fall into each cell of the contingency table. We can then compare the actual counts in each cell with these expected values to compute the chi-squared statistic. If it is larger than the critical value, we can, with high confidence, reject the hypothesis that the variables are independent.

In computing the chi-squared statistic, it is important to correctly compute the degrees of freedom. Recall that for a variable that falls into one of k classes, the number of degrees of freedom is $k - 1$. It can be shown that instead of being known a priori, the number of degrees of freedom is further reduced by each parameter that is estimated from the sample, as the next example shows.

EXAMPLE 2.14: TESTING FOR INDEPENDENCE

Suppose that in a packet trace with a million packets, you obtain the following contingency table:

Packet Size	TCP	UDP	Other	Row Sum
40	12,412	15,465	300	28,177
100	85,646	12,561	15,613	113,820
150	9,846	68,463	4,561	82,870
512	4,865	45,646	23,168	73,679
1,024	48,651	95,965	48,913	193,529
1,200	98,419	59,678	48,964	207,061
1,450	156,461	48,916	51,952	257,329
1,500	16,516	24,943	2,076	43,535
Column sum	432,816	371,637	195,547	1,000,000

Is the packet size independent of the packet type?

Solution:

We do not know the frequency of each packet type in the population (of all IP packets), so we will estimate the population frequencies from this sample, using the column sums as follows:

- $P(TCP) = 432,816/1,000,000 = 0.433$
- $P(UDP) = 371,637/1,000,000 = 0.372$
- $P(Other) = 195,547/1,000,000 = 0.195$

Similarly, we compute the probability of each packet size from the row sums as follows:

- $P(40) = 28,177/1,000,000 = 0.028$
- $P(100) = 113,820/1,000,000 = 0.114$
- ...
- $P(1,500) = 43,535/1,000,000 = 0.043$

If these probabilities were independent, each cell could be computed as follows:

- Count of TCP AND 40 = $P(TCP) * P(40) * 1,000,000 = 0.433 * 0.028 * 1,000,000 = 12,195$

- ...

- Count of Other and 1,500 = P(Other) * P(1,500) * 1,000,000 = 0.195 * 0.043 * 1,000,000 = 8,513

We therefore have both the observed and expected values for each cell. We compute the chi-squared statistic as the sum of squares of the variable (observed value − expected value)^2/(expected value). This value turns out to be 254,326. Here, k is 3 * 8 = 24. Moreover, we have estimated nine parameters from the data; we get two probabilities for free, since probabilities sum to 1. Therefore, the degrees of freedom still left is 24 − 1 − 9 = 14. Looking up the chi-square table with 14 degrees of freedom, we find that the critical value for the 0.001 confidence level to be 36.12. Since the statistic far exceeds this value, we can be more than 99.9% confident that packet type and packet size are *not* independent in the population from which this trace was drawn.

Note that, given the large sample size, even a tiny deviation from the expected values will lead to the null hypothesis of independence being rejected. We discuss this further in Section 2.9.5.

2.5.2 Regression

When two random variables are not independent, one variable sometimes depends on—or can be thought to depend on—the other, in that the value of the second variable is approximately known if the value of the first is known. Let the independent variable X take on specific values, such as x, and let the dependent variable be Y. Then, the **regression** of Y on x is a graph that shows $E(Y|x)$ as a function of x. Note that this graph is defined only when both X and Y are defined on interval or ratio scales.

In the simplest case, we model Y as varying linearly with x. In this case, we define a *best-fit line* that minimizes the sum of squared deviations observed from the estimated values of *y*. If our observations are of the form $\{(x_i, y_i)\}$, the model for the regression line is

$$y = a + bx \qquad \text{(EQ 2.33)}$$

and we therefore seek to minimize

$$S^2 = \sum_{i=1}^{n} (y_i - a - bx_i)^2 \qquad \text{(EQ 2.34)}$$

To find a and b, we set the partial derivative of S with respect to a and b to zero. This gives us

$$a = \bar{y} - b\bar{x}$$

$$b = \frac{\sum (x_i - \bar{x})(y_i - \bar{y})}{\sum (x_i - \bar{x})^2} \qquad \text{(EQ 2.35)}$$

Substituting for a in Equation 2.33, we see that the point $(\bar{x}, \bar{y})$ satisfies the regression equation, so that the regression line always passes through this point, which is also called the *centroid* of the sample. We interpret a as the Y intercept of the best-fit line; b is the mean change in Y with a unit increase in X.

When Y does not depend on X linearly, it is sometimes possible to transform Y so that the dependency is more nearly linear, as the next example demonstrates.

EXAMPLE 2.15: COMPUTING A LINEAR REGRESSION AFTER TRANSFORMATION

Consider the following data set, which shows the packet loss rate for a given buffer size, where three simulations were run for each buffer size setting. Compute the linear regression of the loss rate on the buffer size.

Buffer Size	10 Packets	20 Packets	50 Packets	100 Packets	200 Packets	500 Packets
Run 1	30.20	10.20	5.20	1.10	0.20	0.01
Run 2	27.40	11.30	6.37	1.70	0.23	0.01
Run 3	29.10	9.80	5.82	1.30	0.17	0.01

It is instructive to look at the scatter plot of the data, shown in Figure 2.5(a). It is immediately obvious that the relationship between the loss rate and the buffer size is far from linear. In such cases, it is necessary to transform the data values to extract a more linear relationship. Figure 2.5(b) is a scatter plot that plots the logarithm of the loss rate with respect to the buffer size. It is clear that the relationship is far more linear than before. We

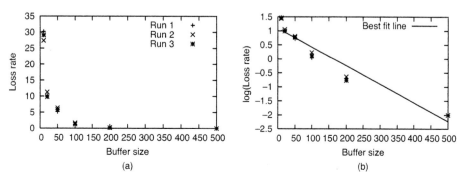

Figure 2.5 Scatter plot of loss rate versus buffer size

compute the best-fit line, using Equation 2.35, as $y = 1.0568 - 0.0066\,x$, which is the regression of Y on x. This best-fit line is also shown in the figure.

The best-fit line, in addition to minimizing the sum of squared errors, has several useful properties. It is the maximum likelihood estimator for the population parameters a and b. Moreover, it is possible to construct confidence intervals for the values of a and b by means of the t distribution.

Note that it is always possible to compute a linear regression of one variable on another, even if the two variables are not linearly related. Therefore, it is always a good idea to use a statistical test for linearity—or the correlation coefficient, described next—to validate that the relationship is reasonably linear before computing the best-fit line.

We now briefly discuss three extensions to simple linear regression.

1. The **least-squares best-fit** approach assumes that the degree of variation in the dependent variable is more or less the same, regardless of the value of the independent variable. In some cases, the greater (or smaller) the value of the independent variable, the greater (or smaller) the variance in the dependent variable. For example, in the preceding example, we see a greater variation in log(loss rate) for smaller values of the buffer size. Such samples are said to be **heteroscedastic**; if the departure from uniform variability is significant, it is necessary to resort to advanced techniques to compute the regression.

2. In some cases, the relationship between the dependent and independent variables is nonlinear even after transformation of the dependent values. In such cases, it may become necessary to perform **nonlinear** regression.

3. Finally, we have considered a dependent variable that depends on only a single independent variable. In general, the dependency may extend to multiple independent variables. This is the subject of **multiple regression**.

These three topics are treated in greater depth in more advanced texts on statistics.

2.5.3 Correlation

When computing a regression, we can use physical considerations to clearly identify independent and dependent variables. In some cases, however, the outcomes of an experiment can be thought of as being mutually dependent. This dependency is captured in the statistical concept of *correlation*. Moreover, as we will see later, even if one variable depends on the other, the correlation coefficient allows us to determine the degree to which variations in the dependent variable can be explained as a consequence of variations in the independent variable.

EXAMPLE 2.16: CORRELATED VARIABLES

Suppose that we transfer a small file over a cellular modem ten times, each time measuring the *round-trip delay* from a ping done just before transferring the file and the *throughput* achieved by dividing the file size by the transfer time. The round-trip delay may be large because the network interface card may have a low capacity, so that even a small ping packet experiences significant delays. On the other hand, the file-transfer throughput may be low because the path delay is large. So, it is not clear which variable ought to be the dependent variable and which variable ought to be the independent variable. Suppose that the measured round-trip delays and throughputs are as shown next:

Throughput (kbps)	46	65	53	38	61	89	59	60	73
Round-trip delay (ms)	940	790	910	1,020	540	340	810	720	830

Figure 2.6(a) shows the scatter plot of the two variables. There appears to be an approximately linear decline in the round-trip delay with an increase in throughput. We arbitrarily choose throughput to be the independent variable

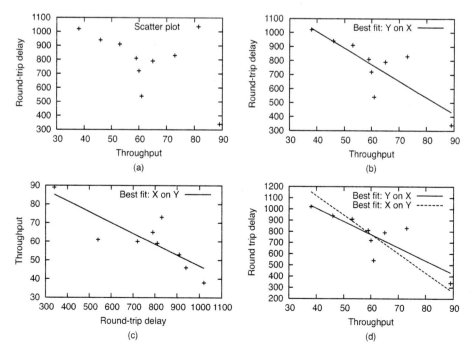

Figure 2.6 Regression and correlation

and do a regression of round-trip delay on it, as shown in Figure 2.6(b). We see that the best-fit line has a negative slope, as expected.

There is no reason why we could not have chosen the round-trip delay to be the independent variable and have done a similar regression. This is shown in Figure 2.6(c). Again, we see that as the round-trip delay increases, the throughput decreases, indicating a negative relationship. We also see the best-fit line with a negative slope.

Note that the two regression lines are not the same! In one case, we are trying to minimize the sum of the squared errors in round-trip delay; in the other, the sum of squared errors in throughput. So, the best-fit lines will, in general, not be the same. This is shown in Figure 2.6(d), where we show both best-fit lines (one drawn with transposed axes).

The reason that two regression lines do not coincide in general is best understood by doing a thought experiment. Suppose that two outcomes of an experiment—say, X and Y—are completely independent. Then, $E(XY) = E(X)E(Y)$, by definition of independence. In the context of a single sample, we rewrite this as

$$E(XY) = \frac{\sum x_i y_i}{n} = E(X)E(Y) = \frac{\sum x_i}{n} \frac{\sum y_i}{n} = \bar{x}\bar{y} \qquad \text{(EQ 2.36)}$$

Recall that $b = \dfrac{\sum (x_i - \bar{x})(y_i - \bar{y})}{\sum (x_i - \bar{x})^2}$. We expand the numerator as

$$\sum x_i y_i - \bar{x}\sum y_i - \bar{y}\sum x_i + n\bar{x}\bar{y}.$$

Rewriting $\sum y_i$ as $n\bar{y}$ and $\sum x_i$ as $n\bar{x}$ and using Equation 2.36, we get

$$b = \frac{\sum x_i y_i - \bar{x}\sum y_i - \bar{y}\sum x_i + n\bar{x}\bar{y}}{\sum (x_i - \bar{x})^2} = \frac{n\bar{x}\bar{y} - n\bar{x}\bar{y} - n\bar{x}\bar{y} + n\bar{x}\bar{y}}{\sum (x_i - \bar{x})^2} = 0, \qquad \text{(EQ 2.37)}$$

so that the regression line has zero slope (i.e., is parallel to the X-axis). Symmetrically, the regression of X on Y will be parallel to the Y axis. Therefore, the two regression lines meet at right angles when the outcomes are independent. Recalling that we can interpret b as the expected increment in Y with a unit change in X, $b = 0$ implies that a unit change in X does not change Y (in expectation), which is consistent with independence.

On the other hand, if one outcome is perfectly linearly related to the other, $Y = tX$. Clearly, $\bar{y} = t\bar{x}$, so that

$$b = \frac{\sum(x_i - \bar{x})(y_i - \bar{y})}{\sum(x_i - \bar{x})^2} = \frac{\sum(x_i - \bar{x})(tx_i - t\bar{x})}{\sum(x_i - \bar{x})^2} = t.$$ Denoting the regression of X on Y

by $x = a' + b'y$, the expression for b' is given by

$$\frac{\sum(x_i - \bar{x})(y_i - \bar{y})}{\sum(y_i - \bar{y})^2} = \frac{\sum(x_i - \bar{x})(tx_i - t\bar{x})}{\sum(tx_i - t\bar{x})^2} = \frac{1}{t}.$$

With transposed axes, this line exactly overlaps the best-fit line for the regression of Y on X. In other words, when there is exact linear dependence between the variables, the best-fit regression lines meet at zero degrees. Thus, we can use the angle between the regression lines as an indication of the degree of linear dependence between the variables.

In practice, the standard measure of dependence, or **correlation**, is the square root of the product bb', denoted r, also called **Pearson's correlation coefficient**, and is given by

$$r = \sqrt{\frac{\sum(x_i - \bar{x})(y_i - \bar{y})}{\sum(x_i - \bar{x})^2}\frac{\sum(x_i - \bar{x})(y_i - \bar{y})}{\sum(y_i - \bar{y})^2}} = \frac{\sum(x_i - \bar{x})(y_i - \bar{y})}{\sqrt{(\sum(x_i - \bar{x})^2)(\sum(y_i - \bar{y})^2)}} \qquad \textbf{(EQ 2.38)}$$

When the slopes are perpendicular, $r = 0$; when the slopes are inverses of each other, so that the regression lines overlap, $r = 1$. Moreover, when X and Y are perfectly negatively correlated, so that $Y = -tX$, $r = -1$. Therefore, we interpret r as the degree of correlation between two variables, ranging from -1 to $+1$, with its sign indicating direction of correlation (positive or negative) and its magnitude indicating the degree of correlation.

EXAMPLE 2.17: CORRELATION COEFFICIENT

Compute the correlation coefficient for the variables in Example 2.16.

Solution:

We compute the mean throughput as 54.4 kbps and the mean delay as 690 ms. Substituting these values into Equation 2.38, we find that $r = -0.56$. This indicates a negative correlation, but it is not particularly linear.

There are many interpretations of the correlation coefficient.[5] One particularly insightful interpretation is based on the sum of squares minimized in a linear

---

5. See Joseph Lee Rodgers and W. Alan Nicewander, "Thirteen Ways to Look at the Correlation Coefficient," *The American Statistician*, Vol. 42, No. 1 (Feb., 1988), pp. 59–66.

regression: $S^2 = \sum_{i=1}^{n} (y_i - a - bx_i)^2$. Substituting for a and b, it is easily shown (see Exercise 9) that

$$S^2 = (1 - r^2) \sum (y_i - \bar{y})^2 \qquad\qquad \text{(EQ 2.39)}$$

That is, r^2 is the degree to which a regression is able to reduce the sum of squared errors, which we interpret as the degree to which the independent variable explains variations in the dependent variable. When we have perfect linear dependency between Y and X, the degree of correlation is 1 in absolute value, and the regression line is perfectly aligned with the data, so that it has zero error.

In computing a correlation coefficient, it is important to remember that it captures only linear dependence. A coefficient of zero does not mean that the variables are independent: They could well be nonlinearly dependent. For example, if $y^2 = 1 - x^2$, for every value of X, there are two equal and opposite values of Y, so that the best-fit regression line is the X-axis, which leads to a correlation coefficient of 0. But, of course, Y is not independent of X! Therefore, it is important to be cautious in drawing conclusions regarding independence when using the correlation coefficient. For drawing such conclusions, it is best to use the chi-square goodness-of-fit test described earlier.

Like any statistic, the correlation coefficient r can have an error due to random fluctuations in a sample. It can be shown that if X and Y are jointly normally distributed; the variable $z = 0.5\log\left(\dfrac{1+r}{1-r}\right)$ is approximately normally distributed with a mean of 0.5 $\log\left(\dfrac{1+\rho}{1-\rho}\right)$ and a variance of $1/(n-3)$. This can be used to find the confidence interval around r in which we can expect to find the population parameter, ρ.

A specific form of correlation that is relevant in the analysis of time series is **autocorrelation**. Consider a series of values of a random variable that are indexed by discrete time: $X_1, X_2, ..., X_n$. Then, the autocorrelation of this series with lag l is the correlation coefficient between the random variable X_i and X_{i-l}. If this coefficient is large (close to 1) for a certain value of l, we can infer that the series has variation on the time scale of l. This is often much easier to compute than a full-scale harmonic analysis by means of a Fourier transform.

Finally, it is important to recognize that correlation is not the same as causality. We must not interpret a correlation coefficient close to 1 or −1 to infer causality. For example, it may be the case that packet losses on a wireless network are positively correlated with mean frame size. One cannot infer that larger frame sizes are more likely to be dropped. It could be the case, for example, that the network is heavily loaded when it is subjected to video traffic, which uses large frames. The increase in the loss rate could be due to the load rather than the frame size. Yet the correlation between these two quantities would be strong.

To go from correlation to causation, it is necessary to determine the physical causes that lead to causation. Otherwise, the unwary researcher may be led to unsupportable and erroneous conclusions.

2.6 Comparing Multiple Outcomes Simultaneously: Analysis of Variance

In the discussion so far, we have focused on comparing the outcomes of experiments corresponding to at most two choices of experimental controls, or *treatments* (Section 2.4.5), and determining dependence and independence between two variables (Section 2.5). Suppose that we wanted to compare outcomes of multiple treatments simultaneously. For example, Examples 2.9 and 2.10 compared the packet loss rate at a queue with 5 buffers with the loss rate at a queue with 100 buffers. Instead, we may want to compare the loss rates with 5, 100, 200, 500, and 1,000 buffers with each other. How should we proceed?

Theoretically, we could perform a set of pairwise comparisons, where each comparison used a normal or t test. For example, we could test the hypothesis that the loss rates with 5 and 100 buffers were identical, the hypothesis that the loss rates with 5 and 200 buffers were identical, and so on. This approach, however, leads to a subtle problem. Recall that when we reject a hypothesis, we are subject to a Type I error, that is, rejecting a hypothesis that is true. If we perform many pairwise comparisons, although the probability of Type I error for any one test is guaranteed to be below 5% (or 1%), the overall probability of making at least one Type I error can be greater than 5% (or 1%)! To see this, think of flipping a coin ten times and looking for ten heads. This has a probability of about $1/1,024 = 0.1\%$. But if we were to flip 1,024 coins, chances are good that we would get at least one run of ten heads. Arguing along similar lines, it is easy to see that, as the number of comparisons increases, the overall possibility of a Type I error increases. What is needed, therefore, is a way to perform a single test that avoids numerous pairwise comparisons. This is achieved by the analysis of variance (ANOVA) technique.

ANOVA is a complex topic with considerable depth. We will discuss only the simplest case of the one-way layout with fixed effects. Multiway testing and random effects are discussed in greater depth in advanced statistical texts.

2.6.1 One-Way Layout

In the analysis of a one-way layout, we group observations according to their corresponding treatment. For instance, we group repeated measurements of the packet loss rate for a given buffer size: say, five buffers. The key idea in ANOVA is that if none of the treatments—such as the buffer size—affect the observed variable, such as the loss rate, all the observations can be assumed to be drawn from the same population. Therefore, the sample mean computed for observations corresponding to each treatment should not be too far from the sample mean computed across all the observations. Moreover, the estimate of population variance computed from each group separately should not differ too much from the variance estimated from the entire sample. If we do find a significant difference between statistics computed from each group separately and the sample as a whole, we reject the null hypothesis. That is, we conclude that, with high probability, the treatments affect the observed outcomes. By itself, that is all that basic ANOVA can tell us. Further testing is necessary to determine which treatments affect the outcome and which do not.

We now make this more precise. Suppose that we can divide the observations into I groups of J samples each. (We assume that all groups have the same number of samples, which is usually not a problem, because the treatments are under the control of the experimenter.) We denote the jth observation of the ith treatment by the random variable Y_{ij}. We model this observation as the sum of an underlying population mean μ, the true effect of the ith treatment α_i, and a random fluctuation ε_{ij}:

$$Y_{ij} = \mu + \alpha_i + \varepsilon_{ij} \qquad \text{(EQ 2.40)}$$

These errors are assumed to be independent and normally distributed with zero mean and a variance of σ^2. For convenience, we normalize the α_is so that $\sum_{i=1}^{I} \alpha_i = 0$. Note that the expected outcome for the ith treatment is $E(Y_{ij}) = \mu + \alpha_i$.

The null hypothesis is that the treatments have no effect on the outcome. If the null hypothesis holds, the expected value of each group of observations would be μ, so that $\forall i, \alpha_i = 0$. Moreover, the population variance would be σ^2.

Let the mean of the ith group of observations be denoted $\overline{Y}_{i.}$ and the mean of all the observations be denoted $\overline{Y}_{..}$. We denote the sum of squared deviations from the mean *within* each sample by

$$SSW = \sum_{i=1}^{I} \sum_{j=1}^{J} (Y_{ij} - \overline{Y}_{i.})^2 \qquad \text{(EQ 2.41)}$$

where $\dfrac{SSW}{I(J-1)}$ is an unbiased estimator of the population variance σ^2 because it sums I unbiased estimators, each given by

$$\frac{1}{J-1} \sum_{j=1}^{J} (Y_{ij} - \overline{Y}_{i.})^2 .$$

Similarly, we denote the sum of squared deviations from the mean *between* samples by

$$SSB = J \sum_{i=1}^{I} (\overline{Y}_{i.} - \overline{Y}_{..})^2 \qquad \text{(EQ 2.42)}$$

where $SSB/(I-1)$ is also an unbiased estimator of the population variance σ^2 because

$$\frac{1}{I-1} \sum_{i=1}^{I} (\overline{Y}_{i.} - \overline{Y}_{..})^2$$

is an unbiased estimator of $\frac{\sigma^2}{J}$. So, the ratio $\frac{SSB/(I-1)}{SSW/(J-1)}$ should be 1 if the null hypothesis holds.

It can be shown that $SSB/(I-1)$ is an χ^2 variable with $I-1$ degrees of freedom and that $SSW/I(J-1)$ is an χ^2 variable with $I(J-1)$ degrees of freedom. The ratio of two χ^2 variables with m and n degrees of freedom follows a distribution called the **F** distribution with (m,n) degrees of freedom. Therefore, the variable $\frac{SSB/(I-1)}{SSW/(J-1)}$ follows the F distribution with $(I-1, I(J-1))$ degrees of freedom, and has an expected value of 1 if the null hypothesis is true.

To test the null hypothesis, we compute the value of $\frac{SSB/(I-1)}{SSW/(J-1)}$ and compare it with the critical value of an F variable with $(I-1, I(J-1))$ degrees of freedom. If the computed value exceeds the critical value, the null hypothesis is rejected. Intuitively, this would happen if SSB is "too large" that is, there is significant variation in the sums of squares between treatments, which is what we expect when the treatment does have an effect on the observed outcome.

EXAMPLE 2.18: SINGLE-FACTOR ANOVA

Continuing with Example 2.9, assume that we have additional data for larger buffer sizes, as follows. Can we still claim that the buffer size plays a role in determining the loss rate?

Loss rate with 5 buffers	1.20%	1.30%	0.90%	1.40%	1.00%	1.80%	1.10%	1.20%	1.50%	1.20%
Loss rate with 100 buffers	0.10%	0.60%	1.10%	0.80%	1.20%	0.30%	0.70%	1.90%	0.20%	1.20%

continues

continued

Loss rate with 200 buffers	0.50%	0.45%	0.35%	0.60%	0.75%	0.25%	0.55%	0.15%	0.35%	0.40%
Loss rate with 500 buffers	0.10%	0.05%	0.03%	0.08%	0.07%	0.02%	0.10%	0.05%	0.13%	0.04%
Loss rate with 1,000 buffers	0.01%	0.02%	0.01%	0.00%	0.01%	0.01%	0.00%	0.02%	0.01%	0.00%

Here, $I = 5$ and $J = 10$. We compute $\overline{Y_{5.}} = 1.26\%$, $\overline{Y_{100.}} = 0.81\%$, $\overline{Y_{200.}} = 0.44\%$, $\overline{Y_{500.}} = 0.07\%$, and $\overline{Y_{1,000.}} = 0.01\%$. This allows us to compute $SSW = 5.13 * 10^{-5}$ and $SSB = 1.11 * 10^{-3}$. The F statistic is therefore $(1.11 * 10^{-3}/ 4)/(5.13 * 10^{-5}/45) = 242.36$. Looking up the F table, we find that even with only $(4, 40)$ degrees of freedom, the critical F value at the 1% confidence level is 3.83. The computed statistic far exceeds this value. Therefore, the null hypothesis is rejected.

The F test is somewhat anticlimactic: It indicates only that a treatment has an effect on the outcome, but it does not quantify the degree of effect. Nor does it identify whether any one treatment is responsible for the failure of the test. These questions can be resolved by post hoc analysis. For example, to quantify the degree of effect, we can compute the regression of the observed effect as a function of the treatment. To identify the treatment that is responsible for the failure of the test, we can rerun the F test, eliminating one treatment at a time. If the F test does not reject the null hypothesis with a particular treatment removed, we can hypothesize that this treatment has a significant effect on the outcome, testing this hypothesis with a two-variable test.

If these approaches do not work, two more advanced techniques to perform multiway comparisons are **Tukey's method** and the **Bonferroni method** (see Section 2.10 for texts that discussed these methods).

2.6.2 Multiway Layouts

It is relatively straightforward to extend the one-way layout to two or more treatments that are simultaneously applied. For instance, we may want to study the joint effect of buffer size and cross-traffic workload on the loss rate. The details of this so-called *two-way layout* are beyond the scope of this text. We will merely point out that in the context of such designs, we have to not only determine the effect of a treatment on the outcome but also deal with the possibility that only certain combinations of treatment levels affect the outcome (e.g., the combination of small buffer size and heavy cross traffic). Such **interaction effects** greatly complicate the analysis of multiway layouts.

2.7 Design of Experiments

The statistically rigorous design of experiments is a complex topic. Our goal here is to give an intuitive understanding of its essentials. Details can be found in more advanced texts devoted to the topic.

The goal of an experiment is, in the words of Sir R. A. Fisher, "to give the facts a chance of disproving the null hypothesis."[6] The first step in designing an experiment is to formulate a precise hypothesis that can be rejected (or not) on the basis of its results. Many experimental studies in the field of computer systems fail to meet even this obvious requirement! The careful choice of a null hypothesis cannot be overemphasized.

Note that our analysis of hypothesis testing assumes that the elements of each sample are independently and randomly selected from the population, so that we can treat the sum of the elements of each sample as the sum of n independent and identically distributed random variables. Therefore, in conducting an experiment, it is necessary to ensure that each observation is as nearly independent of the others as possible. Moreover, observations should be made so that each member of the population has an equal chance of being represented. If observations come from sampling a population, care should be taken that no obvious bias is introduced in the sampling process.

A second consideration in the design of experiments is that enough data be collected so that the hypothesis can be conclusively rejected if necessary. To take a trivial example, it is impossible to reject the hypothesis that a coin is biased from a single coin flip. We can increase the **sensitivity** of an experiment either by collecting more observations within each sample (**enlargement**) or by collecting more samples (**repetition**).

Third, it is necessary to ensure that the experimental conditions be kept as constant as possible (**controlled**) so that the underlying population does not change when making observations. Otherwise, it is impossible to determine the population whose parameters are being estimated by the statistics of the sample. For example, in a wireless network that is subject to random external interference, packet loss rates are determined by the signal strength of not only the transmitter but also the interferer. If an external interferer is not controlled, a study that tries to relate a link-level data rate selection algorithm to the packet loss rate, for example, may draw incorrect conclusions.

Finally, when studying the effect of more than one treatment on the outcome of an experiment, we need to take into account the fact that the treatments may not be independent of each other. If treatments were orthogonal, we would simply need

6. R. A. Fisher, *The Design of Experiments*, Oliver and Boyd, 1935.

to change one treatment at a time, which reduces the analysis of the experiment to analyzing a set of one-way layouts. If they are not, we need to design a set of experiments that explores all combinations of treatments. For example, if both buffer size and cross-traffic workload intensity can affect the packet loss rate at a router, and if these treatments were nonorthogonal, we need to take into account the so-called interaction effects (see Section 2.6.2). A trivial solution to take interactions into account is to perform a **full factorial** design, whereby we set up the cross product of every possible level of each treatment. For example, if we could choose among five buffer sizes and three workload levels, we would need to conduct 15 experiments.

In many cases, a full factorial design is impossible. If so, there is a considerable body of work on the design of **fractional factorial** experiments, whereby we may change two or more treatment levels at the same time, using statistical analysis to identify the effect of each individual treatment. These schemes can be complex, in that they need to consider all possible two-way, three-way, ..., n-way interactions that may affect the observed outcomes. Specifically, the designs must deal with the problem of **aliasing**, that is, not being able to make out the difference between alternative combinations of treatment levels that have the same effect on the output. If certain combinations of levels can be safely ignored or are practically unimportant, we can greatly reduce the number of experiments without affecting the quality of the conclusions.

2.8 Dealing with Large Data Sets

All too often, the problem in the statistical analysis of modern computer systems is not the lack of experimental data but its surfeit. With the extensive logging of system components and the growing number of components in a system, the analyst is often confronted with the daunting task of extracting comprehensible and statistically valid results from large volumes of data. Therefore, the practice of statistical analysis—long focused on the extraction of statistically valid results from a handful of experiments—changes its character. This section discusses a pragmatic approach to the analysis of large data sets, based on the author's own experiences over the past two decades.[7]

Unlike the classical notion of careful experimental design in order to test a hypothesis, the situation in contemporary systems evaluation is to focus, at least initially, on **data exploration**. We typically have access to a large compendium of

---

7. An alternative view from the perspective of computer system performance evaluation can be found in R. Jain, *The Art of Computer Systems Performance Analysis*, Wiley, 2001.

logs and traces, and the questions we would like to answer typically fall into the following broad categories.

- How can the data help us identify the cause of poor overall performance?
- What is the relative performance of alternative implementations of one component of the system?
- Are there implicit rules that describe the data?

In answering these questions, the following procedure has proved useful.

1. *Extract a small sample from the entire data set and carefully read through it.* Even a quick glance at the data will often point out salient characteristics that can be used to speed up subsequent analysis. Moreover, doing so allows a researcher to spot potential problems, such as certain variables not being logged or having clearly erroneous values. Proceeding with a complex analysis in the presence of such defects only wastes time.

2. *Attempt to visualize the* entire *data set.* For example, if every sample could be represented by a point, the entire data set could be represented by a pixellated bitmap. The human eye is quick to find nonobvious patterns but only if presented with the entire data set. If the data set is too large, it may help to subsample it, taking every fifth, tenth, or hundredth sample before visualization. This step will often result in detecting patterns that may otherwise be revealed only with considerable effort.

3. *Look for outliers.* The presence of outliers usually indicates a deeper problem, usually with either data collection or data representation (e.g., due to underflow or overflow). Usually, the analysis of outliers results in the discovery of problems in the logging or tracing software, and the entire data set may have to be collected again. Even if part of the data set can be sanitized to correct for errors, it is prudent to collect the data set again.

4. *Formulate a preliminary null hypothesis.* Choose this hypothesis with care, being conservative in your selection, so that the nonrejection of the hypothesis does not lead you to a risky conclusion.

5. *Use the data set to attempt to reject the hypothesis,* using the techniques described earlier in this chapter.

6. *Frame and test more sophisticated hypotheses.* Often, preliminary results reveal insights into the structure of the problem whose further analysis will require the collection of additional data. The problem here is that if data is collected at different times, it is hard to control extraneous influences. The workload may have changed in the interim, or some system components may

have been upgraded. Therefore, it is prudent to discard the entire prior data set to minimize the effects of uncontrolled variables. Step 6 may be repeated multiple times until the initial problem has been satisfactorily answered.

7. *Use appropriate graphics to present and interpret the results of the analysis.*[8]

When dealing with very large data sets, where visualization is impossible, techniques derived from **data mining** and **machine learning** are often useful. We briefly outline two elementary techniques for data clustering.

The goal of a data-clustering algorithm is to find hidden patterns in the data: in this case, the fact that the data can be grouped into clusters, where each cluster represents closely related observations. For example, in a trace of packets observed at a router interface, clusters may represent packets that fall into a certain range of lengths. A clustering algorithm automatically finds clusters in the data set that, for our example, would correspond to a set of disjoint ranges of packet lengths.

A clustering algorithm takes as input a distance metric that quantifies the concept of a distance between two observations. Distances may be simple metrics, such as packet lengths, or may be more complex, such as the number of edits (that is, insertions and deletions) that need to be made to a string-valued observation to transform it into another string-valued observation. Observations within a cluster will be closer, according to the specified distance metric, than observations placed in different clusters.

In **agglomerative clustering**, we start with each observation in its own cluster. We then merge the two closest observations into a single cluster and repeat the process until the entire data set is in a single cluster. Note that to carry out repeated mergings, we need to define the distance between a point and a cluster and between two clusters. The distance between a point and a cluster can be defined either as the distance from that point to the closest point in the cluster or as the average of all the distances from that point to all the points in the cluster. Similarly, the distance between clusters can be defined to be the closest distance between their points or the distance between their centroids. In either case, we compute a tree such that links higher up in the tree have longer distance metrics. We can therefore truncate the tree at any point and treat the forest so created as the desired set of clusters. This approach usually does not scale beyond about 10,000 observation types on a single server; distributed computation techniques allow the processing of larger data sets.

The **k-means clustering** technique clusters data into k classes. The earliest and most widely used algorithm for k-means clustering is Lloyd's algorithm, in which

---

8. An excellent source for presentation guidelines is E. Tufte, *The Visual Display of Quantitative Information*, 2nd ed., Graphics Press, 2001.

we start with a set of k empty containers. We partition the observations into k sets, either randomly or on the basis of a subsample, allocating one set to each container. For each container, we then compute its centroid, or the point that minimizes the sum of distances from all points in the set to itself. Now, each point is reallocated to the container with the closest centroid. This may result in the container's centroid moving to a different point. We therefore recompute the centroid for each container, reallocating points as before. This process iterates until convergence, when no points move from one cluster to another. In most practical cases, the algorithm is found to converge after a few iterations to a globally optimal clustering. However, convergence may result in a local optimum. Several variants of this algorithm with better convergence properties are described in texts on machine learning and data mining.

2.9 Common Mistakes in Statistical Analysis

We now present some common problems in statistical analysis, especially in the context of computer systems.

2.9.1 Defining Population

A question commonly left unanswered in statistical analyses is a precise statement of the underlying population. As we saw in Section 2.1, the same sample can correspond to multiple underlying populations. It is impossible to interpret the results of a statistical analysis without carefully justifying why the sample is representative of the chosen underlying population.

2.9.2 Lack of Confidence Intervals in Comparing Results

Comparing the performance of two systems simply by comparing the mean values of performance metrics is an all-too-common mistake. The fact that one mean is greater than another is not statistically meaningful and may lead to erroneous conclusions. The simple solution is to always compare confidence intervals rather than means, as described in Section 2.4.5.

2.9.3 Not Stating the Null Hypothesis

Although the process of research necessitates a certain degree of evolution of hypotheses, a common problem is to carry out a statistical analysis without stating the null hypothesis. Recall that we can only reject or not reject the null hypothesis from observational data. Therefore, it is necessary to carefully formulate and clearly state the null hypothesis.

2.9.4 Too Small a Sample

If the sample size is too small, the confidence interval associated with the sample is large, so that even a null hypothesis that is false will not be rejected. By computing the confidence interval around the mean during exploratory analysis, it is possible to detect this situation and to collect larger samples for populations with greater inherent variance.

2.9.5 Too Large a Sample

If the sample size is too large, a sample that deviates even slightly from the null hypothesis will cause the null hypothesis to be rejected because the confidence interval around the sample mean varies as $1/\sqrt{n}$. Therefore, when interpreting a test that rejects the null hypothesis, it is important to take the **effect size** into account, which is the (subjective) degree to which the rejection of the null hypothesis accurately reflects reality. For instance, suppose that we hypothesize that the population mean was 0, and we found from a very large sample that the confidence interval was 0.005±0.0001. This rejects the null hypothesis. However, in the context of the problem, perhaps the value 0.005 is indistinguishable from zero and therefore has a small effect. In this case, we would still not reject the null hypothesis.

2.9.6 Not Controlling All Variables When Collecting Observations

The effect of controlling variables in running an experiment is to get a firm grasp on the nature of the underlying population. If the population being sampled changes during the experiment, the collected sample is meaningless. For example, suppose that you are observing the mean delay from a campus router to a particular data center. Suppose that during data collection, your ISP changed its Tier 1 provider. Then, the observations made subsequent to the change would likely reflect a new population. During preliminary data analysis, therefore, it is necessary to ensure that such uncontrollable effects have not corrupted the data set.

2.9.7 Converting Ordinal to Interval Scales

Ordinal scales, in which each ordinal is numbered, such as the Likert scale—where 1 may represent "poor," 2 "satisfactory," 3 "good," 4 "outstanding," and 5 "excellent"—are often treated as if they are interval scales. So, if one user were to rate the streaming performance of a video player as 1 and another as 3, the mean rating is stated to be 2. This is bad practice. It is hard to argue that the gap between "poor" and "satisfactory" is the same as the gap between "satisfactory" and "good." Yet that is the assumption being made when ordinal scales such as these are aggregated. In such cases, it is better to ask users to rank an experience on a linear scale from 1 to 5. This converts the ordinal scale to an interval scale and allows aggregation without making unwarranted assumptions.

2.9.8 Ignoring Outliers

The presence of outliers should always be a cause for concern. Silently ignoring them or deleting them from the data set altogether not only is bad practice but also prevents the analyst from unearthing significant problems in the data-collection process. Therefore, outliers should never be ignored.

2.10 Further Reading

This chapter only touches on the elements of mathematical statistics. A delightfully concise summary of the basics of mathematical statistics can be found in M. G. Bulmer, *Principles of Statistics*, Oliver and Boyd, 1965, reissued by Dover, 1989. Statistical analysis is widely used in the social sciences and agriculture. The classic reference for a plethora of statistical techniques is G. W. Snedecor and W. G. Cochran, *Statistical Methods*, 8th ed., Wiley, 1989. Exploratory data analysis is described from the perspective of a practitioner in G. Myatt, *Making Sense of Data: A Practical Guide to Exploratory Data Analysis and Data Mining*, Wiley, 2006. Readers who want to learn directly from one of the masters of statistical analysis should refer to R. A. Fisher, *Statistical Methods for Research Workers*, Oliver and Boyd, 1925.

2.11 Exercises

1. **Means**

    Prove that the mean of a sample is the value of x^* that minimizes $\sum_{i=1}^{n} (x_i - x^*)^2$.

2. **Means**

    Prove Equation 2.12.

3. Confidence intervals (normal distribution)

Compute the 95% confidence interval for the following data values (Table 2.2):

Data Value	Frequency
1	5
2	7
3	2
7	2
1,000	1

4. Confidence intervals (t distribution)

Redo Example 2.6, using the t distribution.

5. Hypothesis testing: comparing the mean to a constant

For the following sample, test the null hypothesis that the mean loss rate is 2% at the 95% confidence level.

Loss Rate with 5 Buffers	1.20%	2.30%	1.90%	2.40%	3.00%	1.80%	2.10%	3.20%	4.50%	2.20%

6. Chi-squared test

In Example 2.12, what is the value of n_1 beyond which the hypothesis would be rejected?

7. Fitting a distribution and chi-squared test

Continuing with Example 2.13, consider the following data set. Ignoring the first observation (i.e., (1,18)), find the best Poisson fit for the reduced sample. Use this to compute the expected count for each number of arrivals. What is the chi-squared variate value for this reduced data set? Use this to determine whether the Poisson distribution is indeed a good distribution to describe the reduced data set.

Number of Packet Arrivals	1	2	3	4	5	6	7	8	9	10	11	12	13	14	15	16
Count		18	28	56	105	126	146	164	165	120	103	73	54	23	16	9	5

8. Independence, regression, and correlation

A researcher measures the mean uplink bandwidth of ten desktop computers (in kbps), as well as their mean number of peer-to-peer connections over a period of 1 hour, obtaining the following data set:

Uplink Capacity	202	145	194	254	173	94	102	232	183	198
# Peers	50	31	47	50	41	21	24	50	41	49

a. If the number of peers were independent of the uplink capacity, what is the expected number of peers?

b. Can we conclude, using the chi-squared test, that the number of peers is independent of the uplink capacity, at the 95% and 99.9% confidence levels?

c. Compute the regression of the number of peers on the uplink capacity. What is the slope of the best-fit line?

d. What is the correlation coefficient between the two variates? Does this reinforce your conclusions about independence or dependence?

e. What portion of the variation in the value of the number of peers can be attributed to the uplink capacity?

9. **Correlation coefficient**

   Prove Equation 2.39.

10. **Single-factor ANOVA**

   A university is connected to the Internet through three ISPs. To test their relative performance, the IT staff conducts an experiment by measuring the ping times to a well-known Web site over connections from each of the three providers over a 10-day period. The mean ping time using a connection from each ISP on each day is shown in the following table. Use single-factor ANOVA to test the hypothesis that the ISPs are statistically identical.

Day	ISP1	ISP2	ISP3
1	41.2	50.7	41.1
2	34.9	38.5	48.2
3	43.5	56.3	73.2
4	64.2	54.2	48.4
5	64.0	46.4	61.4
6	54.9	58.4	43.2
7	59.3	61.8	63.9
8	73.1	69.4	54.3
9	56.4	66.3	67.4
10	63.8	57.4	58.4

3

Linear Algebra

This chapter presents the essentials of linear algebra. Starting with a basic introduction to vectors and matrices, we study operations on matrices. Next, we study a linear combination of vectors that underlies the important concepts of matrix rank and independence. We then use these concepts to study the solution of systems of linear equations. Linear algebra plays a critical role in modeling processes as linear transformations, which we study next. We focus on an intuitive understanding of eigenvalues and eigenvectors. We conclude with a description of stochastic matrices that arise frequently in models of computer networking systems.

3.1 Vectors and Matrices

Consider two runs of an experiment in which a researcher collects packet traces on an Internet link. Suppose that the first trace contains 312 TCP and 39 UDP packets and that the second trace contains 432 TCP and 21 UDP packets. We can represent these results in the form of these two ordered tuples: [312, 39] and [432, 21]. Here, the positions in the tuple are implicitly associated with the meaning "TCP count" and "UDP count," respectively. We call this representation of an ordered set of **elements** a **vector**.

A vector with n elements is said to have n **dimensions**. There is a one-to-one mapping from an n-dimensional vector with real-valued elements to a point in an n-dimensional real space. Returning to our example, the vector [432, 21] corresponds to a point in a two-dimensional real space whose X- and Y-axes are "TCP count" and

"UDP count," respectively, and that has coordinates of (432, 21). If one were to add another measurement to the tuple—say, "ICMP count," we could represent the counts in a packet trace by a vector such as [432, 21, 12], which corresponds to a point in a three-dimensional real space.

Vectors can be represented in one of two ways: as **row vectors** of the form [312, 12, 88] and as **column vectors** of the form $\begin{bmatrix} 312 \\ 12 \\ 88 \end{bmatrix}$. We define the **zero vector** of n dimensions, denoted **0**, as the vector [0 0 0 ... 0]. In this book, vectors are shown in lowercase bold italic, and vector elements are shown in italic.

Returning to our example, we can represent packet counts in both traces simultaneously, using an array that looks like this:

$$\begin{bmatrix} 312 & 39 \\ 432 & 21 \end{bmatrix}$$

Such a representation is called a **matrix**. In this book, matrices are shown using uppercase bold italic, and matrix elements are shown using lowercase italic.

Unlike a vector, whose elements may be unrelated, elements in the same column of a matrix are usually related; in our example, all elements in the first column are TCP counts. In general, an array with m rows and n columns is called an $m \times n$ matrix. The element in the ith row and jth column of a matrix named A is usually represented by the symbol a_{ij}. In the preceding example, a_{12} is 39 and a_{21} is 432.

Although vector and matrix representations can be used for arbitrary element types, such as for character strings, in our discussion, we will assume that the elements of a vector or a matrix are members of a mathematical **field**. For completeness, the formal definition of a field is stated below; note that this definition essentially formalizes our intuition of the properties of real numbers: A field F is a finite or infinite **set** along with the **operations** of addition (denoted +) and multiplication (denoted *) on elements of this set that satisfy the following six axioms.

1. **Closure** under addition and multiplication: For a, b in F, if $a + b = c$ and $a * b = d$, then c and d are also in F.

2. **Commutativity** of addition and multiplication: For a, b in F, if $a + b = b + a$ and $a * b = b * a$.

3. **Associativity** of addition and multiplication: For a, b, c in F, $(a + b) + c = a + (b + c)$.

4. Existence of distinct additive and multiplicative **identity** elements in the set: There are distinct elements denoted 0 and 1 in F such that for all a in F, $a + 0 = a$ and $a * 1 = a$.

5. Existence of additive and multiplicative **inverses**: For every a in F, there is an element b also in F such that $a + b = 0$. For every a in F other than 0, there is an element also in F such that $a * c = 1$.

6. **Distributivity** of multiplication over addition: For all a, b, and c in F, the following equality holds: $a * (b + c) = (a * b) + (a * c)$.

3.2 Vector and Matrix Algebra

This section presents some basic operations on vectors and matrices.

3.2.1 Addition

The **sum of two vectors** of the same dimension is a vector whose elements are the sums of the corresponding elements of each vector. Addition is not defined for vectors with different dimensions.

The **sum of two matrices** with the same number of rows and columns is a matrix whose elements are the sums of the corresponding elements of each matrix. Addition is not defined for matrices with different numbers of rows or columns.

Because the elements of a vector or a matrix are drawn from a field and because vector and matrix addition operates element by element, vector and matrix addition inherits the field properties of closure, commutativity, associativity, the existence of an additive inverse, and the existence of an additive identity.

3.2.2 Transpose

The **transpose** of a row vector x—denoted x^T—is a column vector whose jth row is the jth column of x. The transpose of an $m \times n$ matrix A, denoted A^T, is an $n \times m$ matrix whose $[j, i]$th element—denoted a_{ji}—is the $[i, j]$th of A, a_{ij}.

EXAMPLE 3.1: TRANSPOSE

The transpose of $[1,3,5,1]$ is $\begin{bmatrix} 1 \\ 3 \\ 5 \\ 1 \end{bmatrix}$. The transpose of $\begin{bmatrix} 23 & 2 & 9 \\ 98 & 7 & 89 \\ 34 & 9 & 1 \end{bmatrix}$ is $\begin{bmatrix} 23 & 98 & 34 \\ 2 & 7 & 9 \\ 9 & 89 & 1 \end{bmatrix}$.

3.2.3 Multiplication

Multiplying a vector x by a real number, or **scalar**, s results in the multiplication of each element (i.e., **scaling**) of the vector by that real. That is,

$$s\left[x_1, x_2, ..., x_n\right] = \left[sx_1, sx_2, ..., sx_n\right] \tag{EQ 3.1}$$

Similarly, multiplying a matrix A by a real number (scalar) s results in the multiplication of each element of the matrix by that real. That is,

$$s\begin{bmatrix} a_{11} & \cdots & a_{1n} \\ \cdots & \cdots & \cdots \\ a_{m1} & \cdots & a_{mn} \end{bmatrix} = \begin{bmatrix} sa_{11} & \cdots & sa_{1n} \\ \cdots & \cdots & \cdots \\ sa_{m1} & \cdots & sa_{mn} \end{bmatrix} \tag{EQ 3.2}$$

The **product of two vectors** can be defined in terms of either a **dot** product or a **cross** product. The dot product of vector x with elements x_i and vector y with elements y_i is defined as the *scalar s* obtained as the sum of the element-by-element product. That is,

$$s = x, y = \sum_{i=1}^{n} x_i y_i \tag{EQ 3.3}$$

The dot product is undefined if the two vectors do not have the same dimension. The cross product of two vectors is not relevant to computer networking and will not be discussed further.

Unlike the dot product of two vectors, which is a scalar, the product of two matrices is a matrix whose $[i, j]$th element is the dot product of the ith *row* of the first matrix and the jth *column* of the second matrix. That is, if $C = AB$, then

$$c_{ij} = \sum_{k=1}^{n} a_{ik} b_{kj} \tag{EQ 3.4}$$

Note that the number of columns in A (the dimension of each row of A) must equal the number of rows in B (the dimension of each column in B). Thus, the product of an $m \times n$ matrix by an $n \times o$ matrix results in an $m \times o$ matrix. Therefore, the product of a n dimensional row vector—a matrix of size $1 \times n$—with an $n \times n$ matrix is a row vector of dimension n.

EXAMPLE 3.2: MATRIX MULTIPLICATION

The product of $\begin{bmatrix} 23 & 2 & 9 \\ 98 & 7 & 89 \\ 34 & 9 & 1 \end{bmatrix}$ and $\begin{bmatrix} 2 & 5 & -2 \\ 4 & 9 & 8 \\ 3 & 0 & 1 \end{bmatrix}$ is $\begin{bmatrix} 81 & 133 & -21 \\ 491 & 553 & -51 \\ 107 & 251 & 5 \end{bmatrix}$. To obtain c_{11}, for example, we compute $23 * 2 + 2 * 4 + 9 * 3 = 46 + 8 + 27 = 81$.

Matrix multiplication is associative; that is, $(AB)C = A(BC)$ but is *not* commutative. That is, in general,

$$AB \neq BA \qquad \text{(EQ 3.5)}$$

This follows trivially from the observation that although AB may be defined, if the number of columns in B differs from the number of rows in A, then BA may not even be defined. Moreover, if $AB = 0$, it is not necessary that either A or B be the null matrix. This is unlike the case with scalars, where $ab=0$ implies that one of a or b is zero. As a corollary, if $AB = AC$, then B does not necessarily have to be the same as C.

3.2.4 Square Matrices

A matrix A is **square** if it has the same number of rows and columns. A square matrix with nonzero elements only along the main diagonal is called a **diagonal** matrix.

An $n \times n$ square diagonal matrix I with 1 along the main diagonal and 0 elsewhere has the property that multiplication of any $n \times n$ square matrix A with this matrix does not change A. That is, $AI = IA = A$. Hence, I is called the **identity** matrix.

3.2.5 Exponentiation

If a matrix A is square, its product with itself is defined and denoted A^2. If A has n rows and columns, so does A^2. By induction, all higher powers of A are also defined and also have n rows and columns.

EXAMPLE 3.3: EXPONENTIATION

Let A be $\begin{bmatrix} 5 & 0 & 0 \\ 0 & 7 & 0 \\ 0 & 0 & 2 \end{bmatrix}$. Then, $A^2 = \begin{bmatrix} 25 & 0 & 0 \\ 0 & 49 & 0 \\ 0 & 0 & 4 \end{bmatrix}$ and $A^3 = \begin{bmatrix} 125 & 0 & 0 \\ 0 & 343 & 0 \\ 0 & 0 & 8 \end{bmatrix}$. Finding the

higher powers of A in this example is particularly straightforward (why?). Generalizing, we see that if A is a diagonal matrix, the (i,i)th element of the kth power of A is $a_{ii}^{\,k}$.

3.2.6 Matrix Exponential

If a matrix A is square, all higher powers of A are also defined and also have n rows and columns. Then, the **matrix exponential** denoted e^A is defined as the infinite sum

$$e^A = I + A + \frac{A^2}{2!} + \frac{A^3}{3!} + \dots \qquad \text{(EQ 3.6)}$$

3.3 Linear Combinations, Independence, Basis, and Dimension

This section introduces some important foundational concepts that will be used in later sections.

3.3.1 Linear Combinations

Consider a set of k real-valued variables $x_1, x_2,..., x_k$. Suppose that we are given a set of k real-valued weights $w_1, w_2,..., w_k$. Then, we can define the weighted sum of these variables as $s = w_1 x_1 + w_2 x_2 + ... + w_k x_k$. This sum "mixes" the variables in linear proportion to the weights. Therefore, we call s a **linear combination** of the variables.

We can generalize the notion of linear combination to vectors. Here, each x_i is a vector, so that their linear combination, s, is also a vector. Of course, each vector must have the same number of elements. Note that each component of s is a linear combination of the corresponding elements of the underlying vectors.

EXAMPLE 3.4: LINEAR COMBINATION OF SCALARS

Compute the linear combination s of the scalars 2, 4, 1, 5 with weights 0.1, 0.4, 0.25, 0.25.

Solution:

The linear combination is $s = 0.1 * 2 + 0.4 * 4 + 0.25 * 1 + 0.25 * 5 = 0.2 + 1.6 + 0.25 + 1.25 = 3.3$.

EXAMPLE 3.5: LINEAR COMBINATION OF VECTORS

Compute the linear combination of the vectors [2 4 1 5], [3 5 1 2], [5 6 2 1], [9 0 1 3] with weights 0.1, 0.4, 0.25, 0.25.

Solution:

The linear combination is given by $0.1 * [2\ 4\ 1\ 5] + 0.4 * [3\ 5\ 1\ 2] + 0.25 * [5\ 6\ 2\ 1] + 0.25 * [9\ 0\ 1\ 3]$. Clearly, the first element of s is given by $0.1 * 2 + 0.4 * 3 + 0.25 * 5 + 0.25 * 9 = 0.2 + 1.2 + 1.25 + 2.25 = 4.9$. Similarly, the other elements are 3.9, 1.25, and 2.3, so that $s = [4.9\ 3.9\ 1.25\ 2.3]$.

3.3.2 Linear Independence

Consider a set of k vectors $x_1, x_2,..., x_k$. Suppose that we can express one of the vectors—say, x_i—as a linear combination of the others. Then, the value of x_i *depends* on the others: If the remaining vectors assume certain values, the value of x_i is known and cannot be chosen arbitrarily. This means that we have removed some degrees of freedom in assigning arbitrary values to the vectors.

Specifically, suppose that we can express x_i as a linear combination of the remaining $k - 1$ vectors, using an appropriately chosen set of $k - 1$ weights. Then, we can write

$$x_i = w_1 x_1 +... + w_{i-1} x_{i-1} + w_{i+1} x_{i+1} +... + w_k x_k \qquad \text{(EQ 3.7)}$$

Or, transposing terms:

$$w_1 x_1 +... + w_{i-1} x_{i-1} - x_i + w_{i+1} x_{i+1} +... + w_k x_k = 0 \qquad \text{(EQ 3.8)}$$

This leads to the following definition of independence of a set of vectors: We say that a set of vectors is independent if the only set of weights that satisfies Equation 3.8 is $w = 0$.

Note that if a set of vectors is not linearly independent, *any* one of them can be rewritten in terms of the others.

EXAMPLE 3.6: LINEAR INDEPENDENCE

The three vectors

$$x_1 = [3\ 0\ 2]$$
$$x_2 = [-3\ 21\ 12]$$
$$x_3 = [21\ -21\ 0]$$

are not linearly independent, because $6x_1 - x_2 - x_3 = 0$. The first and third vectors are independent because the third element of the first vector cannot be generated by the third vector.

In Section 3.4.6, we will see that if a set of vectors is linearly independent, the matrix formed by the vectors is **nonsingular**, that is, has a nonzero **determinant**.

3.3.3 Vector Spaces, Basis, and Dimension

Given a set of k vectors, suppose that we can identify a subset of r vectors that are linearly independent. That is, the remaining vectors can be written as linear combinations of the r vectors. Then, we call these r vectors the **basis** set of this set of vectors. They form the essential core from which we can derive the rest of the vectors. In this sense, the remaining vectors can be thought to be redundant. For instance, in Example 3.6, the first and third vectors constitute a basis, and the second vector can be generated from the basis set as $x_2 = 6x_1 - x_3$. Note that any linearly independent subset of r vectors can form a valid basis, so the basis set is not unique.

We can now generalize this observation as follows. Suppose that we are given a set of r linearly independent vectors. What is the set of vectors that can be generated as linear combinations of this set? Clearly, there are an infinite number of such vectors. We call this infinite set a **vector space** generated by the basis set. (Note that a vector space is a precisely defined mathematical object; this is only an informal definition of the concept.) The number of basis vectors—the cardinality of the basis set—is called the **dimension** of this space.

EXAMPLE 3.7: BASIS AND DIMENSION

A simple way to guarantee that a set of vectors is linearly independent is to set all but one element in each vector to zero. For instance, the vectors $x_1 = [1\ 0\ 0]$,

$x_2 = [0\ 1\ 0]$, $x_3 = [0\ 0\ 1]$ are guaranteed to be linearly independent. Let us find the vector space generated by this basis set. Consider an arbitrary vector $x = [a\ b\ c]$. This vector can be expressed as a linear combination of the basis set as $x = ax_1 + bx_2 + cx_3$. Therefore, this basis set generates the vector space of all possible vectors with three real-valued elements.

If we think of a vector with three real-valued elements as corresponding to a point in three-dimensional space, where the elements of the vector are its Cartesian coordinates, the basis vectors generate all possible points in three-dimensional space. It is easy to see that the basis vectors correspond to the three ordinal axes. It should now be clear why we call the generated vectors a space and why the cardinality of the basis set is the dimensionality of this space.

3.4 Using Matrix Algebra to Solve Linear Equations

We now turn our attention to an important application of matrix algebra, which is to solve sets of linear equations.

3.4.1 Representation

Systems of linear equations are conveniently represented by matrices. Consider the set of linear equations:

$$3x + 2y + z = 5$$
$$-8x + y + 4z = -2$$
$$9x + 0.5y + 4z = 0.9$$

We can represent this set of equations by the matrix

$$\begin{bmatrix} 3 & 2 & 1 & 5 \\ -8 & 1 & 4 & -2 \\ 9 & 0.5 & 4 & 0.9 \end{bmatrix}$$

where the position of a number in the matrix implicitly identifies it as either a coefficient of a variable or a value on the right-hand side. This representation can be used for any set of linear equations. If the rightmost column is **0**, the system is said to be **homogeneous**. The submatrix corresponding to the left-hand side of the linear equations is called the **coefficient matrix**.

3.4.2 Elementary Row Operations and Gaussian Elimination

Given a set of equations, certain simple operations allow us to generate new equations. For example, multiplying the left- and right-hand sides of any equation by a scalar generates a new equation. Moreover, we can add or subtract the left- and right-hand sides of any pair of equations to also generate new equations.

In our preceding example, the first two equations are $3x + 2y + z = 5$ and $-8x + y + 4z = -2$. We can multiply the first equation by 3 to get the new equation $9x + 6y + 3z = 15$. We can also add the two equations to get a new equation $(3 - 8)x + (2 + 1)y + (1 + 4)z = (5 - 2)$, which gives us the equation $-5x + 3y + 5z = 3$.

We can also combine these operations. For example, we could multiply the second equation by 2 and subtract it from the first one like this:

$$(3 - (-16))x + (2 - 2)y + (1 - 8)z = 5 - (-4)$$
$$19x - 7z = 9$$

In the resulting equation, the variable y has been eliminated (i.e., does not appear). We can similarly multiply the third equation by 4 and subtract it from the first one to obtain another equation that also eliminates y. We now have two equations in two variables that we can trivially solve to obtain x and z. Putting their values back into any of the three equations allows us to find y.

This approach, in essence, is the well-known technique called **Gaussian elimination**. In this technique, we pick any one variable and use multiplications and additions on the set of equations to eliminate that variable from all but one equation. This transforms a system with n variables and m equations to a system with $n - 1$ variables and $m - 1$ equations. We can now recurse to obtain, in the end,[1] an equation with one variable, which solves the system for that variable. By substituting this value back into the reduced set of equations, we solve the system.

When using a matrix representation of the set of equations, the elementary operations of multiplying an equation by a scalar and of adding two equations correspond to two **row operations**. The first row operation multiplies all the elements of a row by a scalar, and the second row operation is the element-by-element addition of two rows. It is easy to see that these are exactly analogous to the operations in the previous paragraphs. The Gaussian technique uses these elementary row operations to manipulate the matrix representation of a set of linear equations so that one row looks like this: $[0\ 0\ \dots\ 0\ 1\ 0\ \dots\ 0\ a]$, allowing us to read off the value of that variable. We can use this to substitute for this variable in the other equations, so that we are left with a system of equations with one less unknown and, by recursion, to find the values of all the variables.

---

1. Assuming that the equations are self-consistent and have at least one solution. More on this later.

EXAMPLE 3.8: GAUSSIAN ELIMINATION

Use row operations and Gaussian elimination to solve the system given by

$$\begin{bmatrix} 3 & 2 & 1 & 5 \\ -8 & 1 & 4 & -2 \\ 9 & 0.5 & 4 & 0.9 \end{bmatrix}$$

Solution:

Subtract row 3 from row 2 to obtain

$$\begin{bmatrix} 3 & 2 & 1 & 5 \\ -17 & 0.5 & 0 & -2.9 \\ 9 & 0.5 & 4 & 0.9 \end{bmatrix}$$

Then subtract 0.25 times row 3 from row 1 to obtain

$$\begin{bmatrix} 0.75 & 1.875 & 0 & 4.775 \\ -17 & 0.5 & 0 & -2.9 \\ 9 & 0.5 & 4 & 0.9 \end{bmatrix}$$

Note that the first two rows represent a pair of equations in two unknowns. Multiply the second row by $1.875/0.5 = 3.75$ and subtract from the first row to obtain

$$\begin{bmatrix} 64.5 & 0 & 0 & 15.65 \\ -17 & 0.5 & 0 & -2.9 \\ 9 & 0.5 & 4 & 0.9 \end{bmatrix}$$

This allows us to read off x as $15.65/66.525 = 0.2426$. Substituting this into row 2, we get $-17 * 0.2426 + 0.5y = -2.9$, which we solve to get $y = 2.4496$. Substituting this into the third row, we get $9 * 0.2426 + 0.5 * 2.4496 + 4z = 0.9$, so that $z = 0.6271$. Checking, $3 * 0.2426 + 2 * 2.4484 - 0.6271 = 4.9975$, which is within rounding error of 5.

In practice, choosing which variable to eliminate first has important consequences. Choosing a variable unwisely may require us to maintain matrix elements to very high degrees of precision, which is costly. There is a considerable body of work on algorithms to carefully choosing the variables to eliminate, which are also called the **pivots**. Standard matrix packages, such as MATLAB, implement these algorithms.

3.4.3 Rank

So far, we have assumed that a set of linear equations always has a consistent solution. This is not always the case. A set of equations has no solution or has an infinite number of solutions if it is either **overdetermined** or **underdetermined**, respectively. A system is overdetermined if the same variable assumes inconsistent values. For example, a trivial overdetermined system is the set of equations $x = 1$ and $x = 2$. Gaussian elimination will fail for such systems.

A system is underdetermined if it admits more than one answer. A trivial instance of an underdetermined system is the system of linear equations $x + y = 1$, because we can choose an infinite number of values of x and y that satisfy this equation. Gaussian elimination on such a system results in some set of variables expressed as linear combinations of the independent variables. Each assignment of values to the independent variables will result in finding a consistent solution to the system.

Given a system of m linear equations using n variables, the system is underdetermined if $m < n$. If m is at least as large as n, the system may or may not be underdetermined, depending on whether some equations are repeated. Specifically, we define an equation as being **linearly dependent** on a set of other equations if it can be expressed as a linear combination of the other equations: The vector corresponding to this equation is a linear combination of the vectors corresponding to the other equations. If one equation in a system of linear equations is linearly dependent on the others, we can reduce the equation to the equation $0 = 0$ by a suitable combination of multiplications and additions. Thus, this equation does not give us any additional information and can be removed from the system without changing the solution.

If of m equations in a system, k can be expressed as a linear combination of the other $m - k$ equations, we really have only $m - k$ equations to work with. This value is called the **rank** of the system, denoted r. If $r < n$, the system is underdetermined. If $r = n$, there is only one solution to the system. If $r > n$, the system is overdetermined and therefore inconsistent. Note that the rank of a matrix is the same as the cardinality of the basis set of the corresponding set of row vectors.

EXAMPLE 3.9: RANK

We have already seen that the system of equations $\begin{bmatrix} 3 & 2 & 1 & 5 \\ -8 & 1 & 4 & -2 \\ 9 & 0.5 & 4 & 0.9 \end{bmatrix}$ has a

unique assignment of consistent values to the variables x, y, and z. Therefore, it has a rank of 3.

Consider the system $\begin{bmatrix} 3 & 2 & 1 & 5 \\ -8 & 1 & 4 & -2 \\ 6 & 4 & 2 & 10 \end{bmatrix}$. We see that the third row is just the first row multiplied by 2. Therefore, it adds no additional information to the system and can be removed. The rank of this system is 2 (it is underdetermined), and the resultant system has an infinity of solutions.

Now, consider the system $\begin{bmatrix} 3 & 2 & 1 & 5 \\ -8 & 1 & 4 & -2 \\ 9 & 0.5 & 4 & 0.9 \\ 3 & 2 & 1 & 4 \end{bmatrix}$. We know that the first three rows are linearly independent and have a rank of 3. The fourth row is inconsistent with the first row, so the system is overdetermined and has no solution. The resulting system has a rank of 4.

Many techniques are known to determine the rank of a system of equations. These are, however, beyond the scope of this discussion. For our purpose, it suffices to attempt Gaussian elimination and report a system to be overdetermined, that is, have a rank of at least n, if an inconsistent solution is found, and to be underdetermined, that is, with a rank smaller than n, if an infinite number of solutions can be found. If the system is underdetermined, the rank is the number of equations that do not reduce to the trivial equation $0 = 0$.

3.4.4 Determinants

We now turn our attention to the study of a determinant of a matrix. Even the most enthusiastic of mathematicians will admit that the study of determinants is a rather dry topic. Moreover, the determinant of a matrix does not, by itself, have much practical value. Although they can compactly represent the solution of a set of linear equations, computing solutions using the determinant is impractical. The real reason to persist in mastering determinants is as a necessary prelude to the deep and elegant area of the eigenvalues of a matrix.

The determinant $D = \det A$ of a two-by-two matrix is a *scalar* defined as follows:

$$D = detA = det\begin{bmatrix} a_{11} & a_{12} \\ a_{21} & a_{22} \end{bmatrix} = \begin{vmatrix} a_{11} & a_{12} \\ a_{21} & a_{22} \end{vmatrix} = a_{11}a_{22} - a_{12}a_{21} \qquad \textbf{(EQ 3.9)}$$

Note the use of vertical lines instead of brackets to indicate the determinant of the matrix rather than the matrix itself. The determinant of a two-by-two matrix is called a determinant of **order** 2.

To describe the determinant of a larger square matrix, we will need the concept of **submatrix** corresponding to an element a_{jk}. This is the matrix A from which the jth row and the kth column have been deleted and is denoted $S_{jk}(A)$. The determinant of this submatrix, $det\ S_{jk}(A) = |S_{jk}(A)|$, is a scalar called the **minor** of a_{jk} and is denoted M_{jk}.

Note that the submatrix of a matrix has one fewer row and column. The determinant of a n-by-n matrix has order n. Therefore, each of its minors has an order $n - 1$.

We now define another auxiliary term, which is the **cofactor** of a_{jk} denoted C_{jk}. This is defined by

$$C_{jk} = (-1)^{j+k} M_{jk} \qquad \text{(EQ 3.10)}$$

We are now in a position to define the determinant of a matrix. The determinant of a matrix is defined recursively as follows:

$$D = \sum_{j=1}^{n} a_{ij} C_{ij} = \sum_{k=1}^{n} a_{ki} C_{ki} \qquad \text{(EQ 3.11)}$$

where i is an arbitrary row or column. It can be shown that D does not change no matter which column or row is chosen for expansion. Moreover, as shown in Section 3.7, the determinant of a matrix does not change if the matrix is transposed. That is, $|A| = |A^T|$.

EXAMPLE 3.10: DETERMINANTS

Compute the determinant of the matrix $\begin{bmatrix} 2 & 5 & -2 \\ 4 & 9 & 8 \\ 3 & 0 & 1 \end{bmatrix}$.

Solution:

We will compute this by expanding the third row so that we can ignore the middle cofactor, corresponding to the element $a_{32} = 0$. The determinant is given by

$$a_{31}C_{31} + a_{33}C_{33} = 3(-1)^{3+1} M_{31} + 1(-1)^{3+3} M_{33}$$

$$= 3\begin{vmatrix} 5 & -2 \\ 9 & 8 \end{vmatrix} + 1\begin{vmatrix} 2 & 5 \\ 4 & 9 \end{vmatrix} = 3(40 - (-18)) + 1(18 - 20) = 174 + (-2) = 172$$

As a check, we expand by the center column to obtain

$$a_{12}C_{12} + a_{22}C_{22} = 5(-1)^{1+2}M_{12} + 1(-1)^{2+2}M_{22}$$

$$= -5\begin{vmatrix} 48 \\ 31 \end{vmatrix} + 9\begin{vmatrix} 2-2 \\ 31 \end{vmatrix} = -5(4-24) + 9(2-(-6)) = 100 + 72 = 172$$

Here are some useful properties of determinants

- A determinant can be computed by expanding any row or column of a matrix. Therefore, if a matrix has a zero column or row, its determinant is 0.
- Multiplying every element in a row or a column of a matrix by the constant c results in multiplying its determinant by the same factor.
- Interchanging two rows or columns of matrix A results in a matrix B such that $|B| = -|A|$. Therefore, if a matrix has identical rows or columns, its determinant must be zero, because zero is the only number whose negation leaves it unchanged.
- A square matrix with n rows and columns has rank n if and only if it has a nonzero determinant.
- A square matrix has an inverse (is **nonsingular**) if and only if it has a non-zero determinant.

3.4.5 Cramer's Theorem

Computing the determinant of a matrix allows us (in theory, at least) to trivially solve a system of equations. In practice, computing the determinant is more expensive than Gaussian elimination, so **Cramer's theorem** is useful mostly to give us insight into the nature of the solution.

Cramer's theorem states that if a system of n linear equations in n variables $Ax = b$ has a nonzero coefficient determinant $D = det\ A$, the system has precisely one solution, given by

$$x_i = D_i/D$$

where D_i is determinant of a matrix obtained by substituting b for the ith column in A. Thus, if we know the corresponding determinants, we can directly compute the x_is by using this theorem, also called **Cramer's rule**.

A system is said to be **homogeneous** if $b = 0$. In this case, each of the D_is is zero, so that each of the x_is is also 0. If the determinant of the coefficient matrix A, or D, is 0, and if the system is homogeneous, Cramer's rule assigns each variable the indeterminate quantity 0/0. However, it can be shown that in this case, *the system does, in fact, have nonzero solutions*. This important fact is the point of departure for the computation of the eigenvalues of a matrix.

3.4.6 The Inverse of a Matrix

The inverse of a square matrix A denoted A^{-1} is a matrix such that $AA^{-1} = A^{-1}A = I$.

EXAMPLE 3.11: INVERSE

Prove that the inverse of a matrix is unique.

Solution:

If A had an inverse B as well as an inverse C, then $AB = BA = AC = CA = I$. So, $B = BI = B(AC) = (BA)C = IC = C$.

Not all square matrices are invertible: A matrix that does not have an inverse is called a **singular** matrix. All singular matrices have a determinant of zero. If a matrix is not singular, its inverse is given by

$$A^{-1} = \frac{1}{|A|}[C_{jk}]^T = \frac{1}{|A|}\begin{bmatrix} C_{11} & C_{21} & \cdots & C_{n1} \\ C_{12} & C_{22} & \cdots & C_{n2} \\ \cdots & \cdots & \cdots & \cdots \\ C_{1n} & C_{2n} & \cdots & C_{nn} \end{bmatrix} \qquad \text{(EQ 3.12)}$$

where C_{jk} is the cofactor of a_{jk}. Note that the cofactor matrix is transposed when compared with A. As a special case, the inverse of a two-by-two matrix

$$A = \begin{bmatrix} a_{11} & a_{12} \\ a_{21} & a_{22} \end{bmatrix} \quad \text{is} \quad A^{-1} = \frac{1}{|A|}\begin{bmatrix} a_{22} & -a_{12} \\ -a_{21} & a_{11} \end{bmatrix} \qquad \text{(EQ 3.13)}$$

EXAMPLE 3.12: INVERSE

Compute the inverse of the matrix $\begin{bmatrix} 2 & 3 \\ 6 & 2 \end{bmatrix}$.

The determinant of the matrix is $2 * 2 - 6 * 3 = -14$. We can use Equation 3.13 to compute the inverse as

$$\frac{1}{-14}\begin{bmatrix} 2 & -3 \\ -6 & 2 \end{bmatrix}$$

3.5 Linear Transformations, Eigenvalues, and Eigenvectors

This section deals with the important problem of linear transformations and their computation, using eigenvalues and eigenvectors.

3.5.1 A Matrix as a Linear Transformation

Recall that the product of an $n \times n$ matrix with an n dimensional column vector—a matrix of size $n \times 1$—is another column vector of dimension n. We can therefore view the matrix as **transforming** the input vector into the output vector.

Note that the kth element of the output column vector is formed by combining all the elements of the input vector, using the weights found in the kth row of the matrix. This is just a *linear combination* of the elements of the input vector. A square matrix that represents (the weights corresponding to) a set of such linear combinations is said to represent a **linear transformation** of the input vector.

EXAMPLE 3.13: MATRIX AS A LINEAR TRANSFORMATION

Consider the matrix $\begin{bmatrix} 2 & 3 \\ 6 & 2 \end{bmatrix}$ and an input vector $\begin{bmatrix} a \\ b \end{bmatrix}$. The multiplication of this

vector with the matrix— $\begin{bmatrix} 2 & 3 \\ 6 & 2 \end{bmatrix} * \begin{bmatrix} a \\ b \end{bmatrix}$ is the output vector $\begin{bmatrix} 2a + 3b \\ 6a + 2b \end{bmatrix}$. The first

element of the output vector can be thought of as combining the input elements a and b with weights 2 and 3 (the first row of the matrix), and the second element of the output vector can be thought of as combining the inputs with weights 6 and 2 (the second row of the matrix).

The definition of matrix multiplication allows us to represent the composition of two linear transformations as a matrix product. Specifically, suppose that the matrix A transforms a column vector x to another column vector x' and that the matrix B is now used to transform x' to another vector x''. Then, $x'' = Bx' = B(Ax) = (BA)x = Cx$, where $C = BA$ is the product of the two transformation matrices. That is, we can represent the composition of the two transformations as the matrix product of the transformation matrices.

EXAMPLE 3.14: COMPOSITION OF LINEAR TRANSFORMATIONS

We have already seen that the matrix $\begin{bmatrix} 2 & 3 \\ 6 & 2 \end{bmatrix}$ transforms a vector $\begin{bmatrix} a \\ b \end{bmatrix}$ to the

vector $\begin{bmatrix} 2a + 3b \\ 6a + 2b \end{bmatrix}$. Suppose that we apply the matrix $\begin{bmatrix} 2 & 0 \\ 0 & 2 \end{bmatrix}$ to this output. The

resultant value is $\begin{bmatrix} 2 & 0 \\ 0 & 2 \end{bmatrix} * \begin{bmatrix} 2a + 3b \\ 6a + 2b \end{bmatrix} = \begin{bmatrix} 4a + 6b \\ 12a + 4b \end{bmatrix}$. Instead, we can compute the

product of the two transformation matrices as $\begin{bmatrix} 2 & 0 \\ 0 & 2 \end{bmatrix} * \begin{bmatrix} 2 & 3 \\ 6 & 2 \end{bmatrix} = \begin{bmatrix} 4 & 6 \\ 12 & 4 \end{bmatrix}$. Then,

applying this product to the initial input gives us

$\begin{bmatrix} 4 & 6 \\ 12 & 4 \end{bmatrix} * \begin{bmatrix} a \\ b \end{bmatrix} = \begin{bmatrix} 4a + 6b \\ 12a + 4b \end{bmatrix}$, as before.

3.5.2 The Eigenvalue of a Matrix

Consider the matrix $\begin{bmatrix} 2 & 0 \\ 0 & 2 \end{bmatrix}$ and an input vector $\begin{bmatrix} a \\ b \end{bmatrix}$. The multiplication of this vec-

tor with the matrix is the output vector $\begin{bmatrix} 2a \\ 2b \end{bmatrix} = 2 * \begin{bmatrix} a \\ b \end{bmatrix}$. Therefore, the matrix repre-

sents a *doubling* transformation on its input: The result of applying this matrix to any vector is equivalent to multiplying the vector by the scalar 2.

When the result of a matrix multiplication with a *particular* vector is the same as a scalar multiplication with that vector, we call the scalar an **eigenvalue** of the matrix and the corresponding vector an **eigenvector**. More precisely, we define an eigenvalue of a square matrix A to be a scalar λ such that, for *some* nonzero column vector x,

$$Ax = \lambda x \qquad \text{(EQ 3.14)}$$

The magnitude of an eigenvalue indicates the degree to which the matrix operation scales an eigenvector: The larger the magnitude, the greater the scaling effect.

EXAMPLE 3.15: EIGENVALUES AND EIGENVECTORS

Compute the eigenvalues and corresponding eigenvectors of the matrix $\begin{bmatrix} 4 & 6 \\ 12 & 4 \end{bmatrix}$.

Solution:

Let the eigenvector be $\begin{bmatrix} x_1 \\ x_2 \end{bmatrix}$. Then, $\begin{bmatrix} 4 & 6 \\ 12 & 4 \end{bmatrix}\begin{bmatrix} x_1 \\ x_2 \end{bmatrix} = \lambda \begin{bmatrix} x_1 \\ x_2 \end{bmatrix}$. Expanding the left-hand side, we get a system of two equations:

$$4x_1 + 6x_2 = \lambda x_1$$
$$12x_1 + 4x_2 = \lambda x_2$$

(EQ 3.15)

Transposing terms, we get

$$(4 - \lambda)x_1 + 6x_2 = 0$$
$$12x_1 + (4 - \lambda)x_2 = 0$$

We recognize this as a homogenous system of two linear equations. Recall from Section 3.4.5 that this system has a nonzero solution if and only if the determinant of the coefficient matrix is zero. That is,

$$\begin{vmatrix} (4 - \lambda) & 6 \\ 12 & (4 - \lambda) \end{vmatrix} = 0$$

We can expand this to get the quadratic:

$$(4 - \lambda)^2 - 72 = 0$$

which we solve to find

$$(4 - \lambda)^2 = 72$$

$$\lambda = 4 \pm \sqrt{72} = 4 \pm 6\sqrt{2}$$

Given these two eigenvalues, we compute the corresponding eigenvectors as follows. First, we substitute the value $\lambda = 4 \pm 6\sqrt{2}$ in Equation 3.15 to get

$$(4 - 4 - 6\sqrt{2})x_1 + 6x_2 = 0$$
$$12x_1 + (4 - 4 - 6\sqrt{2})x_2 = 0$$

$$-6\sqrt{2}x_1 + 6x_2 = 0$$

$$12x_1 - 6\sqrt{2}x_2 = 0$$

which both reduce to the equation

$$\sqrt{2}x_1 - x_2 = 0$$

We have two variables and only one equation, which corresponds to an infinite number of solution eigenvectors, parametrized by a single free variable, represented as $\begin{bmatrix} x_1 \\ \sqrt{2}x_1 \end{bmatrix}$. For instance, if we set $x_1 = 1$, one possible eigenvector is $\begin{bmatrix} 1 \\ \sqrt{2} \end{bmatrix}$. The set of eigenvectors can also be represented as $a\begin{bmatrix} 1 \\ \sqrt{2} \end{bmatrix}$, where a is an arbitrary scalar.

As a check, note that $Ax = \begin{bmatrix} 4 & 6 \\ 12 & 4 \end{bmatrix}\begin{bmatrix} 1 \\ \sqrt{2} \end{bmatrix} = \begin{bmatrix} 4 + 6\sqrt{2} \\ 12 + 4\sqrt{2} \end{bmatrix}$ and $\lambda x = (4 + 6\sqrt{7}) * \begin{bmatrix} 1 \\ \sqrt{2} \end{bmatrix} = \begin{bmatrix} 4 + 6\sqrt{2} \\ 12 + 4\sqrt{2} \end{bmatrix}$.

We interpret this geometrically as follows. Suppose that we represent the Cartesian coordinates of a point (x, y) by the vector $\begin{bmatrix} x \\ y \end{bmatrix}$. Then, the eigenvectors parametrized by x_1 as $\begin{bmatrix} x_1 \\ \sqrt{2}x_1 \end{bmatrix}$ are the set of points that lie on the line $y = \sqrt{2}x$.

Points that lie on this line are transformed by the matrix to other points *also on the same line*, because the effect of the matrix on its eigenvector is to act like a scalar, which does not change the direction of a vector. Moreover, the *degree* of scaling is the associated eigenvalue of $4 + \sqrt{72}$. That is, a point at a unit distance from the origin and on this line (a unit eigenvector) would be scaled to a point on the line that is a distance of $4 + \sqrt{72}$ from the origin. This is shown in Figure 3.1.

To obtain the other eigenvectors, we substitute the value $\lambda = 4 - \sqrt{72}$ in Equation 3.15 to get

$$(4 - 4 + \sqrt{72})x_1 + 6x_2 = 0$$

$$12x_1 + (4 - 4 + \sqrt{72})x_2 = 0$$

$$\sqrt{72}x_1 + 6x_2 = 0$$
$$12x_1 + \sqrt{72}x_2 = 0$$

This gives us the parametrized eigenvector solution, $\begin{bmatrix} x_1 \\ -\sqrt{2}x_1 \end{bmatrix}$, which can be represented as $a\begin{bmatrix} 1 \\ -\sqrt{2} \end{bmatrix}$, where a is an arbitrary scalar.

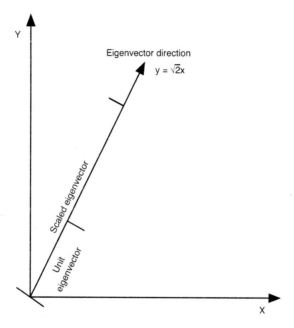

Figure 3.1 The effect of a matrix on an eigenvector is to scale it, preserving its direction.

3.5.3 Computing the Eigenvalues of a Matrix

We can compute the eigenvalues and eigenvectors of a matrix by generalizing the method of the previous example. Consider a matrix A with an eigenvector x and a corresponding eigenvalue λ. We know, by definition, that

$$Ax = \lambda x$$

We rewrite this as

$$(A - \lambda I)x = 0 \tag{EQ 3.16}$$

This is a homogeneous system of equations, so from Section 3.4.5, it has nontrivial solutions only if the determinant of the coefficient matrix is zero:

$$|A - \lambda I| = 0 \qquad \text{(EQ 3.17)}$$

This determinant is called the **characteristic determinant** of the matrix, and Equation 3.17 is called its **characteristic equation**. Expanding the determinant will result, in general, in obtaining a polynomial of the nth degree in λ, which is the **characteristic polynomial** of the matrix. As we have seen, the eigenvalues of the matrix are the roots of the characteristic polynomial. This important result allows us to compute the eigenvalues of any matrix. Note also that the value of the characteristic determinant of a matrix does not change if the matrix is transposed. Hence, the eigenvalues of a matrix and its transpose are identical.

In general, the roots of a polynomial of degree n can be real or complex. Moreover, the fundamental theorem of algebra tells us that there is at least one root and at most n distinct roots. Therefore, a square matrix of degree n has between one and n distinct eigenvalues, some of which may be complex and will form complex conjugate pairs if the matrix is real. Moreover, some eigenvalues may be repeated. Each eigenvalue corresponds to a family of eigenvectors that are parametrized by at least one free variable.

The set of eigenvalues of a matrix are called its **spectrum**. The largest eigenvalue by magnitude is called the **principal eigenvalue**, or the **spectral radius** of the matrix. Each eigenvalue corresponds to a family of eigenvectors. It can be shown that the set of eigenvectors corresponding to a set of *distinct* eigenvalues are always linearly independent of each other. The set of all vectors that can be expressed as a linear combination of the eigenvectors is called the **eigenspace** of the matrix.

EXAMPLE 3.16: COMPLEX EIGENVALUES

Let us compute eigenvalues for the matrix $A = \begin{bmatrix} 0 & 1 \\ -1 & 0 \end{bmatrix}$. We do so by setting the characteristic determinant to 0:

$$\begin{vmatrix} -\lambda & 1 \\ -1 & -\lambda \end{vmatrix} = 0$$

This gives us the characteristic equation

$$\lambda^2 + 1 = 0$$

so that $\lambda = \pm i$. This is the spectrum of the matrix, and the spectral radius is 1.

We find the eigenvector corresponding to $\lambda = i$ by setting

$$\begin{bmatrix} 0 & 1 \\ -1 & 0 \end{bmatrix} \begin{bmatrix} x_1 \\ x_2 \end{bmatrix} = i \begin{bmatrix} x_1 \\ x_2 \end{bmatrix}$$

$$x_2 = ix_1$$

$$-x_1 = ix_2$$

which is a set of equations with rank 1; that is, the second equation just restates the first one. One possible vector that satisfies this is $\begin{bmatrix} 1 \\ i \end{bmatrix}$. To check this, note that $\begin{bmatrix} 0 & 1 \\ -1 & 0 \end{bmatrix} \begin{bmatrix} 1 \\ i \end{bmatrix} = \begin{bmatrix} i \\ -1 \end{bmatrix} = i \begin{bmatrix} 1 \\ i \end{bmatrix}$. The eigenvector corresponding to the eigenvalue $-i$ can be similarly found to be $\begin{bmatrix} x_1 \\ -ix_1 \end{bmatrix}$.

Because both eigenvector families are complex, the matrix never leaves the direction of a real-valued vector unchanged. Indeed, the matrix corresponds to a rotation by 90 degrees, so this is expected. What is unexpected is that the rotation matrix does leave the direction of a complex-valued vector unchanged, which has no obvious intuitive explanation.

EXAMPLE 3.17: EIGENVALUES OF A DIAGONAL MATRIX

Consider a diagonal matrix, such as $A = \begin{bmatrix} a & 0 & 0 \\ 0 & b & 0 \\ 0 & 0 & c \end{bmatrix}$. What are its eigenvalues?

The characteristic equation is

$$\begin{vmatrix} a - \lambda & 0 & 0 \\ 0 & b - \lambda & 0 \\ 0 & 0 & c - \lambda \end{vmatrix} = 0$$

A little work shows that this reduces to the equation

$$(a - \lambda)(b - \lambda)(c - \lambda) = 0$$

which shows that the eigenvalues are simply the diagonal elements a, b, and c. This generalizes: We can read off the eigenvalues as the diagonal elements of any diagonal matrix.

3.5.4 The Importance of Eigenvalues

The eigenvalues of a matrix become important when we consider the *repeated* application of a transformation to an input vector. Suppose that we represent the state of a system by a vector, where each element of the vector corresponds to some aspect of the system, such as the buffer occupancy level (discussed at greater length in Section 8.2.2). Suppose further that we can represent the transformation of the state in one time step as being equivalent to the application of a state transformation operator (and the equivalent matrix) on the state vector. Then, the steady-state, or eventual state, of the system can be obtained by the repeated application of the transformation matrix on the initial vector. It turns out that the eigenvalues of the transformation matrix can be used to characterize the steady state.

To see this, first consider the repeated application of a matrix A to its eigenvector x corresponding to an eigenvalue λ. By definition, a single application of A to $x = Ax = \lambda x$. Applying A n times therefore reduces to computing $\lambda^n x$, which is far simpler!

Now, consider an initial state vector v that can be represented as a linear combination of two eigenvectors of A—say, x_1 and x_2—like so:

$$v = c_1 x_1 + c_2 x_2$$

Suppose that these eigenvectors correspond to the eigenvalues λ_1 and λ_2. Then, $A^n v$ can be found as follows:

$$A^n v = A^n (c_1 x_1 + c_2 x_2) = c_1 A^n x_1 + c_2 A^n x_2 = c_1 \lambda_1^n x_1 + c_2 \lambda_2^n x_2$$

We see that the repeated application of A on v, which is a complex operation, is replaced by the far simpler operation of raising a scalar to the nth power.

This intuition is easily generalized. If we can represent the initial vector as the linear combination of the eigenvectors of a matrix, the repeated application of the matrix can be found with little effort, as the next example shows.

EXAMPLE 3.18: COMPUTING $A^N X$ USING EIGENVECTORS

From the previous example, we know that the matrix $A = \begin{bmatrix} 0 & 1 \\ -1 & 0 \end{bmatrix}$ has two eigen-values i, and $-i$, with corresponding unit eigenvectors $\begin{bmatrix} 1 \\ i \end{bmatrix}$ and $\begin{bmatrix} 1 \\ -i \end{bmatrix}$. Consider a state vector $\begin{bmatrix} 10 \\ 0 \end{bmatrix}$. We can represent this as $5 * \begin{bmatrix} 1 \\ i \end{bmatrix} + 5 * \begin{bmatrix} 1 \\ -i \end{bmatrix}$. Therefore, $\begin{bmatrix} 0 & 1 \\ -1 & 0 \end{bmatrix}^{100}$

$\begin{bmatrix} 10 \\ 0 \end{bmatrix}$, which is computationally complex, reduces to computing $5 * i^{100} * \begin{bmatrix} 1 \\ i \end{bmatrix} +$

$5 * i^{100} * \begin{bmatrix} 1 \\ -i \end{bmatrix} = 5 * \begin{bmatrix} 1 \\ i \end{bmatrix} + 5 * \begin{bmatrix} 1 \\ -i \end{bmatrix} = \begin{bmatrix} 10 \\ 0 \end{bmatrix}$. Geometrically, this makes sense,

because applying A once corresponds to a 90 degree rotation, so applying it for any multiple of four times will leave the initial vector unchanged.

This method of computing the effect of a repeated linear transformation is useful when the initial vector can be written as a linear combination of the eigenvectors. In this context, the following fact is useful: The eigenvectors corresponding to a set of *distinct* eigenvalues form a **linearly independent set**. We have already seen that any set of n linearly independent complex vectors form a basis for the complex hyperspace C^n. Hence, if a square matrix of order n has n distinct eigenvalues, we can express any initial vector as a linear combination of its eigenvectors. This is one reason why knowing the eigenvalues of a matrix is very useful.

What if the initial state vector cannot be written as a linear combination of the eigenvectors? That is, what if the initial state vector is not in the eigenspace of the matrix? It turns out that a somewhat more complex computation, still involving the eigenvalues, allows us to compute $A^n x$.

3.5.5 The Role of the Principal Eigenvalue

Consider a matrix A that has a set of m eigenvalues λ_i, $i = 1, 2, ..., m$ with corresponding unit eigenvectors x_i. Suppose that we choose a vector v in the eigenspace of the matrix such that it is expressed as a linear combination of *all* the eigenvectors:

$$v = \sum_{i=1}^{m} c_i x_i$$

Then, n applications of the matrix to this vector results in the vector

$$\sum_{i=1}^{m} c_i \lambda_i^n x_i$$

As $n \to \infty$, this sum is dominated by the eigenvalue that has the largest magnitude, which is called the **principal**, or **dominant**, eigenvalue. (If more than one eigenvalue has the same magnitude, they are both considered to be the principal eigenvalues.) To first approximation, we can ignore all the other eigenvalues in computing the limit.

EXAMPLE 3.19: PRINCIPAL EIGENVALUE

Consider the matrix $A = \begin{bmatrix} 4 & 6 \\ 12 & 4 \end{bmatrix}$. Recall from Example 3.15 that it has two

eigenvalues, $\lambda = 4 \pm \sqrt{72}$, which evaluate to 12.48 and –4.48. The unit eigen-

vectors of this matrix are $\begin{bmatrix} 1 \\ \sqrt{2} \end{bmatrix}$ and $\begin{bmatrix} 1 \\ \frac{-1}{\sqrt{2}} \end{bmatrix}$. Suppose that we start with an ini-

tial vector $\begin{bmatrix} 0 \\ 3\sqrt{2} \end{bmatrix}$, which we can express as $2 * \begin{bmatrix} 1 \\ \sqrt{2} \end{bmatrix} - 2 * \begin{bmatrix} 1 \\ \frac{-1}{\sqrt{2}} \end{bmatrix}$. Then,

$A^{10} \begin{bmatrix} 0 \\ 3\sqrt{2} \end{bmatrix} = 2 * 12.48^{10} * \begin{bmatrix} 1 \\ \sqrt{2} \end{bmatrix} - 2*(-4.48)^{10} * \begin{bmatrix} 1 \\ \frac{-1}{\sqrt{2}} \end{bmatrix}$. This evaluates to

$\begin{bmatrix} 1.83*10^{11} \\ 2.59*10^{11} \end{bmatrix}$. If we ignore the second term (i.e, the contribution due to the

eigenvalue –4.48), the resulting value changes only in the third decimal place
of precision. It is clear that the dominant eigenvalue is the one that matters.

3.5.6 Finding Eigenvalues and Eigenvectors

Computing the eigenvalues and the eigenvectors of a matrix is important in practice. Here are some facts that help identify the nature of the eigenvalues of a
matrix.

- If a matrix is square and diagonal, its eigenvalues are its diagonal elements.
- If a matrix is square and symmetric (that is, $A^T = A$), its eigenvalues are real.
- **Gerschgorin's "circle" theorem** states that all the eigenvalues of a complex
  matrix lie in the set of disks—on the complex plane—centered on the elements
  of the diagonal, with a radius equal to the sum of the magnitudes of the off-
  diagonal elements. Intuitively, if the off-diagonal elements are "not too large,"
  the eigenvalues of the matrix are its diagonal elements.

EXAMPLE 3.20: FINDING EIGENVALUES

The matrix $A = \begin{bmatrix} 9.1 & 0.8 & 0.3 \\ 0.8 & 5.8 & 0.2 \\ 0.3 & 0.2 & 6.5 \end{bmatrix}$ is symmetric. Hence, its eigenvalues are real. It

has three Gerschgorin disks: (1) center $9.1 + 0i$, radius 1.1, (2) center $5.8 + 0i$ and radius 1.0, and (3) center $6.5 + 0i$ and radius 0.5. Because the eigenvalues are real, they must lie in one of three intervals: [8, 10.2], [4.8, 6.8], and [6, 7]. The second interval overlaps the third, so we know that the eigenvalues lie in either the interval [4.8 7] or the interval [8 10.2].

It is possible to approximately compute the dominant eigenvalue of a matrix[2] by using the **power** method. In this technique, we start with an *arbitrary* initial vector x_0 and repeatedly apply A to it. At each step, we compute the **Rayleigh ratio**
$$\frac{x_k^T A x_k}{x_k^T x_k} = \frac{x^T x_{k+1}}{x_k^T x_k},$$ which converges toward the dominant eigenvalue of the matrix.
The intuitive idea is that applying A to any vector scales it in multiple dimensions, but the dominant eigenvalue dominates the scaling effect. Repeatedly applying A magnifies the contribution of the dominant eigenvalue, exposing it.

EXAMPLE 3.21: POWER METHOD TO COMPUTE THE DOMINANT EIGENVALUE

Use the power method to compute the dominant eigenvalue of the matrix
$$\begin{bmatrix} 4 & 6 \\ 12 & 4 \end{bmatrix}.$$

Solution:

Suppose that we arbitrarily start with the initial vector $x_0 = \begin{bmatrix} 1 \\ 1 \end{bmatrix}$. Applying the

matrix once, we get $x_1 = \begin{bmatrix} 10 \\ 16 \end{bmatrix}$. The Rayleigh ratio evaluates to ([1 1] * $\begin{bmatrix} 10 \\ 16 \end{bmatrix}$)/([1 1] *

$\begin{bmatrix} 1 \\ 1 \end{bmatrix}$) = 26/2 = 13. Repeating, we get $x_2 = \begin{bmatrix} 136 \\ 184 \end{bmatrix}$, and the corresponding Rayleigh

---

2. Usually, but not necessarily, the dominant eigenvalue. It turns out that in nearly all practical cases, this is the one that will be found.

ratio evaluates to 4304/356 = 12.08. After one more iteration, we get $x_3 = \begin{bmatrix} 1648 \\ 2368 \end{bmatrix}$,
and the Rayleigh ratio evaluates to 659840/52352 = 12.60. Recall from Example 3.19 that the dominant eigenvalue is 12.48. We obtain an approximation to within 1% of this value in only three iterations.

It can be shown that the speed of convergence of this method depends on the gap between the dominant and the second-largest eigenvalue. The bigger the gap, the faster the convergence. Intuitively, if the second-largest eigenvalue is close in magnitude to the dominant eigenvalue, its scaling effects do not die down easily, requiring more iterations.

The power method can also be used to find the dominant *eigenvector*. To do so, after each iteration, the vector x_i must be *scaled*. That is, we set its largest element to 1 by dividing each element by the largest element, as demonstrated next.

EXAMPLE 3.22: POWER METHOD FOR COMPUTING THE DOMINANT EIGENVECTOR

Compute the dominant eigenvector of the matrix $\begin{bmatrix} 4 & 6 \\ 12 & 4 \end{bmatrix}$ by using the power method.

Solution:

From Example 3.21, we already know that $x_1 = \begin{bmatrix} 10 \\ 16 \end{bmatrix}$. We rescale it by dividing each element by 16 to get the vector $\begin{bmatrix} 0.625 \\ 1 \end{bmatrix}$. Using this as the new value of x_1, we get $x_2 = \begin{bmatrix} 4 & 6 \\ 12 & 4 \end{bmatrix} * \begin{bmatrix} 0.625 \\ 1 \end{bmatrix} = \begin{bmatrix} 8.5 \\ 11.5 \end{bmatrix}$. We rescale this again to get $x_2 = \begin{bmatrix} 0.739 \\ 1 \end{bmatrix}$. This allows us to compute $x_3 = \begin{bmatrix} 4 & 6 \\ 12 & 4 \end{bmatrix} * \begin{bmatrix} 0.739 \\ 1 \end{bmatrix} = \begin{bmatrix} 8.956 \\ 12.868 \end{bmatrix}$, which is rescaled to $\begin{bmatrix} 0.696 \\ 1 \end{bmatrix}$. Recall that the eigenvector for this eigenvalue is exactly

$\begin{bmatrix} 1 \\ \sqrt{2} \end{bmatrix}$, which we scale to $\begin{bmatrix} 0.707 \\ 1 \end{bmatrix}$. As before, with just three iterations, we are within 1.5% of this final value.

3.5.7 Similarity and Diagonalization

Two matrices are said to be **similar** if they have the same set of eigenvalues. In some cases, given a matrix A, it is useful to be able to compute a similar **diagonal** matrix D. (We show a use case in Example 3.23.)

A sufficient, but not necessary, condition for a matrix of size n to be diagonalizable is that it has n distinct eigenvalues; to see that this condition is not necessary, consider a diagonal matrix with repeated diagonal elements. In this case, let X denote a matrix whose columns are the eigenvectors of A. Then, it can be easily shown, by expansion of the underlying terms, that the matrix

$$D = X^{-1}AX \qquad \text{(EQ 3.18)}$$

is a diagonal matrix whose diagonal elements *are the eigenvalues of A*.

Knowing the diagonalized version of a matrix makes it trivial to compute its mth power. From Equation 3.18, note that

$$D^2 = (X^{-1}AX)(X^{-1}AX) = X^{-1}A^2X$$

A simple induction shows that

$$D^m = X^{-1}A^mX$$

so that

$$A^m = XD^mX^{-1}$$

But the right-hand side is easily computed because D is diagonal. Hence, we can easily compute A^m.

EXAMPLE 3.23: DIAGONALIZATION

Consider the matrix $A = \begin{bmatrix} 4 & 6 \\ 12 & 4 \end{bmatrix}$. Recall from Example 3.15 that it has two

eigenvalues, $\lambda = 4 \pm 6\sqrt{2}$, corresponding to the eigenvectors $\begin{bmatrix} 1 \\ \sqrt{2} \end{bmatrix}$ and $\begin{bmatrix} 1 \\ -\sqrt{2} \end{bmatrix}$.

This allows us to write out the matrix X as $\begin{bmatrix} 1 & 1 \\ \sqrt{2} & -\sqrt{2} \end{bmatrix}$. From Equation 3.13, we

find that $X^{-1} = \dfrac{1}{(-\sqrt{2} - \sqrt{2})}\begin{bmatrix} -\sqrt{2} & -1 \\ -\sqrt{2} & 1 \end{bmatrix}$. Therefore, we diagonalize A as

$$\frac{1}{-2\sqrt{2}}\begin{bmatrix} -\sqrt{2} & -1 \\ -\sqrt{2} & 1 \end{bmatrix}\begin{bmatrix} 4 & 6 \\ 12 & 4 \end{bmatrix}\begin{bmatrix} 1 & 1 \\ \sqrt{2} & -\sqrt{2} \end{bmatrix} = \frac{1}{\sqrt{2}}\begin{bmatrix} \sqrt{2} & 1 \\ \sqrt{2} & -1 \end{bmatrix}\begin{bmatrix} 2 & 3 \\ 6 & 2 \end{bmatrix}\begin{bmatrix} 1 & 1 \\ \sqrt{2} & -\sqrt{2} \end{bmatrix} = \begin{bmatrix} 4 + 6\sqrt{2} & 0 \\ 0 & 4 - 6\sqrt{2} \end{bmatrix}$$

Note that the diagonal elements of A are its eigenvalues.

Given this transformation, we compute A^5 as

$$XD^mX^{-1} = \begin{bmatrix} 1 & 1 \\ \sqrt{2} & -\sqrt{2} \end{bmatrix}\begin{bmatrix} 4 + 6\sqrt{2} & 0 \\ 0 & 4 - 6\sqrt{2} \end{bmatrix}^5 \frac{1}{-2\sqrt{2}}\begin{bmatrix} -\sqrt{2} & -1 \\ -\sqrt{2} & 1 \end{bmatrix}$$

Due to diagonalization, the matrix power computation reduces to computing the exponential of a scalar value. After simplification and maintaining ten digits of precision in the calculations, this reduces to

$$\begin{bmatrix} 150783.99 & 107903.99 \\ 215807.99 & 150783.99 \end{bmatrix}$$

which is within rounding error of the true value of

$$\begin{bmatrix} 150784 & 107904 \\ 215808 & 150784 \end{bmatrix}$$

If the matrix has repeated eigenvalues, it cannot be diagonalized. Instead, the best we can do is to put it in the **Jordan canonical form**, whereby the diagonal elements are the eigenvalues of the matrix, as with a diagonal matrix. However, some elements immediately above the main diagonal may also be 1s. More details on the computation of this form can be found in advanced texts on linear algebra.

3.6 Stochastic Matrices

A **stochastic matrix**, or **Markov matrix**, is a special kind of matrix. A **right stochastic matrix** is a square matrix whose elements are non-negative reals and each of whose *rows* sums to 1. A **left stochastic matrix** is a square matrix whose elements are non-negative reals and each of whose *columns* sums to 1. Unless otherwise specified, when we refer to a stochastic matrix, we refer to a *right* stochastic matrix.

Stochastic matrices are important in the context of computer networking because each row of such a matrix A corresponds to the state of a finite state machine, or Markov chain, representing a networking protocol or a buffer in a router. Each element a_{ij} can be viewed as the probability of entering state j from state i. The summation criterion expresses the fact that the result of a transition from a state is to either remain in the same state or go to some other state. Stochastic matrices arise frequently in the study of Markov chains, stochastic processes, and queueing theory.

EXAMPLE 3.24: STOCHASTIC MATRIX

The matrix $A = \begin{bmatrix} 0.25 & 0.5 & 0.25 \\ 0.1 & 0.9 & 0 \\ 0 & 0 & 1.0 \end{bmatrix}$ is a stochastic matrix because it is square, the

elements are non-negative reals, and each row sums to 1. We interpret row 1 to mean that if the system is in state 1, after one transition, it remains in state 1 with probability 0.25, goes to state 2 with probability 0.5, and goes to state 3 with probability 0.25. Note that if the system enters state 3, it can never leave that state. We call such a state an **absorbing** state.

3.6.1 Computing State Transitions by Using a Stochastic Matrix

Consider a $n \times n$ stochastic matrix A and a column vector p having dimension n with non-negative real elements such that its elements sum to 1. We think of the ith element of p as representing the probability of being in state i at some point in time. Then, $p' = A^T p$ is a vector whose ith element is the probability of being in state i after one transition. (Note the premultiplication not by A but by its transpose.) The reason is that the ith element of p' is given by $p'_i = \sum_{k=1}^{n} p_k a_{ki}$, which, from the law of probability, is the probability of state i after the transition, conditional on the probability of being in each prior state k.

EXAMPLE 3.25: STATE TRANSITIONS

Continuing with the stochastic matrix from Example 3.24, suppose that we start with the system in state 1. What is the probability of being in state 1 after one and two transitions?

Solution:

The initial state vector is $p = [1.0\ 0\ 0]^T$. After one transition, the state vector is given by

$$p = A^T p = \begin{bmatrix} 0.25 & 0.1 & 0 \\ 0.5 & 0.9 & 0 \\ 0.25 & 0 & 1.0 \end{bmatrix} \begin{bmatrix} 1 \\ 0 \\ 0 \end{bmatrix} = \begin{bmatrix} 0.25 \\ 0.5 \\ 0.25 \end{bmatrix}$$

and after two transitions,

$$p = A^T(A^T p) = (A^T)^2 p = \begin{bmatrix} 0.1125 & 0.115 & 0 \\ 0.575 & 0.86 & 0 \\ 0.3125 & 0 & 1.0 \end{bmatrix} \begin{bmatrix} 1 \\ 0 \\ 0 \end{bmatrix} = \begin{bmatrix} 0.1125 \\ 0.575 \\ 0.3125 \end{bmatrix}$$

Thus, after two transitions, the system is in state 1 with probability 0.1125. Note that this probability is larger than the simple probability of staying in state 1, which is just 0.25 * 0.25 = 0.0625, because it takes into account the probability of transitioning from state 1 to state 2 and then back from state 2 to state 1, which has an additional probability of 0.5*0.1 = 0.05.

As this example shows, if A is a stochastic matrix, the $[i,j]$th element of $(A^T)^2$ represents the probability of going from state i to state j in two steps. Generalizing, the probability of going from state i to state j in k steps is given by $(A^T)^k$.

3.6.2 Eigenvalues of a Stochastic Matrix

We now present three important results concerning stochastic matrices.

First, *every* stochastic matrix has an eigenvalue of 1. To prove this, consider the $n \times n$ stochastic matrix A and column vector $x = [1\ 1\ ...\ 1]^T$. Then, $Ax = x$, because each element of Ax multiplies 1 with the sum of a row of A, which, by definition, sums to 1. Because a matrix and its transpose have the same eigenvalues, the transpose of a stochastic matrix also has an eigenvalue of 1. However, the eigenvector of the transposed matrix corresponding to this eigenvalue need not be, and rarely is, the **1** vector.

Second, every possibly complex eigenvalue of a stochastic matrix must have a magnitude no greater than 1. To prove this, consider some diagonal element a_{jj}. Suppose that this element takes the value x. Then, by definition of a stochastic matrix, it must be the case that the sum of the off-diagonal elements is $1 - x$. From Gerschgorin's circle theorem, we know that all the eigenvalues lie within a circle in the complex plane centered at x with radius $1 - x$. The largest-magnitude eigenvalue will be a point on this circle (see Figure 3.2). Although the truth of the proposition is evident by inspection, we now formally prove the result.

Suppose that this point subtends an angle of θ. Then, its coordinates are $(x+(1-x)\cos\theta, (1-x)\sin\theta)$. Therefore, its magnitude is $((x+(1-x)\cos\theta)^2 + ((1-x)\sin\theta)^2)^{1/2}$, which simplifies to $(x^2 + (1-x)^2 + 2x(1-x)\cos\theta)^{1/2}$. This quantity is maximized when $\theta = 0$, so that we merely have to maximize the quantity $x^2 + (1-x)^2 + 2x(1-x)$. Taking the first derivative with respect to x and setting it to zero shows that this expression reaches its maximum of 1 independent of the value of x. So, we can pick x to be a convenient value, such as 1. Substituting $\theta = 0$ and $x = 1$ into $((x+(1-x)\cos\theta)^2 + ((1-x)\sin\theta)^2)^{1/2}$, we find that the magnitude of the maximum eigenvalue is 1.

Third, it can also be shown, although the proof is beyond the scope of this text, that under some mild assumptions,[3] only *one* of the eigenvalues of a stochastic matrix is 1, which also must therefore be its dominant eigenvalue.

These three facts lead to a remarkable insight. Recall that we compute one step in the state evolution of a stochastic system described by the transition matrix A by multiplying the state vector by A^T. We already know that, under some mild assumptions, every stochastic transition matrix A has a unique eigenvalue of 1. We also

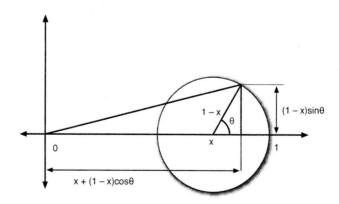

Figure 3.2 Largest-possible eigenvalue of a stochastic matrix

---

3. These assumptions eliminate such matrices as the identity matrix, which is a degenerate Markov matrix in that all its states are absorbing states.

know that a matrix and its transpose have the same eigenvalues. Therefore, A^T also has a unique eigenvalue of 1. What if the state vector was the eigenvector of A^T corresponding to this eigenvalue? Then, one step in the state evolution would leave the corresponding eigenvector *unchanged*. That is, a system in a state corresponding to that eigenvector would never leave that state. We denote this special state by the vector π. It is also called the **stationary probability distribution** of the system. The vector π can be found by solving the system of linear equations given by

$$A^T\pi = \pi \qquad\qquad\qquad \text{(EQ 3.19)}$$

Because every stochastic matrix has an eigenvalue of 1, every stochastic system must have a unique stationary probability distribution, which is the eigenvector corresponding to the unique eigenvalue of 1. Instead of solving a system of linear equations, we can also compute the stationary probability distribution of A by using the power method, because 1 is also its *dominant* eigenvalue. We put these results together to state that *the power method can be used to compute the stationary probability distribution of a stochastic matrix*. In our study of queueing theory, we will examine the conditions on the matrix A that guarantee that its stationary probability distribution is reached independent of the initial state of the system. Roughly speaking, these are the conditions under which the matrix A^T is said to be **ergodic**.

EXAMPLE 3.26: GOOGLE PAGERANK ALGORITHM

The power technique of finding the dominant eigenvector of a stochastic matrix can be used to rank a set of Web pages. More precisely, given a set of Web pages, we would like to identify certain pages as being more important than others. A page can be considered to be important by using the recursive definition that (1) many other pages point to it, and (2) the other pages are also important.

The importance of a page can be quantified according to the actions of a random Web surfer who goes from Web page i to a linked Web page j with probability a_{ij}. If a page is important, a random Web surfer will be led to that page more often than to other, less-important pages. That is, if we consider a population of a large number of surfers, then a larger fraction of Web surfers will be at a more important page, compared to a less-important page. Treating the ratio of the number of Web surfers at a page to the total number of surfers as approximating a probability, we see that the importance of a page is just the stationary probability of being at that page.

To make matters more precise, let the matrix A represent the set of all possible transition probabilities. If the probability of the surfer being at page i at some point is p_i, the probability that the surfer is at page i after one time step is $\mathbf{A}^T p_i$. The dominant eigenvector of $\mathbf{A}^T$ is then the steady state probability of a surfer being at page i. Given that $\mathbf{A}$ is a stochastic matrix, we know that this dominant eigenvector exists and that it can be found by the power method.

What remains is to estimate the quantities a_{ij}. Suppose that page i has links to k pages. Then, we set $a_{ij} = 1/k$ for each page j to which it has a link and set $a_{ij} = 0$ for all other j. This models a surfer going from a page uniformly randomly to one of its linked pages. What if a page has no links? Or if two pages link only to each other? These issues can be approximately modeled by assuming that, with constant probability, the surfer teleports to a randomly chosen page. That is, if there is a link from page i to page j, then $a_{ij} = \alpha /n + (1 - \alpha)/k$, where α is a control parameter; otherwise, $a_{ij} = \alpha /n$. It can be easily shown that these modified a_{ij}s form a stochastic matrix, so that we can extract the dominant eigenvalue, and thus the page rank, by using the power method. A slightly modified version of this algorithm is the publicly described algorithm used by Google to rank Web pages.[4]

3.7 Exercises

1. **Transpose**

   Compute the transpose of $\begin{bmatrix} 4 & 0 & -3 \\ 7 & 82 & 12 \\ 3 & -2 & 2 \end{bmatrix}$.

2. **Matrix multiplications**

   Find the product of the matrices $\begin{bmatrix} 10 & -4 & 12 \\ -5 & 3 & 9 \\ 8 & 0 & -4 \end{bmatrix}$ and $\begin{bmatrix} -4 & 5 & 3 \\ 7 & -2 & 9 \\ 2 & 5 & -4 \end{bmatrix}$.

3. **Exponentiation**

   Prove that if $\mathbf{A}$ is a diagonal matrix, the (i,i)th element of the kth power of $\mathbf{A}$ is a_{ii}^k.

---

4. A rather curious fact is that Google's algorithm to rank pages, called the **PageRank** algorithm, was developed, in part, by its cofounder, Larry Page.

4. Linear combination of scalars

Compute the linear combination of the scalars 10, 5, 2, –4 with weights 0.5, 0.4, 0.25, 0.25.

5. Linear combination of vectors

Compute the linear combination of the vectors [1 2 8 5], [3 7 3 1], [7 2 1 9], [2 6 3 4] with weights 0.5, 0.4, 0.25, 0.25.

6. Linear independence and rank

Are the following three vectors independent?

$$x_1 = [12 \quad 2 \quad -4]$$
$$x_2 = [2 \quad 2 \quad -24]$$
$$x_3 = [2.5 \quad 0 \quad 5]$$

Determine this from the rank of the corresponding coefficient matrix.

7. Basis and dimension

Give two possible bases for the three vectors in Exercise 6. What is the dimension of the vector space generated by these bases?

8. Gaussian elimination

Use row operations and Gaussian elimination to solve the system given by

$$\begin{bmatrix} 6 & 4 & -8 & 5 \\ -8 & 2 & 4 & -2 \\ 10 & 0 & 4 & 1 \end{bmatrix}.$$

9. Rank

Prove that the rank of an $n \times n$ nonzero diagonal matrix is n.

10. Determinant

Compute the determinant of the matrix $\begin{bmatrix} 4 & 0 & -3 \\ 7 & 8 & 12 \\ 3 & -2 & 2 \end{bmatrix}.$

11. Inverse

Compute the inverse of the matrix $\begin{bmatrix} 4 & 0 & -3 \\ 7 & 8 & 12 \\ 3 & -2 & 2 \end{bmatrix}$.

12. Matrix as a transformation

Using the fact that $\sin(A + B) = \sin(A)\cos(B) + \cos(A)\sin(B)$ and $\cos(A + B) = \cos(A)\cos(B) - \sin(A)\sin(B)$, compute the matrix that corresponds to the rotation of a vector joining the origin to the point (x, y) by an angle p.

13. Composing transformations

Compute the composition of a rotation of t degrees followed by a rotation of p degrees.

14. Eigenvalues and eigenvectors

Compute the eigenvalues and corresponding eigenvectors of the matrix $\begin{bmatrix} 1 & 9 \\ 4 & 1 \end{bmatrix}$.

15. Computing $A^n x$

Find the value of $\begin{bmatrix} 1 & 9 \\ 4 & 1 \end{bmatrix}^5 \begin{bmatrix} 8 \\ 0 \end{bmatrix}$.

16. Finding eigenvalues

Bound the interval(s) in which the eigenvalues of the matrix $\begin{bmatrix} 4 & 1 & 0.5 \\ 1 & 6 & 0.3 \\ 0.5 & 0.3 & 5 \end{bmatrix}$ lie.

17. Power method

Use the power method to compute the dominant eigenvalue and corresponding eigenvector of the matrix $\begin{bmatrix} 1 & 9 \\ 4 & 1 \end{bmatrix}$. Iterate four times.

18. Diagonalization

Find the diagonal matrix similar to $\begin{bmatrix} 1 & 9 \\ 4 & 1 \end{bmatrix}$.

19. Stochastic matrix

Determine whether the matrix $\begin{bmatrix} 0.1 & 0.8 & 0.3 \\ 0.5 & 0.1 & 0.4 \\ 0.4 & 0.1 & 0.3 \end{bmatrix}$ is left or right stochastic.

20. State transitions

Consider a system described by the stochastic matrix $\begin{bmatrix} 0.25 & 0.5 & 0.25 \\ 0.1 & 0.9 & 0 \\ 0 & 0 & 1.0 \end{bmatrix}$. Let the

ith row of this matrix correspond to state i. If the initial state is known to be state 1 with probability 0.5 and state 2 with probability 0.5, compute the probability of being in these two states after two time steps.

4

Optimization

This chapter presents an overview of optimization: mathematical techniques that can be used to improve the performance of a computer system. We begin with an overview of techniques for mathematically modeling a system. We then survey the elements of linear optimization, including linear programming and dynamic programming, and conclude with an introduction to some techniques for nonlinear optimization.

4.1 System Modeling and Optimization

A necessary prerequisite to the use of optimization techniques is to **mathematically model** a system. In doing so, it is necessary to identify the following five elements:

1. **Fixed parameters**, system aspects that cannot be changed and that therefore, from the perspective of the model, are constants.

2. **Control parameters**, the settings that can be chosen to optimize the behavior of the system. Control parameters are typically constrained to lie within some range. A set of control parameters where each parameter is within its valid range is called a **feasible set** of control parameters.

3. **Input variables**, the external and uncontrollable inputs to the system. Note that in a *particular* instance of a general model, an input variable can be considered to be a fixed parameter. This is the assumption made in a typical optimization problem. When the inputs may vary over time, the system is better

described using control theory, the topic of Chapter 8. Mathematical modeling from the perspective of control theory is discussed in Section 8.2.

4. **Output variables**, the observable outputs of the system. A subset of the output variables are chosen as **performance metrics** to quantify the performance of the system.

5. **Transfer function**, which maps from fixed parameters, control parameters, and input variables to output variables. Control theory lets us precisely define a transfer function as the Laplace transform of the impulse response function. This is discussed in Section 8.2.2.

Optimization is the process of choosing a feasible set of control parameters so that an **objective function** O defined over the output variables is either maximized or minimized. We use the transfer function to rewrite the objective function as a mathematical function of the fixed parameters, the control parameters, and the input variables. When studying a specific optimization instance, as is the case in this chapter, we can consider the fixed parameters and input variables to be system-defined constants. Therefore, the objective function is typically represented as a function whose variables are the control parameters and whose constants are the fixed parameters and input variables.

EXAMPLE 4.1: MATHEMATICAL MODELING

Consider a source-to-a destination communication path that has a capacity of 100 packets/s so that if packets are sent at a rate $r > 100$ packets/s, packets are dropped at the *drop rate* of $(r - 100)$ packets/s. If this performance is quantified as the difference between the carried load and the drop rate, how fast should a source send to maximize its performance?

Solution:

We model the system as follows:

- *Fixed parameter:* capacity of the path, or 100 packets/s
- *Control parameter:* the source sending rate
- *Input variables:* none
- *Output variables:* carried load, drop rate
- *Objective function:* carried load – drop rate
- *Transfer function:*

$$carried\ load = min(sending\ rate, 100)\ packets/s$$
$$drop\ rate = max(0, sending\ rate - 100)\ packets/s$$

As shown in Figure 4.1, the objective function can be written in terms of the control parameters and fixed parameters as

objective function = carried load − drop rate
$$= \min\ (sending\ rate,\ 100) - (0,\ sending\ rate - 100)\ packets\,/\,s$$

The objective function is maximized when the sending rate is 100 packets/s.

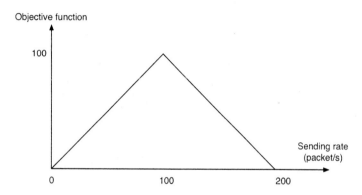

Figure 4.1 The objective function for Example 4.1. The maximum occurs when the control variable is set to 100 packets/s.

Note that the mathematical model in Example 4.1 was easily derived because the underlying system was trivial. In practice, determining an appropriate mathematical model for a complex system is an art that is learned only with experience and a considerable degree of trial and error. Note also that we could easily graph the objective function because it depended only on one control parameter, the sending rate. We cannot easily graph more complex systems that may have many hundreds of control parameters. For such systems, we must resort to a more sophisticated mathematical analysis, which is the topic of the remainder of this chapter.

4.2 Introduction to Optimization

The following example presents an intuitive approach to optimization.

EXAMPLE 4.2: OPTIMIZING A SYSTEM WITH TWO CONTROL PARAMETERS

Consider a system whose objective function O can be expressed in terms of two scalar control parameters x_1 and x_2 as:

$$O = 2x_1 - x_2$$

$$x_{1+}x_2 = 1$$

$$x_1, x_2 \geq 0$$

We can obtain the maximal value of O analytically as follows. The partial derivative of O with respect to x_1 is positive and with respect to x_2 is negative. Hence, O increases when x_1 increases and decreases when x_2 increases. Therefore, to maximize O, we should set x_2 to 0, which is its smallest possible value. This implies that $x_1 = 1$ and that $O = 2$.

Geometrically, as shown in Figure 4.2, we interpret the constraint on the sum of the x_i's to mean that their permissible values lie on a line defined by the points (0,1) and (1,0). At (0,1), O is –1. As we move down the line, x_1 increases and x_2 simultaneously decreases, so that O monotonically increases, reaching its maximum value of 2 at (1,0).

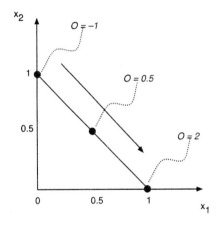

Figure 4.2 Maximizing a function of two variables

EXAMPLE 4.3: OPTIMIZING A SYSTEM WITH THREE VARIABLES

Example 4.2 can be generalized to three variables as follows. Consider the system whose objective function O can be expressed as

$$O = 3x_1 - x_2 - x_3$$

$$x_1 + x_2 + x_3 = 1$$

$$x_1, x_2, x_3 \geq 0$$

Analytically, we see that the partial derivative of O with respect to x_1 is positive and with respect to x_2 and x_3 is negative. Therefore, O attains its maximum when x_1 is as large as possible and x_2 and x_3 are as small as possible. This is at the point $(1,0,0)$, where O attains the value 3.

The geometric interpretation is shown in Figure 4.3. Note that the constraints are of two types. Equality constraints force the solution to lie on a plane. For example, the first equality constraint requires all x_i to lie on a **constraint plane** defined by the three points $(0,0,1)$, $(0,1,0)$, and $(1,0,0)$. In contrast, inequality constraints force the solution to *one side* of a constraint plane. For example, the constraint $x_1 \geq 0$ defines a constraint plane along the x_2 and x_3 axes, and the solution must lie to the right of this plane. A solution that meets all the constraints must, therefore, lie somewhere in the triangular subplane shaded in Figure 4.3.

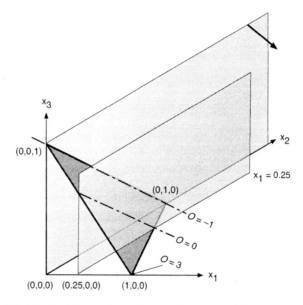

Figure 4.3 Maximizing a function of three variables. The constraint plane is outlined in boldface.

Consider a point in this region that lies on the line defined by the two points $(0,0,1)$ and $(0,1,0)$. This point is at the intersection of the two constraint equations: $x_1 + x_2 + x_3 = 1$ and $x_1 = 0$. Therefore, at every point on this line, $x_2 + x_3 = 1$, which implies that $O = 3x_1 - x_2 - x_3 = 0 - 1 = -1$ at every point on this line. We call such a line along which the objective function is constant an **isoquant**.

Now, consider a point that lies at the intersection of the shaded triangular plane and the plane defined by the equation $x_1 = 0.25$. At every point on this line, $x_2 + x_3 = 1 - 0.25 = 0.75$. Therefore, at every point on this line, $O = 3x_1 - x_2 - x_3 = 0.75 - 0.75 = 0$. This is another isoquant of the system.

Continuing in this manner, we can compute an isoquant for each plane defined by the equation $x_1 = c$, $0 \leq c \leq 1$. As c increases, we can imagine a plane sweeping to the right along the x_1 axis, generating a series of isoquants, with the value of O rising monotonically and attaining its maximum value $O = 3$ when the plane departs from the constraint plane at the vertex $(1,0,0)$.

It is easy to see that for any two points A and B that are both on the constraint plane, one of three conditions must hold. (1) The value of O is the same at both A and B; they are on the same isoquant. (2) O is greater at A. Or (3) O is greater at B. This suggests the following optimization procedure: Start at a random point A on the constraint plane and generate a set of neighbors of this point that are also on the constraint plane. Then evaluate O at those neighbors. If the value of O at A is the same as or higher than at all its neighbors, A is local maximum. Otherwise, the process is repeated from the neighboring point that has the greatest value of O. As long as this process does not get trapped in a local maximum, it finds the optimal value of O. This is the basis of the optimization technique called **hill climbing** that we will return to in Section 4.7.

4.3 Optimizing Linear Systems

We often wish to maximize[1] an objective function O that is a linear combination of the control parameters $x_1, x_2, ... x_n$ and can therefore be expressed as

$$O = c_1 x_1 + c_2 x_2 + ... + c_n x_n \qquad \text{(EQ 4.1)}$$

where the c_i s are real scalars. Moreover, all the x_i are typically constrained by linear constraints in the following **standard form**:

$$a_{11} x_1 + a_{12} x_2 + ... + a_{1n} x_n = b_1 \qquad \text{(EQ 4.2)}$$

$$a_{21} x_1 + a_{22} x_2 + ... + a_{2n} x_n = b_2$$

$$...$$
$$\qquad \text{(EQ 4.3)}$$
$$...$$

$$a_{m1} x_1 + a_{m2} x_2 + ... + a_{mn} x_n = b_m$$

or, using matrix notation:

$$Ax = b \qquad \text{(EQ 4.4)}$$

---

1. In this chapter, we always seek to maximize the objective function. Identical techniques can be used for minimization.

$$x \geq 0 \qquad \text{(EQ 4.5)}$$

where A is an $m \times n$ matrix, and x and b are column vectors with n and m elements, respectively, with $n \geq m$. Let A's rank be r. To allow optimization, the system must be underconstrained with $r < n$, so that some of the x_is can be written as a linear combination of the others, which form a basis for A.[2]

Generalizing from Example 4.3, each equality corresponds to a hyperplane, which is a plane in more than two dimensions. (This is not as intuitive as it sounds; for instance, a three-plane is a solid that fills the entire Euclidean space.) The constraints ensure that valid x_i lie at the intersection of these hyperplanes.

Note that we can always transform an inequality of the form

$$a_{i1}x_1 + a_{i2}x_2 + \ldots + a_{in}x_n \geq b_i$$

to an equality by introducing a new variable s_i, called the **surplus variable**, such that

$$a_{i1}x_1 + a_{i2}x_2 + \ldots + a_{in}x_n - s_i = b_i \qquad \text{(EQ 4.6)}$$

By treating the s_i as virtual control parameters, we can convert a constraint that has a greater-than inequality into the standard form. (We ignore the value assigned to a surplus variable.) Similarly, introducing a **slack** variable converts lesser-than inequalities to equalities. Therefore, any linear system of equal and unequal constraints can be transformed into the standard form that has only equality constraints. Once this is done, we can use **linear programming** (discussed below) to find the value of **x** that maximizes the objective function.

EXAMPLE 4.4: REPRESENTING A LINEAR PROGRAM IN STANDARD FORM

Consider a company that has two network connections to the Internet through two providers (also called *multihoming*). Suppose that the providers charge per byte and provide different delays. For example, the lower-priced provider may guarantee that transit delays are under 50 ms, and the higher-priced provider may guarantee a bound of 20 ms. Suppose that the company has two commonly used applications, A and B, that have different sensitivities to delay. Application A is more tolerant of delay than application B is. Moreover, the applications, on average, generate a certain amount of traffic every day, which has to be carried by one of the two links. The company wants to allocate *all* the traffic from the two applications to one of the two links, maximizing

---

2. To understand this section more fully, the reader may wish to review Section 3.4.

their benefit while minimizing its payments to the link providers. Represent the problem in standard form.

Solution:

The first step is to decide how to model the problem. We must have variables that reflect the traffic sent by each application on each link. Call the lower-priced provider l and the higher priced provider h. Then, we denote the traffic sent by A on l as x_{Al} and the traffic sent by A on h as x_{Ah}. Define x_{Bl} and x_{Bh} similarly. The traffic sent is non-negative, so we have

$$x_{Al} \geq 0\,;\, x_{Ah} \geq 0\,;\, x_{Bl} \geq 0\,;\, x_{Bh} \geq 0\,;$$

If the traffic sent each day by application A is denoted TA, and the traffic sent by B is denoted TB, we have

$$x_{Al} + x_{Ah} = TA\,;\, x_{Bl} + x_{Bh} = TB$$

Suppose that the providers charge c_l and c_h monetary units per byte. Then, the cost to the company is

$$x_{Al}c_l + x_{Bl}c_l + x_{Ah}c_h + x_{Bh}c_h = C$$

What is the benefit to the company? Suppose that application A gains a benefit of b_{Al} per byte from sending traffic on link l and b_{Ah} on link h. Using similar notation for the benefits to application B, the overall benefit (i.e., benefit − cost) that the company should maximize, which is its objective function, is

$$O = (b_{Al} - c_l)x_{Al} + (b_{Ah} - c_h)x_{Ah} + (b_{Bl} - c_l)x_{Bl} + (b_{Bh} - c_h)x_{Bh}$$

Thus, in standard form, the linear program is the preceding objective function, and the constraints on the variables expressed as

$$\begin{bmatrix} 1 & 1 & 0 & 0 \\ 0 & 0 & 1 & 1 \end{bmatrix} \begin{bmatrix} x_{Al} \\ x_{Ah} \\ x_{Bl} \\ x_{Bh} \end{bmatrix} = \begin{bmatrix} TA \\ TB \end{bmatrix}; \begin{bmatrix} x_{Al} \\ x_{Ah} \\ x_{Bl} \\ x_{Bh} \end{bmatrix} \geq \begin{bmatrix} 0 \\ 0 \\ 0 \\ 0 \end{bmatrix}$$

Note that, in this system, $n = 4$ and $m = 2$. To allow optimization, the rank of the matrix A must be smaller than $n = 4$. In this case, the rank of A is 2, so optimization is feasible.

How can we find values of the x_{ij} such that O is maximized? Trying every possible value of **x** is an exponentially difficult task, so we have to be cleverer than that. What we need is an algorithm that systematically chooses the x_i that maximize or minimize O.

To solve a linear system in standard form, we draw on the intuition developed in Examples 4.2 and 4.3. Recall that in Example 4.3, the optimal value of O was reached at one of the vertices of the constraint plane because any other point has a neighbor that lies on a better isoquant. It is only at a vertex that we "run out" of better neighbors.[3] Of course, in some cases, the isoquant can be parallel to one of the hyperedges of a constraint hyperplane. In this case, the O attains a minimum or maximum along an entire edge.

In a general system, the constraint plane corresponds to a mathematical object called a **polytope**, defined as a convex hyperspace bounded by a set of hyperplanes. In such a system, it can be shown that the extremal value of the objective function is attained at one of the vertices of the constraint polytope. It is worth noting that a polytope in more than three dimensions is rather difficult to imagine: For instance, the intersection of two four-dimensional hyperplanes is a three-dimensional solid. The principal fact needed about a polytope when carrying out an optimization is that each of its vertices is defined by n coordinates, which are the values assumed by the x_i at that vertex. The optimal value of O is achieved for the values of the x_i corresponding to the optimal vertex.

The overall approach to finding the optimal vertex is, first, to locate any one vertex of the polytope; second, to move from this vertex to the neighboring vertex where the value of the objective function is the greatest; and finally, to repeat this process until it reaches a vertex such that the value of the objective function at this vertex is greater than the objective function's value at all of its neighbors. This must be the optimal vertex. This algorithm, developed by G. Dantzig, is the famous **simplex** algorithm.

The simplex algorithm builds on two underlying procedures: finding any one vertex of the polytope and generating all the neighbors of a vertex. The first procedure is carried out by setting $n - r$ of the x_i to 0, so that the resulting system has rank n, and solving the resultant linear system using, for example, Gaussian elimination. The second procedure is carried out using the observation that because **A**'s rank is $r < n$, it is always possible to compute a new basis for **A** that differs from the current basis in only one column. It can be shown that this basis defines a neighboring vertex of the polytope.

To carry out simplex in practice, we have to identify whether the program has incompatible constraints. This is easy because, if this is the case, the Gaussian

---

3. For nonlinear objective functions, we could run out of better points even within the constraint plane, so the optimal point may not lie at a vertex.

elimination in the first procedure fails. A more subtle problem is that it is possible for a set of vertices to have the same exact value of O, which can lead to infinite loops. We can eliminate this problem by slightly jittering the value of O at these vertices or using other similar **antilooping** algorithms.

From the perspective of a practitioner, all that needs to be done to use linear programming is to specify the objective function and the constraints to a program called a **Linear Program Solver**, or LP Solver. CPLEX and CS2 are two examples of well-known LP Solvers. A solver returns either the optimal value of the objective function and the vertex at which it is achieved or declares the system to be unsolvable due to incompatible constraints. Today's LP Solvers can routinely solve systems with more than 100,000 variables and tens of thousands of constraints.

The simplex algorithm has been found to work surprisingly well in dealing with most real-life problems. However, in the worst case, it can take time exponential in the size of the input (i.e, the number of variables) to find an optimal solution. Another LP solution algorithm, called the **ellipsoidal method**, is guaranteed to terminate in $O(n^3)$ time, where n is the size of the input, although its performance for realistic problems is not much faster than simplex. Yet another competitor to the simplex algorithm is the **interior point method**, which finds the optimal vertex not by moving from vertex to vertex but by using points interior to the polytope.

Linear programming is a powerful tool. With an appropriate choice of variables, it can be used to solve problems that, at first glance, may not appear to be linear programs. As an example, we now consider how to set up the network-flow problem as a linear program.

4.3.1 Network Flow

The network-flow problem models the flow of goods in a transportation network. Goods may be temporarily stored in warehouses. We represent the transportation network by a graph. Each graph node corresponds to a warehouse, and each directed edge, associated with a capacity, corresponds to a transportation link. The **source** node has no edges entering it, and the **sink** node has no edges leaving it. The problem is to determine the maximum possible throughput between the source and the sink. We can solve this problem by using LP, as the next example demonstrates.

EXAMPLE 4.5: NETWORK FLOW

Consider the network flow graph in Figure 4.4. Here, the node s represents the source and has a total capacity of 11.6 leaving it. The sink, denoted t, has a capacity of 25.4 entering it. The maximum capacity from s to t can be no larger than 11.6 but may be smaller, depending on the intermediate paths.

We can compute the maximal flow that can be sustained on a network-flow graph by using linear programming. Denote the capacity of the link ij from i to j by c_{ij} and the amount of traffic assigned to that link, as part of a flow from s to t, by f_{ij}. For example, in Figure 4.4, $c_{12} = 10.0$, and we may assign $f_{12} = 2.3$

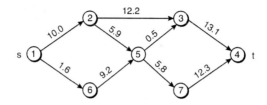

Figure 4.4 Example of a network-flow problem

on it as part of the overall flow from s to t. There are three types of constraints on the f_{ij}s:

1. *Capacity constraints:* The flow on a link cannot exceed its capacity, that is, $f_{ij} \leq c_{ij}$.
2. *Conservation conditions:* All the flow entering a node, other than the sink, must exit it; that is, for all nodes j other than s and t,

$$\sum_{\forall i | \exists ij} f_{ij} = \sum_{\forall k | \exists jk} f_{jk}.$$

3. *Non-negativity:* $f_{ij} \geq 0$.

Given these constraints, the objective function maximizes the flow leaving s. That is $O = \sum_{\forall i | \exists si} f_{si}$. The LP is now easy to frame. It consists of the capacity inequalities, written as equalities after introducing slack variables, the conservation conditions, with the right-hand side carried over to the left and adding slack variables, and the conditions on the flows being non-negative. Some examples of these constraints are: on edge 5–7, $f_{57} \leq 5.8$, and at vertex 3, $f_{23} + f_{53} = f_{34}$.

4.4 Integer Linear Programming

Linear programming allows variables to assume real values. In integer linear programming (ILP), variables are allowed to assume only integer values. Although this difference may appear to be small, it makes the solution of ILP *much* harder. More precisely, though LP can be solved in time polynomial in the size of the input, no polynomial-time solution to ILP is known; on some inputs, an ILP solver can take time exponential in the size of the input. In practice, this means that LP can be used to solve problems with hundreds of thousands of variables, but solving an ILP may take a long time even with a few tens of variables.

Nevertheless, ILP arises naturally in a number of cases. In networking, the most common use of ILP is for the **scheduling** problem, where discrete time slots must be assigned to job requests. Since requests cannot be allocated fractional time slots, the problem is naturally posed as one with integer constraints, as the next example shows.

EXAMPLE 4.6: A SCHEDULING PROBLEM

Two users, Alice and Bob, can schedule jobs on a machine in one of two time periods: Period 1 or Period 2. If Alice schedules a job during Period 1, she gains a benefit of 20 units and incurs a cost of 10 units; during Period 2, she gains a benefit of 10 units and incurs a cost of 20 units. If Bob schedules a job during Period 1, he gains a benefit of 100 units and incurs a cost of 10 units; during Period 2, he gains a benefit of 10 units and incurs a cost of 200 units. Each user may schedule at most one job in one time unit; in each time period, at most one job can be scheduled. There are only four jobs to schedule. Express this system in standard form to maximize the benefit derived from the assignment of user jobs to time periods (also called a **schedule**).

Solution:

The control parameters here are the choice of assignments of user jobs to time periods. We have four jobs and only two time periods. Let x_{ij} be a control parameter that is set to 1 if user i is assigned to schedule a job in time period j. A user can schedule at most two jobs—one in Period 1 and one in Period 2—so

$$x_{11} + x_{12} \le 2$$
$$x_{21} + x_{22} \le 2$$

In each time period, we can have at most one job scheduled, so

$$x_{11} + x_{21} \le 1$$
$$x_{12} + x_{22} \le 1$$

If Alice's job is scheduled in Period 1, the net benefit is $(20 - 10)$, if it isn't, the benefit is 0. The benefit to Alice in time Period 1, therefore, is $x_{11}(20 - 10)$.

Similarly, taking into account the other costs and benefits, the overall objective function is

$$O = x_{11}(20 - 10) + x_{12}(10 - 20) + x_{21}(100 - 10) + x_{22}(10 - 200)$$
$$= 10x_{11} - 10x_{12} + 90x_{21} - 190x_{22}$$

Note that the constraints are not in standard form, because of the inequalities. We can rewrite the constraints by using the slack variables s_1 through s_4 as

$$x_{11} + x_{12} + s_1 = 2$$
$$x_{12} + x_{22} + s_2 = 2$$
$$x_{11} + x_{21} + s_3 = 1$$
$$x_{12} + x_{22} + s_4 = 1$$

or

$$\begin{bmatrix} 1 & 1 & 0 & 0 & 1 & 0 & 0 & 0 \\ 0 & 0 & 1 & 1 & 0 & 1 & 0 & 0 \\ 1 & 0 & 1 & 0 & 0 & 0 & 1 & 0 \\ 0 & 1 & 0 & 1 & 0 & 0 & 0 & 1 \end{bmatrix} \begin{bmatrix} x_{11} \\ x_{12} \\ x_{21} \\ x_{22} \\ s_1 \\ s_2 \\ s_3 \\ s_4 \end{bmatrix} = \begin{bmatrix} 2 \\ 2 \\ 1 \\ 1 \end{bmatrix}$$

$$\begin{bmatrix} x_{11} \\ x_{12} \\ x_{21} \\ x_{22} \\ s_1 \\ s_2 \\ s_3 \\ s_4 \end{bmatrix} \geq \begin{bmatrix} 0 \\ 0 \\ 0 \\ 0 \\ 0 \\ 0 \\ 0 \\ 0 \end{bmatrix}$$

This expresses the system in standard matrix form. Note that all the x_{ij} must be 0 or 1, and therefore the system is an ILP.

There are three alternatives to solving an ILP. One approach is to carefully model the system so that the input size is small, which would minimize the time taken by an ILP solver. A second approach is to not require the solution to be optimal and to accept suboptimal solutions found by using heuristic approaches, such as those discussed in Section 4.7. A third approach, discussed next, allows certain ILPs to be solved as if they were LPs.

4.4.1 Total Unimodularity

An ILP $Ax = b$ can be solved as an LP, ignoring integer constraints, if A is totally unimodular. A square, integer matrix A is called **unimodular** if its determinant is 0, +1 or −1. An integer matrix, which may itself not be square, is called **totally unimodular** if every square, nonsingular submatrix is unimodular.

In practice, there is a simple test for unimodularity.

1. Every entry is 0, 1, or −1.
2. There are zero, one, or two nonzero entries in any *column*.
3. The *rows* can be partitioned into two sets A and B such that

    a. If a column has two entries of the same sign, one of these is in A, and the other is in B.

    b. If a column has two entries of different signs, both entries are in either A or B.

EXAMPLE 4.7: A TOTALLY UNIMODULAR MATRIX

Here is an example of a totally unimodular matrix:

$$\begin{bmatrix} 1 & 1 & 0 & 0 & 1 \\ 0 & -1 & -1 & 0 & 0 \\ 1 & 0 & 0 & 1 & 0 \\ 0 & 0 & -1 & -1 & 0 \end{bmatrix}$$

The matrix can be divided into two sets of two rows (the first and second and the third and fourth) that meet the test for unimodularity.

Like LP, ILP can also be used to model a variety of problems. As an example, we study the use of ILP to solve the weighted bipartite matching problem.

4.4.2 Weighted Bipartite Matching

In a **bipartite** graph, the vertices can be divided into two sets such that all the edges in the graph have one vertex in one set and another vertex in another set (see Figure 4.5). Such graphs arise naturally in many problems. For instance, one set of vertices could represent a set of demands, and the other set could represent a set of resources. Edges then show the resources that could meet each demand. A weight on such an edge could represent the goodness of fit or perhaps the cost of the resource.

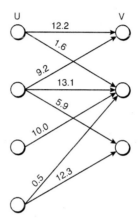

Figure 4.5 Example of a weighted bipartite graph

A **matching** M on a graph is a subset of edges such that no two edges in this set share a common vertex. Each edge in M matches a vertex in one set (say, a demand) to a vertex in another set (say, a resource). A **maximal weighted matching** is such that the sum of the edge weights, summed over the edges in M, is the greatest. If only one such matching exists, it is also the *maximum* weighted matching.

ILP can be used to find the maximal weighted matching in a bipartite graph. Let U and V be the two sets of vertices, and let uv refer to an edge that goes from some element u in U to some element v in V. Let w_{uv} be the weight of such an edge.

Define integer variables x_{uv} that are set to 1 if the corresponding edge is in the matching M and 0 otherwise. The total weight of a matching is $\sum_{u,v} w_{uv} x_{uv}$, which is the value we wish to maximize in the LP (i.e., this is the objective function).

In a matching, there should be at most one edge from an element in U to an element in V and vice versa. (Note that there may be no edge incident at some node in U or V in M if $|U|$ and $|V|$ are not equal.) It is convenient to convert the original graph, where not every element in U has an edge to an element in V, to a *complete* graph, where we add extra zero-weight edges so that every element in U has $|V|$ edges. Then, the constraints are

$$\forall u \sum_k x_{uk} \leq 1$$

$$\forall v \sum_k x_{kv} \leq 1$$

The first constraint ensures that at most one edge in M leaves every node in U. If this is an extra edge, it adds zero weight to M's weight and can be ignored in the final solution. Similarly, the second constraint ensures that at most one edge is incident at every node in V. With these constraints, an ILP solver can be used to solve the maximal weighted matching problem.

4.5 Dynamic Programming

Dynamic programming is a powerful optimization technique applicable when a problem can be decomposed into subproblems such that the optimal solution to the original problem is a composition of the optimal solutions to each subproblem. (This is also called the **optimal substructure** of the problem.) The technique, then, is to decompose the problem into two or more subproblems, solve each subproblem recursively, and then put the solutions together again to obtain the final answer. Of course, the recursion needs to end in a "small" problem that can be easily solved. Moreover, it is critical that the recursion does not result in a proliferation of subproblems.

EXAMPLE 4.8: FIBONACCI COMPUTATION

Although not an optimization problem, the Fibonacci sequence clearly demonstrates the meaning of substructure, composition, and the need to limit the number of subproblems. This sequence is defined by $F(1) = F(2) = 1$, and for $n > 2$, $F(n) = F(n-1) + F(n-2)$. The first few terms of the sequence are 1, 1, 2, 3, 5, 8, 13.

$F(k)$ can be computed by solving two subproblems (computing $F(k-1)$ and computing $F(k-2)$) and composing the solutions by addition. Note that the computation of $F(k-1)$ *reuses* the computation of $F(k-2)$, because $F(k-1) = F(k-2) + F(k-3)$. The solution to $F(k-2)$ is used twice: once to compute $F(k)$ and once to compute $F(k-1)$. In fact, a little thought shows that we need to compute each subproblem (that is, $F(k-i)$ for $i \in [1, k-1]$) only *once*. This makes dynamic programming efficient.

Dynamic programming is useful only when we can strictly limit the number of underlying subproblems. Moreover, it is necessary to remember the solution to the subproblems so that they are not solved repeatedly. This is called **memoization**.

There are two standard approaches to dynamic programming. In the first, **bottom-up** approach, where subproblems are solved starting from the simplest one. They are then composed to find the required solution. In the case of the Fibonacci sequence, this would correspond to computing $F(1)$, $F(2)$, and so on, until $F(k)$ is found. In contrast, the **top-down** approach decomposes problems into subproblems as shown in Example 4.8.

EXAMPLE 4.9: FLOYD-WARSHALL ALGORITHM FOR ALL-PAIRS SHORTEST PATHS

A well-known example of the use of dynamic programming in a networking context is the Floyd-Warshall algorithm for simultaneously computing the shortest paths between all pairs of nodes in a graph in only $O(N^3)$ time. This algorithm uses the bottom-up approach to dynamic programming.

The algorithm operates on an undirected graph G with N nodes whose nodes are numbered $1...N$. Define a *path* as a sequence of nodes such that no node index is repeated. The length of the path is the number of edges in it. We want to find the shortest path from any node i to any node j.

Consider all paths from node i to node j that contains only nodes numbered from $1...k$. Let $s(i,j,k)$ denote the shortest of these paths. For the moment, we will abuse notation and use s to denote both the path and its length. Set $s(i,j,k)$ to ∞ if no such path exists.

Taking the bottom-up approach, assume that $s(i,j,k-1)$, that is, the shortest path from i to j that uses only nodes numbered $1...k-1$, is known. We will use this to compute $s(i,j,k)$.

The solution follows from the following observation: The shortest path from i to j either does or does not include the node numbered k. If it doesn't, $s(i,j,k)$ = $s(i,j,k-1)$. If it does, there must be a path from i to j passing through k, which means that k must be reachable from both i and j using only nodes numbered $1...k-1$. Moreover, the shortest path is composed from the shortest path from i to k using only nodes $1...k-1$ and the shortest path from k to j using only nodes $1...k-1$. Therefore, $s(i,j,k) = s(i,k, k-1) + s(k, j, k-1)$.

We now have the decomposition we need:

$$s(i,j,k) = min(s((i,j,k-1), s(i,k,k-1) + s(k,j,k-1)))$$

To solve the problem, we first compute the values (and paths) $s(i,j,1)$ for all i,j. We can use these values to compute $s(i,j,2)$ for all values of i,j and repeat for increasing values of k, until, when $k = N$, we have the desired solution.

Dynamic programming is effective here because of the optimal substructure, the ease of composition, and the limited number of subproblems.

4.6 Nonlinear Constrained Optimization

So far, we have been examining the use of optimization techniques where the objective function and the set of constraints are both linear functions. We now consider situations in which these functions are not linear.

How does nonlinearity change the optimization problem? In a noninteger constrained linear system, the objective function attains its maximum or minimum value at one of the vertices of a polytope defined by the constraint planes. Intuitively, because the objective function is linear, we can always "walk along" one of the hyperedges of the polytope to increase the value of the objective function, so that the extremal value of the objective function is guaranteed to be at a polytope vertex.

In contrast, with nonlinear optimization, the objective function may both increase and decrease as we walk along what would correspond to a hyperedge (a contour line, as we will see shortly). Therefore, we cannot exploit polytope vertices to carry out optimization. Instead, we must resort to one of a large number of nonlinear optimization techniques, some of which we study next.

Nonlinear optimization techniques fall into roughly into two categories.

1. When the objective function and the constraints are continuous and at least twice differentiable, there are two well-known techniques: Lagrangian optimization and Lagrangian optimization with the Karush-Kuhn-Tucker (KKT) conditions.

2. When the objective functions are not continuous or differentiable, we are forced to use heuristic techniques, such as hill climbing, simulated annealing, and ant algorithms.

We will first look at Lagrangian techniques (Section 4.6.1), a variant called the KKT conditions that allows inequality constraints (Section 4.6.2), and then briefly consider several heuristic optimization techniques (Section 4.7).

4.6.1 Lagrangian Techniques

Lagrangian optimization computes the maximum or minimum of a function f of several variables subject to one or more constraint functions denoted g_i. We will assume that f and all the g_i are continuous, at least twice differentiable, and are defined over the entire domain, that is, do not have boundaries.

Formally, f is defined over a vector $\mathbf{x}$ drawn from R^n, and we wish to find the value(s) of $\mathbf{x}$ for which f attains its maximum or minimum, subject to the constraint function(s): $g_i(\mathbf{x}) = c_i$, where the c_i are real constants.

To begin with, consider a function f of two variables x and y with a single constraint function. We want to find the set of tuples of the form (x,y) that maximize $f(x,y)$ subject to the constraint $g(x,y) = c$. The constraint $g_i(\mathbf{x}) = c_i$ corresponds to a **contour**, or **level, set**—that is, a set of points where g's value does not change. Imagine tracing a path along such a contour. Along this path, f will increase and decrease in some manner. Imagine the contours of f corresponding to $f(\mathbf{x}) = d$ for some value of d. The path on g's contour touches successive contours of f. An extremal value of f on g's contour is reached exactly when g's contour grazes an extremal contour of f. At this point, the two contours are tangential, so that the gradient of f's contour, a vector that points in a direction perpendicular to the contour, has the same direction as the gradient of g's contour, though it may have a different absolute value. More precisely, if the gradient is denoted by $\nabla_{x,y} = \left(\dfrac{\partial}{\partial x}, \dfrac{\partial}{\partial y}\right)$, at the constrained extremal point,

$$\nabla_{x,y}f = -\lambda \nabla_{x,y}g$$

Define an auxiliary function:

$$F(x, y, \lambda) = f(x, y) + \lambda(g(x, y) - c) \qquad \text{(EQ 4.7)}$$

The stationary points of F, that is, the points where $\nabla_{x,y,\lambda}F(x, y, \lambda) = 0$, are points that (1) satisfy the constraint g, because the partial derivative with respect to λ, or $g(x, y) - c$, must be zero, and (2) are also constrained extremal points of f, because $\nabla_{x,y}f = -\lambda \nabla_{x,y}g$. Thus, the extremal points of F are also the points of constrained extrema of f (i.e., minima or maxima). From Fermat's theorem, the maximum or minimum value of any function is attained at one of three types of points: (1) a boundary point, (2) a point where f is not differentiable, and (3) at a stationary point where its first derivative is zero. Because we assume away the first two situations, the maximum or minimum is attained at one of the stationary points of F. Thus, we can simply solve $\nabla_{x,y,\lambda}F(x, y, \lambda) = 0$ and use the second derivative to determine the type of extremum.

This analysis continues to hold for more than two dimensions and more than one constraint function. That is, to obtain a constrained extremal point of f, take the objective function and add to it a constant multiple of each constraint function to get the auxiliary. This constant is called a **Lagrange multiplier**. The resulting system of equations is solved by setting the gradient of the auxiliary function to 0 to find its stationary points.

EXAMPLE 4.10: LAGRANGIAN OPTIMIZATION

Consider a company that purchases capacity on a link to the Internet and has to pay for this capacity. Suppose that the cost of a link of capacity b is Kb. Also suppose that the mean delay experienced by data sent on the link, denoted by d, is inversely proportional to b, so that $bd = 1$. Finally, let the benefit U from using a network connection with capacity b, and delay d, $0 \leq d < \infty$ be described by $U = -Kb - d$; that is, it decreases both with cost and with the delay. We want to maximize U subject to the constraint $bd = 1$. Both U and the constraint function are continuous and twice differentiable. Therefore, we can define the auxiliary function

$$F = -Kb - d + \lambda(bd - 1)$$

Set the partial derivatives with respect to b, d, and λ to zero to obtain, respectively:

$$-K + \lambda d = 0$$
$$-1 + \lambda b = 0$$
$$bd = 1$$

From the second equation, $b = 1/\lambda$, and from the first equation, $d = K/\lambda$, and from the third equation: Substituting the values for b and d, $\lambda = \sqrt{K}$. Substituting these values into the equations for b and d, $b = 1/(\sqrt{K})$ and $d = \sqrt{K}$. This gives a value of U at (b, d) to be $-2\sqrt{K}$. Since U is clearly unbounded in terms of a smallest value (when b approaches 0), this is also its maximum.

4.6.2 Karush-Kuhn-Tucker Conditions for Nonlinear Optimization

The Lagrangian method is applicable when the constraint function is of the form $g(x) = 0$. What if the constraints are of the form $g(x) \leq 0$? In this case, we can use the Karush-Kuhn-Tucker conditions (often called the KKT, or Kuhn-Tucker conditions) to determine whether the stationary point of the auxiliary function is also a global minimum.

As a preliminary, we define what is meant by a **convex** function. A function f is convex if, for any two points x and y in its domain, and for t in the closed interval $[0,1]$, $f(tx + (1 - t)y) \leq tf(x) + (1 - t)y$. That is, the function always lies *below* a line drawn from x to y.

Consider a convex objective function $f: R^n \to R$ with m inequality and l equality constraints. Denote the inequality constraints by $g_i(x) \leq 0, 1 \leq i \leq m$ and the equality constraints by $h_j(\mathbf{x}) = 0$, $1 \le j \le l$. The KKT conditions require all the g_i to be convex and all the h_j to be linear. Then, if a is a point in R^n, and there exist m and l constants, respectively, denoted μ_i and ν_j such that the following conditions hold, we can guarantee that a is a globally constrained minimum of f:

$$\nabla f(a) + \sum_{i=1}^{m} \mu_i \nabla g_i(a) + \sum_{j=1}^{l} \mu_j \nabla h_j(a) = 0$$

$$g_i(a) \le 0 \,\forall i$$

$$h_j(a) = 0 \,\forall j \qquad \text{(EQ 4.8)}$$

$$\mu_i \ge 0 \,\forall i$$

$$\mu_i g_i(a) = 0 \,\forall i$$

If these conditions are met, the stationary points of the auxiliary function (the first equation in the preceding set of equations) yield the minima of f.

4.7 Heuristic Nonlinear Optimization

We now turn to the situation in which the objective function and the constraints are not mathematically "nice," that is, linear or convex. In such cases, we need to rely on heuristic approaches to optimization. Many such approaches have been proposed in the literature. We will outline only two common ones: hill climbing and genetic algorithms.

4.7.1 Hill Climbing

Hill climbing is perhaps the simplest technique for heuristic optimization. Its simplest variant does not even support constraints, seeking only to find the value of x that maximizes $f(x)$. Hill climbing requires two primitives: a way to evaluate $f(x)$ given x and a way to generate, for each point x, another point y, that is near x (assume that x and y are embedded in a suitable metric space).

Start by randomly choosing a point x in the domain of f and labeling it the candidate maximum (we might just get lucky!). Evaluate f on x, then generate a point y that is close to x. If the value of f is higher at y, then y is the new candidate maximum; otherwise, x remains the candidate. We continue to generate and evaluate f on neighboring points of the candidate maximum until we find a point x, all of whose neighbors have a lower value of f than at x. We declare this to be the maximum.

The analogy to climbing a hill is clear. We start somewhere on the hill and take a step in a random direction. If it is higher, we step up. If not, we stay where we are.

This way, assuming that the hill has a single peak, we will eventually get to the top, where every neighboring step must lead downhill.

Although simple, this approach to hill climbing leaves much to be desired. These concerns are addressed by the following variants of the basic approach.

- Generate more than one neighbor of x and choose the one where the value of f is greatest. This variant is also called the **steepest-gradient method**.

- Memorize some or all of the values of y that were discarded in a **tabu list**. Subsequently, if any value in the tabu list is generated, it can be immediately discarded. This variant is called **tabu search**.

- To find the maximum value of f subject to constraint g, choose the initial candidate maximum x to be a value that also satisfies g. Then, when generating neighbors of x, ensure that the neighboring values also satisfy g. This allows the use of hill climbing for constrained optimization.

The single biggest problem with hill climbing is that it fails when f has more than one maximum. In this case, an unfortunate initial choice of x will cause the algorithm to be stuck in a local maximum instead of finding the global maximum. This is illustrated in Figure 4.6, which shows a function with multiple peaks. Starting at the base of any of the lesser peaks will result in hill climbing stopping at a local maximum.

There are several ways to get around this problem. One approach is called **shotgun** hill climbing. Here, the hill-climbing algorithm is started from several randomly chosen candidate maxima. The best result from among these should be the global maximum as well. This approach is widely used.

A second approach, called **simulated annealing**, varies the closeness of a selected neighbor dynamically. Moreover, it allows for some steps of the climb to be downhill. The idea is that if the algorithm is trapped at a local maximum, the only way out is to go down before going up, and therefore, downhill steps should be allowed. The degree to which downhill steps are permitted varies over the climb. At the start, even large downhill steps are permitted. As the climb progresses, however, only small downhill steps are permitted.

More precisely, the algorithm evaluates the function value at the current candidate point x and at some neighbor y. There is also a control variable, called the temperature, T, that describes how large a downhill step is permitted. The **acceptance function** $A(f(x), f(y), T)$ determines the probability with which the algorithm moves from x to y as a function of their values and the current temperature, with a nonzero probability even when $f(y) < f(x)$. Moreover, the acceptance function tends to zero when T tends to zero and $f(y) < f(x)$. The choice of the acceptance function is problem-specific and therefore usually handcrafted.

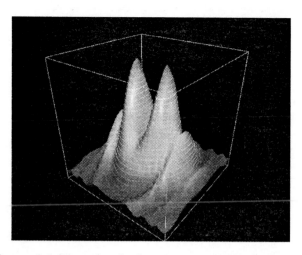

Figure 4.6 Example of a function in which hill climbing
can get stuck in a local maximum

4.7.2 Genetic Algorithms

The term *genetic algorithm* applies to a broad class of approaches that share some
common attributes. The key idea is to encode a candidate maximum value $\mathbf{x}$ as a bit
string. At the start, hundreds or thousands of such candidate values are randomly
generated. The function f is then evaluated at each such value, and the best ones
are **selected** for propagation in one of two ways. With **mutation**, some bits of a
selected candidate value are randomly perturbed to form the next generation of
candidates. With **crossover**, bits from two selected candidate values are randomly
exchanged. In this way, the best **features** of the population are **inherited** by the
next generation. The algorithm proceeds by forming generation after generation of
candidates, until adequate solutions are found.

There is an extensive literature on algorithms for encoding candidates, introducing mutations, and making effective crossovers. Genetic algorithms have been
found to produce surprisingly good results in areas ranging from antenna design to
job scheduling. However, the approach has also been criticized for many shortcom-
ings, such as its sensitivity to numerous tuning parameters and a tendency to converge to local optima.

4.8 Exercises

1. Modeling

You have been hired as the head of a hot air balloon company's flight operations. Too much money is being spent for each flight! Your job is to make flight profitable again. (The number of flights is not negotiable.)

For each flight, you can control where you take off from (there is a finite set of take-off locations) and the duration of the flight, as long as the flight lasts at least 15 minutes. The cost of a flight depends on its duration (to pay for natural gas, the pilot's wages, and for the chase vehicle), where the balloon takes off from, and how far the landing site is from a road (the farther away it is from a road, the more it has to be dragged over a farmer's field). Moreover, you can have at least one pilot and up to nine passengers and can charge them what you wish. Of course, the number of passengers decreases (say, linearly) with the cost of the ticket.

What are the fixed parameters? What are the input and output parameters? What are the control variables? Come up with plausible transfer and objective functions. How would you empirically estimate the transfer function?

2. Optimizing a function of two variables

Consider the following system:

$$O = 10x_1 - 3x_2, \text{where}$$

$$2x_1 - x_2 = 1$$

$$x_1 \geq 0$$

$$x_2 \geq 0$$

Geometrically find the optimal value of O.

3. Optimizing a function of three variables

Geometrically find the optimal value of O where

$$O = 5x_1 + 2x_2 - x_3$$

$$x_1 + x_2 + x_3 = 1$$

$$x_1 \geq 0$$

$$x_2 \geq 0$$

$$x_3 \geq 0$$

4. **Network flow**

   Model the network flow problem of Example 4.5, where the warehouses have finite bounded capacity, as a linear program.

5. **Integer linear programming**

   Generalize Example 4.6 to the case in which n users can schedule jobs on one of k machines, such that each user incurs a specific cost and gains a specific benefit on each machine at each of m time periods. Write out the ILP for this problem.

6. **Weighted bipartite matching**

   Suppose that you have K distinct balls that need to be placed in M distinct urns such that the payoff from placing the kth ball in the mth urn is p_{km}, and no more than two balls can be placed in each urn. Model this as a weighted bipartite matching problem to maximize the payoff.

7. **Dynamic programming**

   You are given a long string L of symbols from a finite alphabet. Your goal is to find the matching substrings of L with a shorter string S from the same alphabet. However, matches need not be exact: You can delete one element of L or S for a penalty of 1, and you can also substitute an element of L for an element of S for a penalty of 1. So, for example, the match between the string L = "text" and S = "tx" is "te" with a penalty of 1 (one substitution), "tex" with a penalty of 1 (one deletion), "ex" with a penalty of 2 (two substitutions), "ext" with a penalty of 2 (one substitution and one deletion), and so on. Use dynamic programming to output all matching substrings of L along with the corresponding penalty.

8. **Lagrangian optimization**

   Use Lagrangian optimization to find the extremal values of $z = x^3 + 2y$ subject to the condition that $x^2 + y^2 = 1$ (i.e., the points (x,y) lie on the unit circle).

9. **Hill climbing**

   Suppose that you know that the objective function you are trying to maximize has no more than K local optima. Outline an algorithm that is guaranteed to find the global optimum using hill climbing.

5

Signals, Systems, and Transforms

This chapter focuses on **transforms**: a family of techniques used to study a series of values, or **signals**. Transforms give insight into the nature of signals and help design effective **systems** to manipulate signals. Transforms form the basis for the study of control theory, discussed in more detail in Chapter 8.

We begin by covering background material on complex numbers and Euler's formula. We then discuss types of signals and systems. Subsequently, the bulk of the chapter is devoted to the study of Fourier series, Fourier transforms, Laplace transforms, and the Z transform.

5.1 Background

5.1.1 Sinusoids

A communication network is formed from communication links. A widely used approach to transferring information over a wired or wireless link is to modify an underlying continuous **carrier** signal to represent the symbol values 0 and 1. In nearly all cases of interest, the carrier signal is **sinusoidal**. That is, it is associated with a time period T such that at time t, the amplitude of the signal is described by the function $\cos\left(\dfrac{2\pi t}{T}\right)$, as shown in Figure 5.1.

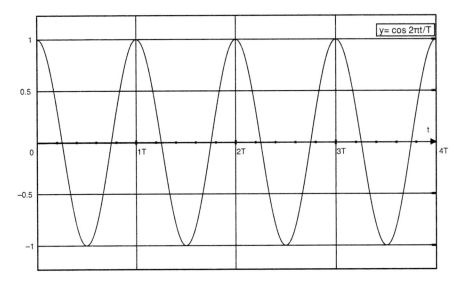

Figure 5.1 A typical carrier wave described by a sinusoidal curve

How can we generate such a time-varying signal? Consider a disk with a radius of one unit that has an axle at its center. Suppose that it rotates in the counterclockwise direction with a uniform angular velocity and with a period of T seconds. Let us paint a small dot on its rim and draw a vector from the center to this dot. The angle that this rotating vector makes with the X-axis at time t is denoted by θ and given by $\theta = \dfrac{2\pi t}{T}$ radians (Figure 5.2). At time t, the distance of the dot from the Y-axis is given by $\cos(\theta) = \cos\left(\dfrac{2\pi t}{T}\right)$, which is precisely the equation describing a sinusoidal carrier. In other words, the unidimensional *time-varying* signal strength of a sinusoidal carrier can be thought of as a projection of a *fixed-length* two-dimensional rotating vector on the X-axis. This warrants a more careful study of the mathematics of rotating two-dimensional vectors.

5.1.2 Complex Numbers

Recall that any vector on a two-dimensional plane can be written as the vector sum of two *basis* vectors, one lying on the X-axis and one parallel to the Y-axis. Let us consider how to represent these basis vectors. A real value x on the number line naturally corresponds to a vector lying on the X-axis drawn from $(0,0)$ to $(0, x)$. Thus, the first of these basis vectors corresponds to, and can be represented by, a

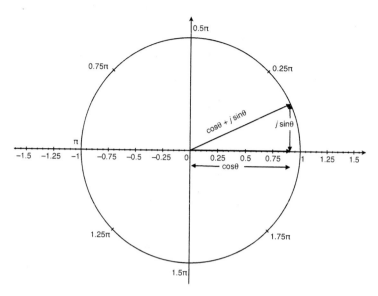

Figure 5.2 Generating a sinusoid from a rotating vector

real number. How can we represent the second vector? Intuitively, we need a way to "raise" a vector off the real axis. Suppose that we denote the operation "rotate a vector counterclockwise by 90 degrees about the origin" by the letter j.[1] Then, the vector $j5$, for example, corresponds to a vector of magnitude 5 lying on the Y-axis. Given this operation, we can denote a vector on the unit disk making an angle θ with the X-axis as the vector sum $\cos(\theta) + j\sin(\theta)$, as shown in Figure 5.2.

We denote the application of the rotation operator j twice in a row like this: $j.j$, or j^2. Note that the application of this combined operator to the vector 1, which is the vector from $(0,0)$ to $(0,1)$, results in the vector -1. We represent this by the equation

$$j.j.1 = j^2.1 = -1$$

(EQ 5.1)

With a slight abuse of notation, we can take the square root of either side to get

$$j = \sqrt{-1}$$

(EQ 5.2)

revealing j to be the unit imaginary vector. It is unfortunate that most students encounter j as a ghostly, ethereal entity rather than as the far more intuitive 90-degree rotation operator.

---

1. Mathematicians and engineers differ in the symbol used for this operation. Engineers use j rather than the mathematician's i because by universal engineering convention, the symbol i represents an electric current.

Given the basis vectors 1 and j, it is easy to see that we can represent a vector from the origin to any point (a,b) on the plane as the vector sum $a + jb$. The corresponding tuple (a,b) is called a **complex** number, with a as its **real** part and b as its **imaginary** part. If $z = a+jb$ is a complex number, we denote $a = \text{Re}(z)$; $b = \text{Im}(z)$. We denote by z^* the **complex conjugate** of z, defined as $z^* = a - jb$.

5.1.3 Euler's Formula

Given the importance of rotating vectors, also called **phasors**, it is desirable to compactly represent the current position of the vector on the unit disk. Of course, this can be easily specified by the single value θ. By tradition, and for sound mathematical reasons that we will see later, we instead represent a rotating vector of magnitude c making an angle θ with the X-axis by using the notation $ce^{j\theta}$. This notation is rather counterintuitive! What does it mean to raise e to an imaginary power? The answer is: It does not matter. All that matters is that the following formula, known as **Euler's formula**,[2] has been found to be consistent with the foundations of real analysis:

$$e^{j\theta} = \cos\theta + j\sin\theta \qquad \text{(EQ 5.3)}$$

EXAMPLE 5.1: EULER'S FORMULA

Use Euler's formula to represent $e^{j\frac{\pi}{2}}$ in the form $a + jb$.

Solution:

By definition, $e^{j\frac{\pi}{2}} = \cos\left(\frac{\pi}{2}\right) + j\sin\left(\frac{\pi}{2}\right) = j$.

EXAMPLE 5.2: EULER'S FORMULA

Use Euler's formula to represent $e^{-j\frac{\pi}{10}} + 2e^{-j\frac{2\pi}{10}}$ in the form $a + jb$.

---

2. The Euler formula has been called the most beautiful formula in mathematics, especially when written for the special value of $\theta = \pi$, where, using standard mathematical convention, it reduces to

$$e^{i\pi} + 1 = 0$$

relating five elementary quantities in mathematics: e, i, 0, 1, and π.

Solution:

$$e^{-j\frac{\pi}{10}} + 2e^{-j\frac{2\pi}{10}}$$

$$= \left(\cos\left(-\frac{\pi}{10}\right) + j\sin\left(-\frac{\pi}{10}\right)\right) + 2\left(\cos\left(-\frac{2\pi}{10}\right) + j\sin\left(-\frac{2\pi}{10}\right)\right)$$

$$= \left(\cos\left(\frac{\pi}{10}\right) + 2\cos\left(\frac{2\pi}{10}\right)\right) - j\left(\sin\left(\frac{\pi}{10}\right) + 2\sin\left(\frac{2\pi}{10}\right)\right)$$

$$= (0.95 + 1.618) - j(0.309 + 1.175)$$

$$= 2.568 + j1.484$$

We have already seen that the projection of a phasor $ce^{j\theta}$ on the X-axis is given by $c\cos(\theta)$, which is the first, or real, component in the expansion of $ce^{j\theta}$ using Euler's formula. We denote this as $\text{Re}(ce^{j\theta})$. Recalling that $\theta = \frac{2\pi t}{T}$, the strength of a carrier signal at time t is therefore given by

$$\text{Re}(ce^{j\left(\frac{2\pi t}{T}\right)}).$$

The factor $\frac{2\pi}{T}$ occurs so frequently in the study of rotating vectors that it has its own symbol, ω, where $\omega = \frac{2\pi}{T}$. The symbol ω has a physical interpretation as the angular frequency of rotation and has units of radians/second. With the notation and concepts built up so far, we can succinctly denote a carrier signal as $\text{Re}(ce^{j\omega t})$.

We have seen two ways of representing a complex number: as a sum $a + jb$, or as a phasor $ce^{j\theta}$. It is straightforward to go from one representation to the other, using the following formulae:

$$\begin{aligned} a &= c\cos\theta & c &= \sqrt{a^2 + b^2} \\ b &= c\sin\theta & \theta &= \text{atan}\left(\frac{b}{a}\right) \end{aligned}$$

(EQ 5.4)

Note that we have arbitrarily described the phasor as rotation in the counterclockwise direction. A sinusoidal carrier can equally well be generated by a phasor rotating in the counterclockwise direction. To distinguish between the two, we denote the angular frequency of a phasor rotating in the clockwise direction as a negative frequency. Thus, a phasor with a frequency of -20π radians/second is rotating 10 times a second in the clockwise direction, and the second hand of a clock has a frequency of $-\frac{\pi}{30}$ radians/second.

EXAMPLE 5.3: KEYING

We now consider how to mathematically represent the transmission of information on a link by modification of the phasor $ce^{j\omega t}$. This is also called **keying**. For simplicity, focus on the problem of sending just one bit: either a 0 or a 1.

In **amplitude shift keying**, we choose two phasor magnitudes c_1 and c_2. To send a 0, the transmitter transmits a signal $c_1\text{Re}(e^{j\omega t})$; to send a 1, it transmits a signal $c_2\text{Re}(e^{j\omega t})$. In practice, this is accomplished by an electronic circuit that sets the degree of amplification of the carrier signal to either c_1 or c_2. If either of the constants c_1 and c_2 is 0, this is also called **on-off keying**.

In **frequency shift keying**, we choose two phasor frequencies ω_1 and ω_2. To send a 0, the transmitter transmits a signal $c\text{Re}(e^{j\omega_1 t})$; to send a 1, it transmits a signal $c\text{Re}(e^{j\omega_2 t})$. In practice, this is accomplished by either coupling the output signal to one of two oscillators tuned to the frequencies ω_1 and ω_2 or sending control signals to a voltage-controlled oscillator.

The **phase** of a sinusoid at time t is the angle it makes with the X-axis at that time. With **phase shift keying**, the transmitter and receiver are assumed to be **phase-locked**; that is, they each have local oscillators that have identical frequencies and phases. The transmitter sends a 0 or a 1 by modifying the phase of the carrier signal. With **binary phase shift keying**, for example, the transmitter transmits the unmodified carrier signal $ce^{j\omega t}$ to send a 0 and $-ce^{j\omega t}$, which is a signal that is exactly 180 degrees out of phase with the receiver's local oscillator, to send a 1. This general idea can be easily extended. For example, with **quadrature phase shift keying**, the transmitter shifts the transmitting phasor's phase by 0, 90, 180, or 270 degrees, using the phasors

$$ce^{j\omega t},\ ce^{j\left(\omega t + \frac{\pi}{2}\right)},\ ce^{j(\omega t + \pi)},\text{ and } ce^{j\left(\omega t + \frac{3\pi}{2}\right)}.$$

These phases allow the receiver to extract *two* bits for each received signal. In practice, phase shift keying is accomplished by slightly delaying the transmitted carrier signal so that it is received out of phase.

One might ask: What is the limit to phase shift keying? Would it be possible to send larger and larger numbers of bits by using more fine-grained phase shifting? Could we send, for example, 32 bits at a time by using 65,536 phases? The answer is that as we increase the number of phase levels, even a slight distortion of a signal along the path from the transmitter to the receiver corrupts the signal. Therefore, the limit to the *capacity* of the path comes from its inherent *noise*. The relationship between the capacity of a channel and its noise characteristics form the basis of *information theory*, which is discussed in Chapter 9.

It is sometimes useful to express sinusoids as complex exponentials. We can do so as follows. First, recall that $\cos(-\theta) = \cos\theta$ and $\sin(-\theta) = -\sin\theta$. Now, because $e^{j\theta} = \cos\theta + j\sin\theta$, it follows that $e^{-(j\theta)} = e^{j(-\theta)} = \cos(-\theta) + j\sin(-\theta) = \cos\theta - j\sin\theta$. Therefore, $e^{j\theta} + e^{-j\theta} = 2\cos\theta$, so that

$$\cos\theta = \frac{1}{2}(e^{j\theta} + e^{-j\theta}) \qquad \text{(EQ 5.5)}$$

Similarly,

$$\sin\theta = \frac{1}{2j}(e^{j\theta} - e^{-j\theta}) \qquad \text{(EQ 5.6)}$$

5.1.4 Discrete-Time Convolution and the Impulse Function

Consider the discrete-time function $x(t)$, where t is a non-negative integer, that represents the number of HTTP requests made to a Web server over intervals of 1 second. Suppose that this function, over an interval of 10 seconds, is given by $x(t)$, $0 \leq t \leq 9$ = 1, 3, 5, 2, 5, 8, 7, 3, 9, 4. That is, in the 0th interval, the Web server receives $x(0)$ = 1 request; in the first interval, it receives $x(1)$ = 3 requests; in the second interval, it receives $x(2)$ = 5 requests; and so on. The histogram of this function is shown in Figure 5.3(a).

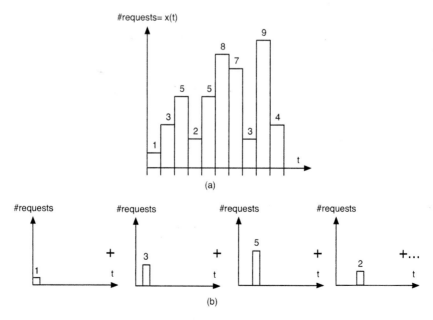

Figure 5.3 Decomposing a discrete-time function

The same histogram can also be represented as the sum of a set of smaller histograms, one per time interval, as shown in Figure 5.3(b). Each smaller histogram is the product of two functions, $x(t)$ and a selector function $sel(t, \tau)$, which is defined as $sel(t, \tau) = 1$ when $t = \tau$ and $= 0$ otherwise. For instance, the first small histogram corresponds to $x(t)*sel(t,0)$ because it is zero everywhere, except when $t = 0$, when $x(t)$ takes the value $x(0)$ and $sel(t,0)$ is 1. Similarly, the second histogram corresponds to $x(t)*sel(t,1)$ and so on. Because their sum is $x(t)$, we can write

$$x(t) = \sum_{\tau = 0}^{\infty} x(t)sel(t, \tau) \qquad\qquad \text{(EQ 5.7)}$$

We make a small digression to consider the relationship between the function $x(t)$ and the function $x(t - a)$. For concreteness, consider the function $x(t)$ shown in Figure 5.3(a) and let $a = 2$. The function $x(t - a)$ is undefined for times before time 2, and, for convenience, we define it to have the value 0. At time 2, $x(t - a) = x(2 - 2) = x(0) = 1$. At time 3, $x(t - a) = x(1) = 3$ and so on. We plot this in Figure 5.4.

Note that $x(t - 2)$ is just $x(t)$ shifted two steps to the right. A little thought shows that, in general, the time series $x(t - a)$ is the time series $x(t)$ shifted by a time interval a to the right.

Now, consider the function $\delta(t)$, also called the **impulse function**, defined as $\delta(0) = 1$ and $\delta(t) = 0$ for all other values of t. We see that, trivially, $sel(t, 0) = \delta(t)$. From our observation about time-shifting, we can define $sel(t, 1) = \delta(t - 1)$, which is the one-step time-shifted version of $\delta(t)$. Generalizing, we see that

$$sel(t, \tau) = \delta(t - \tau) \qquad\qquad \text{(EQ 5.8)}$$

Therefore, we can rewrite Equation 5.7 as

$$x(t) = \sum_{\tau = 0}^{\infty} x(t)\delta(t - \tau) \qquad\qquad \text{(EQ 5.9)}$$

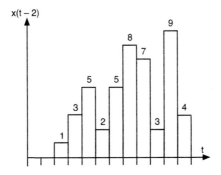

Figure 5.4 Time-shifting a time series

We have already seen that for each term in the summation, the value of the product of $x(t)$ and $\delta(t-\tau)$ is zero except when $\tau = t$, so we can also write the summation as

$$x(t) \;=\; \sum_{\tau = 0}^{\infty} x(\tau)\delta(t-\tau)$$

Finally, for functions $x(t)$ that are defined over both the positive and negative values of t, we can generalize the summation over the entire number line to get

$$x(t) \;=\; \sum_{\tau = -\infty}^{\infty} x(\tau)\delta(t-\tau) \qquad \text{(EQ 5.10)}$$

This summation is called the **convolution** of $x(t)$ with $\delta(t)$ and is denoted $x(t) \otimes \delta(t)$.[3]

In general, the convolution of two discrete functions $x(t)$ and $y(t)$ is defined as

$$x(t) \otimes y(t) \;=\; \sum_{\tau = -\infty}^{\infty} x(\tau)y(t-\tau) \qquad \text{(EQ 5.11)}$$

Note that *each* value of the convolution of $x(t)$ and $y(t)$ (i.e., at time t) is the result of adding *all* product pairs $x(\tau)$ and $y(t-\tau)$. This is clearly a computationally expensive operation. Moreover, we need to be careful in dealing with values of $x(t)$ and $y(t)$ that lie outside their range of definition.

EXAMPLE 5.4: DISCRETE-TIME CONVOLUTION

Compute the convolution of $x(t)$, $0 \le t \le 9$ = 1, 3, 5, 2, 5, 8, 7, 3, 9, 4 and $y(t)$, $0 \le t \le 9$ = 3, 1, 7, 4, 5, 9, 7, 1, 3, 8.

Solution:

By convention, we assume that both functions are zero outside their range of definition. Let $z(t) = x(t) \otimes y(t)$: $z(0) = \sum_{\tau = -\infty}^{\infty} x(\tau)y(-\tau)$. The only value of τ for which both $x(t)$ and $y(t)$ are nonzero is $\tau = 0$, so the sum reduces to $x(0)*y(0) = 3$. $z(1) = \sum_{\tau = -\infty}^{\infty} x(\tau)y(1-\tau)$. The only values of τ for which both $x(t)$

---

3. In electrical engineering texts, convolution is represented by *. Unfortunately, this is universally used in computer science to denote multiplication, thus our choice.

and $y(t)$ are nonzero are $\tau = 0, 1$ so the sum reduces to $x(0) * y(1) + x(1) * y(0) = 1 * 1 + 3 * 3 = 10$. It is left as an exercise to the reader to show that $z(2) = 7 + 3 + 15 = 25$, $z(3) = 4 + 21 + 5 + 6 = 36$, $z(4) = 5 + 12 + 35 + 2 + 15 = 69,....$

5.1.5 Continuous-Time Convolution and the Dirac Delta Function

The definition of convolution can be extended to continuous-time functions. We start, as before, with the definition of a selector function with a parameter τ that picks out the value of $x(t)$ at time τ. Thus, we would like to define a function that is zero everywhere except at a single point, where it has a value of 1. Obviously, such a function is discontinuous at that point, which makes it mathematically troublesome. To avoid this problem, we define the selector function as the limiting case of a rectangular function of unit area defined over a support of length T and with height $1/T$ as $T \to 0$. At the limit, this represents an infinitely tall rectangle that nevertheless has a finite area! Nevertheless, this function is continuous everywhere except at the limit, so that its properties at the limit can be extrapolated from those of the limiting series. Setting aside a mathematically rigorous development, which is beyond the scope of this text, we define the continuous-time impulse function by

$$\int_{-\infty}^{\infty} \delta(t)dt = 1$$

(EQ 5.12)

$$\delta(t) = 0 \text{ for } t \neq 0$$

Intuitively, a continuous-time impulse function has a unit mass concentrated entirely at $t = 0$. It was first defined by the physicist P. A. M. Dirac and therefore is also called the **Dirac delta** in his honor. The Dirac delta is represented graphically by a vertical arrow at the origin. The integral of the delta function is called the **unit-step function** and written $u(t)$. Note that $u(t)$ is zero for $t < 0$ and 1 for $t > 0$. Its value at zero is undefined (Figure 5.5).

For any function $x(t)$ that is continuous in the neighborhood of the origin, the delta function acts as a selector, so that

$$x(t)\delta(t) = x(0)\delta(t)$$

(EQ 5.13)

We interpret this to mean that the multiplication of $x(t)$ with the delta function results in a delta function whose strength is the value of $x(t)$ at the origin. (Compare this with the discrete-time selector function.) Similarly,

$$x(t)\delta(t - \tau) = x(\tau)\delta(t - \tau)$$

(EQ 5.14)

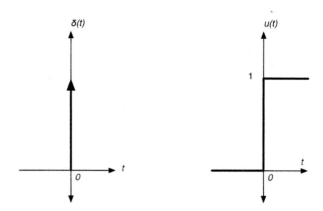

Figure 5.5 The Dirac delta and its integral, the unit-step function

Moreover, analogous to Equation 5.10, we have

$$x(t) = \int_{-\infty}^{\infty} x(\tau)\delta(t - \tau)d\tau$$

(EQ 5.15)

$$x(\tau) = \int_{-\infty}^{\infty} x(t)\delta(t - \tau)dt$$

where the second equation can be obtained by swapping the variables t and τ.

Finally, we can define the convolution of any two continuous-time functions $x(t)$ and $y(t)$ as

$$x(t) \otimes y(t) = \int_{-\infty}^{\infty} x(\tau)y(t - \tau)d\tau$$

(EQ 5.16)

EXAMPLE 5.5: CONTINUOUS-TIME CONVOLUTION

Compute the convolution of the functions $x(t)$ and $y(t)$ defined graphically in Figure 5.6.

Solution:

By convention, we assume that both functions are zero outside their range of definition. Thus,

$$x(\tau) \neq 0 \text{ in the range } -1 \leq \tau \leq 1$$
$$y(t - \tau) \neq 0 \text{ in the range } -1 \leq (t - \tau) \leq 1 \Rightarrow t - 1 \leq \tau \leq t + 1$$

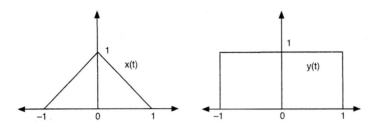

Figure 5.6 Example continuous-time functions for convolution

Therefore, both $x(t)$ and $y(t)$ are simultaneously nonzero only in the range $max(t-1, -1) \le \tau \le min(t+1, 1)$, and

$$x(t) \otimes y(t) = \int_{-\infty}^{\infty} x(\tau)y(t-\tau)d\tau = \int_{max(t-1,-1)}^{min(t+1,1)} x(\tau)y(t-\tau)d\tau$$

It is necessary to evaluate this integral separately in the ranges $[-\infty, -2]$, $[-2, -1]$, $[-1, 0]$, $[0,1]$, $[1,2]$, and $[2, \infty]$. In all the ranges, $y(t) = 1$, but the limits of integration are modified as follows:

$$x(t) \otimes y(t) = \begin{cases} 0 & -\infty \le t \le -2 \\ \int_{-1}^{(t+1)} (1+\tau)d\tau & -2 \le t \le -1 \\ \int_{0}^{(t+1)} (1-\tau)d\tau + \frac{1}{2} & -1 \le t \le 0 \\ \int_{(t-1)}^{0} (1+\tau)d\tau + \frac{1}{2} & 0 \le t \le 1 \\ \int_{t-1}^{1} (1-\tau)d\tau & 1 \le t \le 2 \\ 0 & 2 \le t \le \infty \end{cases}$$

$$x(t) \otimes y(t) = \begin{cases} 0 & -\infty \le t \le -2 \\ \dfrac{(t+2)^2}{2} & -2 \le t \le -1 \\ 1 - \dfrac{t^2}{2} & -1 \le t \le 0 \\ 1 - \dfrac{t^2}{2} & 0 \le t \le 1 \\ \dfrac{(t-2)^2}{2} & 1 \le t \le 2 \\ 0 & 2 \le t \le \infty \end{cases}$$

Note that, in this case, the convolution changes its form across the entire range. Therefore, it is a tricky task to compute it. As we will see later, the use of transforms greatly reduces the complexity of computing the convolution of two functions.

5.2 Signals

A signal is a set of data, usually a function of time. We denote a signal as $x(t)$, where t is nominally time. We have already seen two types of signals: **discrete** signals, where t takes integer values, and **continuous** signals, where t takes real values. In contrast, **digital** signals are those where the signal $x(t)$ takes on one of a quantized set of values, typically 0 and 1, and **analog** signals are those where the signal $x(t)$ takes on real values.

Some signals are **periodic**, so that their values repeat after every time period T. The smallest such period is called the **fundamental period** of the signal. Signals that do not have such a period are called **aperiodic**.

Most signals exist for only a limited period in time and are called **time-limited** signals. Others can be modeled as eternal signals and are called **time-unlimited** signals.

Given a signal $x(t)$, we define a **time-shifted** signal that is time-shifted a time units to the right (i.e., it is delayed by a time units as compared to the original signal) to be $x(t - a)$. Similarly, we define a **time-scaled** signal where the signal is expanded or compressed in time by the scalar value a to be $x(at)$.

Here are some examples of signals that arise in computer networks:

- The series of packet round trip times measured at a network source (discrete, analog, aperiodic, time-limited)

- The buffer occupancy over time at a router (continuous, digital, aperiodic, time-unlimited)

- The samples collected at an analog-to-digital transducer during a voice call (discrete, digital, aperiodic, time-limited)

- The physical carrier signal on a wired or wireless link (continuous, analog, periodic, time-unlimited)

- The number of HTTP requests received at a Web server over intervals of 1 second (discrete, digital, aperiodic, time-unlimited)

- The number of routing updates received by a border gateway protocol (BGP) daemon at a router over intervals of 5 minutes (discrete, digital, aperiodic, time-unlimited)

Digital systems, such as computer networks, approximate a continuous signal by a discrete signal whose time instants are sufficiently closely spaced and an analog signal by a digital signal whose quantization levels are sufficiently closely spaced. We will study what is precisely meant by "sufficiently closely spaced" later in this chapter. For the remainder of this chapter, rather than these specific signals, we will consider signals in the abstract.

5.2.1 The Complex Exponential Signal

A signal that frequently crops up in the study of transforms is the complex exponential signal denoted ke^{st}, where k is a real number and s is a complex quantity that can be written as $s = \sigma + j\omega$. We can expand ke^{st} as $ke^{st} = ke^{(\sigma+j\omega)t} = ke^{\sigma t}e^{j\omega t} = ke^{\sigma t}(\cos\omega t + j\sin\omega t) = ke^{\sigma t}\cos\omega t + jke^{\sigma t}\sin\omega t$. The real and imaginary components of this signal are both exponentially modulated sinusoids having frequency ω. With carefully chosen values of σ, ω, and k, this expression and its conjugate can represent a variety of seemingly unrelated signals:

- When $s = 0$, this reduces to the constant k (Figure 5.7(a)).
- When $\omega = 0$, this reduces to the real monotone exponential $ke^{\sigma t}$ (Figure 5.7(b)).
- When $\sigma = 0$, setting $s = \pm j\omega$ gives us the sum

$$k((\cos\omega t + j\sin\omega t) + (\cos\omega t - j\sin\omega t)) = 2k\cos\omega t,$$

  which is a real sinusoid scaled by a factor k (Figure 5.7(c)).
- When $\sigma \neq 0$, setting $s = \sigma \pm j\omega$ gives us the sum $2ke^{\sigma t}\cos\omega t$, which is a scaled real sinusoid that is modulated by a monotone exponential (Figure 5.7(d)).
- When $\sigma = 0$, the expression reduces to $k(\cos\omega t + j\sin\omega t)$, which is a helix oriented along the t axis, whose projections on the real-t and imaginary-t planes are sinusoids (Figure 5.8(a)).
- In the general case, the function represents an exponentially modulated helix oriented along the t axis, whose projections on the real-t and imaginary-t planes are exponentially modulated sinusoids (Figure 5.8(b)).

It is worth studying these figures carefully because they provide deep insight into the nature of a complex exponential that will greatly help in understanding the nature of transforms.

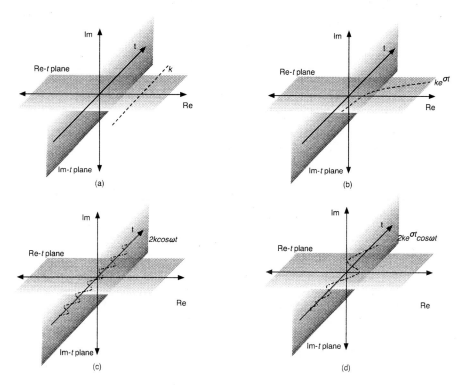

Figure 5.7 Elementary cases of the complex exponential signal

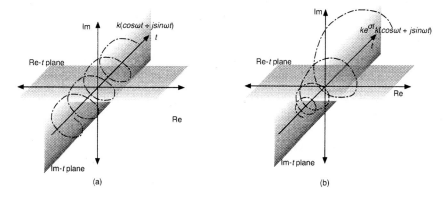

Figure 5.8 More general cases of the complex exponential signal

5.3 Systems

A system is an entity that acts on a set of input signals to produce a set of output signals. Mathematically speaking, a system is a function whose domain and ranges are both sets of functions. We typically denote the input to the system by the vector function $x(t)$ and its output by the vector function $y(t)$. The **transfer function** $H(.)$ converts the input to the output, so that $y(t) = H(x(t))$.[4]

When studying a system, we have one of two goals in mind: (1) to determine the output from an existing system when it receives a specific input (the **analysis** problem) or (2) to design a system that exhibits a desired transformation from a set of input signals to a set of output signals (the **design** problem). In both cases, we use transforms as an essential analytical and design tool. This chapter focuses on the tools of analysis; Chapter 8, on control theory, focuses on design.

As with signals, systems can be categorized in several ways: **continuous time** and **discrete time**, and **analog** and **digital**. Their definitions mirror those for signals. We discuss four categories in more detail.

Causal systems act only on inputs from the past. That is, they cannot know the future. In contrast, **acausal** systems are aware of the future. Although acausal systems sound improbable, they are rather easy to build if they operate on logs or traces of inputs rather than on inputs presented to the system in real time.

Memoryless systems act only on the inputs presented at any point in time. By contrast, the output of a **dynamic** system may depend on both current and past inputs.

A **time-invariant** system is one whose parameters do not change with time. So, if the system has an output $y(t)$ at time t for an input $x(t)$, it has the output $y(t - T)$ for an input $x(t - T)$. That is, if $y(t) = H(x(t))$, then $y(t - T) = H(x(t - T))$.

Finally, and most important, a **linear** system is one that exhibits the properties of **additivity** and **homogeneity**.

- A system is **additive** if, given that input x_1 leads to output y_1 and input x_2 leads to output y_2, the input $(x_1 + x_2)$ leads to the output $(y_1 + y_2)$. That is, if $y_1 = H(x_1)$ and $y_2 = H(x_2)$, then $y_1 + y_2 = H(x_1 + x_2)$.
- A system is **homogeneous (scalar)** if, given that the input x leads to the output y, the input kx, where k is a scalar, leads to the output ky. That is, if $y = H(x)$, then $ky = H(kx)$.

These two conditions can be combined into the single condition of **superposition**. A system exhibits superposition if, given that the input x_1 leads to output y_1

---

4. We are using the term *transfer function* loosely. As discussed in Section 8.2.2, in the context of control theory, the transfer function is more precisely described as the Laplace transform of the impulse response of the system. At this stage, however, this loose but intuitively appealing description of the transfer function suffices.

and input x_2 leads to output y_2, then for all constants k_1 and k_2, the input $(k_1x_1 + k_2x_2)$ leads to the output $(k_1y_1 + k_2y_2)$. That is, if $y_1 = H(x_1)$ and $y_2 = H(x_2)$, then $k_1y_1 + k_2y_2 = H(k_1x_1 + k_2x_2)$.

EXAMPLE 5.6: LINEAR SYSTEM

Is the system defined by the transfer function $H(x) = x^2$ linear?

Solution:

$H(k_1x_1 + k_2x_2) = (k_1x_1 + k_2x_2)^2$, which is not the same as $k_1y_1 + k_2y_2 = k_1^2x_1^2 + k_2^2x_2^2$. Hence, the system is not linear.

Note that any system that limits the output to some maximum or minimum is not linear, because such a system is not homogeneous. But in practice, outputs are almost always bounded—that is, they *saturate* at some limiting value—due to physical limitations. Therefore, most real systems are not linear. However, it is often possible to model the system behavior, around its operating point, as being approximately linear. Specifically, we can use the first-order Taylor expansion of the transfer function in the region of the operating point to approximate the behavior of the system. This technique, called **linearization**, is discussed in Section 8.2.2.

5.4 Analysis of a Linear Time-Invariant System

The class of linear time-invariant (**LTI**) systems is important both because it is relatively easy to analyze and because many common systems can be approximated by LTI systems. Here, we study three aspects of an LTI system: the effect of an LTI system on a complex exponential input, the output of an LTI system with a zero input, and the output of an LTI system for an arbitrary input. We will revisit the third topic later to demonstrate the power of using transform domain techniques in analysis.

Note that the discussion here is for continuous time systems. The analysis of discrete time systems is nearly identical, and we defer this discussion to our study of control theory in Chapter 8.

5.4.1 The Effect of an LTI System on a Complex Exponential Input

Consider an LTI system that is described by

$$y(t) = H(x(t))$$

where y and x are, in general, vector functions of time, and H is the transfer function. For simplicity of exposition, in the remainder of this discussion, we will assume that both x and y are scalar functions of time and so will no longer use bold-face to represent them. Suppose that the input is a complex exponential function of time, so that $x(t) = ke^{st}$, where s is complex and k is real. Then,

$$y(t) = H(ke^{st}) \qquad \text{(EQ 5.17)}$$

Now, consider the input $(e^{s\tau})(ke^{st})$, where τ is independent of t. Because the system is LTI and $e^{s\tau}$ is a scalar with respect to t, the corresponding output is $(e^{s\tau})y(t)$. But note that the input $(e^{s\tau})(ke^{st})$ can be rewritten as $ke^{s(t+\tau)}$, which we recognize as a time-shifted input (i.e., t is replaced by $t+\tau$). Therefore, the corresponding output, because of time invariance, must be $y(t+\tau)$. This gives us the relationship

$$y(t + \tau) = e^{s\tau}y(t) \qquad \text{(EQ 5.18)}$$

This must hold for all t, so it is true for $t = 0$, where

$$y(\tau) = e^{s\tau}y(0) \qquad \text{(EQ 5.19)}$$

Differentiating both sides with respect to τ, we get

$$\frac{dy(\tau)}{d\tau} = sy(0)e^{s\tau} = sy(\tau) \qquad \text{(EQ 5.20)}$$

where, for the last step, we invoke Equation 5.19. Using standard techniques for the solution of ordinary differential equations, it is easy to show that the unique solution to this differential equation is given by

$$y(t) = f(s)e^{st} \qquad \text{(EQ 5.21)}$$

where $f(s)$ is an arbitrary function independent of t. This is an important result! It shows that for *any* LTI system, if the input is a complex exponential, so too is the output. It is impressive that we can characterize all LTI systems so simply: After all, we have absolutely no idea what the system looks like on the inside, yet we are able to state how it will respond to a complex exponential input.

We can gain additional insight into the nature of this phenomenon by comparing Equations 5.21 and 5.17. We see that for the special input $x(t) = ke^{st}$, the effect of the LTI system is to act as a scalar multiplier, with the multiplication factor being $f(s)/k$. Therefore, $x(t) = ke^{st}$ is an **eigenfunction** of an LTI system: that is, an input function such that the effect of the system is simply to scale it. The corresponding **eigenvalue** is $f(s)/k$.

We can summarize this discussion by stating that the input $x(t) = ke^{st}$ is an eigenfunction of any LTI system for any value of s. Therefore, if we can represent an arbitrary input as the sum of such eigenfunctions, the corresponding output will be the sum of the scaled inputs. From this perspective, the transforms we are about to study can be viewed as a way to represent an arbitrary input as the sum of complex exponentials.

5.4.2 The Output of an LTI System with a Zero Input

A wide range of LTI systems can be described in the form of a **linear differential equation**, whose general form is

$$\frac{d^N y(t)}{dt^N} + a_1 \frac{d^{N-1} y(t)}{dt^{N-1}} + \ldots + a_{N-1}\frac{dy(t)}{dt} + a_N y(t)$$

$$= b_{N-M}\frac{d^M x(t)}{dt^M} + b_{N-M+1}\frac{d^{M-1} x(t)}{dt^{M-1}} + \ldots + b_{N-1}\frac{dx(t)}{dt} + b_N x(t)$$

(EQ 5.22)

In nearly all practical systems, $M > N$. Here, we study the output of this class of LTI system when its input $x(t)$ is zero, so that the right-hand side is zero. Using the operator D to denote differentiation, with D^N representing $\frac{d^N}{dt^N}$, we can rewrite the equation, for zero input, as

$$(D^N + a_1 D^{N-1} + \ldots + a_{N-1}D + a_N)y(t) = 0$$

where the polynomial in D on the left-hand side is called the **characteristic polynomial** of the system. Note that this characteristic polynomial is of degree N. Therefore, from the fundamental theorem of algebra, it can be factorized as

$$((D - \lambda_1)(D - \lambda_2)\ldots(D - \lambda_N))y(t) = 0$$

where the λ_i (in general complex quantities) are the roots of the polynomial, and some of the roots may be repeated. Assume for the moment that the roots are distinct. In this case, each solution of this equation (that is, a value of $y(t)$ for which the equation is true) is given by

$$(D - \lambda_i)y(t) = 0$$

which we can expand as

$$\frac{dy(t)}{dt} = \lambda_i y(t)$$

Comparing this with Equation 5.20, we see that the solution of this equation is given by

$$y(t) = c_i e^{\lambda_i t}$$

where c is a constant independent of t but may be a function of λ_i. Because each root of the equation generates a solution of this form, and the system is linear, by superposition the general solution (assuming distinct roots) is given by their sum:

$$y(t) = \sum_{i=1}^{N} c_i e^{\lambda_i t} \qquad \text{(EQ 5.23)}$$

We interpret this as follows: If a linear differential LTI system, irrespective of its internal organization, receives no input and if the roots of its characteristic polynomial are distinct, its output can be expressed as the sum of complex exponentials. Recall that any complex exponential has an intrinsic frequency. Each root of Equation 5.23 corresponds to a **natural frequency** of the LTI system: a frequency at which the system vibrates given zero input. The solution in Equation 5.23 is therefore also called the **natural response** of the system. If a system is subjected to an input that then ceases, such as a burst of packets entering a router's buffer, the subsequent response of the system, because there is no additional input, will be its natural response. The natural response is a combination of its natural frequencies, which are intrinsic to the system.

A system that is given an input at a frequency that coincides with one of its natural frequencies will *resonate*, amplifying the input. This important phenomenon is widely employed in practical systems. For example, the basis of radio reception is to tune the resonant frequency[5] of an electronic circuit so that it selectively amplifies signals corresponding to a desired transmitter, ignoring the rest of the radio spectrum.

EXAMPLE 5.7: REAL NATURAL RESPONSE OF AN LTI SYSTEM

Compute the natural response of the LTI system given by

$$\frac{d^2y(t)}{dt^2} + \frac{5dy(t)}{dt} + 6y(t) = 8x(t).$$

Solution:

The natural response is given by the differential equation $(D^2 + 5D + 6)y(t) = 0$, which can be factored as $((D+3)(D+2))y(t) = 0$. Thus, the natural response is given by $c_1 e^{-3t} + c_2 e^{-2t}$, where the two constants can be determined from the initial conditions $y(0)$ and $\dot{y}(0)$. The two phasors corresponding to this solution have no complex component, and therefore both correspond to a natural frequency of 0 (i.e., do not have an oscillatory behavior).

---

5. Strictly speaking, we tune the receiver to a range centered on the resonant frequency.

EXAMPLE 5.8: COMPLEX NATURAL RESPONSE OF AN LTI SYSTEM

Compute the natural response of the LTI system given by $\dfrac{d^2y(t)}{dt^2} + y(t) = 8x(t)$.

Solution:

The natural response is given by the differential equation $(D^2 + 1)y(t) = 0$, which can be factored as $((D+j)(D-j))y(t) = 0$. Thus, the natural response is given by $c_1 e^{-jt} + c_2 e^{jt}$, where the two constants can be determined from the initial conditions $y(0)$ and $\dot{y}(0)$. To get more insight into this solution, we use Euler's equation to expand this solution as

$$c_1(\cos(-t) + j\sin(-t)) + c_2(\cos(t) + j\sin(t))$$
$$= c_1(\cos(t) - j\sin(t)) + c_2(\cos(t) + j\sin(t))$$
$$= (c_1 + c_2)\cos(t) + j(c_2 - c_1)\sin(t)$$

For this solution to be real, it is necessary that $(c_1 + c_2)$ have no imaginary component and that $(c_2 - c_1)$ have no real component. This is possible only if $c_1 = a + jb$ and $c_2 = a - jb$, where a and b are real numbers. Recall that pairs of numbers of this form are called **complex conjugate pairs**. In general, for practical systems, the constants associated with the natural response come in complex conjugate pairs.

Continuing with our solution, we therefore substitute $a \pm jb$ for the constants to get the natural response as $2a\,\cos(t) + 2b\,\sin(t)$. We recognize this as an *oscillatory* response, with an angular frequency of 1 radian/second. Interestingly, this natural response does not decay: The system oscillates indefinitely at this frequency of its own accord!

We have thus far assumed that the roots of the characteristic equation are distinct. This need not necessarily be the case. For example, if the characteristic equation is $D^2 + 2D + 1$, the roots are -1 and -1, which are repeated. In the case of repeated roots, the form of the solution is slightly different. For a root λ that is repeated r times, it can be shown that the corresponding solution is given by

$$y(t) = (c_1 e^{\lambda t} + c_2 t e^{\lambda t} + \ldots + c_r t^{r-1} e^{\lambda t}) \qquad \textbf{(EQ 5.24)}$$

5.4.3 The Output of an LTI System for an Arbitrary Input

We now study how an LTI system responds to a nonzero input. We use the notation $x(t) \to y(t)$ to denote that if the input to a system is $x(t)$, its output is $y(t)$. Suppose that we are given $h(t)$, the **impulse response** of the system. This is the response to the system when the input is the Dirac delta $\delta(t)$. Using our notation, we write

$$\delta(t) \rightarrow h(t) \qquad \text{(EQ 5.25)}$$

What does the impulse response look like? By definition, because it is a delta function, the input ceases immediately after time 0. Therefore, the response of the system is its natural response (other than at time 0 itself). We have already seen how to compute this response.

Recall from Equation 5.13 that multiplying $\delta(t)$ by $x(t)$ results in scaling the impulse by the value $x(0)$; that is, $x(t)\delta(t) = x(0)\delta(t)$. Because the system is linear, the response of the system to the scaled impulse $x(0)\delta(t)$ will be the scaled output $x(0)h(t)$, so that

$$x(t)\delta(t) \rightarrow x(0)h(t). \qquad \text{(EQ 5.26)}$$

Recall from Equation 5.14 that if we time-shift the impulse, we select a different "slice" of $x(t)$. Specifically, $x(t)\delta(t-\tau) = x(\tau)\delta(t-\tau)$. Because the system is both linear and time-invariant, the response to this time-shifted scaled impulse $x(\tau)\delta(t-\tau)$ will be the scaled and time-shifted impulse response $x(\tau)h(t-\tau)$, so that

$$x(\tau)\delta(t-\tau) \rightarrow x(\tau)h(t-\tau). \qquad \text{(EQ 5.27)}$$

Finally, Equation 5.15 tells us that we can assemble $x(t)$ by integrating these small "slices" together, so that $x(t) = \int\limits_{-\infty}^{\infty} x(\tau)\delta(t-\tau)d\tau$. Clearly, this will result in the integration of the corresponding responses together as follows:

$$x(t) = \int\limits_{-\infty}^{\infty} x(\tau)\delta(t-\tau)d\tau \rightarrow \int\limits_{-\infty}^{\infty} x(\tau)h(t-\tau)d\tau = x(t) \otimes h(t) \qquad \text{(EQ 5.28)}$$

This important result tells us that if we know the impulse response $h(t)$ of an LTI system, we can compute its response to *any* input $x(t)$ by convolving the input signal with the impulse response. Therefore, it is important to be able to compute the convolution of any two functions. This, however, is a difficult and complicated operation, as we saw in Section 5.1.5. An important outcome of transform domain techniques is to convert the difficult convolution operation to a simple multiplication.

5.4.4 Stability of an LTI System

We briefly consider the stability of an LTI system. This topic is covered in more detail in Section 8.8. Intuitively, a system is stable if, when all inputs are removed, the output either eventually dies down or, at most, oscillates with a bounded amplitude. Here, we study how to characterize the stability of an LTI system.

We have seen that the behavior of an LTI system is described by its natural frequencies, which are expressed as complex exponentials. In Section 5.2.1, we saw that a complex exponential can show only one of three behaviors over time: grow without bound, decay to zero, or oscillate with a constant amplitude and frequency. Therefore, an LTI system can be characterized as stable, oscillatory (or marginally stable), or unstable.

Consider the complex exponential $ke^{(\sigma + j\omega)t}$, which represents a root: a solution to an LTI system's characteristic polynomial. If $\sigma > 0$, this exponential grows without bound. On the other hand, if $\sigma < 0$, the exponential decays to zero. Finally, if $\sigma = 0$, the exponential reduces to a pure sinusoidal oscillation.

Given this observation, we can now easily characterize the stability of an LTI system. If *all* its roots have a value of $\sigma < 0$, the system is **asymptotically stable**. If even one root has a value of $\sigma > 0$, it is **unstable**. Finally, if all the values of σ are 0, the behavior of the system depends on whether there are repeated roots. If there are no repeated roots, the system is **purely oscillatory**. On the other hand, if there are repeated roots, the system is unstable.

This observation allows us great insight into the design of stable LTI systems: We must ensure that the system is such that all the roots of the characteristic polynomial (also called the **poles** of the system) lie in the left half of the complex plane. This lies at the heart of control theory and we will consider it in more detail in Chapter 8.

5.5 Transforms

We are finally ready to embark on a study of transforms. Before plunging in, it is worth recapitulating why transforms are important. Transforms allow us to achieve three goals.

1. The convolution of two functions, which arises in the computation of the output of an LTI system, can be computed more easily by transforming the two functions, multiplying the transformed functions, and then computing the inverse transform.

2. Transforms convert a linear differential equation into a simpler algebraic equation.

3. They give insight into the natural response of a system: the natural frequencies at which it oscillates. This allows us to quickly determine whether there are special frequencies at which the system becomes unstable, whether there are special frequencies that cause the system output to become zero, and the frequencies at which most of the output magnitude can be found.

Table 5.1 Summary of Transforms Described in This Chapter

Transform	Signal Type	Transform Description
Fourier series	Continuous, periodic	Sum of sinusoids
Fourier	Continuous, periodic or aperiodic	Integral of sinusoids
Discrete-time Fourier	Discrete, periodic or aperiodic	Sum of sinusoids
Laplace	Continuous, periodic or aperiodic	Integral of complex exponentials
Z	Discrete, periodic or aperiodic	Sum of complex exponentials

We will consider five transforms: the Fourier series, the Fourier transform, the discrete Fourier transform, the Laplace transform, and the Z transform. All the transforms share some common properties. For now, we observe that a transform converts a function of time into either an infinite sum or an integral of exponentials of a complex quantity. The transforms differ in whether the complex quantity is a pure sinusoid or an exponentially modulated sinusoid and whether the input signal is continuous or discrete, as shown in Table 5.1. Although this may appear confusing at first glance, these concepts should become clear by the end of this chapter.

5.6 The Fourier Series

We first study **eternal periodic** signals, that is, signals that last for an infinitely long duration and whose values repeat identically after every period of duration T_0. All signals are, of course, time-limited, so this signal cannot be achieved in practice. However, they are still worth studying because the insight gained from the Fourier series allows us to define the Fourier transform for aperiodic signals.

Fourier showed that nearly every periodic signal $x(t)$, other than some pathological signals, can be represented at nearly every value of t as an infinite sum of sinusoids, as follows:

$$x(t) = a_0 + \sum_{k=1}^{\infty} (a_k \cos k\omega_0 t + b_k \sin k\omega_0 t) \qquad \text{(EQ 5.29)}$$

where the **fundamental angular frequency** ω_0 is given by

$$\omega_0 = \frac{2\pi}{T_0} \qquad \text{(EQ 5.30)}$$

and the constants a_0, a_k, and b_k are real numbers uniquely determined by $x(t)$. This remarkable equation shows that *any* periodic function, not just a function that looks sinusoidal, can be represented as the sum of sinusoids. It is as fundamental as the observation that any natural number can be denoted using only the ten symbols 0–9. More formally, using the appropriate vector space, we can show that the set of pairs of sinusoids in a Fourier series form an infinite orthogonal basis set, so that every vector—corresponding to an eternal periodic function—can be represented as a linear combination of this basis.

Each pair of terms in the series has a frequency that is a multiple of the fundamental frequency and is therefore called a **harmonic** of that frequency. Once the potentially infinite set of values associated with the constants a_0, a_k, and b_k is known, the function itself is completely specified and can be synthesized from them alone. The accuracy of representation quickly improves with the number of terms.[6]

Note that the constant a_0 can be viewed as a degenerate sinusoid with zero frequency. It is called the **DC** component of the signal by analogy to a direct-current electrical system that, unlike an alternating-current, or AC, system, does not have a sinusoidally oscillating voltage or current.

A graphical interpretation of a Fourier series may add some additional insight. Recall from Section 5.1.1 that a sinusoid can be thought of as a being generated by a rotating phasor. We see that each harmonic in the Fourier series corresponds to two rotating phasors that are offset by 90 degrees and with a common rotational frequency of $k\omega_0$ with magnitudes of a_k and b_k, respectively. The sinusoid generated by these phasors add up in just the right way to form $x(t)$.

So far, we have studied only the form of the Fourier series. We do, of course, need a way to determine the constants corresponding to each term in a Fourier series. It can be shown that these are given by the following equations:

$$a_0 = \frac{1}{T_0}\int_0^{T_0} x(t)dt$$

$$a_k = \frac{2}{T_0}\int_0^{T_0} x(t)\cos k\omega_0 t dt \qquad \text{(EQ 5.31)}$$

$$b_k = \frac{2}{T_0}\int_0^{T_0} x(t)\sin k\omega_0 t dt$$

where the integral is taken over any period of length T_0 (because they are all the same).

---

6. However, note that due to the **Gibb's phenomenon**, the Fourier series can have an error of about 10%, even with many tens of terms, when representing a sharply changing signal, such as a square wave.

The form of the Fourier series presented so far is called the **sinusoidal form**. These sinusoids can also be expressed as complex exponentials, as we show next. Note that the kth term of the Fourier series is

$$x_k(t) = a_k \cos k\omega_0 t + b_k \sin k\omega_0 t$$

Using Equations 5.5 and 5.6, we can rewrite this as

$$x_k(t) = \frac{a_k}{2}(e^{jk\omega_0 t} + e^{-jk\omega_0 t}) + \frac{b_k}{2j}(e^{jk\omega_0 t} - e^{-jk\omega_0 t})$$

Collecting like terms, and defining $c_0 = a_0$, $c_k = \frac{1}{2}(a_k - jb_k)$, $c_{-k} = \frac{1}{2}(a_k + jb_k)$, $k>0$,

we can rewrite this as

$$x(t) = c_0 + \sum_{k=1}^{\infty} c_k e^{jk\omega_0 t} + \sum_{k=1}^{\infty} c_{-k} e^{j(-k)\omega_0 t}$$

(EQ 5.32)

$$x(t) = \sum_{k=-\infty}^{\infty} c_k e^{jk\omega_0 t}$$

This compact notation shows that we can express $x(t)$ as an infinite sum of complex exponentials. Specifically, it can be viewed as a sum of an infinite number of phasors, each with a real magnitude c_k and a rotational frequency of $k\omega_0$. It can be shown that the constants c_k can be found, if we are given $x(t)$, by the relation

$$c_k = \frac{1}{T_0} \int_0^{T_0} x(t) e^{-jk\omega_0 t} dt$$

(EQ 5.33)

EXAMPLE 5.9: FOURIER SERIES

Find the Fourier series corresponding to the series of rectangular pulses shown in Figure 5.9.

Solution:

The kth coefficient of the Fourier series corresponding to this function is given by

$$c_k = \frac{1}{T_0} \int_0^{T_0} x(t) e^{-jk\omega_0 t} dt \ .$$

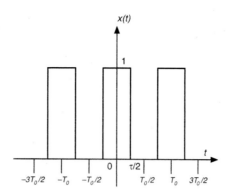

Figure 5.9 An infinite series of rectangular pulses

Instead of choosing the limits from 0 to T_0, we will choose the limits from $-T_0/2$ to $T_0/2$ because it is symmetric about 0. Note that in this range, the function is 1 in the range $[-\tau/2, \tau/2]$ and 0 elsewhere. Therefore, the integral reduces to

$$c_k = \frac{1}{T_0}\int_{-\frac{\tau}{2}}^{\frac{\tau}{2}} e^{-jk\omega_0 t}\,dt = -\frac{1}{jk\omega_0 T_0}e^{-jk\omega_0 t}\Big|_{-\frac{\tau}{2}}^{\tau/2} = \frac{1}{jk\omega_0 T_0}\left(e^{jk\omega_0 \frac{\tau}{2}} - e^{-jk\omega_0 \frac{\tau}{2}}\right) \quad \textbf{(EQ 5.34)}$$

Using Equation 5.6 and multiplying the numerator and denominator by $\tau/2$, we can rewrite this as

$$c_k = \frac{\tau}{T_0}\left(\frac{\sin\left(\dfrac{k\omega_0\tau}{2}\right)}{\dfrac{k\omega_0\tau}{2}}\right) \quad \textbf{(EQ 5.35)}$$

Note that the coefficients c_k are real functions of τ (not t), which is a parameter of the input signal. For a given input signal, we can treat τ as a constant. Observing that $T_0 = \dfrac{2\pi}{\omega_0}$, the coefficients can be obtained as the values taken by a continuous function of ω, defined as

$$X(\omega) = \frac{\tau\omega_0}{2\pi}\frac{\sin\left(\dfrac{\omega\tau}{2}\right)}{\dfrac{\omega\tau}{2}} \quad \textbf{(EQ 5.36)}$$

for the values $\omega = k\omega_0$. That is, $c_k = X(k\omega_0)$. Thus, c_k is a *discrete* function of ω defined at the discrete frequency values $\omega = k\omega_0$, as shown in Figure 5.10.

The function $sin(x)/x$ arises frequently in the study of transforms and is called the **sinc** function. It is a sine wave whose value at 0 is 1 and elsewhere is the sine function linearly modulated by distance from the Y-axis. This function forms the envelope of the Fourier coefficients, as shown in Figure 5.10. Note that the function is zero (i.e., has zero-crossings) when a sine function is zero, that is, when $\omega\tau/2 = m\pi$, $m \neq 0$, or $\omega = 2m\pi/\tau$, $m \neq 0$.

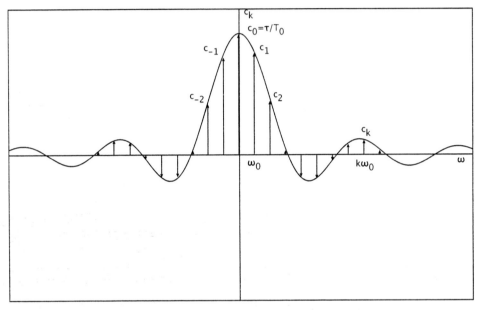

Figure 5.10 The sinc function as a function of ω

5.7 The Fourier Transform and Its Properties

A Fourier series can represent any *eternal* periodic function as an infinite sum of real sinusoids. However, it cannot be used to represent aperiodic functions. These are represented, instead, using a Fourier transform.

To motivate the Fourier transform, consider the behavior of the pulse series of Example 5.9 when increasing the interpulse spacing T_0 while keeping the pulse width τ constant. Recall that for this signal, the kth Fourier series coefficient c_k is given by

$$X(\omega) = \frac{\tau}{T_0} \frac{\sin\left(\frac{\omega\tau}{2}\right)}{\frac{\omega\tau}{2}} \text{ for } \omega = k\omega_0 \text{ where } \omega_0 = \frac{2\pi}{T_0}.$$

As T_0 increases, ω_0 decreases, which brings the coefficients under the sinc curve, which are spaced ω_0 apart, closer together (see Figure 5.10). In the limit, as $T_0 \to \infty$, the periodic pulse train becomes a single pulse, and the coefficients are spaced infinitely closely together, converging with the sinc curve. Thus, in the limit, the sinc curve corresponds to the Fourier series representing a single pulse and is called its **Fourier transform**.

Arguing along the same lines, we can analyse the limiting behavior of the generic kth Fourier series coefficient

$$c_k = \frac{\omega_0}{2\pi} \int_0^{\frac{2\pi}{\omega_0}} x(t)e^{-jk\omega_0 t}dt$$

as $\omega_0 \to 0$ to define the Fourier transform of a signal $x(t)$ as

$$X(j\omega) = \int_{-\infty}^{\infty} x(t)e^{-j\omega t}dt \qquad \text{(EQ 5.37)}$$

This transforms a signal (a function of time) to a function of the complex quantity $j\omega$. The value of the transform for a specific value of $\omega = w$ can be viewed as the amount of signal energy at the frequency w. The magnitude at $\omega = 0$, for example, is the DC component of the signal. We represent the fact that $X(j\omega)$ is the transform of the signal $x(t)$ as

$$x(t) \overset{\mathcal{F}}{\leftrightarrow} X(j\omega) \qquad \text{(EQ 5.38)}$$

The double-headed arrow indicates that $x(t)$ can be recovered from its transform, $X(jw)$, using the *inverse Fourier transform* discussed later.

EXAMPLE 5.10: FOURIER TRANSFORM

Compute the Fourier transform of a single rectangular pulse of height 1 and width τ centered on the origin (Figure 5.11). This signal is also denoted $rect(t/\tau)$.

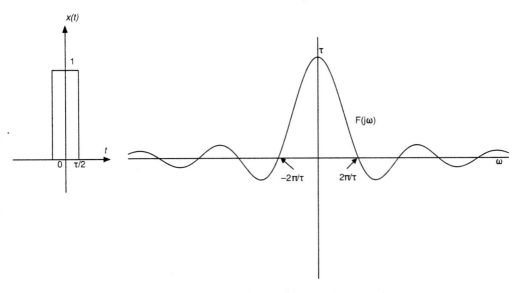

Figure 5.11 A single pulse and its Fourier transform

Solution:

The Fourier transform of this signal $x(t)$ is given by

$$X(j\omega) = \int_{-\infty}^{\infty} x(t)e^{-j\omega t}dt.$$

The function is zero outside the interval $[-\tau/2, \tau/2]$ and 1 inside this interval. Therefore, the function reduces to

$$X(j\omega) = \int_{\frac{-\tau}{2}}^{\frac{\tau}{2}} e^{-j\omega t}dt = \frac{-e^{-j\omega t}}{jw}\bigg|_{\frac{-\tau}{2}}^{\tau/2} = \frac{e^{j\omega\frac{\tau}{2}} - e^{-j\omega\frac{\tau}{2}}}{j\omega}$$

Multiplying the numerator and denominator by $\frac{\tau}{2}$ as before, and using Euler's formula, we can rewrite this as

$$X(j\omega) = \tau\frac{\sin\left(\frac{\omega\tau}{2}\right)}{\frac{\omega\tau}{2}} = \tau\mathrm{sinc}\left(\frac{\omega\tau}{2}\right) \qquad \text{(EQ 5.39)}$$

Therefore, the Fourier transform of $rect\left(\frac{t}{\tau}\right)$ is a sinc function that has a peak of height τ at the origin and zero crossings when $\omega\frac{\tau}{2} = k\pi$, $k \neq 0$: that is, when $\omega = \frac{2k\pi}{\tau}$, as shown in Figure 5.11. Note that the signal has no energy at frequencies corresponding to its zero crossings. This allows us to introduce a narrow-frequency signal at these frequencies and not interfere with the signal. This is the basis of **orthogonal frequency division multiplexing (OFDM)**, which is widely used in such technologies as 4G and WiFi.

The Fourier transform of a signal may not always exist. The existence of a transform is guaranteed by the **Dirichlet conditions**.

- The signal $x(t)$ is **absolutely integrable**, that is, $\int_{-\infty}^{\infty} |x(t)| dt < \infty$.
- The signal $x(t)$ has a finite number of maxima and minima and a finite number of discontinuities in any finite interval.

These conditions are satisfied by most signals that arise in practical situations. Note that signals with "jumps," such as rectangular pulses, do have Fourier transforms, as we have already seen. Indeed, we can even compute the Fourier transform of a highly discontinuous function, such as an impulse, as in the next example.

EXAMPLE 5.11: FOURIER TRANSFORM OF AN IMPULSE

Compute the Fourier transform of an impulse.

Solution:

The transform is given by

$$X(j\omega) = \int_{-\infty}^{\infty} \delta(t)e^{-j\omega t}dt.$$

From Equation 5.15, setting $\tau = 0$, we see that this integral is simply $X(\tau) = e^{-j\omega\tau}|_0 = 1$. Thus, the Fourier transform of an impulse is the constant 1, or $\delta(t) \overset{\mathcal{F}}{\leftrightarrow} 1$.

Given a transformed signal, we can recover it by using the inverse Fourier transform, given by

$$x(t) = \frac{1}{2\pi} \int\limits_{-\infty}^{\infty} X(j\omega)e^{j\omega t}d\omega \qquad\qquad \textbf{(EQ 5.40)}$$

Compare this with Equation 5.32 to see how the summation in the Fourier series is transformed into its limiting integral.

EXAMPLE 5.12: INVERSE FOURIER TRANSFORM

What is the signal corresponding to the transformed signal $\delta(\omega - \omega_0)$?

Solution:

The signal is given by

$$x(t) = \frac{1}{2\pi} \int\limits_{-\infty}^{\infty} \delta(\omega - \omega_0)e^{j\omega t}d\omega \,.$$

But, from Equation 5.15, the integral reduces to $e^{j\omega_0 t}$. Therefore, we have

$$\frac{e^{j\omega_0 t}}{2\pi} \overset{\mathscr{J}}{\leftrightarrow} \delta(\omega - \omega_0), \text{ or } e^{j\omega_0 t} \overset{\mathscr{J}}{\leftrightarrow} 2\pi\delta(\omega - \omega_0).$$

We now turn to some useful properties of the Fourier transform. Proofs of these properties can be derived from first principles, using the definition of the transform, and can be found in standard textbooks on the subject. These properties, along with the table of Fourier transforms in (Table 5.2) allow us to compute the transforms of most functions that arise in practice without having to compute the integral in Equation 5.37 explicitly.

1. **Linearity:** If $x_1(t) \overset{\mathscr{J}}{\leftrightarrow} X_1(j\omega)$ and $x_2(t) \overset{\mathscr{J}}{\leftrightarrow} X_2(j\omega)$, then for any constants a and b, $ax_1(t) + bx_2(t) \overset{\mathscr{J}}{\leftrightarrow} aX_1(j\omega) + bX_2(j\omega)$. Note that a and b can be complex numbers.

EXAMPLE 5.13: LINEARITY OF THE FOURIER TRANSFORM

Compute the Fourier transform of the eternal sinusoid $\cos(\omega_0 t)$.

Solution:

We use Equation 5.5 to rewrite $\cos(\omega_0 t) = \frac{1}{2}(e^{j\omega_0 t} + e^{-j\omega_0 t})$. From the previous

example and the linearity property, we get $\cos(\omega_0 t) \overset{\mathcal{F}}{\leftrightarrow} \pi(\delta(\omega + \omega_0) + \delta(\omega - \omega_0))$.

Thus, a sinusoid in the time domain corresponds to two impulses in the frequency domain. These are at the two frequencies ω_0 and $-\omega_0$ and represent counterrotating phasors with the same frequency. The imaginary components of these phasors are always equal and opposite, and their sum is therefore a real sinusoid.

---

2. **Time-shifting:** If $x(t) \overset{\mathcal{F}}{\leftrightarrow} X(j\omega)$, then $x_1(t - t_0) \overset{\mathcal{F}}{\leftrightarrow} e^{-j\omega t_0}X_1(j\omega)$. That is, shifting the signal forward in time by t_0 units results in multiplying the transform by $e^{-j\omega t_0}$.

EXAMPLE 5.14: FOURIER TRANSFORM OF A TIME-SHIFTED IMPULSE

Compute the Fourier transform of an impulse that occurs at time t_0.

Solution:

Since $\delta(t) \overset{\mathcal{F}}{\leftrightarrow} 1$, we immediately get $\delta(t - t_0) \overset{\mathcal{F}}{\leftrightarrow} e^{-j\omega t_0}$.

---

3. **Time-scaling:** If $x(t) \overset{\mathcal{F}}{\leftrightarrow} X(j\omega)$ then $x(at) \overset{\mathcal{F}}{\leftrightarrow} \frac{1}{|a|}X\left(\frac{j\omega}{a}\right)$, where a is an arbitrary constant. Intuitively, $x(at)$ is a times "faster" than $x(t)$. This results in the transform's having a magnitude that is a times smaller and a frequency scale that is a times "slower." For instance, if $a = 5$, what happens at time 10 in the unscaled function happens at time 2 in the scaled function. In contrast, a feature present at 100 radians/second in the unscaled transform is present at 500 radians/second in the scaled transform.

EXAMPLE 5.15: FOURIER TRANSFORM OF A SCALED FUNCTION

Compute the Fourier transform of a rectangular pulse as in Figure 5.11 but with a pulse width of 2τ.

Solution:

The transform of a pulse of width τ is $\tau\mathrm{sinc}\left(\frac{\omega\tau}{2}\right)$. When the pulse is twice as wide, the pulse starts at time $-\tau$ instead of at time $-\frac{\tau}{2}$, expanding the time scale by a factor of 2, so that $a = 1/2$. The transform of the longer pulse is $2\tau\mathrm{sinc}(\omega\tau)$. This has zero crossings when $\omega\tau = k\pi$, that is, when $\omega = \frac{k\pi}{\tau}$, which is twice as fast as before.

---

4. **Duality:** If $x(t) \overset{\mathcal{F}}{\leftrightarrow} X(j\omega)$, then $X(t) \overset{\mathcal{F}}{\leftrightarrow} 2\pi x(-j\omega)$ and $X(jt) \overset{\mathcal{F}}{\leftrightarrow} 2\pi x(-\omega)$. This property allows us to use knowledge of a transform to compute new transforms.

EXAMPLE 5.16: DUALITY

What is the Fourier transform of the constant function $1(t)$?

Solution:

Since $\delta(t) \overset{\mathcal{F}}{\leftrightarrow} 1$, $1(t) \overset{\mathcal{F}}{\leftrightarrow} 2\pi\delta(-j\omega)$. But $\delta(.)$ is symmetric about the origin, so, we have $1(t) \overset{\mathcal{F}}{\leftrightarrow} 2\pi\delta(j\omega)$, which is an impulse centered on the origin, or at zero frequency. This means that all the energy of the constant function is at a frequency of 0, which is what one would expect.

---

5. **Differentiation:** If $x(t) \overset{\mathcal{F}}{\leftrightarrow} X(j\omega)$, then $\dfrac{dx^n(t)}{dt^n} \overset{\mathcal{F}}{\leftrightarrow} (j\omega)^n X(j\omega)$.

EXAMPLE 5.17: FOURIER TRANSFORM OF A DERIVATIVE

Compute the Fourier transform of the signal $j\omega_0 e^{j\omega_0 t}$.

Solution:

Since $j\omega_0 e^{j\omega_0 t} = \dfrac{de^{j\omega_0 t}}{dt}$, then $j\omega_0 e^{j\omega_0 t} \overset{\mathcal{F}}{\leftrightarrow} 2\pi(j\omega)\delta(\omega - \omega_0)$.

Table 5.2 presents some standard transform pairs. These are derived using both first principles and the properties of the Fourier transform discussed earlier.

Table 5.2 Some Standard Fourier Transforms

No.	$x(t)$	$X(j\omega)$	Notes
1	$\delta(t)$	1	
2	1	$2\pi\delta(\omega)$	
3	$e^{j\omega_0 t}$	$2\pi\delta(\omega - \omega_0)$	
4	$\cos\omega_0 t$	$\pi(\delta(\omega + \omega_0) + \delta(\omega - \omega_0))$	The Fourier transform of a cosine results in impulses in both the positive and negative frequency axes.
5	$\sin\omega_0 t$	$j\pi(\delta(\omega - \omega_0) - \delta(\omega + \omega_0))$	See preceding note.
6	$u(t)$	$\pi\delta(\omega) + \dfrac{1}{j\omega}$	
7	$e^{-at}u(t)$	$\dfrac{1}{a + j\omega}$	$a > 0$, and this is an exponential defined only for positive time values.
8	$\cos(\omega_0 t)u(t)$	$\dfrac{\pi}{2}(\delta(\omega + \omega_0) + \delta(\omega - \omega_0)) + \dfrac{j\omega}{\omega_0^2 - \omega^2}$	This is a sinusoid defined only for positive time values.
9	$\sin(\omega_0 t)u(t)$	$\dfrac{\pi}{2j}(\delta(\omega - \omega_0) - \delta(\omega + \omega_0)) + \dfrac{\omega_0}{\omega_0^2 - \omega^2}$	This is a sinusoid defined only for positive time values.
10	$rect\left(\dfrac{t}{\tau}\right)$	$\tau\,\text{sinc}\left(\dfrac{\omega\tau}{2}\right)$	This is a pulse symmetric about the origin with width τ.

6. **Convolution property:** If

$$x_1(t) \overset{\mathcal{J}}{\leftrightarrow} X_1(j\omega), \ x_2(t) \overset{\mathcal{J}}{\leftrightarrow} X_2(j\omega), \ y(t) \overset{\mathcal{J}}{\leftrightarrow} Y(j\omega), \text{ and } y(t) = x_1(t) \otimes x_2(t),$$

then $Y(jw) = X_1(jw)X_2(jw)$. That is, convolution in the time domain corresponds to multiplication in the transform domain. For an LTI system with an impulse response of $h(t)$, we know from Equation 5.28 that an input of $x(t)$ leads to an output of $y(t) = x(t) \otimes h(t)$. Therefore, $Y(jw) = X(jw)H(jw)$. We can recover $y(t)$ from this by taking the inverse transform.

The symmetric convolution property also holds: Multiplication in the time domain corresponds to convolution in the transform domain. That is, if

$$x_1(t) \overset{\mathcal{J}}{\leftrightarrow} X_1(j\omega), \ x_2(t) \overset{\mathcal{J}}{\leftrightarrow} X_2(j\omega), \ y(t) \overset{\mathcal{J}}{\leftrightarrow} Y(j\omega), \text{ and } y(t) = x_1(t)x_2(t),$$

then $Y(jw) = \dfrac{1}{2\pi} X_1(jw) \otimes X_2(jw)$.

EXAMPLE 5.18: USING CONVOLUTION TO SOLVE A SYSTEM

Consider a system such that the Fourier transform $H(j\omega)$ of its transfer function $h(t)$ is $\dfrac{1}{j\omega + 2}$. What is its response to the input $e^{-t}u(t)$?

Solution:

Because $x(t) = e^{-t}u(t)$, from row 7 of Table 5.2, $X(j\omega) = \dfrac{1}{1 + j\omega}$. Therefore,

$Y(j\omega) = \dfrac{1}{(1 + j\omega)(2 + j\omega)}$. Using the method of partial fractions (i.e., writing

the expression as $\dfrac{a}{1 + j\omega} + \dfrac{b}{2 + j\omega}$ and solving for a and b),[7] we find that

$Y(j\omega) = \dfrac{1}{1 + j\omega} - \dfrac{1}{2 + j\omega}$. To find the inverse transform, recall that the Fourier

transform is linear, so we need to find only the inverse transform of each term in isolation. From row 7 of Table 5.2 again, we get $y(t) = (e^{-t} - e^{-2t})u(t)$.

---

7. More generally, for $F(x) = \dfrac{P(x)}{(x - \lambda_1)(x - \lambda_2)...(x - \lambda_r)}$, we can write

$F(x) = \dfrac{k_1}{(x - \lambda_1)} + ... + \dfrac{k_r}{(x - \lambda_r)}$, where $k_r = [(x - \lambda_r)F(x)]\big|_{x = \lambda_r}$. Also see Section 8.11.

It is clear that the Fourier transform greatly simplifies the analysis of LTI systems: Instead of having to deal with the complex convolution operator, we need merely to deal with multiplying two transforms and then taking the inverse. In general, we can always find the inverse of the product from first principles by using Equation 5.40. However, because the Fourier transform may not always exist, system analysis is typically performed using the Laplace transform.

This concludes our discussion of the Fourier transform. We now turn our attention to the more general Laplace transform, which shares most of the properties of the Fourier transform and can also be applied to a wider range of functions.

5.8 The Laplace Transform

The Fourier transform gives us insight into the frequencies in which a signal's energy is concentrated and simplifies the computation of convolutions. Its main problem is that it is not guaranteed for functions that do not satisfy the Dirichlet conditions. We now study the Laplace transform, which shares most of the properties of the Fourier transform and, additionally, is defined for a wider class of functions.

Recall that the Fourier transform is defined by $X(j\omega) = \int\limits_{-\infty}^{\infty} x(t)e^{-j\omega t}dt$. The Laplace transform is defined by

$$X(s) = \int\limits_{-\infty}^{\infty} x(t)e^{-st}dt \qquad \text{(EQ 5.41)}$$

where $s = \sigma + j\omega$. Intuitively, instead of taking the limiting sum of a series of pure sinusoids, as with the Fourier transform, the Laplace transform takes the limiting sum of a series of complex exponentials. Alternatively, writing e^{-st} as $e^{-\sigma t}e^{-j\omega t}$, we can write

$$X(s) = \int\limits_{-\infty}^{\infty} (x(t)e^{-\sigma t})e^{-j\omega t}dt \qquad \text{(EQ 5.42)}$$

so that the Laplace transform is identical to the Fourier transform of the function $(x(t)e^{-\sigma t})$. Intuitively, given a signal $x(t)$ that does not satisfy the Dirichlet conditions, we multiply it by an exponentially decreasing function $e^{-\sigma t}$, so that the product becomes absolutely integral. Note that, in this process, we must be careful to select a value of σ large enough to ensure convergence. Therefore, unlike the Fourier transform, in specifying the Laplace transform, it is essential to give the **region of convergence**, that is, the values of σ for which the Laplace transform is defined.

As with the Fourier transform, we denote the relationship between a signal $x(t)$ and its transform $X(s)$ by using the notation

$$x(t) \overset{\mathcal{L}}{\leftrightarrow} X(s) \tag{EQ 5.43}$$

Note that the Laplace transform of a signal is, in general, a *complex* function, with both real and imaginary parts, hence its representation as $X(s)$.

The inverse Laplace transform is given by

$$x(t) = \frac{1}{2\pi j} \int\limits_{(\sigma - j\infty)}^{(\sigma + j\infty)} X(s)e^{st}ds \tag{EQ 5.44}$$

The limits of the integral denote integrating from $-\infty$ to ∞ along the imaginary axis for a value of σ chosen in the transform's region of convergence. In practice, the inverse operation is rarely performed from first principles, because the inverse can be found from a table of standard transforms and the (nice!) properties of the Laplace transform.

5.8.1 Poles, Zeroes, and the Region of Convergence

We now examine in greater depth the somewhat mysterious notion of a region of convergence by referring to a concrete example. Observe that the unit step signal $u(t)$ is not absolutely integrable because the area under this signal is infinite. Therefore, it does not satisfy the Dirichlet conditions, and a Fourier transform is not guaranteed. Nevertheless, it can be shown that its Fourier transform is $\pi\delta(\omega) + \frac{1}{j\omega}$. In the next example, we will compute its Laplace transform.

EXAMPLE 5.19: LAPLACE TRANSFORM OF A UNIT STEP

Compute the Laplace transform of the unit step signal.

Solution:

By definition,

$$X(s) = \int\limits_{-\infty}^{\infty} u(t)e^{-st}dt = \int\limits_{0}^{\infty} e^{-st}dt = \frac{e^{-st}}{-s}\bigg|_{0}^{\infty}.$$

Now, $e^{-s\infty} = 0$ if $Re(s) > 0$. Assuming that this is the case, we can evaluate the integral as

$$\frac{1}{s} \qquad Re(s) > 0.$$

Thus,

$$u(t) \overset{\mathcal{L}}{\leftrightarrow} \frac{1}{s} \qquad Re(s) > 0.$$

The region of convergence of this transform is the set of all values of s where the condition $Re(s) > 0$ holds. Recall that s is complex, so this is the right-half plane of the complex plane.

The next example reinforces this notion.

EXAMPLE 5.20: LAPLACE TRANSFORM OF A REAL EXPONENTIAL

Compute the Laplace transform of the signal $x(t) = u(t)e^{at}$, where a is a real constant.

Solution:

By definition,

$$X(s) = \int_{-\infty}^{\infty} u(t)e^{at}e^{-st}dt = \int_{0}^{\infty} e^{-(s-a)t}dt = \frac{e^{-(s-a)t}}{-(s-a)}\Big|_{0}^{\infty}.$$

As before, $e^{-(s-a)\infty}$ is 0 if $Re(s-a) > 0$, that is, $Re(s) > a$. If this condition holds, the integral evaluates to $\frac{1}{(s-a)}$. Therefore,

$$u(t)e^{-at} \overset{\mathcal{L}}{\leftrightarrow} \frac{1}{(s-a)} \qquad Re(s) > a.$$

In this case, the region of convergence is the complex half-plane defined by $Re(s) > a$.

What if $s = a$? In this case, the denominator becomes zero, and the transform's value is infinite. This is called a **pole** of the system. (The pole in the previous example was at 0.)

It is easy to show that the transform pair is valid even for a complex a, where $a = \sigma + j\omega$, as long as $Re(s) > \sigma$.

The values of s for which the transform vanishes are called the **zeroes** of the transform. This is illustrated by the next example.

EXAMPLE 5.21: LAPLACE TRANSFORM OF A SINUSOID

Compute the Laplace transform of the sinusoid $u(t)\cos\omega_1 t$.

Solution:

We use Euler's formula to rewrite the signal as $u(t)\left(\dfrac{e^{j\omega_1 t} + e^{-j\omega_1 t}}{2}\right)$. By definition,

$$X(s) = \int_{-\infty}^{\infty} u(t)\left(\frac{e^{j\omega_1 t} + e^{-j\omega_1 t}}{2}\right) e^{-st}dt$$

$$= \frac{\left(\displaystyle\int_{0}^{\infty} e^{j\omega_1 t} e^{-st}dt + \int_{0}^{\infty} e^{-j\omega_1 t} e^{-st}dt\right)}{2}$$

$$= \frac{1}{2}\left(\frac{1}{s - j\omega_1} + \frac{1}{s + j\omega_1}\right),$$

where, in the last step, we used the result from the previous example, and we are assuming that $Re(s) > 0$. This reduces to $\dfrac{s}{s^2 + \omega_1^2}$, with the region of convergence as $Re(s) > 0$. Note that the transform becomes infinite for $s = \pm j\omega_1$ —the poles of the transform—and is zero for $s = 0$, which is the zero of the transform.

It is important to keep track of the region of convergence of the transform. Two time-domain functions that are completely different may have an identical transform and may differ only in their region of convergence. Therefore, the Laplace transform is unique only if the region is also specified.

If the region of convergence of the Laplace transform of a signal includes the imaginary axis, the Fourier transform of the signal is defined and can be obtained by setting $s = j\omega$. Otherwise, the Laplace transform of the signal exists but not its Fourier transform.

5.8.2 Properties of the Laplace Transform

The Fourier transform is a special case of the Laplace transform. Therefore, almost all the properties of the Fourier transform—namely, linearity, time-shifting, time-scaling, differentiation, and the convolution property—also hold for the Laplace transform, though in a slightly different form. We summarize the corresponding properties in Table 5.3.

Table 5.3 Properties of the Laplace Transform

Property	Precondition	Postcondition	Notes
Linearity	$x_1(t) \overset{L}{\leftrightarrow} X_1(s) \quad \alpha_1 < Re(s) < \beta_1$ $x_2(t) \overset{L}{\leftrightarrow} X_2(s) \quad \alpha_2 < Re(s) < \beta_2$	$a x_1(t) + b x_2(t) \overset{L}{\leftrightarrow} a X_1(s) + b X_2(s)$ $max(\alpha_1, \alpha_2) < Re(s) < min(\beta_1, \beta_2)$	Both a and b are arbitrary constants and can be complex.
Time scaling	$x(t) \overset{L}{\leftrightarrow} X(s) \quad \alpha < Re(s) < \beta$	$x(at) \overset{L}{\leftrightarrow} \dfrac{1}{|a|} X\left(\dfrac{s}{a}\right)$ $a\alpha < Re(s) < a\beta$	A compression in the time scale expands the frequency scale.
Frequency scaling	$x(t) \overset{L}{\leftrightarrow} X(s) \quad \alpha < Re(s) < \beta$	$\dfrac{1}{|a|} x\left(\dfrac{t}{a}\right) \overset{L}{\leftrightarrow} X(as)$ $\dfrac{\alpha}{a} < Re(s) < \dfrac{\beta}{a}$	A compression in the frequency scale expands the time scale.
Time-shifting	$x(t) \overset{L}{\leftrightarrow} X(s) \quad \alpha < Re(s) < \beta$	$x(t - t_0) \overset{L}{\leftrightarrow} e^{-s t_0} X(s)$ $\alpha < Re(s) < \beta$	Delaying by a time t_0 multiplies the transform by $e^{-s t_0}$.
Frequency-shifting	$x(t) \overset{L}{\leftrightarrow} X(s) \quad \alpha < Re(s) < \beta$	$e^{at} x(t) \overset{L}{\leftrightarrow} X(s - a)$ $\alpha - Re(a) < Re(s) < \beta - Re(a)$	Note the change in the region of convergence due to frequency shifting.
Differentiation	$x(t) \overset{L}{\leftrightarrow} X(s) \quad \alpha < Re(s) < \beta$	$\dfrac{d^n x(t)}{d t^n} \overset{L}{\leftrightarrow} s^n X(s)$ $\alpha < Re(s) < \beta$	Differentiation in the time domain corresponds to multiplication by a factor of s in the transform domain.

continues

Table 5.3 Properties of the Laplace Transform (*Continued*)

Property	Precondition	Postcondition	Notes
Integration	$x(t) \overset{\mathcal{L}}{\leftrightarrow} X(s)$ $\alpha < Re(s) < \beta$	$\int_{-\infty}^{t} x(r)dr \overset{\mathcal{L}}{\leftrightarrow} \dfrac{X(s)}{s}$ $max(\alpha, 0) < Re(s) < \beta$	Integration in the time domain corresponds to division by a factor of s in the transform domain. Note that the region of convergence also changes.
Convolution in time domain	$x_1(t) \overset{\mathcal{L}}{\leftrightarrow} X_1(s)$ $\alpha_1 < Re(s) < \beta_1$ $x_2(t) \overset{\mathcal{L}}{\leftrightarrow} X_2(s)$ $\alpha_2 < Re(s) < \beta_2$ $y(t) = x_1(t) \otimes x_2(t)$	$y(t) \overset{\mathcal{L}}{\leftrightarrow} Y(s)$ $Y(s) = X_1(s)X(s)_2$ $max(\alpha_1, \alpha_2) < Re(s) < min(\beta_1, \beta_2)$	The value $y(t)$ is a convolution of two functions $x_1(t)$ and $x_2(t)$. The product of their transforms $X_1(s)$ and $X_2(s)$ determine $Y(s)$, the transform of $y(t)$, and its region of convergence.
Multiplication in time domain	$x_1(t) \overset{\mathcal{L}}{\leftrightarrow} X_1(s)$ $\alpha_1 < Re(s) < \beta_1$ $x_2(t) \overset{\mathcal{L}}{\leftrightarrow} X_2(s)$ $\alpha_2 < Re(s) < \beta_2$ $y(t) = x_1(t)x_2(t)$	$y(t) \overset{\mathcal{L}}{\leftrightarrow} Y(s)$ $Y(s) = \dfrac{1}{2\pi j} X_1(s) \otimes X_2(s)$ $\alpha_1 + \alpha_2 < Re(s) < \beta_1 + \beta_2$	The value $y(t)$ is a product of two functions $x_1(t)$ and $x_2(t)$. The convolution of their transforms $X_1(s)$ and $X_2(s)$ determines $Y(s)$, the transform of $y(t)$, and its region of convergence.
Final value theorem	$X(s)$	$\lim_{t \to \infty} x(t) = \lim_{s \to 0} sX(s)$	The limiting value of $x(t)$ in the time domain as $t \to \infty$ is given by finding the limit of $sX(s)$ as $s \to 0$ in the transform domain.

Table 5.4 Some Standard Laplace Transforms

No.	Signal	$x(t)$	$X(s)$	Region of Convergence
1	Delta or unit impulse	$\delta(t)$	1	All s
2	Unit step	$u(t)$	$1/s$	$Re(s) > 0$
3	Delayed delta	$\delta(t - t_0)$	$e^{-t_0 s}$	All s
4	Ramp	$tu(t)$	$\dfrac{1}{s^2}$	$Re(s) > 0$
5	Exponential decay	$e^{\alpha t} u(t)$	$\dfrac{1}{s - \alpha}$	$Re(s) > \alpha$
6	Nth power decay	$\dfrac{t^n}{n!} e^{\alpha t} u(t)$	$\dfrac{1}{(s - \alpha)^{n+1}}$	$Re(s) > \alpha$
7	Sine	$\sin(\omega t) u(t)$	$\dfrac{\omega}{s^2 + \omega^2}$	$Re(s) > 0$
8	Cosine	$\cos(\omega t) u(t)$	$\dfrac{s}{s^2 + \omega^2}$	$Re(s) > 0$
9	Exponentially modulated sine	$e^{\alpha t} \sin(\omega t) u(t)$	$\dfrac{\omega}{(s - \alpha)^2 + \omega^2}$	$Re(s) > \alpha$
10	Exponentially modulated cosine	$e^{\alpha t} \cos(\omega t) u(t)$	$\dfrac{s - \alpha}{(s - \alpha)^2 + \omega^2}$	$Re(s) > \alpha$

These properties, along with the table of common transforms (Table 5.4) allow us to derive the transform of many common signals without having to derive them from first principles. Note that these transforms are defined for functions that exist only for $t > 0$, so that the Laplace integral has limits from 0 to ∞. This is also called the **unilateral** Laplace transform. In a practical system, a *causal* signal is 0 for $t < 0$, so the unilateral transform suffices for all practical systems.

EXAMPLE 5.22: USING THE LAPLACE TRANSFORM TO SOLVE A SYSTEM

Consider a system such that the Laplace transform $H(s)$ of its transfer function $h(t)$ is $\dfrac{1}{s + 2}$. What is its response to the input $e^{-t} u(t)$?

Solution:

Since $x(t) = e^{-t}u(t)$, from row 5 of Table 5.4, $X(s) = \dfrac{1}{s+1}$. Therefore,

$Y(s) = \dfrac{1}{(1+s)(2+s)}$. Using the method of partial fractions, i.e., writing the

expression as $\dfrac{a}{1+s} + \dfrac{b}{2+s}$ and solving for a and b—also see Section 8.11—we

find that $Y(s) = \dfrac{1}{1+s} - \dfrac{1}{2+s}$. To find the inverse transform, recall that the

Laplace transform is linear, so we need only find the inverse transform of each term in isolation. From row 5 of Table 5.4 again, we get $y(t) = (e^{-t} - e^{-2t})u(t)$.

This analysis assumes that the system is at rest at time zero. If this is not the case, the actual response would be the sum of the natural response, which is the way the system behaves if there is no external input, and the forced response, which is the way the system behaves assuming that its initial state, is at rest. The details of this analysis are beyond the scope of this text.

This concludes our study of the Laplace transform. We now focus on two transforms that deal with *discrete* signals rather then continuous signals, as we have done so far.

5.9 The Discrete Fourier Transform and Fast Fourier Transform

Most signals in computing systems take on values only at discrete moments in time. Specifically, the signal is defined only at times nT, where n is an integer, and T, a real, is the inverse of the clock frequency. We denote such a signal as $x[nT]$ in contrast to a continuous signal, which is denoted $x(t)$.

5.9.1 The Impulse Train

We define an impulse train $s_T(t)$ with parameter T to be a signal that consists of an infinite series of delta signals with time-separation T. An impulse train is denoted as

$$s_T = \sum_{n=-\infty}^{\infty} \delta(t - nT) \qquad \text{(EQ 5.45)}$$

What is the Fourier transform of an impulse train? By the linearity property of the Fourier transform, the transform of the infinite sum in Equation 5.45 is the sum of the individual transforms. From Example 5.12, $\delta(t - nT) \overset{\mathcal{J}}{\leftrightarrow} e^{-j\omega nT}$. Therefore, the Fourier transform of an impulse train is given by

$$s_T \overset{\mathcal{J}}{\leftrightarrow} \sum_{n = -\infty}^{\infty} e^{-j\omega nT}$$

(EQ 5.46)

5.9.2 The Discrete-Time Fourier Transform

We now consider the Fourier transform of the discrete signal $x[nT]$. We start by studying the product of an impulse train with a *continuous* signal $x(t)$, given by

$$x(t)s_T(t) = x(t) \sum_{n = -\infty}^{\infty} \delta(t - nT)$$

$$= \sum_{n = -\infty}^{\infty} x(t)\delta(t - nT)$$

(EQ 5.47)

From Equation 5.14, we can rewrite this as

$$x(t)s_T(t) = \sum_{n = -\infty}^{\infty} x(nT)\delta(t - nT)$$

(EQ 5.48)

We thus interpret the product of a signal with an impulse train as an impulse train whose value at time nT is an impulse of height $x(nT)$, the value of $x(t)$ at that time. This is called a **modulated** impulse train.

We now return to the function $x[nT]$, defined only at the discrete times nT. We argue that this function is equivalent to a modulated impulse train of a function $x(t)$ if the value of $x(t)$ matches the value of $x[nT]$ at every discrete time. From a strictly mathematical perspective, this is not quite correct: $x[nT]$ is discrete and therefore undefined between sample times, whereas the product $x(t)s_T(t)$ is defined for all times. However, in the interests of developing intuition, we will ignore this distinction, writing

$$x[nT] = x(t)s_T(t) = \sum_{n = -\infty}^{\infty} x(nT)\delta(t - nT)$$

(EQ 5.49)

$$= \sum_{n = -\infty}^{\infty} x[nT]\delta(t - nT)$$

(EQ 5.50)

where, in the second step, we use the fact that at the discrete times nT, $x(nT) = x[nT]$. Let us compute the Fourier transform of $x[nT]$. Because of the linearity of the Fourier transform, we can simply compute the transform of a single value $x[nT]\delta(t - nT)$ for a particular value of n and then sum these. Note that the first term in this expression, $x[nT]$, is *independent* of t. Therefore, from the perspective of the transform, it is a constant multiple of $\delta(t - nT)$. Moreover, from Example 5.12, $\delta(t - nT) \overset{\mathcal{F}}{\leftrightarrow} e^{-j\omega nT}$. Therefore, we have

$$x[nT] \overset{\mathcal{F}}{\leftrightarrow} \sum_{n = -\infty}^{\infty} x[nT]e^{-j\omega nT} \qquad \text{(EQ 5.51)}$$

This defines the **discrete-time Fourier transform** of the discrete function $x[nT]$ and is denoted $\tilde{X}(j\omega)$.

EXAMPLE 5.23: DISCRETE-TIME FOURIER TRANSFORM OF A DISCRETE EXPONENTIAL SIGNAL

Compute the discrete-time Fourier transform of the signal $a^n u[nT]$, where $0 < a < 1$.

Solution:

The transform is given by $\displaystyle\sum_{n = -\infty}^{\infty} a^n u(nT)e^{-j\omega nT} = \sum_{n = 0}^{\infty} (ae^{-j\omega T})^n$. We recognize this as a geometric series with parameter $ae^{-j\omega T}$. Now, $e^{-j\omega T}$ is a phasor with unit magnitude, and we already know $|a| < 1$, so this parameter is < 1, and the geometric series sums to $\dfrac{1}{1 - ae^{-j\omega T}}$, which is the desired transform.

The corresponding inverse transform is given by

$$x[nT] = \frac{1}{\omega_s} \int_0^{\omega_s} \tilde{X}(j\omega)e^{j\omega nT}d\omega \qquad \text{(EQ 5.52)}$$

where $\omega_s = \dfrac{2\pi}{T}$.

5.9.3 Aliasing

The sampled version of a signal may not be unique. Two nonidentical signals whose sampled versions are identical are said to be **aliases** of each other. We now study the conditions under which aliasing is possible.

To understand the problem, we need to reexamine the nature of an impulse train, s_T. Recall that this is a periodic function with a period of T. Therefore, its fundamental angular frequency is

$$\omega_s = \frac{2\pi}{T} \tag{EQ 5.53}$$

Any periodic signal can be expressed as a Fourier series by using Equation 5.32, restated here:

$$s_T = \sum_{k=-\infty}^{\infty} c_k e^{jk\omega_s t} \tag{EQ 5.54}$$

The kth term of this series is given by

$$c_k = \frac{1}{T} \int_{-\frac{T}{2}}^{\frac{T}{2}} s_T e^{-jk\omega_s t} dt$$

$$= \frac{1}{T} \int_{-\frac{T}{2}}^{\frac{T}{2}} \sum_{n=-\infty}^{\infty} \delta(t - nT) e^{-jk\omega_s t} dt \tag{EQ 5.55}$$

where, in the second step, we expand s_T by using Equation 5.45. Note that the integration limits are in the range $[-T/2, T/2]$. In this range, the only nonzero delta signal in the summation is $\delta(t)$. So, the infinite sum reduces to a single term,

$$\delta(t)e^{-jk\omega_s t}.$$

Moreover, because $\delta(t)$ is zero valued other than at the origin, we can expand the integral to cover the entire real line, to get

$$c_k = \frac{1}{T} \int_{-\infty}^{\infty} \delta(t)e^{-jk\omega_s t} dt \tag{EQ 5.56}$$

But from Equation 5.15, the integral is simply the value of $e^{-jk\omega_s t}$ at $t = 0$, which is 1, so $c_k = \dfrac{1}{T}$, and we can rewrite Equation 5.54 as

$$s_T = \sum_{k=-\infty}^{\infty} \frac{1}{T} e^{jk\omega_s t} \qquad \text{(EQ 5.57)}$$

Let us use this to compute the Fourier transform of the impulse train. From the linearity property, we need to compute only the transform of $e^{jk\omega_s t}$. From row 3 of Table 5.2, this is given by $2\pi\delta(\omega - k\omega_s)$. Therefore, we have

$$s_T \overset{\mathcal{F}}{\leftrightarrow} \sum_{k=-\infty}^{\infty} \frac{2\pi}{T} \delta(\omega - k\omega_s) \qquad \text{(EQ 5.58)}$$

$$s_T \overset{\mathcal{F}}{\leftrightarrow} \omega_s \sum_{k=-\infty}^{\infty} \delta(\omega - k\omega_s) \qquad \text{(EQ 5.59)}$$

This is an alternative form of the transform in Equation 5.46. However, this form gives us additional insight. Note that the transform is an infinite series of frequency-domain impulses that are separated by the fundamental frequency ω_s. In other words, it is an impulse train in the transform domain. Therefore, we have the beautiful result that the *discrete-time Fourier transform of an impulse train in the time domain is an impulse train in the transform domain!*

We can use this result to explain the need for bandlimiting $x(t)$. From Equation 5.49, we see that the discrete (sampled) signal $x[nT]$ is the product of $x(t)$ and s_T. Therefore, from the convolution property of the Fourier transform, $\tilde{X}(j\omega)$, the transform of $x[nT]$, which we previously computed in Equation 5.51, can also be written as

$$\tilde{X}(j\omega) = \frac{1}{2\pi} X(j\omega) \otimes \omega_s \sum_{k=-\infty}^{\infty} \delta(\omega - k\omega_s)$$

$$= \frac{\omega_s}{2\pi} \sum_{k=-\infty}^{\infty} X(j\omega) \otimes \delta(\omega - k\omega_s) \qquad \text{(EQ 5.60)}$$

$$= \frac{1}{T} \sum_{k=-\infty}^{\infty} X(j\omega) \otimes \delta(\omega - k\omega_s)$$

Carefully examine the expression within the summation, which is the convolution of $X(j\omega)$ with a frequency-shifted impulse. From Equations 5.15 and 5.16, we see that this reduces to $X(j\omega - k\omega_s)$, which is the (continuous) Fourier transform of $x(t)$ shifted in frequency by ω_s. Therefore, the summation represents the addition of scaled and frequency-shifted replicas of $X(j\omega)$ (see Figure 5.12). That is, sampling a signal $x(t)$ with a sampler of period T to produce $x[nT]$ causes the transform of the sampled signal to infinitely replicate the transform of the original signal with a frequency spacing of ω_s.

Suppose that the support of $X(j\omega)$—the range of values for which it is nonzero—is smaller than ω_s. Then, the shift-and-add operation will result in creating multiple replicas of $X(j\omega)$ that do not touch each other. We can pick any one copy—by multiplying it with a pulse of width ω_s in the frequency domain, also called a **band-pass filter**—and take the inverse transform to recover $x(t)$. In other words, the original *continuous* signal can be recovered despite *digital* sampling! This is quite a neat trick, for we have gone from the continuous domain to a discrete domain with no loss of information. The corresponding condition is called the **Nyquist criterion**.

To get some insight into this condition, recall that the Fourier transform of a cosine signal of frequency ω_L (row 4 of Table 5.2) results in the creation of two symmetric impulses at $\pm\omega_L$. Because any signal can be represented as an integral of sinusoids using the Fourier transform, intuitively, if the signal has a highest inherent frequency component of ω_L, its Fourier transform will have a bandwidth of $2\omega_L$ (see Figure 5.12). Sampling such a signal in a way that preserves all the information of the original signal requires $\omega_s > 2\omega_L$. This is an alternative statement of the Nyquist criterion and can be remembered as: *To prevent aliasing, the sampling function should have a frequency that is at least twice that of the highest frequency component of a signal.*

This result is widely applicable to computer networking, where we are nearly always dealing with sampled signals. It is important to ensure that, given an esti-

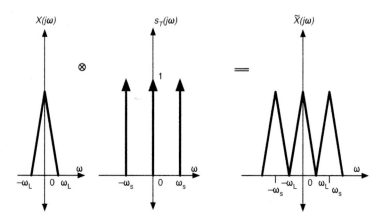

Figure 5.12 The effect of sampling on the Fourier transform of a signal

mate of the highest estimated frequency of the underlying signal, the sample rate is at least twice as fast. Recall that any signal with a sharp transition, such as a pulse signal, has a Fourier transform that has an infinite support, so that it is not band-limited. Sampling any such function is guaranteed to introduce aliasing. Therefore, it is important to ensure, in practice, that most of the signal energy lies within $\pm\omega_s$.

5.9.4 The Discrete-Time-and-Frequency Fourier Transform

So far, we have placed no restrictions on the form of the transformed signal. In the discrete-time Fourier transform, for example, the transformed signal extends over all frequencies. Suppose that we introduce the restriction that the transformed signal must be represented by a finite set of discrete frequencies. In other words, the transformed signal must modulate a finite impulse train in the frequency domain. In this case, we call the transform the discrete-time-and-frequency Fourier transform, or simply discrete Fourier transform (DFT).

It can be shown that the DFT of a discrete-time function cannot be uniquely defined unless the function is either time-limited or, if eternal, periodic with a finite period. Moreover, the duration of the function or its period must be an integer multiple of the sampling period T. We have already seen that a discrete-time function can be represented as a modulated impulse train whose discrete-time Fourier transform is a modulated impulse train in the frequency domain. This fact can be used to show that a time-limited or periodic discrete-time function with N samples per period is discrete and periodic in the transform domain with N component frequencies.

We denote the discrete-time signal, which needs to be specified at N instants, as $x[0], x[T], x[2T],..., x[(N-1)T]$. We denote the period of the signal as T_0, with $T_0 = NT$. Then, the sampling frequency is given by

$$\omega_s = \frac{2\pi}{T} \qquad \text{(EQ 5.61)}$$

and the signal frequency, corresponding to the period over which the signal repeats, is given by

$$\omega_0 = \frac{2\pi}{T_0} \qquad \text{(EQ 5.62)}$$

The kth frequency of the DFT of this signal is denoted $X[jk\omega_0]$, where the term $jk\omega_0$ indicates that the transform domain is complex and discrete, with a fundamental frequency of ω_0. This term of the DFT is given by

$$X[jk\omega_0] = \frac{1}{NT} \sum_{n=0}^{N-1} x[nT]e^{-jk\omega_0 nT} \qquad \text{(EQ 5.63)}$$

The corresponding inverse transform is given by

$$x[nT] = T \sum_{k=0}^{N-1} X[jk\omega_0]e^{jk\omega_0 nT}$$ (EQ 5.64)

EXAMPLE 5.24: DFT

Compute the DFT of the function shown in Figure 5.13. (Assume that $T = 1$, $T_0 = 9$).

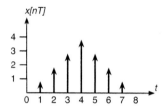

Figure 5.13 Figure for Example 5.24

Solution:

We have $x[0] = 0$, $x[1] = 1$, $x[2] = 2$, $x[3] = 3$, $x[4] = 4$, $x[5] = 3$, $x[6] = 2$, $x[7] = 1$, $x[8] = 0$. Also, $N = \dfrac{T_0}{T} = 9$, and $\omega_0 = \dfrac{2\pi}{9}$.

The first Fourier value, $X[0]$, is given by

$$\frac{1}{NT} \sum_{n=0}^{N-1} x[nT]e^{-j0.\omega_0 nT} = \frac{1}{N} \sum_{n=0}^{N-1} x[nT] = \frac{1}{9}(1+2+3+4+3+2+1) = \frac{16}{9}$$

This is also the arithmetic mean of the input signal; the first DFT coefficient is always the average of the signal values because this represents the DC value of the signal.

The second Fourier value, with $k = 1$, $X\left[j\dfrac{2\pi}{9}\right]$, is given by

$$\frac{1}{9} \sum_{n=0}^{8} x[nT]e^{-j1.\omega_0 n} = \frac{1}{9}\left(1e^{-j\frac{2\pi}{9}} + 2e^{-j\frac{4\pi}{9}} + 3e^{-j\frac{6\pi}{9}} + \ldots + 2e^{-j\frac{12\pi}{9}} + 1e^{-j\frac{14\pi}{9}}\right)$$

Recall that this can be reduced to a complex quantity of the form $a + jb$ by expanding each term, using Euler's formula.

The third Fourier value, with $k = 2$, $X\left[j\dfrac{4\pi}{9}\right]$, is given by

$$\frac{1}{9}\sum_{n=0}^{8} x[nT]e^{-2 \cdot j\omega_0 n} = \frac{1}{9}\left(1e^{-j\frac{4\pi}{9}} + 2e^{-j\frac{8\pi}{9}} + 3e^{-j\frac{12\pi}{9}} + \dots + 2e^{-j\frac{24\pi}{9}} + 1e^{-j\frac{28\pi}{9}}\right)$$

The remaining values are computed similarly.

5.9.5 The Fast Fourier Transform

The fast Fourier transform (FFT) is a clever technique for rapidly computing the terms of a DFT. The FFT draws on the observation that the terms in this transform follow a regular recursive structure, as described next.

To see the hidden structure of a DFT, we start by simplifying the notation. Suppose that time is normalized so that the sampling period T has a unit duration so that $T = 1$ and $T_0 = NT = N$. Then, $\omega_0 = \dfrac{2\pi}{T_0} = \dfrac{2\pi}{N}$. Denote by ω_N the value $e^{j\frac{2\pi}{N}}$.

Finally, we write the signal as $x[n]$ and its transform by $X[k]$. Then, we can rewrite $X[jk\omega_0] = \dfrac{1}{NT}\displaystyle\sum_{n=0}^{N-1} x[nT]e^{-jk\omega_0 nT}$ as $X[k] = \dfrac{1}{N}\displaystyle\sum_{n=0}^{N-1} x[n]\omega_N^{-kn}$. We expand the right-hand side as

$$\frac{1}{N}(x[0] + x[1]\omega_N^{-k} + x[2]\omega_N^{-2k} + x[3]\omega_N^{-3k} + \dots + x[N-1]\omega_N^{-k(N-1)}) \qquad \textbf{(EQ 5.65)}$$

Obtaining this value is computationally difficult because we need to compute N powers of the complex quantity ω_N. The heart of the FFT algorithm is to reduce this computational overhead.

For simplicity, assume that N is even. Then, we can partition this expression into two equal-length series: one with the odd terms and one with the even terms. The even terms form the series

$$\frac{1}{N}(x[0] + x[2]\omega_N^{-2k} + x[4]\omega_N^{-4k} + \dots + x[N-2]\omega_N^{-k(N-2)})$$

Denote by ω_E the value ω_N^2. Then, we can rewrite this series as

$$\frac{1}{N}\left(x[0] + x[2]\omega_E^{-k} + x[4]\omega_E^{-2k} + \dots + x[N-2]\omega_E^{-\frac{k(N-2)}{2}}\right) \qquad \textbf{(EQ 5.66)}$$

We can interpret this as the DFT of a series with only $N/2$ terms, therefore requiring only $N/2$ powers of ω_E. Now, let us consider the odd terms of Equation 5.65:

$$\frac{1}{N}(x[1]\omega_N^{-k} + x[3]\omega_N^{-3k} + x[5]\omega_N^{-5k} + \ldots + x[N-1]\omega_N^{-k(N-1)})$$

We can rewrite this as

$$\frac{\omega_N^{-k}}{N}(x[1] + x[3]\omega_N^{-2k} + x[5]\omega_N^{-4k} + \ldots + x[N-1]\omega_N^{-k(N-2)})$$

$$= \frac{\omega_N^{-k}}{N}\left(x[1] + x[3]\omega_E^{-k} + x[5]\omega_E^{-2k} + \ldots + x[N-1]\omega_E^{-\frac{k(N-2)}{2}}\right)$$

(EQ 5.67)

Note that the powers of ω_E on the right-hand side are exactly the same as in Equation 5.66. Therefore, once we compute the $N/2$ powers of ω_E to compute Equation 5.66, we can obtain the sum of the odd terms with only one additional multiplication.

It is easy to see how this structure can be made to recurse: We rewrite Equations 5.66 and 5.67 as odd and even terms, reducing the number of exponentials by another factor of 2. If N is a power of 2, we can continue in this fashion until we get to the trivial case of computing the DFT of a series with only two terms, which is given by $\frac{1}{2}(x[0] + x[1]\omega_N^{-k})$. We can then unwind the recursion to find the required transform. This is illustrated by the following example.

EXAMPLE 5.25: FAST FOURIER TRANSFORM

Use the FFT technique to compute the discrete Fourier transform of the signal $x[i] = i$ for $0 \le i \le 7$.

Solution:

We have $N = 8$. Denote by ω_N the value $e^{j\frac{2\pi}{8}}$. The kth term of the transform is given by

$$\frac{1}{8}(\omega_N^{-k} + 2\omega_N^{-2k} + 3\omega_N^{-3k} + 4\omega_N^{-4k} + 5\omega_N^{-5k} + 6\omega_N^{-6k} + 7\omega_N^{-7k})$$

$$= \frac{1}{8}(2\omega_N^{-2k} + 4\omega_N^{-4k} + 6\omega_N^{-6k}) + \frac{\omega_N^{-k}}{8}(1 + 3\omega_N^{-2k} + 5\omega_N^{-4k} + 7\omega_N^{-6k})$$

Let $\omega_E = \omega_N^2 = e^{j\frac{4\pi}{8}}$. Then, we can rewrite this sum as

$$= \frac{1}{8}(2\omega_E^{-k} + 4\omega_E^{-2k} + 6\omega_E^{-3k}) + \frac{\omega_N^{-k}}{8}(1 + 3\omega_E^{-k} + 5\omega_E^{-2k} + 7\omega_E^{-3k})$$

$$= \frac{1}{8}((4\omega_E^{-2k}) + (2\omega_E^{-k} + 6\omega_E^{-3k})) + \frac{\omega_N^{-k}}{8}((1 + 5\omega_E^{-2k}) + (3\omega_E^{-k} + 7\omega_E^{-3k}))$$

Let $\omega_F = \omega_E^2 = e^{j\frac{8\pi}{8}}$. Then, we can continue to rewrite the series as

$$= \frac{1}{8}((4\omega_F^{-k}) + \omega_E^{-k}(2 + 6\omega_F^{-k})) + \frac{\omega_N^{-k}}{8}((1 + 5\omega_F^{-k}) + \omega_E^{-k}(3 + 7\omega_F^{-k})) \qquad \textbf{(EQ 5.68)}$$

To evaluate this, for each k, we compute ω_F^{-k}, ω_E^{-k}, and ω_N^{-k} and substitute in Equation 5.68. For example, for $k = 2$, we compute the transform value as follows:

$$\omega_N^{-k} = e^{-j\frac{4\pi}{8}} = \cos\left(-\frac{\pi}{2}\right) + j\sin\left(-\frac{\pi}{2}\right) = -j$$

$$\omega_E^{-k} = \omega_N^{-2k} = -1$$

$$\omega_F^{-k} = \omega_E^{-2k} = 1$$

We substitute this in Equation 5.68 to find the value to be

$$\frac{1}{8}((4) - 1(2 + 6)) + \left(-\frac{j}{8}\right)((1 + 5) - 1(3 + 7)) = \frac{1}{8}(-4) + \left(-\frac{j}{8}\right)(-4) = -0.5 + j0.5$$

5.10 The Z Transform

The Z transform generalizes the DFT in roughly the same way that the Laplace transform generalizes the Fourier transform. The integral in the Fourier transform can be viewed as the limiting sum of a series of unmodulated complex exponentials as their interfrequency separation tends to zero. The Laplace transform generalizes this by taking the limiting sum over a series of modulated complex exponentials. In the same way, the DFT is a finite sum of unmodulated complex exponentials. The Z transform generalizes this to an infinite sum of modulated complex exponentials.[8]

8. A careful reader may note that we are simultaneously generalizing in two dimensions: from a finite sum to an infinite sum and from a sum of unmodulated complex exponentials to a sum of modulated complex exponentials. Indeed, an intermediate step, the discrete Laplace transform, corresponds to a finite sum of modulated complex exponentials, which we have glossed over in this exposition.

However, the notation of the Z transform is particularly simple because the complex transform variable, denoted z, is written in the $a + jb$ form rather than the equivalent modulated complex exponential form.

We will consider only causal signals, that is, signals $x[k]$ such that $x[k] = 0$ for $k < 0$. We define the Z transform of such a signal as the infinite sum $\sum_{k=0}^{\infty} x[k]z^{-k}$, which we denote by

$$x[k] \overset{Z}{\leftrightarrow} X(z) = \sum_{k=0}^{\infty} x[k]z^{-k} \qquad \text{(EQ 5.69)}$$

As with the Laplace transform, the infinite series defining the Z transform converges only for certain values of z, which define its **region of convergence**.

The inverse Z transform is given by

$$x[k] = \frac{1}{2\pi j} \oint_C X(z)z^{k-1} dz$$

$$\text{(EQ 5.70)}$$

where C is a circle with its center at the origin of the z plane such that all values z such that $X(z)z^{k-1} = \infty$ (its poles) are inside this circle. As with the Laplace transform, the inverse is usually found from a table of standard transforms and the properties of the Z transform. Similarly, the concepts of poles and zeroes introduced for the Laplace transform continue to hold for the Z transform, as the next examples show.

EXAMPLE 5.26: Z TRANSFORM OF A UNIT STEP

Compute the Z transform of the discrete unit step signal defined by $x[k] = 1$ for $k \geq 0$.

Solution:

By definition, $X(z) = \sum_{k=0}^{\infty} z^{-k} = \frac{1}{1-z^{-1}} = \frac{z}{z-1}$, which converges when $|z| > 1$, which is the region of convergence of this transform. Recall that z is complex, so this is the set of points outside a unit circle in the complex plane centered on the origin. Note that, unlike the Laplace transform, in the case of the Z transform, the region of convergence is expressed in terms of circular regions or their intersections, rather than half-planes.

EXAMPLE 5.27: Z TRANSFORM OF A DISCRETE EXPONENTIAL

Compute the Z transform of the signal $x[k] = e^{-ak}$ where a is a complex constant and $k \geq 0$.

Solution:

By definition,

$$X(z) = \sum_{k=0}^{\infty} e^{-ak} z^{-k} = \sum_{k=0}^{\infty} (e^{-a} z^{-1})^k = \frac{1}{1 - e^{-a} z^{-1}} = \frac{z}{z - e^{-a}}.$$

The series converges and the transform is defined for the region where $|e^{-a} z^{-1}| < 1 \Rightarrow |z| > |e^{-a}|$, which is a circle of radius $|e^{-a}|$ centered at the origin. What if $|z| = |e^{-a}|$? In this case, the denominator becomes zero and the transform's value is infinite. This is called a **pole** of the system. (The pole in the previous example was at 1.) Intuitively, the series e^{-ak} diverges when $|a| < 1$. We can ensure convergence by modulating this signal with the complex value z^{-1}, but only when the absolute value of z is greater than $|e^{-a}|$.

The values of z for which the transform vanishes are called the *zeroes* of the transform, illustrated by the next example.

EXAMPLE 5.28: Z TRANSFORM OF A SINUSOID

Compute the Z transform of the discrete sinusoid $\cos[\omega k]$.

Solution:

We use Euler's formula to rewrite the signal as $\left(\dfrac{e^{j\omega k} + e^{-j\omega k}}{2} \right)$. By definition,

$$X(z) = \sum_{k=0}^{\infty} \left(\frac{e^{j\omega k} + e^{-j\omega k}}{2} \right) z^{-k} = \frac{1}{2} \sum_{k=0}^{\infty} e^{j\omega k} z^{-k} + \frac{1}{2} \sum_{k=0}^{\infty} e^{-j\omega k} z^{-k}$$

$$= \frac{1}{2} \left(\frac{1}{1 - e^{j\omega} z^{-1}} + \frac{1}{1 - e^{-j\omega} z^{-1}} \right),$$

where, in the last step, we used the result from the previous example, and we are assuming that $|z| > e^{-j\omega}$. This reduces to $\dfrac{z^2 - z \cos\omega}{z^2 - 2z \cos\omega + 1}$, with the region of convergence $|z| > |e^{-j\omega}| = 1$ (the entire z plane excluding a disk of radius 1). Note that the transform becomes infinite for $z = e^{\pm j\omega}$ (the poles of the transform) and is zero for $z=0$ (the zero of the transform).

It is important to keep track of the region of convergence of the transform. As with the Laplace transform, it can be shown that two completely different time-domain functions may have an identical transform, other than the region of convergence. The transform is unique only if the region is also specified. In general, the region of convergence of the Z transform is given by the annulus in the complex plane specified by $\alpha < |z| < \beta$.

5.10.1 Relationship between Z and Laplace Transforms

(This section can be skipped during a first reading.) The Z transform is a compact representation of the Laplace transform of a discrete-time signal. We now discuss how the Z transform's z auxiliary variable relates to the s auxiliary variable used in the Laplace transform.

Recall the following facts.

- The Laplace transform of a continuous signal is the Fourier transform of the signal after it has been modulated by the real exponential $e^{-\sigma t}$.

- A discrete-time signal whose values are separated in time by T seconds can be viewed as the product of a corresponding continuous-time signal and an impulse train with impulses spaced T seconds apart.

- The transform of a discrete-time impulse train with impulses spaced T seconds apart is an impulse train in the frequency domain with impulses spaced $\frac{2\pi}{T}$ Hz apart.

- The Fourier transform of the product of two signals is the convolution of their Fourier transforms.

- The convolution of a signal with an impulse train replicates the signal.

Given these facts, we see that the Laplace transform of a discrete-time signal with values spaced apart by T seconds results in infinitely replicating the transform of the signal modulated by the real exponential $e^{-\sigma t}$ with a period of $2\frac{\pi}{T}$. Therefore, it is possible to fully describe the signal in the frequency domain considering only frequencies in the range $0 \pm \frac{\pi}{T}$. This corresponds to values of the Laplace variable $s = \sigma + j\omega$ that lie in band $\sigma - j\frac{\pi}{T} \le s \le \sigma + j\frac{\pi}{T}$, as shown by the two dashed horizontal lines in Figure 5.14.

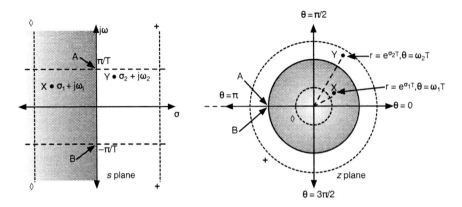

Figure 5.14 Mapping from the s plane to the z plane

The Z transform denotes these values with the z variable, using the relationship $z = e^{sT} = e^{\sigma T}e^{j\omega T}$. Representing z in the form $z = Ae^{j\theta}$, we see that

$$A = e^{\sigma T}$$
$$\theta = \omega T$$

(EQ 5.71)

As a result of this mapping, lines parallel to the Y-axis in the s plane correspond to circles in the z plane, and lines parallel to the X-axis in the s plane correspond to radial lines in the z plane. This is shown in Figure 5.14, where the two vertical lines marked by a diamond and a cross in the s plane are transformed to corresponding circles in the z plane, and the two horizontal dashed lines marked A and B map to the same radial line in the z plane.

The Y-axis in the s plane corresponds to the unit circle in the z plane. The left half-plane in the s domain corresponds to points within the unit circle in the z plane. Note that the vertical line marked with a diamond lies in the left half-plane of the s plane and therefore lies within the unit circle in the z plane. Similarly, point X in the s plane, which lies in the left half-plane, is mapped to a point within the unit circle in the z plane, and point Y in the s plane, which lies in the right half-plane, is mapped to a point outside the unit circle. Moreover, Y has a larger ω value than X and so rotated further in the anticlockwise direction in the z plane than X.

EXAMPLE 5.29: MAPPING FROM THE s PLANE TO THE Z PLANE

What is the z value corresponding to the s value $3 + j2$, assuming that $T = 1$? Express this value in both polar and Cartesian coordinates.

Solution:

The z value $Ae^{j\theta}$ is given by $e^{sT} = e^{3+j2} = e^3e^{j2} = 20.08e^{j2}$. Using Euler's formula, we can write this as $20.08(\cos(2) + j\sin(2)) = 20.08(-0.42 + j(0.91)) = (-8.36 + j18.26)$.

5.10.2 Properties of the Z Transform

The Z transform shares many of the properties of the Fourier and Laplace transforms: linearity, time-shifting, time-scaling, differentiation, and the convolution property, though in a slightly different form. Table 5.5 summarizes some important properties. For simplicity, we implicitly assume that signal values are spaced a unit time step apart: $T = 1$.

These properties, along with the table of common transforms (Table 5.6) allow us to derive the transform of most common signals without having to derive them from first principles.

EXAMPLE 5.30: USING THE Z TRANSFORM TO SOLVE A SYSTEM

Consider a discrete-time system such that the Z transform $H(z)$ of its transfer function $h[k]$ is $\dfrac{1}{1-z^{-1}}$. What is its response to the input $2^{-k}u[k]$?

Solution:

Since $x[k] = 2^{-k}u[k]$, from row 5 of Table 5.6,

$$X(z) = \frac{1}{1 - \dfrac{z^{-1}}{2}}. \text{ Therefore, } Y(z) = \frac{1}{(1-z^{-1})\left(1 - \dfrac{z^{-1}}{2}\right)}.$$

Using the method of partial fractions (i.e., writing the expression as $\dfrac{a}{1-z^{-1}} + \dfrac{b}{1 - \dfrac{z^{-1}}{2}}$ and solving for a and b), we find that $Y(z) = \dfrac{2}{1-z^{-1}} - \dfrac{1}{1 - \dfrac{z^{-1}}{2}}$.

To find the inverse transform, recall that the Z transform is linear, so we need only find the inverse transform of each term in isolation. From row 3 and row 5 of Table 5.6, we get $y[k] = 2u[k] - \left(\dfrac{1}{2}\right)^k u[k]$, which is a discrete unit step of height 2 to which is added a decaying discrete exponential.

Table 5.5 Some Properties of the Z Transform

Property	Precondition	Postcondition	Notes
Linearity	$x_1[k] \overset{Z}{\leftrightarrow} X_1(z) \quad \alpha_1 < |z| < \beta_1$ $x_2[k] \overset{Z}{\leftrightarrow} X_2(z) \quad \alpha_2 < |z| < \beta_2$	$ax_1[k] + bx_2[k] \overset{Z}{\leftrightarrow} aX_1(z) + bX_2(z)$ $max(\alpha_1, \alpha_2) < |z| < min(\beta_1, \beta_2)$	Arbitrary constants a and b can be complex. This assumes that no pole-zero cancellations are involved.
Time-shifting	$x[k] \overset{Z}{\leftrightarrow} X(z) \quad \alpha < |z| < \beta$	$x[k-a] \overset{Z}{\leftrightarrow} z^{-a}X(z) \quad \alpha < |z| < \beta,$ $\text{except } z = 0 \text{ if } a > 0$ $\text{and } z = \infty \text{ if } a < 0$	Shifting a signal a steps forward multiplies its transform by z^{-a}.
Scaling in the z domain	$x[k] \overset{Z}{\leftrightarrow} X(z) \quad \alpha < |z| < \beta$	$a^k x[k] \overset{Z}{\leftrightarrow} X\left(\frac{z}{a}\right) \quad 1(|a|\alpha < |z| < |a|\beta)$	An expansion in the frequency scale compresses the time scale.
Time reversal	$x[k] \overset{Z}{\leftrightarrow} X(z) \quad \alpha < |z| < \beta$	$x[-k] \overset{Z}{\leftrightarrow} X(z^{-1}) \quad \frac{1}{\beta} < |z| < \frac{1}{\alpha}$	Reversing the direction of a signal is equivalent to using z^{-1} instead of z in the expression of the transform.
Time-domain convolution	$x_1[k] \overset{Z}{\leftrightarrow} X_1(z) \quad \alpha_1 < |z| < \beta_1$ $x_2[k] \overset{Z}{\leftrightarrow} X_2(z) \quad \alpha_2 < |z| < \beta_2$	$x_1[k] \otimes x_2[k] \overset{Z}{\leftrightarrow} X_1(z)X_2(z)$ $max(\alpha_1, \alpha_2) < |z| < min(\beta_1, \beta_2)$	Convolution in the time domain corresponds to multiplication in the transform domain.
First difference	$x[k] \overset{Z}{\leftrightarrow} X(z) \quad \alpha < |z| < \beta$	$x[k] - x[k-1] \overset{Z}{\leftrightarrow} (1 - z^{-1})X(z)$ $max(\alpha, 0) < |z| < \beta$	The first difference is equivalent to differentiation in the time domain.

Table 5.6 Some Standard Z Transforms

No.	Signal	$x[k]$	$X[z]$	Region of Convergence
1	Delta or unit impulse	$\delta[k]$	1	All z
2	Delayed delta	$\delta[k - k_0]$	z^{-k_0}	$z \neq 0$
3	Unit step	$u[k]$	$\dfrac{1}{1 - z^{-1}}$	$|z| > 1$
4	Ramp	$ku[k]$	$\dfrac{z^{-1}}{(1 - z^{-1})^2}$	$|z| > 1$
5	Exponential	$a^k u[k]$	$\dfrac{1}{1 - az^{-1}}$	$|z| > |a|$
6	Sine	$\sin(\omega_0 k)u[k]$	$\dfrac{z^{-1}\sin(\omega_0)}{1 - 2z^{-1}\cos(\omega_0) + z^{-2}}$	$|z| > 1$
7	Cosine	$\cos(\omega_0 k)u[k]$	$\dfrac{1 - z^{-1}\cos(\omega_0)}{1 - 2z^{-1}\cos(\omega_0) + z^{-2}}$	$|z| > 1$
8	Exponentially modulated sine	$a^k \sin(\omega_0 k)u[k]$	$\dfrac{az^{-1}\sin(\omega_0)}{1 - 2az^{-1}\cos(\omega_0) + a^2 z^{-2}}$	$|z| > |a|$
9	Exponentially modulated cosine	$a^k \cos(\omega_0 k)u[k]$	$\dfrac{1 - az^{-1}\cos(\omega_0)}{1 - 2z^{-1}\cos(\omega_0) + (a^2 z)^{-2}}$	$|z| > |a|$

5.11 Further Reading

An excellent text that delves more deeply into the material covered in this chapter using a unique graphical approach is P. Kraniuskas, *Transforms in Signals and Systems*, Addison-Wesley, 1992. A more traditional approach can be found in B. P. Lathi, *Linear Systems and Signals*, Oxford, 2005. A lucid description of complex numbers and the Fourier transform, along with historical anecdotes, can be found in P. J. Nahin, *Dr. Euler's Fabulous Formula*, Princeton University Press, 2006.

5.12 Exercises

1. **Complex arithmetic**

   Compute $e^{-j\frac{\pi}{2}} + e^{j\frac{\pi}{2}}$.

2. **Phase angle**

   What is the phase angle corresponding to the complex number $1+j$?

3. **Discrete convolution**

   Let $z(t)$ be the convolution of $x(t)$, $0 \le t \le 9$ = 1, 3, 5, 2, 5, 8, 7, 3, 9, 4 and $y(t)$, $0 \le t \le 9$ = 3, 1, 7, 4, 5, 9, 7, 1, 3, 8. Compute $z(5)$.

4. **Signals**

   Give an example of a signal that is continuous, digital, aperiodic, and time-unlimited.

5. **Complex exponential**

   Describe the Im-t projection of the curve $5e^t(\cos 3t + j\sin 3t)$.

6. **Linearity**

   Is the system defined by the transfer function $H(x) = 5\dfrac{dx}{dt} + 1$ linear?

7. **LTI system**

   What is the output of an LTI system when the input is a real sinusoid?

8. **Natural response**

   Compute the natural response of the LTI system given by

   $$2\frac{d^2y(t)}{dt^2} + 11\frac{dy(t)}{dt} + 15y(t) = 32x(t).$$

9. **Natural response**

   Determine the exact natural response of the system described by

   $$2\frac{d^2y(t)}{dt^2} + y(t) = 32x(t); \quad y(0) = 0, \; \dot{y}(0) = 1. \text{ What is its frequency?}$$

10. **Stability**

   Characterize the stability of the system in Exercise 9.

11. **Fourier series**

   Find the Fourier series corresponding to the infinite series of isosceles triangular pulses of base width 2τ and height 1 spaced apart T_0 seconds. Use the fact

   that $\int xe^{ax}dx = \dfrac{axe^{ax} - e^{ax}}{a^2} + C$.

12. **Fourier series**

   Compute the third coefficient of the Fourier series representing a periodic rectangular pulse of width $1s$ spaced apart by 10s.

13. **Fourier transform**

   Find the Fourier transform of a single left-triangular pulse defined by $1 - t$ in
   $[0,1]$.

14. **Inverse Fourier transform**

   Compute the inverse Fourier transform of the function $\pi(\delta(\omega + \omega_0) + \delta(\omega - \omega_0))$
   from first principles.

15. **Computing the Fourier transform**

   Use the properties of the Fourier transform to compute the transform of the
   function $\cos(\omega_0(t + t_0)) + \sin(\omega_0(t - t_0))$.

16. **Laplace transform**

   Compute the Laplace transform of the sinusoid $u(t)\sin \omega_0 t$ from first principles. Locate its pole(s) and zero(es).

17. **Laplace transform**

   Find the Laplace transform of the signal $u(t)\sin \omega_0(t - t_0)$.

18. **Using the Laplace transform to solve a system**

   Consider a system whose impulse response $h(t)$ is given by $\cos(\omega_0 t)$. What is
   its response to the input $e^{-t}u(t)$?

19. Discrete-time Fourier transform

Compute the discrete-time Fourier transform of the signal $0.5^n u[nT]$, where $0 < a < 1$.

20. Discrete-time-and-frequency Fourier transform

Compute the fourth Fourier term for the signal shown in Figure 5.13.

21. Z transform

Compute the Z transform of the discrete ramp $ku[k]$ from first principles.

22. Z transform

Compute the Z transform of the signal $x[k] = e^{a(k-k_0)}$, where a is a complex constant and $k \geq 0, k_0 > 0$.

Stochastic Processes and Queueing Theory

6.1 Overview

Queues arise naturally when entities demanding service, or **customers**, interact asynchronously with entities providing service, or **servers**. **Service requests** may arrive at a server when it is either unavailable or busy serving other requests. In such cases, service demands must be either queued or dropped. A server that queues demands instead of dropping them can smooth over fluctuations in the rate of service and in the rate of request arrivals, leading to the formation of a queueing system. The study of the probabilistic behavior of such systems is the subject of queueing theory.

Here are some examples of queueing systems.

1. The arrival and service of packets at the output queue of a switch. Packets may arrive when the output link is busy, in which case the packets, which are implicit service requests, must be buffered (i.e., queued).

2. The arrival and service of HTTP requests at a Web server. If the Web server is busy serving a request, incoming requests are queued.

3. The arrival of telephone calls to a switch-control processor in the telephone network. The processor may be unable to service the call because the switch is busy. In this case, the call is queued, awaiting the release of network resources.

Given a queueing system, we would like to compute certain quantities of interest, such as

- The **queueing delay**: the expected waiting time for a service request
- The **backlog**: the mean number of service requests that are awaiting service
- The **utilization factor**: the expected fraction of time that the server is busy
- The **drop rate**: the expected fraction of service requests that must be dropped because there is no more space left in the queue
- The mean length of a busy or idle period

Queueing theory allows us to compute these quantities—both for a single queue and for interconnected networks of queues—as long as the incoming traffic and the servers obey certain simplifying conditions. Unfortunately, measurements show that traffic in real networks does *not* obey these conditions. Moreover, we cannot mathematically analyze most networks that are subjected to realistic traffic workloads. Nevertheless, it is worth studying queueing theory for two important reasons. First, it gives us fundamental insights into the behavior of queueing systems. These insights apply even to systems that are mathematically intractable. Second, the solutions from queueing theory—even from unrealistic traffic models—are a reasonable first approximation to reality. Therefore, as long as we keep in mind that results from queueing theory are only approximate and are meant primarily to give an insight into a real system, we can derive considerable benefit from the mathematical theory of queues.

6.1.1 A General Queueing System

We now introduce some standard notation. A **queue** is formed when **customers** present **service requests**, or **jobs**, to one or more **servers**. Customers arrive at a rate of λ customers/second at times t, and the time between arrivals is described by the **interarrival time distribution** $A(t) = P$(time between arrivals $\leq t$). We denote the service time by x, which has a **service-time distribution** $B(x) = P$(service time $\leq x$) with a mean service rate of μ customers/second. Customers are assumed to wait in the queue with a **mean waiting time** T. Note that in this chapter, we will study primarily a single queue in isolation.

6.1.2 Little's Theorem

Little's theorem is a fundamental result that holds true for *all* arrival and service processes. The theorem states that the mean number of customers in a queueing system is the product of their mean waiting time and their mean arrival rate.

Proof of Little's Theorem: Suppose that customers arrive to an empty queue[1] at a mean rate of λ customers/second. An average of λt customer arrive in t seconds. Let T denote the mean waiting time in seconds of a newly arriving customer. The total time spent waiting in the queue across all customers during the time interval is therefore λTt customer-seconds.

Let N denote the mean number of customers in the queue. In 1 second, these N customers accumulate N customer-seconds of total waiting time. Thus, in t seconds, they accumulate a total of Nt customer-seconds of waiting time. This must equal λTt, which implies that $N=\lambda T$.

Note that this argument is independent of the length of the time interval t. Moreover, it does not depend on the order of service of customers, the number of servers, or the way in which customers arrive. Thus, it is a powerful and general law applicable to all queueing systems.

EXAMPLE 6.1: LITTLE'S THEOREM

Suppose that you receive e-mail at the average rate of one message every 5 minutes. If you read all your incoming mail instantaneously once an hour, what is the average time that a message remains unread?

Solution:

The mean message arrival rate is 12 messages/hour. Because you read e-mail once an hour, the mean number of unread messages is 6 (the expected number of messages received in half an hour). By Little's theorem, this is the product of the mean arrival rate and the mean waiting time, which immediately tells us that the mean time for a message to be unread is $\dfrac{6}{12}$ hours = 30 minutes.

EXAMPLE 6.2: LITTLE'S THEOREM

Suppose that 10,800 HTTP requests arrive at a Web server over the course of the busiest hour of the day. If the mean waiting time for service should be under 6 seconds, what should be the largest allowed queue length?

Solution:

The arrival rate $\lambda = 10,800/3600 = 3$ requests/second. We want $T \leq 6$. Now, $N = \lambda T$, so $T = N/\lambda$. This means that $N/\lambda \leq 6$ or that $N \leq 6 * 3 = 18$. So, if the mean

---

1. The same reasoning applies when customers arrive to a nonempty queue, but arrivals to an empty queue simplifies the analysis.

queueing delay is to be no larger than 6 seconds, the mean queue length should not exceed 18. In practice, the Web server could return a server-busy response when the queue exceeds 18 requests. This is conservative because then 18 is the *maximum* queue length rather than its mean.

6.2 Stochastic Processes

The foundation of queueing theory is the mathematical study of a **stochastic process**. Such a process is used to model the arrival and service processes in a queue. We will both intuitively and mathematically define a stochastic process and then study some standard stochastic processes.

EXAMPLE 6.3: DETERMINISTIC AND STOCHASTIC PROCESSES

Consider a staircase with ten steps numbered 1 through 10 and a person standing on the first step, which is numbered 1. Suppose that a clock next to the staircase ticks once a second starting at time 1. Finally, assume that it takes zero time to climb each step.

If the person were to climb one step at each clock tick, we can predict exactly where the person would be at each time step. At time 0, the person is on step 1 and would stay there until just before time 1. When the clock ticks and time increments to 1, the person would be at step 2 and would stay there until just before time 2. At time 2, the person would be on step 3, and so on. We therefore call the act of climbing the staircase in this fashion a **deterministic** process.

In contrast, suppose that the person climbs one step or goes down one step or stays on the same step with some (potentially zero) probability. With this change, we lose predictability. That is, we no longer know exactly where the person will be at any moment in time; we can only attach probabilities to the set of places where the person *could* be at that time. The process is no longer deterministic but instead **stochastic**.

We capture this by means of a random variable X_i that denotes the step the person is on immediately after the ith clock tick. The random variable is associated with the probability distribution $\pi(i)$ over the positions where the person could be immediately after that time. For instance, at time 0, the person is at step 1 with probability 1, so the distribution of X_0 over the domain {1, 2,...,10} is given by the discrete probability distribution $\pi(0)$ = {1.0, 0,..., 0}. Suppose that the probability that the person goes up is p, that the person goes down is q, and that the person stays on the same step is $1 - p - q$, except at step 1, where the probability of going up is p, and the probability of staying on the same step is $1 - p$. Then, immediately after time 1 (after the first clock tick), $\pi(1) = \{1 - p, p, 0,...,0\}$. Similarly, $\pi(2) = \{(1 - p)^2 + pq, p(1 - p - q) + (1 - p)p, p^2, 0,...,0\}$, and so on. To compute $\pi(i)$ given $\pi(i - 1)$, we determine the different ways that we can reach each particular step, summing the probability over all possible ways to reach that step.

Note that we distinguish between the distribution of the random variables at each time step and the actual trajectory taken by a person. For a given trajectory, at each time instant, the person is, of course, only on one step of the staircase. The trajectories are created by sampling from the distributions $\pi(i)$. A trajectory is also therefore called a **sample path**.

This example suggests the following definition of a **stochastic process**: a family of random variables X_i that are indexed by the time index i. The value of the random variable in a particular trajectory is also called the **state** of the stochastic process at that point in time. Without loss of generality, we can think of the states as being chosen from the integers from 1 to N. Thus, we can imagine the process as "moving" from the state corresponding to the value taken by random variable X_i in a given trajectory to the state corresponding to the value taken by random variable X_{i+1} at time $i+1$, just like the person moves from one stair to another. As we have shown, given the probabilities of moving from one step to another, we can, in principle, compute the distribution of each X_i: the distribution of the stochastic process over the state space at that time.

Time is discrete in this example. In other situations, a system is better modeled when time is continuous. In this case, the family of random variables corresponding to the stochastic process consists of the variables $X(t_1)$, $X(t_2)$,..., where the t_i represent the times at which the state transitions occur. Given the probability of moving from step to step, we can compute $\pi(t_{i+1})$, the distribution of $X(t_{i+1})$, from $\pi(t_i)$ the distribution of $X(t_i)$.

In the example, the person's movements were limited to moving up or down one step on each clock tick. We could, instead, allow the person to go from a given step to any other step—not just the steps above and below—with some probability. Indeed, this distribution of probabilities could differ at different steps and even differ at each clock tick! And, finally, the person could be on a ramp, so that the amount of movement could be a real positive or negative quantity rather than an integer. These variations are all within the scope of definition of a stochastic process, but the analysis of the corresponding processes is progressively more difficult. We will first describe some standard types of stochastic processes and then focus on the simplest ones.

6.2.1 Discrete and Continuous Stochastic Processes

A stochastic process can be classified as a discrete or a continuous process in two ways. (1) The values assumed by the random variables, or the **state space**, can be discrete or continuous, and (2) the index variable, or time, also can be discrete or continuous.

A **discrete-space process** is one in which the random variables X_i take on discrete values. Without loss of generality, we can think of the state in a discrete-space process as being indexed by an integer in the range 1,2,...N.

EXAMPLE 6.4: DISCRETE-SPACE PROCESS

Continuing with Example 6.3, we see that the set of possible states is the set of stairs, which forms a discrete set.

A **continuous-space process** is one in which the random variables take on values from a finite or infinite continuous interval or a set of such intervals.

EXAMPLE 6.5: CONTINUOUS-STATE PROCESS

Continuing with Example 6.3, consider a person walking up and down a ramp rather than a stair. This would allow movements by real amounts. Therefore, the random variable corresponding to the state of the process can take on real values, and the corresponding stochastic process would be a continuous-space process.

In a **discrete-time** process, the indices of the random variables are integers. We can think of the stochastic process in a particular trajectory as moving from one state to another at these points in time.

EXAMPLE 6.6: DISCRETE-TIME PROCESS

Continuing with Example 6.3, this corresponds to a person moving from one step to another exactly at each clock tick. Such a stochastic process is also called a **stochastic sequence**.

In a **continuous-time** process, the times when the process can move to a new state are chosen from a real interval.

EXAMPLE 6.7: CONTINUOUS-TIME PROCESS

Continuing with Example 6.3, this corresponds to a person moving from stair to stair at will, independent of the clock.

Stochastic processes corresponding to all four combinations of {discrete space, continuous space} and {discrete time, continuous time} are well known.

6.2.2 Markov Processes

An important aspect of a stochastic process is how the probability of transitioning from one state to another is influenced by past history. Continuing with our staircase example—a discrete-time and discrete-space stochastic process—consider a person who is allowed to go from any stair to any other stair. Moreover, we will ask the person to obey the following rules: If he or she arrives at stair 5 from stair 6, move to stair 3. If, however, he or she arrives at stair 5 from stair 3, move to stair 9. In all other cases, move to stair 1. Suppose that at some point in time, we see that the person is on stair 5. What happens next?

The answer is: We don't know. It depends on where the person was in the previous time step. Stated more precisely, the distribution of the random variable X_{n+1} (i.e., $\pi(n+1)$) when $X_n = 5$ depends on the value of X_{n-1}. Generalizing from this example, we can define more complex stochastic processes for which $\pi(n+1)$ depends not only on X_n but also on $X_{n-1}, X_{n-2},..., X_1$. Such systems are inherently complex, and there is little we can say about them.

In an attempt to curb this complexity, consider the following rule:

$$\pi(n+1) \text{ depends only on the value of } X_n$$

This rule simplifies the situation: If the person is on step 5 at time n, we know π_{n+1} *independent of the prior history*. As we will see, this allows us to easily compute many quantities of interest about the process. Moreover, many naturally occurring stochastic processes obey this rule. Owing to these two facts, stochastic processes that obey this rule are given a special name: **Markov processes**, in honor of A. N. Markov, who first studied them in 1907.

Formally, for the case of discrete-time stochastic processes, we state the **Markov property** as

$$P(X_{n+1} = j \mid X_n = i_n, X_{n-1} = i_{n-1}, X_{n-2} = i_{n-2}, X_{n-3} = i_{n-3}, ..., X_1 = i_1)$$
$$= P(X_{n+1} = j \mid X_n = i_n)$$

(EQ 6.1)

The conditional probability $P(X_{n+1} = j | X_n = i_n)$ is called the **transition probability** to go from state i_n to state j.

EXAMPLE 6.8: MARKOV PROCESS

Consider a discrete-time discrete-space Markov process whose state space is {1,2,3}. Let $P(X_3 = 1 | X_2 = 1) = 0.2$; $P(X_3 = 2 | X_2 = 1) = 0.4$; $P(X_3 = 3 | X_2 = 1) = 0.4$. Suppose that we know that $P(X=1) = 1$. Then, the Markov property allows us to compute $\pi(3)$ no matter which path was taken to reach the state 1 at time 2.

Note that for a discrete-time stochastic process at time step n, we already know the sequence of prior states. At time n, we are usually interested in computing $\pi(n + 1)$ given this past history. The Markov property allows us to forget everything about history except the value of the current random variable, which encapsulates all past history. This is similar in spirit to the memorylessness property of the exponential distribution (see Section 1.6.3).

A similar property holds true for continuous-time stochastic processes. For simplicity, we will first study discrete-time processes that obey the Markov property, also known as **discrete-time Markov chains**, before considering continuous-time Markov processes.

6.2.3 Homogeneity, State-Transition Diagrams, and the Chapman-Kolmogorov Equations

A stochastic process may satisfy the Markov property even if its transition probabilities vary over time. A process with time-dependent transition probabilities is called a **nonhomogeneous Markov process**. Of course, this greatly complicates the analysis, but we can simplify it by decreeing that the transition probabilities should be time-independent. In our example, this means that when the person is on a particular step—say, step 4—the probability of going to any other step is always the same, no matter *when* the person got to step 4. Such a process is called a **homogeneous Markov process**. For a homogeneous Markov process, we define the *time-independent* transition probability between state i and state j as $p_{ij} = P(X_n = j | X_{n-1} = i)$ for any n.

EXAMPLE 6.9: HOMOGENEOUS MARKOV PROCESS

Consider the discrete-time discrete-space stochastic process in Example 6.8. If this process were homogeneous, we need not consider exactly one point in time, such as time 2. Instead, if $P(X_{n+1}= 1 \mid X_n = 1) = 0.2$; $P(X_{n+1}=2 \mid X_n = 1) = 0.4$; $P(X_{n+1} = 3 \mid X_n = 1) = 0.4$, we can compute the distribution X_{n+1} given X_n for all values of n.

The state-transition probabilities for a homogeneous Markov chain with N states have two equivalent representations. The first is in the form of an $N \times N$ transition matrix $\mathbf{A}$ whose elements are the probabilities p_{ij}. This representation has the attractive property that the probability of going from any state i to state j in two steps is given by the elements of $\mathbf{A}^2$. The second is as a graph (see Example 6.10). In this representation, vertices represent states, and the annotation on an edge from vertex i to vertex j is p_{ij}. This visually represents a Markov chain. Note that a non-homogeneous Markov chain requires such a state-transition diagram for each time step.

EXAMPLE 6.10: REPRESENTING A HOMOGENEOUS MARKOV PROCESS

Continuing with Example 6.9: We have already seen that $p_{11} = 0.2$, $p_{12} = 0.4$, $p_{13} = 0.4$. Suppose that $p_{21} = 1.0$, $p_{22} = 0$, $p_{23} = 0$, and $p_{31} = 0.5$, $p_{32} = 0.25$, $p_{33} = 0.25$. Then, we can represent it in two ways as follows and as shown in Figure 6.1.

$$A = \begin{bmatrix} 0.2 & 0.4 & 0.4 \\ 1.0 & 0 & 0 \\ 0.5 & 0.25 & 0.25 \end{bmatrix}$$

where A is a right stochastic matrix (see Section 3.6).

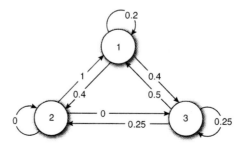

Figure 6.1 State-transition diagram for Example 6.10

Given the set of transition probabilities p_{ij} for a homogeneous Markov chain, we can define the m-step transition probability from state i to state j denoted $p_{ij}^{(m)}$ by

$$p_{ij}^{(m)} = P(X_{n+m}=j \mid X_n = i) = \sum_k p_{ij}^{(m-1)} p_{kj} \qquad m = 2,3,\ldots \qquad \textbf{(EQ 6.2)}$$

where the sum of products form comes from summing across independent events (that of going to some intermediate state in $m-1$ steps), and each term is a product because it is the combination of two independent events (going from state i to state k and from state k to state m). These relations exist only because of the Markovian nature of the chain. They are important enough that they are given their own name: the **Chapman-Kolmogorov** equations, which can also be stated as:

$$p_{ij}^{(m)} = P(X_{n+m}=j \mid X_n = i) = \sum_k p_{ik} p_{kj}^{(m-1)} \qquad m = 2,3,\ldots \qquad \textbf{(EQ 6.3)}$$

Comparing the two, we see that the first formulation traces the trajectory of the process as it goes from state i to state k in $m-1$ steps and from state k to state j in one step. The second formulation traces the trajectory of the process as it goes from state i to state k in one step and from state k to state j in $m-1$ steps. Clearly, these are equivalent recursions.

6.2.4 Irreducibility

If every state of a stochastic process can be reached from every other state after a finite number of steps, the process is called **irreducible**; otherwise, it is **reducible**. Moreover, if states of a stochastic process can be separated into subsets that are mutually unreachable, we call each such set a **separable subchain**.

EXAMPLE 6.11: A REDUCIBLE MARKOV CHAIN

Consider the Markov chain in Figure 6.2. Here, the transition probabilities p_{ij} for i even and j odd or i odd and j even are 0. Therefore, if the initial state of the process is an even-numbered state, the trajectory of process is confined to even-numbered states. Alternatively, a process that starts from an odd-numbered state will forever stay in odd-numbered states. The even-numbered states are unreachable from the odd-numbered steps' states, and the chain, therefore, is reducible. Indeed, we could separate the even-numbered and odd-numbered states into separate chains that would equivalently describe the process. We can generalize this idea to construct stochastic processes that can be decomposed into as many subchains as we wish.

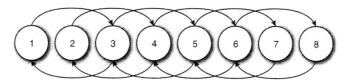

Figure 6.2 A reducible Markov chain

6.2.5 Recurrence

For every state j of a stochastic process, one of two conditions must hold: After entering state j, either the probability of reentering state j after a finite number of steps is 1, or there is some nonzero probability that the state is not reentered after a finite number of steps. In Example 6.3, this is equivalent to saying that after stepping on a stair—say, stair 6—it either is certain that the person will return to stair 6, or there is a nonzero probability that the person will not return to stair 6. If return to a state is certain, we call the state **recurrent**; otherwise, we call it **transient**.

Let f_j^n denote the probability that the *first* return to state j is after n steps. State j is recurrent if $\sum_{n=1}^{\infty} f_j^n = 1$ and transient otherwise.

Although a state is recurrent, its expected recurrence period, defined as $\sum_{n=1}^{\infty} n f_j^n$, may be infinite. This sum may diverge if f_j^n is sufficiently large for large values of n. In such cases, the mean recurrence period is infinite, and the state is called **recurrent null**. Otherwise, it is called **recurrent non-null**.

6.2.6 Periodicity

Given a recurrent state j, suppose that the only way to return to that state is to take r, $2r$, $3r$... steps, with $r \geq 2$. We then call the state j **periodic**, with a period r. Periodic states arise when the Markov chain has a cycle. A trivial way to check whether a state is periodic is to see whether it has a self-loop, that is $p_{jj} > 0$. If so, the state can be reentered with any desired number of steps, which makes $r = 1$ and the state **aperiodic**. For an irreducible Markov chain, if *any* state has a self-loop, all states are aperiodic.

EXAMPLE 6.12: PERIODIC AND APERIODIC MARKOV CHAINS

The Markov chain in Figure 6.2 is periodic with period 2, and the chain in Figure 6.1 is aperiodic.

6.2.7 Ergodicity

The sequence of states visited by a stochastic process is called its **trajectory**. For example, a valid trajectory for the chain in Figure 6.1 is $1 \to 2 \to 1 \to 3 \to \ldots$. Given a trajectory, we can compute a statistic on it, such as the fraction of the trajectory spent in a particular state. This statistic is the limiting ratio of the number of occurrences of that state to the length of the trajectory. Because trajectories can be made as long as we desire, if the limiting statistic exists, it can be approximated as closely as we wish. We call such a limit a **time average**.

Now, consider a set of instances of the same stochastic process. At each time step, each instance changes state according to the same transition probabilities. Nevertheless, the trajectory associated with any pair of processes in the ensemble may differ owing to their stochastic nature. Suppose that we want to compute a statistic on the ensemble of trajectories at any time step. For instance, we may wish to compute the fraction of trajectories in state 1 at time step 10. If the limiting statistic exists, we can approximate this statistic as closely as we wish by making the ensemble sufficiently large. We call such a limit an **ensemble average**.

An interesting question is whether a statistic computed as a time average is the same as a statistic computed as an ensemble average. As the next example shows, this need not necessarily be the case!

EXAMPLE 6.13: TIME AND SPACE AVERAGES

Consider the stochastic process shown in Figure 6.2. Suppose that the initial state is 1 and that the statistic we wish to compute is the fraction of time spent in an odd-numbered state. Clearly, no matter how long the length of the trajectory, this time average will be 1.0. Now, consider an ensemble of instances of this process where the initial state is chosen equally probably as 1 or 2. For this ensemble, the limiting value of the statistic at any time step will be 0.5 and is the ensemble average. For this stochastic process, the time average differs from the ensemble average.

Intuitively, a stochastic process is **ergodic** if every statistic computed as a time average over a sufficiently long single trajectory can also be computed as an ensemble average over a sufficiently large number of trajectories. For this to be true, the sequence of states visited by the stochastic process over time should look statistically identical to the set of states occupied by an ensemble of processes at a single time step. We now consider the conditions under which a stochastic process is ergodic.[2]

---

2. Many mutually incompatible definitions of ergodicity exist in the literature. The definition presented here was chosen because it has a simple intuitive basis.

To begin with, we define a *state j* to be ergodic if it is recurrent non-null and aperiodic. Continuing with Example 6.3, it is a stair that the person will return to (recurrent), with a mean recurrence period that is finite (non-null), and such that the returning times do not have a least common divisor larger than 1 (aperiodic). If all the states in a Markov chain are ergodic, other than for a finite set of transient states, the chain itself is ergodic.[3] It can be shown that a finite aperiodic irreducible Markov chain is always ergodic. (In other words, all states of a finite irreducible Markov chain are recurrent non-null.)

EXAMPLE 6.14: ERGODIC MARKOV CHAIN

The Markov chain in Figure 6.1 is finite, aperiodic, and irreducible. Therefore, it is also ergodic.

A chain that is ergodic is insensitive to its initial state $\pi(0)$: Independent of its initial state, $\pi(n)$, the distribution of X_n (for reasonably large values of n) is the same. Nonergodic chains are (1) recurrent null (so that they may take a long time to return to some state), or (2) reducible (so that some parts of the chain do not communicate with others), or (3) periodic (so that quantities of interest also share the same period).

6.2.8 A Fundamental Theorem

We now have enough terminology to state (without proof) a fundamental theorem of queueing theory.

Theorem 6.11: The states of an irreducible Markov chain are one of the following: all transient, all recurrent null, or recurrent non-null. If any state is periodic, all states are periodic with the same period *r*.

Intuitively, this categorizes all Markov chains into a few types. The first are those where the process goes from state to state but never returns to any state. In this case, all states are transient. In the second and third types of chain, the process returns to at least one of the states. But the chain is irreducible, and so we can go from that state to all other states. Therefore, if the process can return to any one state, it can by definition return to all other states, which makes all states recurrent. In the second type, the transition probabilities are such that the expected recurrence period is infinite, so that all states are recurrent null. In the third type,

---

3. We allow a finite number of transient states in the chain because over sufficiently long trajectories or for a sufficiently large ensemble, their contribution to any statistic is negligible.

the expected recurrence period for all states is finite. For this type, we have two subtypes: the periodic recurrent non-null chains, whose states all share the same period, and the aperiodic recurrent non-null (ergodic) chains, for which no such period can be defined.

6.2.9 Stationary (Equilibrium) Probability of a Markov Chain

Recall that for a homogeneous Markov chain, the state-transition probabilities are time-independent. For a homogeneous chain, we expect that the probability of *being* in any particular state to also be time-independent. (If the probability of going from one state to another does not depend on time, the probability of being in any state shouldn't either.)

Of course, the probability of being in a particular state may depend on the initial state, especially for nonergodic chains, which are sensitive to their initial conditions. We define the **stationary probability distribution** of a Markov chain as follows: Suppose that we start with the initial distribution $\pi(0) = \pi^*$. Then, π^* is also the stationary distribution of the chain, if for all n, $\pi(n) = \pi^*$. Intuitively, if we start with the probability of being in each state j as defined by the stationary distribution, the transitions from each state according to the transition probabilities do not change the probability of being in each state.

EXAMPLE 6.15: STATIONARY DISTRIBUTION

Compute the stationary distribution of the Markov chain in Figure 6.3.

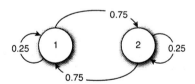

Figure 6.3 A simple Markov chain

Solution:

By symmetry, we guess that the stationary probability of being in state 1 is 0.5 and of being in state 2 is 0.5; that is, $\pi(0) = \pi^* = [0.5\ 0.5]$. After one time step, the probability of being in state 1 is 0.25*0.5 + 0.75*0.5, where the first term is the probability of remaining in state 1, and the second term is the probability of going from state 2 to state 1; we sum these probabilities because these are independent events. As expected, this sums to 0.5, so that the probability of being in state 1 in time step 2 is also 0.5. Symmetrically, if the probability of being in state 2 at time 1 is 0.5, the probability of being in state 2 at time 2 is also 0.5. Therefore, the stationary probability distribution of this chain is indeed $\pi^* = [0.5 \ 0.5]$.

6.2.10 A Second Fundamental Theorem

We now state a second fundamental theorem that allows us to compute stationary probabilities for any Markov chain.

Theorem 6.2: In an irreducible and aperiodic homogeneous Markov chain, the limiting probability distribution

$$\pi^* = \lim_{n \to \infty} \pi(n)$$

(EQ 6.4)

always exists and is independent of the initial state probability distribution $\pi(0)$. Moreover, if all the states are ergodic (being recurrent non-null, in addition to being aperiodic), then π_j^*, the stationary probability of being in state j, is nonzero and can be uniquely determined by solving the following set of equations:

$$\sum_j \pi_j^* = 1$$
$$\pi_j^* = \sum_i \pi_i^* p_{ij}$$

(EQ 6.5)

This theorem provides us with a simple set of equations to determine the stationary probability that the Markov chain is in any particular state. We need only verify that the set of states is finite, memoryless (i.e., satisfies the Markov property), irreducible (all states can be reached from each other), and aperiodic (e.g., because of at least one self-loop). These properties can be verified through simple inspection. Then, we can solve the preceding system of equations to obtain the stationary probability of being in each state.

EXAMPLE 6.16: STATIONARY PROBABILITY OF A MARKOV CHAIN

Compute the stationary probability for the Markov chain in Figure 6.1.

Solution:

Note that this chain is ergodic, so we can use Theorem 6.2 to obtain the following equations:

$$\pi_1^* = 0.2\pi_1^* + 1\pi_2^* + 0.5\pi_3^*$$

$$\pi_2^* = 0.4\pi_1^* + 0\pi_2^* + 0.25\pi_3^*$$

$$\pi_3^* = 0.4\pi_1^* + 0\pi_2^* + 0.25\pi_3^*$$

$$1 = \pi_1^* + \pi_2^* + \pi_3^*$$

We solve this system of equations by using, for example, Gaussian elimination (see Section 3.4.2) to obtain $\pi_1^* = 15/31$; $\pi_2^* = 8/31$; $\pi_3^* = 8/31$, which is the stationary probability distribution of the chain.

6.2.11 Mean Residence Time in a State

Besides knowing the stationary probability of being in a particular state of a Markov chain, we would also like to know how long the process spends in each state. This duration can be computed by first obtaining the probability P(system stays in state j for m additional steps given that it just entered state j). The probability that the system stays in the same state after one time step is clearly p_{jj}. Moreover, after one time step, being Markovian, the process has no memory that it was in that state earlier. Therefore, the probability of staying in the state for m steps is given by $p_{jj}^{m}(1 - p_{jj})$, which is a geometrically distributed random variable with parameter $(1 - p_{jj})$ (see Section 1.5.3). This allows us to compute the mean of the distribution: the expected residence time in state j, as $1/(1 - p_{jj})$.

EXAMPLE 6.17: RESIDENCE TIME

Compute the residence times in each state of the Markov chain shown in Figure 6.1.

Solution:

$p_{11} = 0.2$, so E(residence time in state 1) = $1/(1 - 0.2) = 1/0.8 = 1.25$.

$p_{22} = 0$, so E(residence time in state 1) = $1/(1 - 0) = 1$.

$p_{33} = 0.25$, so E(residence time in state 1) = $1/(1 - 0.25) = 1/0.75 = 1.33$.

6.3 Continuous-Time Markov Chains

Our discussion so far has focused on discrete-time Markov chains, where state transitions happen every clock tick. We now turn our attention to continuous-time chains, where state transitions can happen independent of clock ticks. Most of the intuitions developed for discrete-time chains carry through to continuous-time chains, with a few modifications. The main point of difference is that we need to consider the time instants t_1, t_2,... when state transitions occur, rather than assuming that a state transition occurs at every clock tick. We briefly state the main results for a continuous-time stochastic process and then focus on a specific type of continuous-time process: the birth-death process.

6.3.1 Markov Property for Continuous-Time Stochastic Processes

We first state the Markov property for continuous-time stochastic processes. The stochastic process $X(t)$ forms a continuous-time Markov chain if for all integers n and for any sequence of times t_1, t_2,...,t_{n+1} such that $t_1 < t_2 < ... < t_{n+1}$:

$$P(X(t_{n+1}) = j \mid X(t_1) = i_1, X(t_2) = i_2,...,X(t_n) = i_n) = P(X(t_{n+1} = j) \mid X(t_n) = i_n) \quad \text{(EQ 6.6)}$$

Intuitively, this means that the future $(X(t_{n+1}))$ depends on the past only through the current state i_n.

The definitions of homogeneity, irreducibility, recurrence, periodicity, and ergodicity introduced for discrete-time Markov chains in Section 6.2.3 continue to hold for continuous-time chains with essentially no change, so we will not restate them here.

6.3.2 Residence Time in a Continuous-Time Markov Chain

Analogous to the geometric distribution of residence times in a discrete-time chain, residence times are exponentially distributed for a continuous-time Markov chain for essentially the same reasons. If we denote the residence time in state j by R_j, the exponential distribution gives us the memorylessness property:

$$P(R_j > s + t | R_j > s) = P(R_j > t) \quad \text{(EQ 6.7)}$$

6.3.3 Stationary Probability Distribution for a Continuous-Time Markov Chain

The definition of the stationary probability of a continuous-time Markov chain closely follows that of a discrete-time Markov chain. Therefore, we omit the intermediate details and present the set of equations necessary to compute the stationary probability of a continuous-time homogeneous Markov chain.

Define the transition probability of going from state i to state j by

$$p_{ij}(t) = P(X(s + t) = j | X(s) = i) \quad \text{(EQ 6.8)}$$

Intuitively, this means that if the process is at state i at any time s, the probability that it will get to state j after a time interval t is given by $p_{ij}(t)$. This is independent of the value of s because the process is homogeneous.

Define the quantity q_{ij}, which denotes the **rate** at which the process departs from state i to state j (where j and i differ) when in state i:

$$q_{ij} = \lim_{\Delta t \to 0} p_{ij}(\Delta t)/\Delta t \qquad \text{(EQ 6.9)}$$

That is, the probability that the process transitions from i to j during any interval of length Δt time units, conditional on its already being at state i, is $q_{ij}\Delta t$. We also define the negative quantity q_{ii} by

$$q_{ii} = -\sum_{j \neq i} q_{ij} \qquad \text{(EQ 6.10)}$$

Then, $-q_{ii}$ is the rate at which the process does *not* stay in state i (i.e., departs to some other state) during an interval of length Δt time units. Because $\sum_j p_{ij}(t) = 1$ (at any time t, the chain transitions to *some* state, including the current state), we see that

$$\sum_j q_{ij}(t) = 0 \qquad \text{(EQ 6.11)}$$

With these quantities in hand, we can define the time evolution of the probability of being in state j at time t, defined as $\pi_j(t)$, by

$$\frac{d\pi_j(t)}{dt} = q_{jj}\pi_j(t) + \sum_{k \neq j} q_{kj}\pi_k(t) \qquad \text{(EQ 6.12)}$$

For ergodic continuous-time Markov chains, as $t \to \infty$, these probabilities converge to the stationary probability distributions π_j^*, which are implicitly defined by

$$q_{jj}\pi_j^* + \sum_{k \neq j} q_{kj}\pi_k^* = 0$$
$$\sum_j \pi_j^* = 1 \qquad \text{(EQ 6.13)}$$

Note that this is Equation 6.12 with the rate of change of the probability set to 0—which is what one would expect for a stationary probability—and with the time-dependent probabilities replaced by their time-independent limiting values.

This ends our brief summary of continuous-time Markov processes. Instead of studying general continuous-time processes, we instead focus on a smaller but very important subclass: continuous-time birth-death processes.

6.4 Birth-Death Processes

This section discusses a special class of continuous-time homogenous Markov chains having the property that state transitions are permitted from state j only to states $j - 1$ and $j + 1$ (if these states exist). This class is well suited to describe such processes as the arrival and departure of customers from a queue (the subject of queueing theory, after all!), where the state index corresponds to the number of customers awaiting service. More precisely, if the number of customers in the system is j, the Markov chain is considered to be in state j. Customer arrivals cause the number of customers in the system to increase by one, which moves the process to state $j + 1$, and this happens at a rate $q_{j,j+1}$. Similarly, customer departures (due to service) cause the process to move from state j to state $j - 1$, and this happens at the rate $q_{j,j-1}$. In keeping with standard terminology, we denote:

$$\lambda_j = q_{j,j+1}$$
$$\mu_j = q_{j,j-1}$$

(EQ 6.14)

as the **birth** and **death rates**, respectively. Note that these rates can be state-dependent but cannot be time-dependent, owing to homogeneity. Also, by definition, at state i, the transition rates q_{ij} are 0 for all j other than i, $i - 1$, and $i + 1$. Given this fact, Equation 6.11, and Equation 6.14, we find that

$$q_{jj} = -(\lambda_j + \mu_j)$$

(EQ 6.15)

For a birth-death process, being in state j has the intuitive meaning that the population size is j; that is, there are j customers in the queueing system. Note that when $j = 1$, we have one customer in the system—the customer that is receiving service—and *none* are in the queue. Generalizing, in state j, we have one customer receiving service and $j - 1$ in the queue awaiting service.

6.4.1 Time-Evolution of a Birth-Death Process

Because a birth-death process is a continuous-time Markov chain, the time evolution of $\pi_j(t)$ is given by Equation 6.12. We substitute Equation 6.14 and Equation 6.15 to find

$$\frac{d\pi_j(t)}{dt} = -(\lambda_j + \mu_j)\pi_j(t) + \lambda_{j-1}\pi_{j-1}(t) + \mu_{j+1}\pi_{j+1}(t) \qquad j \geq 1$$

(EQ 6.16)

$$\frac{d\pi_0(t)}{dt} = -\lambda_0\pi_0(t) + \mu_1\pi_1(t) \qquad j = 0$$

This describes the time evolution of a birth-death system. In practice, solving these equations is complex and does not give too many insights into the structure of the system. These are better obtained from the stationary probability distribution, which we study next.

6.4.2 Stationary Probability Distribution of a Birth-Death Process

Because a birth-death process is an ergodic continuous-time Markov chain, its stationary probability distribution is given by Equation 6.13. Denoting the stationary probability of being in state j by $\pi_j^* P_j$ and substituting Equation 6.14 and Equation 6.15 into Equation 6.13, we obtain the following equations:

$$0 = -(\lambda_j + \mu_j)\pi_j^* + \lambda_{j-1}\pi_{j-1}^* + \mu_{j+1}\pi_{j+1}^* \qquad j \geq 1$$
$$0 = -\lambda_0\pi_0^* + \mu_1\pi_1^* \qquad\qquad\qquad\qquad j = 0 \qquad \textbf{(EQ 6.17)}$$
$$\sum_j \pi_j^* = 1$$

In matrix form, we can write the first two equations as

$$PQ = 0 \qquad\qquad \textbf{(EQ 6.18)}$$

where

$$P = \begin{bmatrix} \pi_0^* & \pi_1^* & \pi_2^* & \cdots \end{bmatrix}$$

$$Q = \begin{bmatrix} -\lambda_0 & \lambda_0 & 0 & \cdots & \cdots \\ \mu_1 & -(\lambda_1 + \mu_1) & \lambda_1 & \cdots & \cdots \\ 0 & \mu_2 & -(\lambda_2 + \mu_2) & \lambda_2 & \cdots \\ \cdots & \cdots & \cdots & \cdots & \cdots \end{bmatrix} \qquad \textbf{(EQ 6.19)}$$

The two matrices are infinite-dimensional if the population size is unbounded. Moreover, by defining $P(t)$ as

$$P(t) = \begin{bmatrix} \pi_0(t) & \pi_1(t) & \pi_2(t) & \cdots \end{bmatrix}$$

we can rewrite Equation 6.16 as

$$dP(t)/dt = P(t)Q \qquad\qquad \textbf{(EQ 6.20)}$$

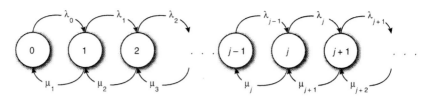

Figure 6.4 State-transition-rate diagram for a birth-death process

6.4.3 Finding the Transition-Rate Matrix

The Q matrix defined by Equation 6.19 is also called the **transition-rate matrix**. It is important because it allows us to derive both the time-dependent evolution of the system (i.e., $P_j(t)$), through Equation 6.20, and the long-term probability of being in state j, through Equation 6.18. Thus, in practice, the first step in studying a birth-death process is to write down its Q matrix.

Consider the representation of a generic birth-death process in Figure 6.4. Here, we represent each state j by a circle, and we label the arc from state j to state k with the transition rate q_{jk}. From this figure, we can determine Q for a birth-death process as follows. Note that the diagonal elements of Q (i.e., q_{jj}) are the negative of the quantities *leaving* state j. Focusing on the jth column, the $q_{j-1,j}$th elements, immediately above the diagonal, such as element q_{01}, are the rates entering state j from state $j - 1$, i.e., λ_{j-1} and the $q_{j+1,j}$th elements, such as element q_{32}, immediately below the diagonal, are the rates entering state j from state $j + 1$. All other elements are 0. In each row, the quantities sum to zero, due to Equation 6.11.

Thus, given the state-transition-rate diagram, it is possible to quickly construct Q and use it to obtain the time-dependent and time-independent (stationary) probabilities of being in each state. We now use this approach to study some standard birth-death systems. Note that this inspection approach also applies to all continuous-time Markov chains, where we can determine the elements of the Q matrix by inspecting the corresponding state-transition-rate diagram, then solving for P and $P(t)$ by using Equation 6.18 and Equation 6.20, respectively.

EXAMPLE 6.18: TRANSITION-RATE MATRIX FOR A BIRTH-DEATH PROCESS

Consider the state-rate-transition diagram in Figure 6.5. What are the P and Q matrices for this system? What are the equations for its time evolution and the long-term probability of being in each state?

The P matrix is $\begin{bmatrix} \pi_0^* & \pi_1^* & \pi_2^* & \pi_3^* \end{bmatrix}$ and $P(t) = \begin{bmatrix} \pi_0(t) & \pi_1(t) & \pi_2(t) & \pi_3(t) \end{bmatrix}$. By inspection, we can write the Q matrix as

$$\mathbf{Q} = \begin{bmatrix} -1 & 1 & 0 & 0 \\ 5 & -10 & 5 & 0 \\ 0 & 8 & -12 & 4 \\ 0 & 0 & 10 & -10 \end{bmatrix}$$

Therefore, the time evolution of state probabilities is given by

$$\frac{d}{dt}\left(\begin{bmatrix} \pi_0(t) & \pi_1(t) & \pi_2(t) & \pi_3(t) \end{bmatrix}\right) = \begin{bmatrix} \pi_0(t) & \pi_1(t) & \pi_2(t) & \pi_3(t) \end{bmatrix} \begin{bmatrix} -1 & 1 & 0 & 0 \\ 5 & -10 & 5 & 0 \\ 0 & 8 & -12 & 4 \\ 0 & 0 & 10 & -10 \end{bmatrix}$$

$$\begin{bmatrix} \dot{\pi}_0(t) & \dot{\pi}_1(t) & \dot{\pi}_2(t) & \dot{\pi}_3(t) \end{bmatrix} = \begin{bmatrix} \pi_0(t) & \pi_1(t) & \pi_2(t) & \pi_3(t) \end{bmatrix} \begin{bmatrix} -1 & 1 & 0 & 0 \\ 5 & -10 & 5 & 0 \\ 0 & 8 & -12 & 4 \\ 0 & 0 & 10 & -10 \end{bmatrix}$$

which is a system of differential equations that can be solved to give the evolution of the time-varying probabilities $\pi_i(t)$.

The long-term probability of being in each state is given by

$$\begin{bmatrix} \pi_0^* & \pi_1^* & \pi_2^* & \pi_3^* \end{bmatrix} \begin{bmatrix} -1 & 1 & 0 & 0 \\ 5 & -10 & 5 & 0 \\ 0 & 8 & -12 & 4 \\ 0 & 0 & 10 & -10 \end{bmatrix} = 0$$

which is a system of linear equations in four variables that can be solved to obtain the stationary probability distribution of the chain.

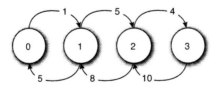

Figure 6.5 A simple birth-death process

6.4.4 A Pure-Birth (Poisson) Process

Consider a system in which $\lambda_j = \lambda$ for all j (the departure rate from all states is the same) and $\mu_j = 0$ for all j (the death rate is 0). This represents a **Poisson** process whose population grows without bound and whose rate of growth is λ independent of the population size, that is, we expect the population to grow by 1 every $1/\lambda$ seconds independent of the current population size.

We study two properties of this process: the probability of being in state j at time t, which corresponds to having j arrivals in time t, and the distribution of interarrival times, that is, the expected time between going from any state to the adjacent state.

We can derive the probability of being in any state directly from Equation 6.16. Substituting the values for λ and μ in this equation, we get

$$\frac{d\pi_j(t)}{dt} = -\lambda\pi_j(t) + \lambda\pi_{j-1}(t) \qquad j \geq 1$$

$$\frac{d\pi_0(t)}{dt} = -\lambda\pi_0(t)$$

(EQ 6.21)

The second equation is a trivial differential equation whose solution is given by

$$\pi_0(t) = e^{-\lambda t}$$

(EQ 6.22)

We substitute this into the first equation to get

$$\frac{d\pi_1(t)}{dt} = -\lambda\pi_1(t) + \lambda e^{-\lambda t}$$

(EQ 6.23)

whose solution is

$$\pi_1(t) = \lambda e^{-\lambda t}$$

(EQ 6.24)

By repeatedly substituting this into the first equation, we obtain

$$\pi_j(t) = \frac{(\lambda t)^j}{j!} e^{-\lambda t}$$

(EQ 6.25)

which is the density function for the Poisson distribution (see Section 1.5.4) with parameter λt. Thus, for a Poisson process with parameter λ, the probability of j arrivals in time t, which is also the probability of being in state j at time t, is given by a Poisson distribution with parameter λt. Because the mean of the Poisson distribution is also its parameter, the expected number of arrivals in time t is λt. This is intuitively pleasing: The arrival rate is λ, so in time t we should see, on average, λt arrivals.

EXAMPLE 6.19: POISSON PROCESS

Consider packets arriving to a link as a Poisson process at a mean rate of five packets/second. What is the probability that the link receives two packets after 2 seconds and ten packets after 2 seconds?

Solution:

We have $\lambda = 5$ and $t = 2$, so the Poisson parameter is 10. The probability of having two packets arrive to the link after 2 seconds is $\pi_2(2) = (10^2/2!)\,e^{-10} = 50 * e^{-10} = 2.26 * 10^{-3}$. This is a rather unlikely event.

The probability of having ten packets arrive to the link after 2 seconds is $\pi_{10}(2) = (10^{10}/10!)\,e^{-10} = 0.125$. Note that the expected number of packet arrivals after 2 seconds is ten, yet the probability that the expected number of packets is actually achieved is only 1 in 8!

We now derive the interarrival time distribution for a Poisson process. Let a denote the continuous random variable that represents the time between any two arrivals: We seek the distribution for a. Consider the cumulative density function of a, given by the probability $P(a \leq t) = 1 - P(a > t)$. But $P(a > t)$ is just $P(0$ customer arrivals in time $(0, t)) = 1 - \pi_0(t) = 1 - e^{-\lambda t}$, $t \geq 0$. The density function is given by differentiating this expression to get

$$a(t) = \lambda e^{-\lambda t} \tag{EQ 6.26}$$

We recognize this as an exponential distribution (see Section 1.6.3). This gives us the following important result:

> The interarrival times for a Poisson process
> are drawn from an exponential distribution.

We note that the exponential distribution is memoryless. Thus, for a Poisson process, not only is the rate of transitioning to the next state (the birth rate) independent of the current population size, but also the *time* at which this transition occurs does not depend on how long the process has been at the current population size.

6.4.5 Stationary Probability Distribution for a Birth-Death Process

We now return to computing the stationary probability distribution for a general birth-death process, using Equation 6.17. From the second equation, we immediately obtain

$$\pi_1^* = \frac{\lambda_0}{\mu_1}\pi_0^*$$

(EQ 6.27)

Substituting this into the first equation, we find that

$$\pi_2^* = \frac{\lambda_0\lambda_1}{\mu_1\mu_2}\pi_0^*$$

(EQ 6.28)

Repeating this substitution, we find that P_j is given by

$$\pi_j^* = \frac{\lambda_0\lambda_1\ldots\lambda_{j-1}}{\mu_1\mu_2\ldots\mu_j}\pi_0^* = \pi_0^*\prod_{i=0}^{j-1}\frac{\lambda_i}{\mu_{i+1}}$$

(EQ 6.29)

We therefore obtain the long-term probabilities of being in any state j as a function of the probability of being in state 0 and the system parameters. Knowing that these probabilities sum to 1, we can determine

$$\pi_0^* = \frac{1}{1 + \displaystyle\sum_{j=1}^{\infty}\prod_{i=0}^{j-1}\frac{\lambda_i}{\mu_{i+1}}}$$

(EQ 6.30)

This can be substituted back into Equation 6.29 to obtain the long-term probability of being in any state j. Of course, we need to ensure that the series in the denominator of Equation 6.30 actually converges! Otherwise, π_0^* is undefined, and so are all the other π_i^*. It turns out that the condition for convergence, as well as for the chain to be ergodic, is the existence of a value j_0 such that for all values of $j > j_0$, $\lambda_j < \mu_j$. We interpret this to mean that after the population reaches some threshold j_0, the rate of departures must exceed the rate of arrivals. This makes intuitive sense: Otherwise, the population size will grow (in expectation) without bound, and the probability of any particular population size will be 0.

EXAMPLE 6.20: GENERAL EQUILIBRIUM SOLUTION

Find the equilibrium probabilities of being in each state for the birth-death process shown in Figure 6.5.

Solution:

From Equation 6.30, we get

$$\pi_0^* = 1/[1 + 1/5 + (1 * 5)/(5 * 8) + (1 * 5 * 4)/5 * 8 * 10)] = 0.73$$

This can be substituted into Equation 6.29 to obtain

$$\pi_1^* = 1/5 \; \pi_0^* = 0.2 * 0.73 = 0.146.$$

$$\pi_1^* = 1/8 \; \pi_0^* = 0.125 * 0.73 = 0.09.$$

$$\pi_2^* = 1/20 \; \pi_0^* = 0.05 * 0.73 = 0.0365.$$

As a check, $0.73 + 0.146 + 0.09 + 0.0365 = 1.0025$, which is within the rounding error.

6.5 The M/M/1 Queue

The M/M/1 queue is the simplest nontrivial queueing system. Here, the a/b/c notation, also called **Kendall notation**, denotes the following.

- The "a" portion in the notation, the arrival process, is Markovian; it is a Poisson process with exponentially distributed interarrival times.
- The "b" portion in the notation, the departure process, is Markovian; it is a Poisson process with exponentially distributed interdeparture times.
- The "c" portion in the notation, the system is a single server.

Extended forms of the notation describe the size of the buffers available—we assume an infinite number—as well as the service discipline—we assume first come, first served—and other queueing parameters. However, the three-parameter version of the notation is the one that is commonly used.

The M/M/1 queueing system is a birth-death Markov process with a state-independent arrival rate λ and a state-independent departure rate μ. These rates are therefore also independent of the population size. This is counterintuitive, in that the rate of departure from a small population is the same as the rate of departure from a large population.

We study the long-term behavior of the M/M/1 queue by removing state dependence (the subscript j) in the transition rates in the analysis of Section 6.4.5. From Equation 6.29, we find that

$$\pi_j^* = \pi_0^* \prod_{i=0}^{j-1} \frac{\lambda}{\mu} = \pi_0^* \left(\frac{\lambda}{\mu}\right)^j \qquad j \geq 0 \qquad \text{(EQ 6.31)}$$

To obtain π_0^*, we use Equation 6.30 to obtain

$$\pi_0^* = \frac{1}{\left(1 + \sum_{j=1}^{\infty} \left(\frac{\lambda}{\mu}\right)^j\right)}$$ (EQ 6.32)

When $\lambda < \mu$, the infinite sum in the denominator converges, and the denominator reduces to $\left(\dfrac{1}{1 - \dfrac{\lambda}{\mu}}\right)$, so that

$$\pi_0^* = 1 - \frac{\lambda}{\mu}$$ (EQ 6.33)

The ratio λ/μ represents the intensity of the arrival rate as a fraction of the service rate and can be viewed as the utilization of the system. The value is important enough that it deserves its own symbol, ρ, which allows us to write Equation 6.33 as

$$\pi_0^* = 1 - \rho$$ (EQ 6.34)

This equation has the intuitive meaning that the probability that the system is idle (i.e., π_0^*) is (1 − utilization). It can be shown that this relationship is true for *all* queueing systems whose population size is unbounded.

We now use Equation 6.31 to obtain the stationary probability of being in any state j as

$$\pi_j^* = \rho^j(1 - \rho)$$ (EQ 6.35)

Note that this is a geometric distribution.

EXAMPLE 6.21: M/M/1 QUEUE

Consider a link to which packets arrive as a Poisson process at a rate of 300 packets/sec such that the time taken to service a packet is exponentially distributed. Suppose that the mean packet length is 500 bytes and that the link capacity is 1.5 Mbps. What is the probability that the link's queue has one, two, and ten packets, respectively?

Solution:

The packet length is 500 bytes = 4,000 bits, so the link service rate of 1,500,000 bits/sec = 375 packets/sec. Therefore, the utilization is 300/375 = 0.8. When the link queue has one packet, it is in state j = 2, because one packet is being served at that time. Thus, we need $\pi_2^* = 0.8^2 * 0.2 = 0.128$. For the queue having two packets, we compute $\pi_3^* = 0.8^3 * 0.2 = 0.1$. For ten packets in the queue, we compute $\pi_{11}^* = 0.8^{11} * 0.2 = 0.0067$, a fairly small quantity. Thus, even when the utilization is high (80%), the queue size is quite small, rarely exceeding ten packets.

Note that the long-term probability that the population size is j depends only on the utilization of the system. As the utilization increases, the probability of reaching larger population sizes increases. To see this analytically, consider the mean number of customers in the system, which is also the mean population size, denoted $\overline{N}$ defined by

$$\overline{N} = \sum_{j=0}^{\infty} j\pi_j^* \qquad \text{(EQ 6.36)}$$

It can be shown that when this sum converges (i.e., when $\lambda < \mu$):

$$\text{Mean number of customers in the system} = \overline{N} = \frac{\rho}{(1-\rho)} \qquad \text{(EQ 6.37)}$$

EXAMPLE 6.22: MEAN NUMBER OF CUSTOMERS IN THE QUEUE

Compute the mean number of packets in the system of Example 6.19.

Solution:

The utilization is 0.8, so the mean number of packets in the system is $0.8/(1-0.8)$ = 0.8/0.2 = 4. Of these, we expect three to be in the queue, and one to be in service.

It is obvious from Equation 6.37 that as $\rho \to 1$, $\overline{N} \to \infty$. That is, as the arrival rate approaches the service rate, the expected number of customers in the system grows without bound. This is somewhat unexpected: After all, the arrival rate is smaller than the service rate. Why, then, should the number of customers grow? The reason is that we are dealing with stochastic processes. Even though the arrival rate, on average, is lower than the service rate, there will be time periods when the short-term arrival rate exceeds the service rate. For instance, even if the mean arrival rate is one customer per second, there will be short intervals during which two or even three customers may arrive in 1 second. During this time, the queue builds up and is drained when the service rate exceeds the arrival rate. In fact, there is an interesting asymmetry in the system: When the short-term arrival rate exceeds the short-term service rate, the queue builds up, but when the service rate exceeds the arrival rate, if the queue is empty, the system does not build up "service credits." The server is merely idle. Thus, the system tends to build up queues that are drained only over time. This is reflected in the fact that as the utilization of the system increases, the mean number of customers in the system increases sharply.

It is remarkable that this fundamental insight into the behavior of a real queueing system can be derived with only elementary queueing theory. Moreover, this insight carries over to all other queueing systems: As the utilization approaches 1, the system becomes **congested**. The behavior of the mean queue length, which also corresponds to the waiting time, through Little's theorem, is shown in Figure 6.6.

It is clear that the queue length asymptotes to infinity as the utilization approaches 1. In networking terms, this means that as the arrival rate approaches a link's capacity, the queue at the immediately preceding router or switch will grow without bound, causing packet loss. This analysis allows us to derive a practical guideline: We should provision enough service capacity so that the system utilization never exceeds a threshold of around 70%. Alternatively, if this threshold is exceeded, either service requests should be dropped, or new service capacity should be made available so that the utilization decreases.

Another related quantity of interest for this queue is the mean waiting time in the queue. From Little's theorem, the mean number of customers in the system is the product of their mean waiting time and their mean arrival rate, so $\frac{\rho}{(1-\rho)}c =$ mean waiting time $*\lambda$, which means that

$$\text{Mean waiting time} = \frac{\frac{\rho}{\lambda}}{(1-\rho)} = \frac{\frac{1}{\mu}}{(1-\rho)} \qquad \text{(EQ 6.38)}$$

This quantity also grows without bound as the utilization approaches 1.

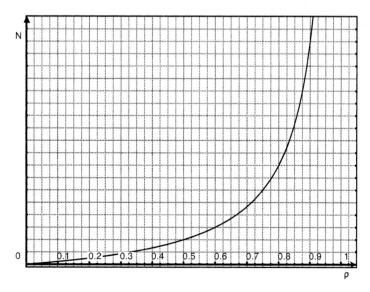

Figure 6.6 Mean queue length as a function of utilization

EXAMPLE 6.23: M/M/1 QUEUE WAITING TIME

What is the mean waiting time for a packet in the queue described in Example 6.20?

Solution:

For this queue, $\mu = 375$ and $\rho = 0.8$. So, the mean waiting time is $(1/375)/(1 - 0.8) = 5/375$ seconds = 13.3 ms.

6.6 Two Variations on the M/M/1 Queue

We now briefly consider two variations on the M/M/1 queue, essentially to give insight into how one proceeds with the analysis of a queueing system.

6.6.1 The M/M/∞ Queue: A Responsive Server

Suppose that a provider of service capacity brings on a new server to serve every arriving customer. This is like a private bank where new agents are brought on to provide individual attention to each customer when she or he arrives. This system can be modeled as a queue with an infinite number of servers, though, at any time, the number of servers is finite.

We can model and analyze this queue by using the same techniques as with an M/M/1 queue. We start with the state-transition-rate diagram shown in Figure 6.7. Note that μ_j, the rate of departure from the jth queue, is $j\mu$, which models the fact that when there are j customers, there are j servers. From the diagram, we can directly invoke Equation 6.29 to write down π_j^*, the stationary probability of being in state j, as

$$\pi_j^* = \pi_0^* \prod_{i=0}^{j-1} \frac{\lambda}{(i+1)\mu} = \pi_0^* \left(\frac{\lambda}{\mu}\right)^j \frac{1}{j!} \qquad \text{(EQ 6.39)}$$

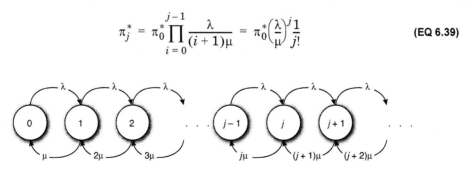

Figure 6.7 State-transition-rate diagram for an M/M/∞ queue

We solve for π_0^* by using Equation 6.30, as

$$\pi_0^* = \frac{1}{\left[1 + \sum\limits_{j=1}^{\infty} \left(\frac{\lambda}{\mu}\right)^j \frac{1}{j!}\right]}$$

(EQ 6.40)

Recalling the standard expansion $e^x = \sum\limits_{j=0}^{\infty} \frac{x^j}{j!}$, we see that

$$\pi_0^* = e^{-\frac{\lambda}{\mu}}$$

(EQ 6.41)

and

$$\pi_j^* = \pi_0^* \prod\limits_{i=0}^{j-1} \frac{\lambda}{(i+1)\mu} = e^{-\frac{\lambda}{\mu}} \left(\frac{\lambda}{\mu}\right)^j \frac{1}{j!}$$

(EQ 6.42)

Equation 6.42 shows that the stationary probability of being in state j is given by the Poisson distribution with parameter λ/μ. Thus, with "infinite" servers, the number of customers in the queue follows the Poisson distribution. This allows us to compute the expected number of customers in the queue as the mean of the Poisson, which is its parameter: λ/μ. All other parameters of interest for this queueing system can be derived from Equation 6.42.

EXAMPLE 6.24: RESPONSIVE SERVER

Suppose that customers arrive at a private bank, modeled as a responsive server, as a Poisson process at the rate of ten customers/hour. Suppose that a customer's needs can be met on average in 20 minutes and that the service-time distribution is exponentially distributed. What is the probability that there are five customers in the bank at any point in time?

Solution:

We have $\lambda = 10$ and $\mu = 3$ (i.e., three customers can be served an hour, on average, by a server). Thus, $\pi_0^* = e^{-10/3} = 0.036$. We need to find $\pi_5^* = 0.036 * (10/3)^5 * 1/5! = 0.123$. Thus, there is a nearly one in eight chance that there will be five customers in the bank at any given time.

6.6.2 M/M/1/K: Bounded Buffers

Suppose that the queueing system has only $K - 1$ buffers. In this case, the population size, including the customer in service, cannot grow beyond K, and arrivals when the system is in state K are lost, similar to packet loss when arriving at a full queue. To model this, we can simply ignore arrivals to state K, which means that we will never enter states $K + 1$, $K + 2$,.... This results in a state-transition-rate diagram shown in Figure 6.8.

The state transition rates are therefore

$$\lambda_j = \begin{cases} \lambda & j < K \\ 0 & j \geq K \end{cases}$$ (EQ 6.43)

and

$$\mu_j = \mu \qquad j=1,2,...,K$$

We can therefore use Equation 6.29 to write π_j^* as

$$\pi_j^* = \begin{cases} \pi_0^*\left(\frac{\lambda}{\mu}\right)^j & j \leq K \\ 0 & j > K \end{cases}$$ (EQ 6.44)

We use Equation 6.30 to obtain

$$\pi_0^* = \frac{1}{\left[1 + \sum_{j=1}^{K} \left(\frac{\lambda}{\mu}\right)^j\right]}$$ (EQ 6.45)

Given the standard result $\sum_{k=0}^{n-1} r^k = \frac{1-r^n}{1-r}$, we can simplify this to

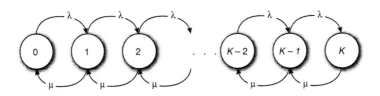

Figure 6.8 State-transition-rate diagram for an M/M/1/K queue

$$\pi_0^* = \frac{1 - \dfrac{\lambda}{\mu}}{1 - \left(\dfrac{\lambda}{\mu}\right)^{K+1}}$$ (EQ 6.46)

So, we can now write Equation 6.44 as

$$\pi_j^* = \begin{cases} \dfrac{1 - \dfrac{\lambda}{\mu}}{1 - \left(\dfrac{\lambda}{\mu}\right)^{K+1}} \left(\dfrac{\lambda}{\mu}\right)^j = \dfrac{1 - \rho}{1 - \rho^{K+1}} \rho^j & j \le K \\ 0 & j > K \end{cases}$$ (EQ 6.47)

As before, given these probabilities, we can compute all quantities of interest about the queueing system, such as the distribution of the queue length, the mean number of customers in the queue, and the mean waiting time. In particular, the intuitive meaning of π_K^* is the probability that the system is "full" when it has a buffer of size $K - 1$. So, π_K^* can be interpreted as the **blocking probability** of an M/M/1/K queue. We can then choose K as a sizing parameter to make π_K^* as small as desired.

Note that in this system, $\pi_0^* \ne 1 - \rho$, because the system size is bounded. Therefore, the number of customers served in a chosen time period may be lower than what the utilization indicates, because customer arrivals when the queue is full are lost. Moreover, the system is stable by definition, independent of the utilization, because excess arrivals are automatically dropped.

EXAMPLE 6.25: M/M/1/K QUEUE

Consider the system of Equation 6.21 but with the restriction that the queue has only four buffers. What is the probability that three of these are in use? How many buffers should we provision to ensure that the blocking probability is no more than 10^{-6}?

Solution:

We have $K = 5$, and $\dfrac{\lambda}{\mu} = 0.8$. From Equation 6.46, $\pi_0^* = (1 - 0.8)/(1 - 0.8^6) = 0.27$. If three buffers are in use, the system is in state $j = 4$. From Equation 6.44, we get $\pi_4^* = 0.27(0.8)^4 = 0.11$.

To size the buffer, we have to choose K such that $\pi_K^* < 10^{-6}$. We solve for K^* by using the inequality $10^{-6} > ((0.2)(0.8)^K)/(1 - 0.8^{K+1})$, to obtain $K^* = 55$. Thus, we need 54 buffers to satisfy this blocking probability.

6.7 Other Queueing Systems

Advanced texts of queueing theory describe queueing systems that go beyond the Markovian and exponential framework. Those queueing systems become much more difficult to analyze, so we will merely state two important results.

6.7.1 M/D/1: Deterministic Service Times

Consider a queueing system in which arrivals are from a Poisson process, but service times are deterministic. That is, as long as the queue is nonempty, the interdeparture time is deterministic rather than exponentially distributed. Representing the interdeparture time (a constant) by μ and the utilization by $\rho = \lambda/\mu$, it can be shown that the system is stable (i.e., the queue length is finite) as long as $\lambda < \mu$. Moreover, the long-term probability that the number of customers in the system is j (i.e., P_j) is given by

$$\pi_j^* = \begin{cases} 1-\rho & j = 0 \\ (1-\rho)(e^\rho - 1) & j = 1 \\ (1-\rho)\left(\displaystyle\sum_{i=0}^{j} \frac{(-1)^{j-i}(i\rho)^{j-i-1}(i\rho+j-i)e^{i\rho}}{(j-1)!}\right) & j > 1 \end{cases} \quad \text{(EQ 6.48)}$$

This allows us to derive the mean number of customers in the system as

$$\text{Mean customers in the system} = \rho + \frac{\rho^2}{2(1-\rho)} \quad \text{(EQ 6.49)}$$

and the mean response time as

$$\text{Mean response time} = \frac{1}{\mu} + \frac{\rho}{2\mu(1-\rho)} \quad \text{(EQ 6.50)}$$

Other quantities of interest regarding the M/D/1 queue can be found in standard texts on queueing theory.

6.7.2 G/G/1

Once the arrival and service processes become non-Poisson, the analysis of even a single queue becomes challenging. For such systems, few results are available other than Little's theorem, and if the queue size is unbounded, $\pi_0^* = 1 - \rho$. A detailed study of such queues is beyond the scope of this text.

6.7.3 Networks of Queues

So far, we have studied the behavior only of a single queue. This is like studying a network with a single router: not very interesting! What happens when we link the output of a queue to the input of another queue, as we do in any computer network? Intuitively, we are making the departure process of one queue the arrival process for the second queue. Moreover, we may have more than one departure process mix to form the arrival process. Can this be analyzed?

We represent this composite system, also called a *tandem of queues* as shown in Figure 6.9. Here, each queue is shown by a buffer (with customers or jobs in it) and a server (represented by a circle). Jobs served by the servers on the left enter the queue of the server on the right. Each queue and associated server is also called a *node* (drawing on the obvious graph analogy).

If all the queues on the left are M/M/1 queues, recall that their departure processes are Poisson. Moreover, it can be shown that the mixture of Poisson processes is also a Poisson process whose parameter is the sum of the individual processes. Therefore, the input to the queue on the right is a Poisson process that can be analyzed as an M/M/1 queue. This leads to the fundamental insight that a tandem of M/M/1 queues is analytically tractable. Because the departure process of an M/M/m queue (i.e., a queue with m servers) is also Poisson, this result holds true for tandems of M/M/m queues.

We can make things a bit more complicated: We can allow customers to enter *any* queue (node) as a Poisson process, and we can also allow customers that leave a node to exit the system altogether with some probability or join any other node in the system with some probability. Note that this can potentially lead to cycles, where customers go through some set of nodes more than once. Nevertheless, in 1963, the American mathematician J. R. Jackson was able to show that these networks behave as if each M/M/m queue was being fed by a single Poisson stream. Such networks are also called **Jacksonian** networks in his honor. For a Jacksonian network, we have a strong result: Let $\pi^*_{k_1 k_2 \ldots k_n}$ denote the long-term probability

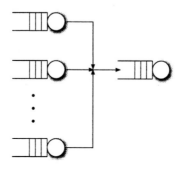

Figure 6.9 A network of queues

that there are k_1 customers at the first node, k_2 customers at the second node, and so on. Then:

$$\pi^*_{k_1 k_2 \ldots k_n} = \pi^*_{k_1} \pi^*_{k_2} \ldots \pi^*_{k_n} \tag{EQ 6.51}$$

That is, the joint probability of having a certain number of customers in each queue is the product of the individual probabilities. We interpret this to mean that each queue in the system acts as if it were independent of the others. This **product form** of the probability distribution greatly simplifies analysis.

Despite the elegance and power of Jacksonian network analysis, it can be rarely applied to study practical computer networks, because customers (packets) in real networks rarely arrive as a Poisson process. Thus, the output process is also non-Poisson, which makes subsequent analysis complex. In recent years, the development of network calculus and stochastic network calculus has allowed significant inroads into the study of the performance of non-Jacksonian networks.

6.8 Further Reading

The definitive introductory text on queueing theory is the two-volume text by L. Kleinrock, *Queueing Systems*, Wiley Interscience, 1975. A modern and thorough treatment of Markov chains can be found in P. Bremaud, *Markov Chains*, Springer, 1999. Further details on network calculus can be found in J.-Y. Le Boudec and P. Thiran, *Network Calculus*, Springer, 2001.

6.9 Exercises

1. **Little's theorem**

   Patients arriving at the Grand River Hospital Emergency Room have a mean waiting time of 3 hours. It has been found that, averaged over the period of a day, patients arrive at the rate of one every 5 minutes.

   a. How many patients are awaiting treatment on average at any given point in time?

   b. What should the size of the waiting room be so that it can always accommodate arrivals?

2. **A stochastic process**

   Consider that in Example 6.3, a person is on an infinite staircase on stair 10 at time 0 and potentially moves once every clock tick. Suppose that the person moves from stair i to stair $i + 1$ with probability 0.2, and from stair i to stair $i - 1$ with probability 0.2 (the probability of staying on stair i is 0.6). Compute the probability that the person is on each stair at time 1 (after the first move), time 2, and time 3.

3. **Discrete- and continuous-state and time processes**

   Come up with your own examples for all four combinations of discrete state/discrete time/continuous state/continuous time processes.

4. **Markov process**

   Is the process in Exercise 2 a Markov process? Why or why not?

5. **Homogeneity**

   Is the process in Exercise 2 homogeneous? Why or why not?

6. **Representation**

   a. Represent the process in Exercise 2 by using a transition matrix and a state transition diagram.
   b. Do the rows in this matrix have to sum to 1? Do the columns in this matrix have to sum to 1? Why or why not?
   c. Now, assume that the staircase has only four steps. Make appropriate assumptions (what are these?) to represent this finite process as a transition matrix and a state-transition diagram.

7. **Reducibility**

   Is the chain in Exercise 2 reducible? Why or why not?

8. **Recurrence**

   Is state 1 in the chain in Exercise 6(c) recurrent? Compute f_1^1, f_1^2, and f_1^3.

9. **Periodicity**

   Is the chain in Exercise 2 periodic? If not, give an example of a chain with period N for arbitrary $N > 1$.

10. **Ergodicity**

    Is any state in the chain of Exercise 6(c) nonergodic? Why or why not?

11. Stationary probability

Compute the stationary probability distribution of the chain in Exercise 6(c).

12. Residence times

Compute the residence time in each state of the Markov chain in Exercise 6(c).

13. Stationary probability of a birth-death process

Consider the following state-rate-transition diagram.

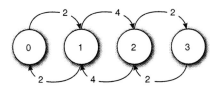

a. Compare this with the state-transition probability diagram in Exercise 6(c). What features are the same, and what differ?

b. Write down the Q matrix for this system.

c. Use the Q matrix to compute the stationary-probability distribution of this chain.

14. Poisson process

Prove that the interdeparture time of a pure-death process is exponentially distributed.

15. Stationary probabilities of a birth-death process

Use Equation 6.30 to compute the stationary probability of the birth-death process in Exercise 13.

16. M/M/1 queue

Is the birth-death process in Exercise 13 M/M/1? Why or why not?

17. M/M/1 queue

Consider a link to which packets arrive as a Poisson process at a rate of 450 packets/sec such that the time taken to service a packet is exponentially distributed. Suppose that the mean packet length is 250 bytes and that the link capacity is 1 Mbps.

a. What is the probability that the link's queue has one, two, and ten packets respectively?

    b. What is the mean number of packets in the system? What is the mean number in the queue?

    c. What is the mean waiting time?

18. Responsive (M/M/∞) server

Compute the ratio of π_j^* for a responsive server to the same value for an M/M/1 queue. How does this ratio behave as a function of j?

19. M/M/1/K server

Assume that the queueing system in Exercise 17 has ten buffers. Compute an upper bound on the probability of packet loss.

20. M/D/1 queue

Compute the mean number of customers in an M/D/1 system that has a utilization of 0.9.

    a. How does this compare with a similarly loaded M/M/1 system?

    b. Compute the ratio of the mean number of customers as a function of ρ.

    c. Use this to compare the behavior of an M/D/1 queue with that of an M/M/1 queue under heavy load.

7

Game Theory

Mathematical game theory is the study of the behavior of decision makers who are conscious that their actions affect one another and who may have imperfect knowledge of both one another and the future. Game theory originated with the mathematical study of such traditional games as bridge and chess, in which each player makes moves in response to, and in active consideration of, the moves of the other players. The concepts that arise in the study of such parlor games are widely applicable and are particularly relevant when a scarce resource has to be shared among many entities, each of which tries to maximize its own share: a situation that frequently occurs in computer networks.

The difference between a game and classical mathematical optimization can be intuited from an example. Suppose that you are looking for a particular store in an unfamiliar mall. This is an optimization problem: You could choose a search strategy that minimizes the time taken to find the store, given the set of actions available to you, such as walking past every store, looking for a directory, or asking for help. In contrast, suppose that you are looking for your lost friend in a mall. Should you stay in a central location so that your friend can find you? Or should you move around, with some risk that you may never meet? Introducing a second locus of decision making completely changes the problem!

The origin of game theory, due almost entirely to von Neumann and Morgenstern in the first half of the twentieth century, was part of a larger project applying mathematics to sociology to solve societal problems that had eluded centuries of past effort by qualitative sociologists. This worldview, especially the use of game theory to model policies for global nuclear warfare, gave the theory a (perhaps deserved) bad reputation, though it was routinely used to study microeconomic problems. In recent years, game theory has given deep insights into the operation of the Internet and in the design of decentralized algorithms for resource sharing, especially the theory known as *mechanism design*. Hence, there has been a resurgence of interest in these topics. This chapter describes the terminology of game theory, focuses on algorithmic aspects of mechanism design, and concludes with a sketch of the limitations of this approach.

7.1 Concepts and Terminology

7.1.1 Preferences and Preference Ordering

The ultimate basis of game theory is **utility theory**, which in turn is grounded in the axiomatization of the preference relationships of an agent.[1] The axioms of preferences refer to **goods**: concrete objects, such as a bar of soap or a meal at a restaurant, as well as more abstract quantities, such as the mean end-to-end delay, measured over intervals of 1 second and over the course of a given hour, between a particular browser and a Web server.

Here are the six **axioms of preferences**:

1. **Orderability:** Given two goods, an agent must prefer one to the other or view them both as being equally preferable. There is no option to "pass." Therefore, in any set of goods, there must exist a set of equivalent most-preferred and least-preferred goods.

2. **Transitivity:** An agent that prefers good A to good B and good B to good C prefers good A to good C.

3. **Continuity:** We assume that if an agent prefers good B more than good A and less than good C, it is always possible to define a lottery whereby with probability p, the agent would win prize A and with the remaining probability would win prize C, such that the agent equally prefers B and the lottery. We say that the agent is indifferent between B and a lottery with outcome $pA + (1 - p)C$ (see Example 7.1).

4. **Substitutability:** If an agent prefers good A and B equally, we should be able to replace one with the other in any lottery.

---

1. The term *agent* is widely used in the area of artificial intelligence to denote either a human being or software acting on a human's behalf.

5. **Monotonicity:** Given two lotteries with the same outcomes A and C, defined by $pA + (1 - p)C$, $qA + (1 - q)C$, respectively; an agent preferring A to C and if $p > q$, the agent prefers the first lottery to the second.

6. **Decomposability:** A **compound lottery** is run in two stages, where the winners of the first stage enter a second lottery and may subsequently either win again or lose. Decomposability means that such a compound lottery is equivalent to an appropriately defined single-stage lottery: If the outcome of the first lottery is $pA + (1 - p)B$ and of the second lottery is $qC + (1 - q)D$, and outcome B of the first lottery is participation in the second, the outcome of the compound lottery is $pA + (1- p)qC + (1 - p)(1 - q)D$.

EXAMPLE 7.1: CONTINUITY OF PREFERENCES

Consider an agent that prefers an apple (A) to a banana (B) and a banana to a carrot (C). Suppose that the agent participates in the following lottery: We divide the circumference of a circle into two sections, marked A and C, where the fraction of the circumference that is marked A is denoted p. A pointer pinned to the center of the circle is spun. If the pointer stops spinning at a part of the circle marked A, which happens with probability p, the agent wins A. Otherwise, it wins C. Continuity of preferences implies that there exists a value p such that the agent is equally happy with B and the results of this lottery. Intuitively, when p is 1, the agent always wins A, so it should prefer the lottery to B. Conversely, when p is 0, the agent always wins C, so it should prefer B to the lottery. Therefore, it seems plausible that there is some intermediate point where the agent equally prefers the lottery and B.

These axioms of preference allow us to express the preference an agent may have for any element of a set of goods as a lottery over the preferences for the least- and most-preferred elements. We can do more: Suppose that we assign numerical values to the least- and most-preferred element: say, 0 and 1. Then, we can assign the numerical value p to the preference of a good G, where the agent equally prefers G and a lottery where the agent wins the most-preferred element with probability p and the least-preferred element with probability $1 - p$. We can therefore think of p as being a numerical value for the preference for G. Note that the preference for G is a **linear combination** of the preferences for the least- and most-preferred goods.[2]

More generally, a **utility function** that assigns numerical values to preferences over goods allows us to numerically compare the preference expressed by an agent

---

2. For a mathematical definition of a linear combination, refer to Section 3.3.1.

among these goods. Denoting the least-preferred good by L and the most-preferred good by M, we can then define a utility function U by $U(L) = 0$, $U(M) = 1$, and for all other goods G, $U(G) = p$, where the agent equally prefers G and a lottery among L and M with odds p. With a slight change of perspective, we can imagine that U assigns **utilities** to goods, such that higher utilities correspond to more-preferred goods. This assumes, of course, that the agent's preferences are consistent.[3]

Utilities are useful for modeling competing objectives in **multiobjective optimization**. Suppose that we wish to optimize a system in which there is an inherent conflict among the objectives. For example, in most systems, increased performance comes at increased cost. We desire both better performance and lower cost. These competing objectives can be modeled with a utility function that increases with performance and decreases with cost, where the cost itself may depend on the performance. This naturally models the preferences we have over the goods of performance and cost. By maximizing this utility function, we can find the choice of system parameters that makes the most desirable trade-off between performance and cost.

EXAMPLE 7.2: UTILITY FUNCTION

Consider an ISP that charges \$1.25/GB for transfers that exceed a monthly quota and a customer of this ISP who would like to transfer unlimited amounts of data but also would not like to pay a large monthly bill. We can model the customer's preferences by using a utility function as follows. The customer prefers more data transfer to less data transfer and smaller monthly payments to larger monthly payments. Let $d(x)$ denote the utility of x gigabytes of transfer, where d is an increasing function of x, and let $p(y)$ denote the (dis-) utility of y dollars of payment, where p is an increasing function of y. Of course, y itself is a function of x, so we can write it as $y(x)$. The overall utility, U, increases with d and decreases with p, modeling the conflict in the underlying objectives.

A typical form assumed for U is $U = ad(x) - p(y(x))$, where a is a tuning parameter that is chosen to balance the relative utilities of data transfer and money. This is true for all values of U. So, by setting U to 0, we find that $a = p(y(x))/d(x)$. That is, we can determine a by finding the amount of data transfer at which the cost of transfer just balances the gain. Of course, U can be far more complicated. Note that U is a linear function of d and p: a simplifying assumption.

---

3. In the real world, sadly, consistency of preferences rarely holds. We discuss this in more detail in Section 7.4.

Linear utility functions are rather unrealistic: Most people experience diminishing returns with increases in the quantity of a good, which is better modeled by a nonlinear curve of the form $1 - e^{-x}$, where x denotes the quantity of the good.

Before leaving the topic of utility functions, we remark on two important properties. First, **utilities are unique only up to an affine transform**. Utility functions establish only preference *orderings*, so the utility functions U_1 and aU_1+b, where a and b are real constants, are identical. A consequence is that utility functions are **personal**, and the utility functions of two individuals are incomparable in a deep sense. So, if one agent were to assign a utility of 15 to some good, and another agent were to assign a utility of 7 to the same good, it does *not* mean that the first agent prefers it more. The second agent could easily have assigned the good a utility of 5,000, for example, with an affine translation. Therefore, any scheme that assumes the ability to perform interpersonal utility comparison is simply wrong. Unfortunately, the game-theory literature has many examples of published papers that make this fundamental error.

7.1.2 Terminology

We model the interaction of decision makers in the form of a **game**. Each decision maker, or **player**, takes **actions** chosen from a finite or infinite set in response to prior actions by other players, as well as expectations about how their action will "play out" in the other players' minds. These actions may be **simultaneous** or **sequential**.

When the game ends—that is, all the actions are carried out—each player is given a reward, or **outcome**, that depends on his or her actions. We assume that each player has a utility function that establishes a preference ordering among the outcomes: The utility of an outcome is called the **payoff**.

Players are assumed to be **rational**; that is, they take actions that will assure them the best possible payoff. The **principle of maximum expected utility** states that a rational player takes actions that maximize its expected utility from the game. Moreover, player rationality is assumed to be **common knowledge**: Each player knows that every other player is rational, and this fact itself is known by everyone, with infinite recursion. (This is perhaps one of the most controversial assumptions made by game theory.)

This chapter assumes that players are **noncooperative**; that is, they do not collude or form coalitions. Note that noncooperation is not the same as adversarial or malicious behavior. The assumption of noncooperation holds true for game-theoretic models commonly used in computer networking problems: It is relaxed when studying cooperative game theory, a topic that we will, however, not touch on.

A critical factor in distinguishing among different types of games is the degree of information each player has about other players and about the game. In games of **perfect information**, players may be able to observe every action and may also precisely know every player's possible actions and objectives. A canonical example is the game of chess, where all possible actions of each player are codified by the rules of chess, and all actions are visible to the players. In other games, players may not be able to see other players' actions, not know other players' objectives, and, in some cases, may not even know how many other players are playing the game. For example, in the card game of bridge, each player's hand is private, so a player cannot know the set of potential next actions of the other players. These limitations, naturally, limit the degree to which we can model the games and predict their outcomes. In some cases, such as when a player does not know the initial state of the game—for instance, any card game in which the deck has been shuffled so no player knows what the other players' hands contain—we can think of there being a special player called "Nature" that makes a randomizing initial move, after which the players play the actual game.

7.1.3 Strategies

A player's actions typically depend on not only prior actions of the other players— the **history** of the game—but also expectations about the responses this action may elicit from the other players. A player's **strategy** is a full description of the player's actions during the game. A strategy should be detailed enough that a player can give it to a disinterested third party and walk away or, equivalently, give it to a computer for execution. A strategy describes the player's actions, taking into account every possible action by every other player. A full description of a strategy is impossible other than for the simplest games. Nevertheless, the concept of a strategy is both useful, in that it allows us to precisely model a player's actions, and necessary, to determine the expected outcome of a game, which is expressed in the form of each player's preferred strategy. In game-theoretic analysis, a critical modeling step is to enumerate the set of strategies available to each player.

Strategies are of two types. **Pure strategies** deterministically describe the actions a player makes at each stage of the game. In contrast, **mixed strategies** associate probabilities with two or more pure strategies. The strategy that is played is chosen according to these probabilities. In this sense, a pure strategy is a mixed strategy, with the entire probability mass concentrated at a single point in the domain of strategies. Note that with a mixed strategy, once a specific pure strategy is chosen, the player cannot introduce any additional randomness: Every action is made deterministically according to the pure strategy. In a repeated game, where a game is played repeatedly, a different probabilistic choice can be made for each underlying game instance.

EXAMPLE 7.3: PURE AND MIXED STRATEGIES

Consider the simple game of **Matching Pennies**. In this game, two players each have a coin that they simultaneously place on a table. Subsequently, each observes both coins. One player wins if the coins are both heads or both tails, and the other player wins otherwise. A player has two pure strategies: play heads or play tails. However, we can also define an infinite number of mixed strategies, parametrized by a real number $p \in [0, 1]$, each of which corresponds to the strategy: Play heads with probability p and tails with probability $1 - p$. We will show later that the optimal strategy for both players is to choose $p = 0.5$.

We denote the strategy adopted by player i by s_i. Thus, we can denote an entire game played by n players by the tuple of adopted strategies $(s_1, s_2,...,s_n)$, called the **strategy profile**. The payoff to player i as a result of the game is denoted $\pi_i(s_1, s_2,...,s_n)$ and represents the utility to player i when the game is played with that particular strategy profile.

EXAMPLE 7.4: STRATEGY PROFILE

For the game of Matching Pennies, suppose that we denote the action "play head" by H and the action "play tail" by T. Then, the set of possible pure strategies is {HH, HT, TH, TT}, where each element is a strategy profile. Suppose that for both players, winning has utility 1 and losing has utility –1. Also, let player 1 win if the coins match and player 2 win otherwise. Then, we can write down the payoffs as:

$$\pi_1(HH) = 1, \pi_1(HT) = -1, \pi_1(TH) = -1, \pi_1(TT) = 1;$$

$$\pi_2(HH) = -1, \pi_2(HT) = 1, \pi_2(TH) = 1, \pi_2(TT) = -1;$$

In this example, the utility of player 2, for each strategy, is exactly the opposite of player 1. In other words, player 1 wins if and only if player 2 loses. Such a game is called a **zero-sum** game.

7.1.4 Game Representation

Games can be represented in two standard forms: **normal form** and **extensive form**. In normal form, a game with n players is represented by an n-dimensional array, where each dimension corresponds to the set of pure strategies of each player, and each matrix element is an n-tuple that corresponds to the outcome for each player; the ith element of each tuple is the payoff (utility) to the ith player.

This array is also called the **payoff matrix**. Note that all the strategies are assumed to be played simultaneously.

EXAMPLE 7.5: NORMAL FORM: MATCHING PENNIES

Table 7.1 shows the Matching Pennies game in normal form, where player 1's pure strategies are along the rows, and player 2's pure strategies are along the columns.

Table 7.1 The Payoff Matrix for Matching Pennies

	H	T
H	(1,–1)	(–1,1)
T	(–1,1)	(1,–1)

EXAMPLE 7.6: NORMAL FORM: WIFI GAME

In the 802.11 (WiFi) protocol, each station with data to send contends for airtime. For simplicity, assume that time is slotted and that each packet transmission takes exactly one time slot. If a station does not send data in a slot, airtime is wasted. If only one station sends data, it succeeds. If both send, both fail, and both must try again.

Consider an 802.11 wireless LAN with two active stations. We can model this as a game with two players. Consider actions over a single time slot. For each player, the possible actions are "send" (S) and "don't send" (D). We need to model the payoffs to each player. Assume that a station prefers success to a wasted time slot, and prefers a wasted time slot to a collision, because on a collision, no progress is achieved but also energy is wasted. We can express these preferences by assigning a utility of –1 to a collision, 0 to a wasted time slot, and 1 to success. This allows us to represent the game in normal form in Table 7.2:

Table 7.2 The Payoff Matrix for the WiFi Game

	S	D
S	(–1,–1)	(1,0)
D	(0,1)	(0,0)

The following example demonstrates a quirk with representing games in normal form. Consider a two-person game in which the row player can play pure strategies A or B; and if it plays A, it wins and the game is over. On the other hand, if it plays B, the column player can play Y or N, and the row player can then play C or D. What is the row player's strategy space? By convention, it is not {A, BC, BD} but {AC, AD, BC, BD}. That is, even though the game ends after the row player plays A, we represent the alternatives AC and AD explicitly in the normal form.

In extensive form, the game is represented by a **game tree**, in which each node corresponds to the player whose turn it is to move, and each departing edge represents a possible action that can be taken at that stage of the game. We identify each node in the tree with the past history of the game. Leaves correspond to outcomes of the game and are associated with the payoff to the players for that outcome. Games with sequential actions by the players are more naturally represented in extensive form.

EXAMPLE 7.7: EXTENSIVE FORM: THE PRICING GAME

Suppose an Internet service provider wants to roll out a new service with a price that could be low (L), medium (M), or high (H). Suppose that the prices are 1, 2, and 3, respectively, and the utility that the customer derives from the service is a. For each price, the customer can say yes (Y) or no (N). If the customer says yes, the ISP gets a payoff corresponding to the price, and the customer gets the payoff $a - price$ for some constant value a. If the customer says no, the payoff to both parties is 0. In extensive form, we represent the game as shown in Figure 7.1.

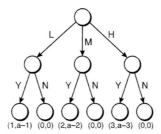

Figure 7.1 Extensive form of the pricing game

The extensive-form representation has an inherent problem with representing simultaneity. Consider a game, such as Matching Pennies, in which two players act simultaneously. If we arbitrarily choose nodes corresponding to player 1's actions as the first level of nodes, when player 2 plays, it can see what player 1 did. This, of course, makes the game pointless. Making the alternative choice does not remedy the situation. What we need is a way to hide a player's actions from the other player, that is, make the information available to it less than "perfect." We can do so by placing a subset of nodes in the game tree in the same **information set**. From the perspective of a player, all nodes in the set are equivalent; the player cannot distinguish between them. Graphically, we draw a dashed line between equivalent nodes. This allows us to easily represent simultaneous actions, as the next example shows.

EXAMPLE 7.8: REPRESENTING SIMULTANEOUS ACTIONS IN EXTENSIVE FORM

Figure 7.2 shows the extensive-form representation of the Matching Pennies game. Note that player 2 cannot determine whether player 1 played H or T.

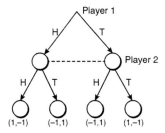

Figure 7.2 Representing simultaneity in an extensive-form game

It can be shown that, with the use of information sets, the normal- and extensive-form representations are equivalent. Therefore, from now on, we will not distinguish between the two.

Both normal and extensive forms grow exponentially in size with the number of actions and number of players. If there is only limited interaction between the players, we can use a compact **graphical game** representation instead.

A graphical game with n players is represented by an undirected graph with n vertices and a set of n payoff matrices, with one vertex and one matrix corresponding to each player. If node i has neighbors j and k, player i's payoffs are only a function of i, j, and k's actions, and therefore the payoff matrix at node i has entries only for i, j, and k's actions. The overall game is composed from the individual subgames. Note that we are not ruling out global impact of a player's actions. However, this occurs only through the propagation of local influences. This is similar in principle to Bayesian networks, whereby the joint probability distribution over all the underlying random variables is a product of the local conditional probability distributions at each node, and where the absence of edges between two vertices denotes independence.

Kearns et al. proposed this model in 2001 (see Section 7.5), and it is rapidly gaining popularity because it can represent games that cannot be compactly represented in normal or extensive form. Note that a graphical game is equivalent to a normal-form game: It is compact because it does not represent outcomes corresponding to simultaneous actions taken by noninteracting players.

7.1.5 Response and Best Response

Consider a two-player game with players labeled A and B. Recall that A's strategy s_A encapsulates this player's actions for the entire game. The strategy chosen by B *conditional on A playing s_A* is called B's **response** to s_A. Given the set of possible strategies that B could play, at least one of them will have a payoff as good as or better than all the others. We call this B's **best response** to s_A.

We can generalize this to n players as follows. Let $(s_1, s_2,...,s_n)$ be a strategy profile. We denote by s_{-i} the tuple $(s_1, s_2,...,s_{i-1}, s_{i+1},...,s_n)$, that is, the strategy profile excluding i's strategy. Then, the best response of player i to s_{-i} denoted s_i^* are the strategies (there may be more than one) that give i the highest possible payoff. That is:

$$\pi_i(s_i^*, s_{-i}) \geq \pi_i(s_i^j, s_{-i}) \qquad \forall s_i^j \neq s_i^* \qquad \text{(EQ 7.1)}$$

EXAMPLE 7.9: BEST RESPONSE

Consider the WiFi game in Example 7.6. If the row player (station 1) plays S, the column player's (station 2's) best response is D because the payoff for SD is 0 and for SS is −1. On the other hand, if the row player plays D, the best response is S because the payoff for DS is 1 and for DD is 0.

7.1.6 Dominant and Dominated Strategy

In some games, it is possible to determine that a rational player should play a particular strategy no matter what the other players do. This is called a **dominant strategy** for that player. Mathematically, we say that a strategy s_i^* is a dominant strategy for player i if

$$\pi_i(s_i^*, s_{-i}) \geq \pi_i(s_i^j, s_{-i}) \qquad \forall s_{-i}, \forall s_i^j \neq s_i^* \qquad \text{(EQ 7.2)}$$

Compared to the best response, there is an additional universal quantifier over all s_{-i}, which indicates that the dominant strategy is the best response no matter what strategies the other players pick. If the inequality is strict, the strategy is **strongly dominant**; otherwise, if it is strict for at least one s_{-i} but not for all of them, it is **weakly dominant**.

Symmetrically, a strategy whose payoff is lower (strictly lower) than another strategy is weakly (strongly) dominated by the other strategy.

EXAMPLE 7.10: DOMINANT STRATEGY

In the WiFi game of Example 7.6, the column player's best response is S or D, depending on what the row player does. Therefore, this game does not have a dominant strategy for the column player. Symmetrically, the game also does not have a dominant strategy for the row player.

Wireless networks can exhibit the *capture effect*, whereby a transmission from a station succeeds even if there are competing transmissions, because the signal strength from that station is so strong that it overpowers the competition. In this case, the payoff matrix is as shown in Table 7.3. Transmissions from the column player (station) always succeed due to the capture effect. In this case, the dominant strategy for the column player is S: No matter what the row player does, the column player is better off doing S than D.

Table 7.3 Payoff Matrix for WiFi Game with Capture Effect

	S	D
S	(–1,1)	(1,0)
D	(0,1)	(0,0)

7.1.7 Bayesian Games

We stated earlier that a critical factor in any game is the amount of information available to each player. In a game with perfect information, each player knows the other players, their past history of actions, the actions available to the other players, and the utility to the other players from each outcome. Consider a card game that starts with the deck being shuffled and dealt. No player knows the other players' hands, so they cannot know their possible actions. This is, therefore, a game with **imperfect information**.

A **Bayesian** game is a form of game with imperfect information, where each player can be from a set of possible **types**. If all players know each others' types, the game becomes one of perfect information. Therefore, all the uncertainty is encapsulated in the selection of player types. In a card game, each player's hand corresponds to that person's type. The **state** of the game is the set of player types for that game.

A Bayesian game starts with a move by Nature that results in each player being randomly assigned a type, according to some probability mass function. We can also view this as Nature selecting some state of the game. At this point, it is possible that all players receive a **signal** that may give information about each other. Specifically, the signal eliminates some possible states. Thus, the conditional probability that a player has a particular type, given a signal, can differ from the unconditional probability of that type.

In an extensive-form game, imperfectness can be represented by putting more than one node in an equivalence class, where a player is unable to distinguish between nodes in the same equivalence class (they are in the same information set). The effect of a signal is to potentially reduce the size of an equivalence class.

EXAMPLE 7.11: BAYESIAN WIFI GAME

Consider the 802.11 game of Example 7.6, where the row player does not know the column player's signal strength. If the column player's signal strength is low, the capture effect is absent, and the payoff matrix is the one shown in Table 7.2. Otherwise, with the capture effect, the payoff matrix is shown in Table 7.3. We can model this as a Bayesian game where the column player has one of two types: "strong signal" and "weak signal." In the first move by Nature, the column player is assigned one of the two types according to some probability distribution: say, with probability 0.1, the player is strong; with probability 0.9, the player is weak.

To incorporate the notion of a signal, assume that the row player can measure the received signal strength of the column player's transmission. Suppose that, given that the signal strength is high, the column player has 0.95 probability of being strong and 0.05 probability of being weak. Similarly, assume that if the signal strength is low, the column player has a 0.1 probability of being strong and 0.9 probability of being weak. We can see that the signal allows the row player to better judge the type of the column player, potentially allowing it to improve its chances in the game.

7.1.8 Repeated Games

Nearly any game can be repeated. Each repetition of a game is called a **stage**. With a finite number of repetitions, the overall game can be thought of as a single game with a much larger strategy profile space, because each player can change strategies at each repetition, perhaps taking into account the outcome of the previous stage. Analysis of finite repeated games is thus more complex and does not necessarily give much more insight into the problem.

Paradoxically, the analysis of repeated games is somewhat simpler when games are repeated an infinite number of times. The reason is that in such a case, every stage is equivalent: We do not have a final stage that needs to be specially handled. In a game with infinite repetitions, both the normal and extensive forms are undefined. The payoff matrix in the normal form is infinite-dimensional, which means that we cannot represent the payoffs. Similarly, in the extensive form, there are no leaves, so we cannot assign payoffs to leaves, as we normally do. Moreover, if the player were to get a small positive payoff with two strategies in each stage, *both* of them will result in infinite payoffs with infinite stages, so that they are equivalent. This doesn't make intuitive sense! To get around the problem, with infinitely repeated games, we represent the payoff of a potentially infinitely long strategy as the average payoff per stage, assuming the limit exists. Alternatively, we can **discount** future expected payoffs at each stage by a factor b that lies in $(0,1)$. That is, the payoff at the ith stage is multiplied by b^i. This often results in a payoff that is finitely bounded.

EXAMPLE 7.12: REPEATED GAME

Consider the two-stage version of the WiFi game in Example 7.6. With one stage, there are only two strategies for each player (S and D) and four strategy profiles (SS, SD, DS, and DD). With two stages, they have four strategies each (SS, SD, DS, and DD), and therefore the normal-form payoff matrix has 16 entries. The number of strategies for each player grows as s^i, where s is the number of strategies available to each player, and i is the number of stages. The payoff matrix has s^{2i} entries. Thus, repeated games are cumbersome to represent even with a few stages.

The infinitely repeated WiFi game can be similarly defined, with each player's strategy being an infinite string chosen from the alphabet {S, D}. Assume that the discount factor is 0.8. Then, if the expected payoffs for the row player are $r_0, r_1, r_2,...$, the discounted net payoff for that player is

$$\sum_{i=0}^{\infty} r_i 0.8^i .$$

There are many possible strategies for infinite-repeated games. A simple one is to always play the same pure strategy. A more interesting strategy is **tit for tat**, whereby each player plays what the other player played in the previous stage.

7.2 Solving a Game

7.2.1 Solution Concept and Equilibrium

Intuitively, the **solution** of a game is the set of strategies we expect rational players to adopt, given the payoff matrix. The solution of a game is also called its **equilibrium** point. The solution of a game *need not* be the strategy profile whose payoff to each player is greater than the payoff from any other strategy profile: As we will see shortly, rational players may sometimes be forced to play a strategy that gives them less payoff than some other strategy does! In common parlance, this is a lose-lose situation.

The **solution concept** is the line of reasoning adopted in determining a solution or equilibrium. For the same game, different solution concepts can yield different equilibria. Game theorists usually make the simplifying assumption that all the players implicitly agree on using the same solution concept. If different players use different solution concepts, the outcome is unpredictable.

7.2.2 Dominant-Strategy Equilibria

The dominant-strategy solution concept is used in games in which each player has a strongly or weakly dominant strategy. The idea is simple: If each player has a strategy it should play irrespective of actions by other players, it is reasonable to assume that the players will play this strategy. Note that the dominant strategy for a player may be a mixed strategy, which is a random variable defined over the domain of the pure strategies. When such an equilibrium exists, it is the preferred solution concept because it makes the fewest demands on assumptions of player rationality.

EXAMPLE 7.13: DOMINANT-STRATEGY SOLUTION FOR WIFI WITH CAPTURE

It is easy to solve a game when there is a dominant strategy for one of the players. Consider the capture-effect WiFi game of Example 7.10. We saw that the dominant strategy for the column player was S. This is known to both the column player and the row player. Therefore, the row player can assume that, as a rational player, the column player will play S. Given this, the row player's best response is D. Therefore, the solution to the game is DS: The row player plays D and the column player plays S.

EXAMPLE 7.14: DOMINANT-STRATEGY SOLUTION FOR MATCHING PENNIES

Consider the game of Matching Pennies introduced in Example 7.3. We stated without proof that the best strategy for both players was a mixed strategy that equally randomized between H and T. This is also the dominant-strategy solution of the game. Intuitively, this makes sense because any deviation of either player from a 50% choice of H or T gives the other player a winning edge in the long run, assuming that the game is repeated sufficiently often. The only way to counteract this is for both players to play randomly, with an equal chance of playing H or T.

As an interesting aside, the Matching Pennies game also models penalty kicks in a soccer game. If the kicker and the goalkeeper both go left (L) or right (R), the goalkeeper wins; otherwise, the kicker wins. The best strategy for both, therefore, is to choose L or R with equal probability.

EXAMPLE 7.15: DOMINANT-STRATEGY SOLUTION FOR DELAY-SENSITIVE WIFI

Consider the WiFi game with delay-sensitive stations, for which the cost of waiting one slot (–2) is worse than the cost of a collision (–1). This game is represented in Table 7.4 in the normal form. Note that for the row player, strategy S always returns higher payoffs than strategy D, no matter whether the column player plays S or D. So, S is a dominant strategy for this player. Symmetrically, S is also the dominant strategy for the column player. Therefore, the dominant-strategy solution for this game is SS. This is a bad outcome because no progress will be made, owing to repeated collisions. System designers must be careful that their systems do not admit such unproductive outcomes. It is also interesting to note that a slight change in the payoff matrix completely changes the outcome of the game!

Table 7.4 The Payoff Matrix for the WiFi Game with Delay-Sensitive Stations

	S	D
S	(–1,–1)	(1,–2)
D	(–2,1)	(–2,–2)

EXAMPLE 7.16: DOMINANT-STRATEGY SOLUTION FOR PRISONER'S DILEMMA

In the game known as the **Prisoner's Dilemma**, two prisoners in two isolated cells are offered a bargain by the warden. If each prisoner informs on the other prisoner (defects, or D), both are set free, and the other prisoner is given four more years of prison. If neither informs on the other (showing solidarity, or S), they get only a year of prison each. If both defect, they both get three years of prison each. What should each prisoner do?

Solution:

The payoff matrix is shown in Table 7.5. Note that the dominant strategy for the row player is to play D (because $0 > -1$ and $-3 > -4$). By symmetry, D is also the dominant strategy for the column player. Therefore, the dominant-strategy equilibrium is DD. This game is called a dilemma because the best-possible outcome is SS. Nevertheless, the inexorable logic of game theory dictates that both prisoners will defect, a lose-lose situation. We will see later that, using the solution concept of correlated equilibria, this sad outcome can be averted, as long as both prisoners agree to change their solution concept from dominant strategy to a correlated equilibrium.

Table 7.5 The Payoff Matrix for the Prisoner's Dilemma Game

	S	D
S	(–1,–1)	(4,0)
D	(0,–4)	(–3,–3)

7.2.3 Iterated Removal of Dominated Strategies

In some games, not all players have dominant strategies, so it is not possible to find a dominant-strategy equilibrium. However, even if only one player has one or more dominant strategies—strategies whose payoffs are the same and whose payoffs are greater than the player's other strategies—it may be possible to find a plausible equilibrium by deletion of *dominated* strategies. Specifically, if player i has a set of dominant strategies—say, $\{s_i^*\}$—then the other players can reason that player i will certainly play one of these strategies. Therefore, all their own strategies incompatible with this set can be eliminated, which may then yield a dominant-strategy set for one of the other players: say, j. This, in turn, allows us to remove the dominated strategies for j and so on. In the end, we hope to be left with a single strategy for each player, which is the equilibrium.

EXAMPLE 7.17: ITERATED REMOVAL OF DOMINANT STRATEGIES

Consider the WiFi game with capture (Table 7.3). Recall that here, the column player has a dominant strategy S. The row player can reason as follows: "Column will certainly play S. If Column plays S and I play S, I get –1 and if I play

D, I get 0, so I should play D." Thus, with this solution concept, we can find the equilibrium DS.

As with dominant strategies, not all games are guaranteed to have a dominant-strategy equilibrium even with the iterated removal of dominated strategies. Also, applying this concept is tricky because a pure strategy may be dominated by a mixture of other pure strategies, where none of the strategies in the mixture dominate the pure strategy, but none of the strategies in the mixture can be dominated by the pure strategy, either.

7.2.4 Maximin Equilibrium

The **maximin equilibrium** and its dual, the **minimax equilibrium**, are among the earliest and best-studied solution concepts. They both arise from the concept of **security level**, which is the guaranteed payoff to a particular player even if the other players coordinate their actions to minimize that player's payoff. The idea is for each player to choose a strategy that maximizes this guaranteed payoff, thus maximizing its security level. It is a pessimistic or perhaps even a paranoid way to play a game, in the sense that it does not even assume that the opponents are rational; they may even be willing to reduce their own payoffs in order to harm other players. Nevertheless, no matter what the other players do, the maximin payoff is guaranteed.

Mathematically, define $s_{-i}^{\min}(s_i)$ to be the tuple of other player strategies that minimize the payoff to i when playing s_i. Then, the maximin strategy for i is s_i^*, where $\pi(s_{-i}^{\min}(s_i^*), s_i^*) > \pi(s_{-i}^{\min}(s_i^j), s_i^j) \ \forall s_i^* \neq s_i^*$. Note that the maximin strategy for a player can be pure or mixed.

EXAMPLE 7.18: MAXIMIN STRATEGY

Consider the WiFi game of Example 7.6. If the row player plays S, the column player can play S to give it a payoff of −1, but if Row plays D, the worst payoff is only 0. So, the maximin strategy for Row is D. Similarly, the maximin strategy for Column is also D. Therefore, the maximin equilibrium for this game is DD. Note that there is no dominant-strategy equilibrium for this game.

EXAMPLE 7.19: GRAPHICAL REPRESENTATION OF A MAXIMIN STRATEGY

Consider the payoff matrix shown in Table 7.6 for a two-player zero-sum game. We would like to compute the maximin strategy for both players. In general, this strategy is a mixed strategy, so assume that the row player plays strategy R1 with probability p and R2 with probability $(1 - p)$. If the Column player plays C1, then Row gets a payoff of $3p + 2(1 - p) = p + 2$. If Column plays C2, Row gets $p + 4(1 - p) = 4 - 3p$. This is shown graphically in Figure 7.3, where the X-axis is the choice of p and the Y-axis is Row's payoff. It can be shown that if Row uses any value of p other than 0.5, it may obtain a payoff lower than 2.5 (see Exercise 14). It can be shown that even if Column plays a mixed strategy, Row can guarantee itself a payoff of 2.5 by playing 0.5R1 + 0.5R2. Similarly, it can be shown that Column can hold Row down to 2.5 by playing 0.75C1 + 0.25C2. If Column plays any other strategy, Row can obtain a greater payoff, and, because this is a zero-sum game, Column will get a lower payoff. Therefore, the maximin strategy for Column is 0.75C1 + 0.25C2, and the mixed-strategy profile (0.5R1 + 0.5R2, 0.75C1 + 0.25C2) is the maximin equilibrium for this game.

Table 7.6 A Zero-Sum Game

	C1	C2
R1	(3,–3)	(1,–1)
R2	(2,–2)	(4,–4)

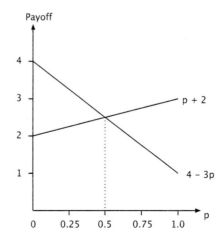

Figure 7.3 Maximin strategy for the row player in Example 7.19

In a two-person game, the equilibrium point is also called a **saddle** point. Any deviation from this point by the row or the column player will decrease its guaranteed minimum payoff.

The dual of the maximin strategy is the minimax strategy. In the two-player version, a player acts so as to minimize the best-possible payoff that the other player receives. In this sense, the player acts to maximally punish the other player without regard to its own payoff. The n-player version of this solution concept is somewhat more tricky to state and requires the players to act as if they form a coalition to punish a given player. This solution concept is therefore of only theoretical interest, in that it is the dual of the maximin strategy, so we will not consider it any further.

One of the earliest theorems in game theory was stated and proved by von Neumann in 1928 and is called the **minimax theorem**. It states that in every finite, two-person, zero-sum game, player 1 is guaranteed a payoff of at least v independent of player 2's strategy, and, symmetrically, player 2 can restrict player 1 to a value of at most v, independent of player 1's strategy. This value may require players to play mixed strategies. The strategy corresponding to this guaranteed payoff is the maximin strategy. Because player 1 is guaranteed to get at least v, and player 2, being an opponent in a zero-sum game and thus receiving a payoff of $-v$ would never want player 1 to get any payoff higher than v, this is an equilibrium. Thus, another way to view this theorem is that it asserts that every finite, two-person, zero-sum game has an equilibrium that results from both players playing the maximin strategy.

7.2.5 Nash Equilibria

Although dominant-strategy equilibria are preferred, many games do not allow such a solution. For instance, there is no dominant-strategy solution for the Matching Pennies game or the WiFi game of Example 7.6. In such games, we turn to a different solution concept, called the **Nash equilibrium** concept.

The key idea in a Nash equilibrium is that players have no incentive to deviate from it. That is, *assuming that every other player* is playing the strategy corresponding to the Nash equilibrium strategy profile, no player's payoffs are better by choosing any other strategy. Mathematically, a strategy profile $(s^*_1, s^*_2,...,s^*_n)$ is a (weak[4]) Nash equilibrium if

$$\pi_i(s^*_i, s^*_{-i}) \geq \pi_i(s_i, s^*_{-i}) \qquad \forall s_i \neq s^*_i \tag{EQ 7.3}$$

---

4. The equilibrium is strict if the inequality is strict.

In a Nash equilibrium, each player plays its best response, assuming that all other players play their Nash strategy. This exposes both the power and the weakness of the concept. The concept is powerful because it intuitively matches our expectations of a rational player who plays the best response to the other players' actions. Moreover, we need only identify a potential Nash strategy profile (it doesn't matter how) and check whether any player has an incentive to deviate, which is straightforward. However, a Nash equilibrium presupposes that all players are going to play according to this solution concept. Worse, it is not unique: A game may have more than one Nash equilibrium. In this case, players need to either guess which Nash equilibrium will be chosen by the others or coordinate their actions by using an external signal.

Every dominant-strategy equilibrium, by definition, is also a Nash equilibrium, though the converse is not true. For instance, in Prisoner's Dilemma, DD is both a dominant strategy and a Nash equilibrium. On the other hand, SS is not a Nash equilibrium, because if a player assumes that the other player is going to play S, it pays for it to defect. Similarly, every maximin equilibrium is also a Nash equilibrium.

Note that a Nash equilibrium may involve mixed strategies, as the next example shows.

EXAMPLE 7.20: NASH EQUILIBRIUM FOR MATCHING PENNIES

Recall the Matching Pennies game (shown in Table 7.1). We will prove that the Nash equilibrium is for both players to play a mixed strategy with the probability of H (or T) = 0.5 (represented as 0.5H + 0.5T).

Consider the situation for the row player. Assume that the column player plays 0.5H + 0.5T. Let the row player play $pH + (1 - p)T$. Row plays H with probability p. We have two cases: Column plays either H or T. (1) Column plays H with probability 0.5, giving Row a payoff of 1, so that the expected payoff for Row in this case is p. (2) Column plays T with probability 0.5, giving Row a payoff of −1, so that the expected payoff for Row in this case is $-p$. Thus, the expected payoff when Row plays H is 0. Arguing along the same lines, the expected payoff for Row when it plays T is also 0. So, we have the interesting situation that, if Column plays 0.5H + 0.5 T, no matter what Row does, its expected payoff is 0. By symmetry, if Row plays 0.5H + 0.5T, the expected utility of Column is 0, no matter what it does. Therefore, Equation 7.3 holds (albeit with equality rather than inequality), and this is therefore a (weak) Nash equilibrium.

EXAMPLE 7.21: FINDING NASH EQUILIBRIA: BATTLE OF THE SEXES

Consider the following **coordination game** (Table 7.7), popularly called the
Battle of the Sexes. A couple wants to choose between going to a prizefight F,
which the row player wants, and going to a ballet B, which the column player
wants.[5] Both would rather be with each other than by themselves.

Table 7.7 The Payoff Matrix for the Battle of the Sexes Coordination Game

	F	B
F	(2,1)	(0,0)
B	(0,0)	(1,2)

It is obvious that the two pure-strategy Nash equilibria are FF and BB.
There is, however, also a mixed-strategy Nash equilibrium whereby Row plays
$2/3F + 1/3B$ and Column plays $1/3F + 2/3B$. To see this; assume that Column
plays $1/3F + 2/3B$ and Row plays $pF + (1 - p)B$. Then, Row's expected payoff is
$p(1/3 * 2) + (1 - p)(2/3 * 1) = 2p/3 + 2/3 - 2p/3 = 2/3$, independent of p. Symmetrically, it can be shown that when Row plays $2/3F + 1/3B$, Column always gets
$2/3$ independent of its strategy. Therefore, Equation 7.3 holds with equality,
and this is a weak Nash equilibrium. It is worth noting that this mixed equilibrium gives a lower payoff than either of the pure equilibria.

In 1951, J. Nash proved a famous theorem that earned him the Nobel Prize in
Economics. The theorem states that every game with a finite number of players and
actions has at least one Nash equilibrium. Thus, we can always find at least one
Nash equilibrium for finite normal-form games. The Nash theorem, however, proves
only the existence of an equilibrium—by relying on a fixed-point property of iterated maps described by the Brouwer fixed-point theorem—rather than telling us
how to find this equilibrium. Therefore, in practical cases, finding the equilibrium
can be challenging. In doing so, however, it is useful to rely on the following fact: If
a mixed strategy uses strategy s, then s cannot be strongly dominated by any other
strategy; otherwise, you could remove this strategy from the mixture and increase
the payoff.

So far, we have considered Nash equilibria in games with discrete actions. However, a player's actions may be chosen from a subset of the real line. Finding Nash

---

5. This being the twenty-first century, we'll leave the sex of the row and column players unspecified.

equilibria in such games is essentially the same as finding *local* maxima of a vector-valued function of a vector of real variables. More precisely, consider the mapping G from a vector $\mathbf{x}$ in $\mathbf{R}^n$, corresponding to the action chosen by each player, to the payoff vector π, which determines the corresponding payoff to each player. We say that a payoff vector π^i dominates payoff vector π^j if every element of π^i is greater than or equal to the corresponding members of π^j. At each local maximum $\mathbf{x}^m$ of G, $\pi^m = G(\mathbf{x}^m)$ dominates $\pi_j = G(\mathbf{x}^j)$ for all $\mathbf{x}^j$ in the neighborhood of $\mathbf{x}^m$. We can use any standard optimization technique, even a heuristic such as hill climbing, to find these local maxima. If G is globally convex—that is, there is a single global maximum—then *any* hill-climbing technique will find the global maximum. In many papers on game theory, G is assumed to be convex, so that this approach can be used. It is a contentious point, however, whether this convexity assumption holds in the real world.

7.2.6 Correlated Equilibria

A fundamental problem with the Nash equilibrium concept arises when a game has more than one Nash equilibrium, when each player has to somehow guess which of the game's equilibria the others pick. Even if there is a unique equilibrium, each player has to know exactly which strategy every other player is going to play. If the other players are playing mixed strategies, each player also has to know exactly how all the other players are going to mix each of their pure strategies. This isn't very realistic!

A hint to a possible solution lies in the formulation of a Bayesian game, whereby a move by Nature decides player types and each player has the same subjective probability distribution over the types chosen by Nature. (Once the player types are chosen, however, the rest of the game is a standard game and is solved using a standard solution concept.) The key idea of a correlated equilibrium is to extend the subjective probability distribution of each player not just to player types but also to player *strategies,* given a *shared* view on the current state of the world. That is, each player has a subjective probability distribution over possible strategies of the other players, conditional on a random variable called the "state of the world," and tries to maximize his or her own payoff conditional on this distribution. In the original formulation of this solution concept, the shared common view on the state of the world was expressed in the form of an external, globally trusted, correlating agent who tells each player what to do. Such an agent is not really necessary. Nevertheless, it is easier to discuss a correlated equilibrium assuming such an agent, and we shall do so as well.

More precisely, we assume the existence of an external agent that, based on some probability distribution, chooses a strategy profile for the game. Each player is assumed to know the probability distribution used to choose the strategy profile and only its own pure strategy corresponding to this strategy profile. The external agent does not tell the player, however, what it told the other agents. This models the fact that all the players have their own subjective probability distributions on their pure strategies as a function of the state of the world. The player then plays this strategy. We say that the resulting strategy profile is a **correlated equilibrium** if the players do not have any incentive to deviate from this strategy.

EXAMPLE 7.22: SIMPLE CORRELATED EQUILIBRIA

Recall from Example 7.16 that in the Prisoner's Dilemma (Table 7.5) both the dominant strategy and the Nash equilibria are DD, with payoff (–3,–3). Suppose that we introduce correlation through a coin toss. If the coin lands heads up, the players are told to play DS; if tails up, they are told to play SD. Note that when told to play S, Row would gain by playing D instead! So, it has an incentive to deviate, and this is *not* a correlated equilibrium.

In contrast, consider the Battle of the Sexes game (Table 7.7). Suppose that an outside agent told each player to play FF or BB, based on the results of a coin toss. Consider the row player's point of view. If told to play F, it does pay for Row to deviate and play B. Symmetrically, neither does Column gain from deviation. Therefore, this is a correlated equilibrium. If the coin is fair, both can achieve an expected gain of 0.5 * 2 + 0.5 * 1 = 1.5, which is more than they can gain from a mixed Nash strategy, which gives them only 2/3 each.

Correlated equilibria can be complex if the correlating device does not allow a player to determine exactly what the other players would do, as was the case with the Battle of the Sexes. This is illustrated by the following game.

EXAMPLE 7.23: CORRELATED EQUILIBRIUM FOR CHICKEN

The following game models the game of chicken in which two racers rush toward each other at full speed. The first person to pull away is the chicken and loses. Of course, if neither pulls away, both lose. The game matrix is given in Table 7.8, where D stands for "dare" and C for "chicken."

Table 7.8 Payoff Matrix for the Chicken Game

	D	C
D	(0,0)	(7,2)
C	(2,7)	(6,6)

We assume the existence of an external agent and that both players know that the external agent says CC with probability 1/3, DC with probability 1/3, and CD with probability 1/3 (and never says DD). Suppose that Row is told to play D. Then, it knows that Column was asked to play C. Row goes from 7 to 6 by deviating, so it will not deviate. Suppose that Row is told to play C. Then, there is probability 1/2 that the other player was told to play D and probability 1/2 the other player was told to play C. Assuming that the other player does not deviate from the correlated equilibrium, the expected utility of deviating and playing D is 0(1/2) + 7(1/2) = 3.5, and the expected utility of listening to the agent and playing C is 2(1/2) + 6(1/2) = 4. So, the player would prefer to play C: not deviate. From the symmetry of the game, the same argument holds for Column. Therefore, neither player will deviate from the suggestion of the agent, and this is a correlated equilibrium.

Note that in a correlated equilibrium, we have a free variable: the probability with which the adviser asks each player to play each pure strategy, from which none of the players will deviate. By choosing different values for this distribution, we can achieve a range of payoffs to each player.

The correlated-equilibrium concept is more appealing than a Nash equilibrium because it does not require players to know the exact strategy for every player, just that they will condition on the same state of the world. Moreover, every Nash equilibrium—whether using pure or mixed strategies—can be shown to be a correlated equilibrium that advises only pure strategies. Therefore, correlated equilibria are the more powerful solution concept, especially if an external correlating agent can be naturally found in the problem domain.

7.2.7 Other Solution Concepts

Our treatment of solution concepts is necessarily limited. Several concepts, such as rationizability, subgame perfectness, trembling-hand perfectness,[6] ε-Nash equilibria, and evolutionary stability have been studied in the literature. More detail on these can be found in a standard texts on game theory (see Section 7.5).

7.3 Mechanism Design

Traditionally, game theory studies the behavior of players when the game has already been specified. In contrast, **mechanism design** sets up the rules of a game

---

6. This intriguing term refers to a game in which a player, owing to a "trembling hand" may occasionally make a suboptimal move.

such that rational utility-maximizing players, in equilibrium, will behave as the designers intended. The key idea is to choose the rules of the game so that each player's attempt to maximize utility also achieves the desired outcome *without* the designer's knowing each player's utility function. Intuitively, the game is set up so that the players do what the designers want them to do because the players themselves want to do it!

7.3.1 Practical Mechanisms

Mechanism design arises naturally in some common situations. Consider the owner of a good who wants to sell it to the buyer who will pay the most for it, who is also the buyer who values the good most highly. This can be achieved by an **English auction**, in which the good is simultaneously presented to all buyers and the price of the good is gradually raised until all but one buyer drops out. If we treat the bidders as players in a game, it is easy to see that in equilibrium, this auction mechanism ensures that a player's bid reflects the player's true valuation.

As another example, consider an election officer who wants to choose one of the candidates running for office as the winner. Presumably, the winner should, in some way, reflect the wishes of society. The electoral officer implements what is known, in the literature, as a **social-choice function**. Again, we desire a mechanism such that, assuming that such a social choice exists in the first place, all voters reveal their true preferences instead of voting other than for their choice in an attempt to influence the final outcome.

It turns out that similar considerations arise in several networking problems. For instance, if several users want to download a file using BitTorrent, how can we ensure that all users do their fair share in downloading and sharing the torrent? Similarly, if we have a group of mobile phone users sharing content using ad hoc phone-to-phone data propagation, how can we make sure that all users have an incentive to participate in the scheme despite the depletion of their scarce battery resources? The general area of mechanism design addresses these issues. Here, we will merely touch on the main concepts.

7.3.2 Three Negative Results

In using mechanism design to achieve social choices, it is useful to keep three negative results in mind: the Condorcet paradox, Arrow's theorem, and the Gibbard-Satterthwaite theorem

The **Condorcet paradox** demonstrates that even an election with just three voters and three candidates does not have a self-consistent majority, or "social" choice. Consider an election with three candidates a, b, and c. Let voter 1 prefer a to b and b to c. Let voter 2 prefer b to c and c to a. Finally, let voter 3 prefer c to a and

a to b. Now, note that voters 1 and 3 prefer a to b. So, the majority prefer a to b, and in the social choice, it must certainly be the case the a is preferred to b. However, the voter preferences are rotationally symmetric, so a majority also prefers b to c and c to a. If preferences are transitive, which is necessary for consistency, we find that a majority prefers a to b to c to a! Thus, in reflecting a society's choice of candidates, we have to give up majority (i.e., have a dictatorship) or consistency or transitivity. These choices are not appealing. One may think that the problem here is that we are using a simple majority rule. What if this were replaced with something more sophisticated, such as proportional representation? Indeed, several schemes, called **voting methods**, have been proposed in the literature that are more sophisticated than majority and remedy some of its problems. Although they each have their strengths, they all run afoul of a fundamental theorem of social choice called Arrow's theorem.

Arrow's theorem states that under some very general conditions, we cannot reasonably compose individual *strict* orderings of alternatives—orderings in which every alternative has a definite rank, though multiple alternatives may have the same rank—to form a global strict ordering. The theorem assumes that individual preferences are arbitrary: One individual may rank alternative 1, for example, as his or her most-preferred alternative, but another individual may rank the same alternative as his or her least-preferred alternative.

Define a **social-welfare function** as a function that maps from a set of individual strict orderings of a finite set of alternatives to a global ordering. We say that a social-welfare function satisfies **unanimity** if it orders alternative a higher than b if every individual ranks a higher than b. A social-welfare function satisfies **independence of irrelevant alternatives** if the aggregate ranking of two alternatives a and b depends only on how each individual ranks a and b. That is, the other alternatives could be arbitrarily ranked, but as long as every individual ranks a higher than b, so too should the social-welfare function. Finally, we call a social-welfare function a **dictatorship** if there is an individual i such that the social-welfare function's choice of the top-ranked alternative is that individual's choice of the top-ranked alternative, no matter what the other individuals desire.[7]

Arrow's theorem, for which he won the Nobel Prize, states that every social-welfare function over a set of more than two alternatives that satisfies unanimity and independence of irrelevant choices is a dictatorship! This is troublesome, in that we have to give up either unanimity or independence of irrelevant choices to avoid dictatorship.

---

7. This is a weak form of dictatorship, in that if the other individuals were to change their preference orderings, the identity of the dictator could change. The idea is that any voting method that meets Arrow's criteria necessarily transfers the power to decide the social choice, or cast the "deciding vote," one of the (perhaps unwitting) individuals.

The third minefield in the design of social-choice functions is called the **Gibbard-Satterthwaite theorem**, which can also be formulated as an extension of Arrow's theorem. Recall that social-choice functions decide on a choice of a specific alternative rather than an ordering on alternatives. We call a social-choice function **strategically manipulable** by an individual if that individual can influence the outcome of the social-choice function in his or her favor by lying about his or her preference ordering. A social-choice function that *cannot* be manipulated by an individual in this manner is called **incentive compatible**. We will now show that if we have an election with two candidates, standard majority voting is incentive compatible. To see this, note that a voter can manipulate the outcome if and only if there are an odd number of voters and this voter is casting the deciding vote. If the voter lies when casting the deciding vote, that voter does not influence the election in his or her favor: The outcome is the opposite of what the voter wants. Therefore, the outcome is non-manipulable, or incentive compatible. The Gibbard-Satterthwaite theorem states that if f is any incentive-compatible social-choice function that decides between more than two alternatives, f is a dictatorship; that is, there is some individual who can control the outcome of the election. The consequence of this theorem is that even the most sophisticated scheme for aggregating individual choices can either be manipulated or be dictated to! This is a strong negative result.

There are several ways out of this quandary. One of them, which turns out is the basis of most approaches to mechanism design, is to introduce the notion of money. Specifically, in Arrow's framework, the utility of each individual is expressed only through that person's preferred ordering. Such a simplistic notion of utility is necessary for the Gibbard-Satterthwaite theorem. If, however, we assume that an individual's utility is **quasilinear**, that is, the utility depends not only on the alternative selected but also on an additional monetary side payment, preferences for alternatives cannot be arbitrary, and both Arrow's and the Gibbard-Satterthwaite theorem can be avoided. In the context of voting, this means that an individual whose choice did not affect the final outcome would be compensated by a certain amount of money. So, the greater the attempt by a voter to change other voters' choices, the more it will cost. Therefore, assuming that everyone has the same amount of money, we can avoid manipulation (or at least, buying elections will only be for the rich).

7.3.3 Examples of Mechanism Design

To fix ideas, we first study two simple examples of mechanism design in which a **principal** designs a game so that the players, or **agents**, carry out the principal's wishes.

EXAMPLE 7.24: PRICE DISCRIMINATION

Suppose that a manufacturer of a communication device called the uPhone (the principal) sells to one of two types of customers (the agents). Chatters (C) need only one uPhone, because most of their friends already have one, and Antediluvians (A) need at least two, one for each party making a call. What price should be set for them?

A naive solution would be to price the uPhone at, say, $100, so that C pays $100 and A pays $200. Suppose that the internal value C ascribes to a uPhone is $50, and the internal value that A ascribes to two uPhones is $300. By pricing it at $100, no C will buy it, and every A who buys it would have been willing to pay $150 per uPhone, so that manufacturer is leaving money on the table. Can it do better?

If it knew that the internal valuation of C for a uPhone was c and of A was a and if $2a > c$, the manufacturer could price the uPhones as follows:

$$\text{One uPhone costs } c \text{ but two cost } \min(2a, 2c)$$

This way, Chatters would pay c, so the manufacturer would not lose sales to them. Moreover, because $2a > c$, Chatters are never tempted to get two when they don't need it. If $2a > 2c$, and the price of two uPhones were greater than $2c$, Antediluvians would just buy two uPhones individually, so there would be no point in setting the price for two uPhones any higher than $2c$. On the other hand, if the price for two uPhones was more than $2a$, no As would buy uPhones. So, the price for two should be the smaller of $2a$ and $2c$. This **discriminative pricing scheme** gives a seller the most possible profit and the largest-possible customer base.

Note that for this scheme to work, we need to know the internal valuation of each type of customer. But this is private information: How can a seller determine it? A hint to a solution can be found in the **Vickrey**, or **second price**, auction.

EXAMPLE 7.25: VICKREY AUCTION

Consider the sale of a good by auction. Unlike in the previous example, assume that the seller does not know the internal valuations of the buyers, in which case the solution is trivial. The Vickrey auction awards the good to the highest bidder but charges the winner the second-highest bid. We now prove that this results in each buyer's telling the seller its true internal valuation.[8]

---

8. It does not, unfortunately, result in the seller's getting the best price. If the second-highest bid is very low, the seller may end up with essentially nothing, although there was a willing buyer at a higher price.

Suppose that the valuation of a bidder for a good is v, the price it bids is b, and the highest price bid by any other bidder is p. The utility of a bid b is given by $v - b$ if $b > p$ and the bidder wins and 0 if $b < p$ and the bidder loses. If a bidder is going to tell a lie, either (A) $b > v$ or (B) $b < v$. Suppose that $b > v$. Now we have two more cases: Either (A.1) the bidder wins the auction, so that $b > p$, or (A.2) the bidder loses, so $b < p$. Suppose case A.1 holds:

- (A.1.a): If $p < v$, the bidder gains a utility of $v - p$. But it would have obtained the same gain by telling the truth, so telling a lie doesn't help.

- (A.1.b): If $p > v$, the bidder loses utility of $p - v$, so lying hurts.

With case A.2, telling a lie does not help, since the utility from the transaction is zero.[9]

Now, suppose that the bidder bids a lower valuation (i.e., $b < v$). Again, we have two subcases: Either the bidder wins (B.1) or it loses (B.2).

- (B.1): If it wins, it pays the second price, and by reasoning along the same lines as cases A.1.a and A.1.b, we can see that telling a lie either hurts or has the same payoff as telling the truth.

- (B.2): If it loses, the bidder loses utility of $p - v$, so lying hurts.

We have shown, therefore, that in all cases, telling a lie is either as good as or worse than telling the truth. Therefore, a rational player would tell the truth and reveal its true internal valuation to the seller. This is called **truth revelation**.

Note that the price obtained by the seller is not as high as in the previous example, where the seller would have obtained the internal valuation of the highest bidder. Nevertheless, this simple scheme has the remarkable property that the design of the mechanism makes it incentive compatible for a rational player to reveal the truth. This is at the heart of all mechanism design.

Importantly, we require the players to care about how much money they bid, that is, their utilities are quasilinear. Otherwise, owing to the Gibbard-Satterthwaite theorem, we would end up with a dictatorship, where only one player would decide who gets the good, or would have the price of the good strategically manipulable by one or more players.

---

9. Of course, a player who knows the internal valuation of other players could artificially boost up their price to just below that of the (known) winning bid, to hurt the winner. However, this violates the assumption that internal valuations are secret.

7.3.4 Formalization

We now formalize the intuitions we have developed so far. Assume that principal P is designing a mechanism with n agents, indexed by i. Assume that the mechanism is associated with a set O of one of $|O|$ outcomes chosen by the principal, with each action called o. For instance, in the uPhone example, one agent at any given time is playing the game (the customer in the store), so $n = 1$. The set of possible outcomes O is $\{(0,.), (1,c), (2,\min(2a, 2c))\}$, where the first tuple represents "don't purchase," the second outcome represents "purchase 1 for c," and the third outcome represents "purchase 2 for $\min(2a, 2c)$." We assume that each agent has a type t_i that captures all the private information relevant to its decision making. For instance, in the uPhone example, the type was A or C. Each t_i is drawn from a set of all possible types for the ith player, T_i. We assume that each agent has a preference ordering over the outcomes, which are represented in the form of private, quasilinear utility functions $U_i(o, t_i)$. For example, the utility function of a Chatter is $U_c((1,c), c) = c - c = 0$; $U_c((2, \min(2a, 2c)), c) = \min(2a, 2c) - c < 0$.

We define the possible states of the world as the product of all possible agent types and denote it $T = T_1 \times T_2 \times ... \times T_n$, where x is the cross product. A **social-choice function** is a mapping f from T to O, which describes, for each possible state of the world, the desired outcome. This is outcome that the principal would have chosen *assuming that it knew the true state of the world*. In the uPhone example, a single agent (customer) at any given time has type A or C. The social-choice function f maps C to $(1, c)$ and A to $(2, \min(2c, 2a))$. Of course, a principal does not know the true type of an agent. So, we seek a mechanism that results in the right outcome without knowledge of the state of the world.

A **mechanism** is an n-tuple of strategy spaces, also called message, or action, spaces, $S = S_1 \times S_2 \times ... \times S_n$ and an **outcome function** g that maps from S to O. Each S_i represents the possible strategies, or actions, allowed to an agent in the mechanism, that is, the rules of the corresponding game. In the uPhone example, $S_A = S_C = \{$buy nothing, buy one uPhone, buy two uPhones$\}$. The function g represents the outcome as a function of the agent's strategies. In the uPhone example, this is the pricing schedule, which maps from "buy one" to price c and from "buy two" to price $\min(2a, 2c)$. Recall that each player has utilities over these outcomes.

A mechanism $M = (S_1,...,S_n, g(.))$ is said to **implement** social-choice function $f(T)$ if there is an equilibrium-strategy profile $s^* = (s_1^*(t_1), s_2^*(t_2), ..., s_n^*(t_n))$ of the game induced by M such that

$$g(s_1^*(t_1), s_2^*(t_2), ..., s_n^*(t_n)) = f(t_1, ..., t_n) \qquad \text{(EQ 7.4)}$$

The equilibrium of the game depends on the underlying solution concept. The most widely used concept is dominant strategy. However, in some cases, a Nash equilibrium—no agent will deviate from the equilibrium—or a Bayes-Nash equilibrium—

the expected gain to each agent at the Nash equilibrium exceeds the expected utility from deviation—is also used. We will study only dominant-strategy solutions here because they are usually thought to be more plausible than the other solution concepts. In this solution concept, let s_{-i} represent the strategies of players other than i:

$$u_i(g(s_i^*(t_i), s_{-i}^*(t_{-i})), t_i) \geq u_i(g(\tilde{s}_i(t_i), \tilde{s}_{-i}(t_{-i})), t_i) \quad \forall i, \forall t_i, \forall \tilde{s}_i \neq s_i^*, \forall \tilde{s}_{-i} \qquad \text{(EQ 7.5)}$$

This implies that for player i, no matter what the other players play, the utility from the dominant strategy is as much as or greater than any other strategy.

7.3.5 Desirable Properties of a Mechanism

We now define certain desirable properties of any mechanism. Note that these are not mutually compatible: We need to balance between them in any practical mechanism.

- **Individual rationality:** No agent should be forced to participate in the mechanism; every agent should receive a greater utility from participation than nonparticipation. (For Bayesian agents, these would be expectations rather than actual utilities, conditioned on each agent's prior knowledge of (potentially) its type and the types of the other agents.)

- **Incentive compatibility:** A mechanism is incentive compatible if it is in the best interests of each agent to cooperate. More precisely, if the designer of the mechanism would like agent i to play strategy s_i^* in a dominant-strategy equilibrium, the mechanism is incentive compatible if, in such an equilibrium, the payoff to agent i when it plays s_i^* is as good as or better than the payoff with any other strategy.

- **Strategy-proofness:** A mechanism is strategy-proof if it is incentive compatible and the equilibrium is a dominant-strategy equilibrium.

- **Efficiency:** A mechanism is efficient if the selected outcome maximizes the total utility. At first glance, this seems impossible: After all, a player's utility is private! However, recall our assumption that the principal knows the form of the utility function of each player and all it does not know is a single type parameter. As we will see, this permits the desired maximization. A second objection is whether summing utilities is meaningful given that utilities are defined only up to an affine transform. The introduction of a common "money" parameter that all agents value allows us to plausibly maximize the sum of the utilities.

- **Budget balance:** In general, a mechanism may require transfers of money between agents. With a budget-balanced mechanism, these net transfers across agents are zero, so that the principal does not have to inject money into the system. (When dealing with Bayesian agents, we need to distinguish between *ex ante* budget balance, which means that the budget is balanced only in expectation, and *ex post* budget balance, which means that the budget is always balanced.)

- **Fairness:** In some cases, we would like the mechanism to select the outcome that minimizes the variance in the utilities of the agents. This is defined as *fairness*.

- **Revenue maximization:** Obviously, the designer of the mechanism would like to get the most possible revenue from the mechanism.

- **Pareto optimality:** A mechanism is Pareto optimal if it implements outcomes such that increasing the utility of any agent would necessarily decrease the utility of some other agent. That is, there is no "slack" in the system.

7.3.6 Revelation Principle

Mechanism design permits players to adopt arbitrarily complex strategies. Yet consider the following particularly simple strategy called **direct revelation**: Agent i tells the principal its type t_i. Of course, the agent could lie. Nevertheless, it should be clear that revelation greatly restricts the strategy spaces and simplifies the mechanism.

Formally, a direct-revelation mechanism $M = (T_1,...,T_n, g(.))$ is a mechanism where $S_i = T_i$, the strategy space for agent i, is its set of valid types. A direct-revelation mechanism is incentive compatible if, in equilibrium, the chosen strategy is to tell the truth, $s_i(t_i) = t_i$ for all t_i in T_i. Note that in a direct-revelation mechanism, the outcome function g is the same as the social-choice function f, because they both operate on the same space of agent types.

Suppose that we restrict mechanisms to those in which the only strategy allowed to an agent is direct revelation. Are there mechanisms that are more complex and can therefore achieve outcomes that this simple mechanism cannot? The surprising answer is that there are not! Every mechanism, no matter how complex, that achieves its goals through a dominant-strategy equilibrium can be reduced to a mechanism whereby the only strategy for an agent is direct revelation and the solution concept is dominant-strategy equilibrium.

To see this, note that the complex mechanism must require the player to play *some* strategy $s_i^*(t_i)$ in equilibrium. The strategies that are allowed each agent are not only under the control of the principal but also can depend only on t_i. Therefore, the principal could always simulate s_i if it were told t_i. Thus, no matter how complex s_i, all that the agent i needs to tell the principal is t_i, and the principal would compute the same outcome in equilibrium as would the complex mechanism. The preceding reasoning, with a modicum of mathematical formalism, is known as the **revelation principle**.

Given this principle, we need study only mechanisms of the direct-revelation type. Moreover, we would like to design mechanisms where truth telling is the dominant strategy, or, in short, direct-revelation incentive-compatible mechanisms. But, do any such mechanisms exist? The answer is affirmative, as the next section shows.

7.3.7 Vickrey-Clarke-Groves Mechanism

The Vickrey-Clarke-Groves (**VCG**) mechanism[10] is a direct-revelation mechanism that makes truth telling incentive compatible. Because all mechanisms that use dominant strategy as a solution concept can be reduced to an equivalent direct-revelation mechanism, the VCG mechanism is a widely used building block in the design of dominant-strategy mechanisms.

In the VCG mechanism, each agent tells the principal its (purported) type. Based on these types, the principal computes an outcome x (i.e., the social choice) and asks each agent to make a payment p_i. The agent would not like to pay the principal any money, so its utility declines with increasing payments. By choosing payments carefully, the principal can make truth telling the dominant-strategy equilibrium of the game, so that the social choice that is computed based on reported types is the true social choice.

Specifically, given an outcome x, the VCG mechanism assumes that agents have quasilinear utility functions of the form

$$u_i(x, p_i, t_i) = v_i(x, t_i) - p_i \qquad \text{(EQ 7.6)}$$

where the principal knows the form of v_i but not the parameter t_i. The **valuation function** v describes how highly each agent values the outcome ("public good") x, based on its type. Agent i of true type t_i tells the principal that its type is $\hat{t}_i$.

The principal computes the social choice, or outcome x^*, as

$$x^* = g(\hat{t}_1, ..., \hat{t}_n) = \overset{\arg\max}{\underset{x}{}} \sum_i v_i(x, \hat{t}_i) \qquad \text{(EQ 7.7)}$$

Thus, x^* is chosen to maximize the sum of individual valuations as a function of the reported types. Note that this potentially makes x^* strategically manipulable, in that an agent may report a type that would make $v_i(x^*, \hat{t}_i)$ be more in line with i's

---

10. The Clarke, Groves, and Vickrey mechanisms differ slightly in their generality. For simplicity, we will refer to all three interchangeably as VCG mechanisms.

wishes, making i a dictator. To avoid this, the VCG mechanism asks each player to make a payment p_i, where

$$p_i = h_i(\hat{t}_{-i}) - \sum_{j \neq i} v_j(x^*, \hat{t}_j)$$

(EQ 7.8)

where $h(.)$ is any function that is independent of t_i. The key idea is to pay agent i an amount equal to the sum of the other player's valuations. So, given that the social choice is x^*, the agent i's utility becomes

$$
\begin{aligned}
u_i(x^*, p_i, t_i) &= v_i(x^*, t_i) - p_i \\
&= v_i(x^*, t_i) - \left(h_i(\hat{t}_{-i}) - \sum_{j \neq i} v_j(x^*, \hat{t}_j) \right) \\
&= -h_i(\hat{t}_{-i}) + v_i(x^*, t_i) + \sum_{j \neq i} v_j(x^*, \hat{t}_j)
\end{aligned}
$$

(EQ 7.9)

Of these three terms, agent i has no control over the first term, because h does not depend on i, and has no control over the third term, which sums over the valuations of the other agents. Agent i can control only the second term, by its choice of reporting its type. Agent i should therefore report a type that maximizes the value of $v_i(x^*, t_i)$. How can it do that? Recall that the mechanism finds x as the value that maximizes

$$\sum_i v_i(x, \hat{t}_i) = v_i(x^*, \hat{t}_i) + \sum_{j \neq i} v_j(x^*, \hat{t}_j).$$

Comparing this with Equation 7.9, we see that agent i can maximize its utility by making $v_i(x^*, t_i)$ the same as $v_i(x^*, \hat{t}_i)$, and this will happen only if $\hat{t}_i = t_i$, that is, it tells the truth.

Essentially, the VCG mechanism forces each agent's utility function to be the sum of the reported valuations of all the users. Thus, every agent reports its type truthfully so that the overall maximization is in its own favor. This makes truth telling incentive compatible, so VCG is not strategically manipulable. Moreover, this is the only known mechanism that provides both individual rationality and Pareto efficiency.

We have thus far left $h(.)$ undefined. Different choices of $h(.)$ can achieve different outcomes. For example, it can be used to achieve **weak budget balance**—the principal may net revenue but will never have to pay money out—or individual rationality—no agent will be worse off participating than not participating. There is a particularly well-chosen value of h, called the **Clarke Pivot** value, that guarantees individual rationality while also maximizing revenue for the principal but not necessarily budget balance, that we describe next.

First, define x^{-i} as the social choice computed without taking agent i's input into account:

$$x^{-i} = \underset{x}{\arg\max} \sum_{j \neq i} v_j(x, \hat{t}_j) \qquad \text{(EQ 7.10)}$$

Then, the Clarke Pivot price that i pays, p_i, is given by

$$p_i = \sum_{j \neq i} v_j(x^{-i}, \hat{t}_j) - \sum_{j \neq i} v_j(x^*, \hat{t}_j) \qquad \text{(EQ 7.11)}$$

With this definition of p_i, we find that agent i's utility is given by

$$u_i(x^*, p_i, t_i) = v_i(x^*, t_i) - p_i = v_i(x^*, t_i) - \left(\sum_{j \neq i} v_j(x^{-i}, \hat{t}_j) - \sum_{j \neq i} v_j(x^*, \hat{t}_j) \right)$$

$$\qquad \text{(EQ 7.12)}$$

$$= \left(\sum_{j \neq i} v_j(x^*, \hat{t}_j) + v_i(x^*, t_i) \right) - \sum_{j \neq i} v_j(x^{-i}, \hat{t}_j)$$

The first term (in the parentheses) can be viewed as the overall utility from social choice x^* and the second term as the utility due to the social choice made considering everyone but i. Therefore, the VCG mechanism gives agent i a utility that corresponds to its own contribution to the overall utility, or social welfare.

EXAMPLE 7.26: VCG MECHANISM

Consider a company in which three departments would like to purchase and share a single enterprise router that costs $3,000. The department IT heads get together with the CIO, who wants to know whether they really value the router enough to justify having the company spend $3,000 on it. If the CIO simply asked the department IT heads (the agents) how much they value the router, they have no incentive to tell the truth, so they would all insist that they needed it. The CIO could, instead, implement a VCG mechanism as follows. Suppose that agent 1 thinks that its department's share of the router is worth $500, agent 2 thinks that its department's share is also worth $500, and agent 3 thinks that its department's share of the router is worth $2,500. We represent this as $v_1 = v_2 = 500$; $v_3 = 2,500$. Since they sum to more than $3,000, the router should be bought, assuming that the agents tell the truth. That is, $x^* =$ "purchase."

To ensure truthfulness, the CIO demands payments from each agent (this could be from the departmental IT budget). Assume that the CIO uses the Clarke Pivot payment rule described in Equation 7.11. We see that $x^{-1} =$ "purchase", $x^{-2} =$ "purchase", and $x^{-3} =$ "do not purchase." Obviously, v_i is 0 if the decision is "do not purchase" and the valuation described earlier if the decision is "purchase." This allows us to compute $p_1 = (500 + 2500) - (500 + 2500) = 0$, which is also the same as p_2. However, $p_3 = (0) - (500 + 500) = -1000$. In other words, p_3 receives a net payment of $1,000 from the CIO! We see that with the Clarke Pivot value, the VCG mechanism does not achieve budget balance. We do achieve individual rationality: Everyone is better off participating in the mechanism than not.

In general, if the nonparticipation of a single agent can affect the outcome, as it can here, we cannot achieve budget balance with a VCG mechanism. Nevertheless, it is important to note that the VCG mechanism makes truth telling a dominant strategy, so the CIO can expect that each department head will tell the truth.

Despite its lack of budget balance, the VCG mechanism can be proved to be individually rational, efficient, and strategy proof. Moreover, under some weak conditions, including the assumption that no single agent can affect the outcome, the VCG mechanism can also achieve weak budget balance. Therefore, it is the most widely used dominant-strategy mechanism.

7.3.8 Problems with VCG Mechanisms

The VCG mechanism has two important properties. First, it allows us to design and analyze practical network protocols and algorithms by using game theory. It is, therefore, the most engineering-oriented aspect of game theory, thus appealing to computer scientists and engineers. Second, it is remarkable in that it makes agents reveal their true types. This is intimately connected to Byzantine agreement, a classic problem in distributed computer algorithm design. Nevertheless, there are many drawbacks of the VCG approach that we briefly discuss next.

- *Information requirements:* The VCG mechanism assumes that the principal knows the form of the utility function of each agent so that revelation of the agent's type is sufficient to compute its utility. This is a strong assumption. It may not always be possible for principals to know agent utilities, which, after all, reflect their complex inner motivations.

- *Complexity of valuation function:* The computation of the optimal social choice requires the principal to compute the valuation for each agent for each possible alternative. Consider a principal that wants to sell m different goods, where players can buy any subset of the goods and value each subset differently. This is called a *combinatorial auction* and may reflect the fact that agents may benefit only from purchasing two or three specific goods rather than from each good individually. Then, each agent needs to specify up to 2^m different values, and the principal would need to compute sums over all possible partitions of the m goods and their allocation to the agents, an enormous task.

- *Centralization:* The social-choice function in a VCG is computed by a single centralized principal that receives inputs from all the agents. Imagine a resource-allocation problem with hundreds or thousands of agents: This would require the principal to perform a very large optimization, which is computationally expensive. It would be preferable to have this computation broken up into smaller, distributed computations.

- *Nonapproximability:* In dominant strategies, at least, the VCG mechanism requires that the principal compute the exact optimal value of the sum of the agent valuations. If this is not the optimal value, agents lose incentive compatibility. However, finding the optimal point of the sum of valuations is complex and may be only approximable, leaving the mechanism potentially open to manipulation.

- *Fairness:* The VCG scheme assumes that all agents have the same value for money. If this is not true—if, for example, richer agents care less for money than poorer agents do—fairness is not assured.

- *Budget balance:* We would like any mechanism to be net budget balanced, so that there are no net payments made to the principal or to the agents. At least, it should not cost the principal money to run the mechanism. However, if a single player can affect the outcome, VCG is not even weakly budget balanced. It turns out that a different solution concept, called the Bayes-Nash equilibrium, can guarantee budget balance. The corresponding mechanism, called **d'Asprement-Gerard-Varet** (AGV) after its inventors, lets each agent compute expected utilities as a function of their prior subjective probabilities on the types of the other agents. However, this budget balance comes at the expense of individual rationality; some agents would be better off not participating in the mechanism.

7.4 Limitations of Game Theory

Having studied some aspects of game theory, we now outline some of its limitations.

- Perhaps the biggest problem with using game theory in real life is ensuring that all players are aware of the others' utilities from each outcome. In real life, players often do not know what actions other players are permitted, their payoffs for each outcome, and the utility they gain from these payoffs.

- A second problem has to do with modeling time. A normal-form game is played simultaneously by all players, and an extensive-form game is played sequentially. In neither case, however, do we model the timing of the underlying events. Time and delay are critical factors in most networking problems. For example, in a wireless LAN, a station's transmission is known to others only after a nontrivial delay. Therefore, each player may see a different view of the world at each point in time. This affects the outcome of the game but is not modeled by classical game models.

- Almost all games assume that players are rational. However, considerable experimental evidence shows that people are not rational and sometimes do not even have consistent preferences, undermining utility functions as valid descriptions of user satisfaction.

- Most game models assume that the number of players does not change over time. However, in most typical networks, the number of players—endpoints sharing a resource—may vary over time. An endpoint usually does not know who else is sharing a given resource, let alone their utilities and payoffs.

- Any social-welfare function that maximizes sums of utilities is implicitly performing interpersonal utility comparisons. This is fundamentally invalid. The standard justification is that all players have the same value for money, but this is certainly an unrealistic assumption.

- As we have seen with mechanism design, games may require massive communication among players or between agents and the principal. For instance, to form Bayesian expectations on the other players' types, a player may need to observe their past behavior in great detail. This is both an invasion of privacy and expensive to communicate.

We conclude that it is unlikely that the results of game theory can be used directly in practical situations. However, it provides deep insights into modeling the behavior of selfish, rational agents and into the design of communication protocols that cannot be manipulated to subvert the designer's intentions. These make it well worth our study.

7.5 Further Reading

The classic original text on game theory, J. Von Neumann and O. Morgenstern, *The Theory of Games and Economic Behaviour*, Princeton University Press, 1944 (or the 60th anniversary edition released in 2004) is still a wonderful and insightful read. Another classic is R. D. Luce and H. Raiffa, *Games and Decisions*, Wiley, 1957. A more recent introductory text is M. J. Osborne and A. Rubinstein, *A Course in Game Theory*, MIT Press, 1994.

A brief overview of contemporary game theory can be found in K. Leyton-Brown and Y. Shoham, *Essentials of Game Theory*, Morgan and Claypool, 2008. A computer science perspective on game theory and, in particular, mechanism design, can be found in N. Nisan, T. Roughgarden, E. Tardos, and V. V. Vazirani, *Algorithmic Game Theory*, Cambridge University Press, 2007.

Graphical games were introduced and discussed in more detail in M. Kearns, M. Littman, and S. Singh, "Graphical Models for Game Theory," *Proceedings of the Conference on Uncertainty in Artificial Intelligence*, 2001. A critique of VCG mechanisms can be found in M. H. Rothkopf, "Thirteen Reasons the Vickrey-Clarke-Groves Process Is Not Practical," *Operations Research* 55, no. 2, (2007): 191–197.

7.6 Exercises

1. Preferences

Suppose that you equally like a banana and a lottery that gives you an apple 30% of the time and a carrot 70% of the time. Also, you equally like a peach and a lottery that gives you an apple 10% of the time and a carrot 90% of the time.

a. What can you say about your relative preferences for bananas and peaches?

b. If you had a lottery whose payoffs were bananas and carrots, what probability of winning a banana or a carrot would be equally preferred to a peach?

2. Utility functions

Your cable company gives you 10 GB of free data transfer a month and charges $5/GB thereafter. Suppose that your utility from transferring x GB of data is $100(1 - e^{-0.25x})$ and that your disutility from paying $1 is 1. Graphically evaluate how much data should you transfer in a month to maximize your utility.

3. Pure and mixed strategies

Consider the game of tic-tac-toe. What are the possible actions for the first move of the first player (ignore symmetries)? What would constitute a pure strategy? What would constitute a mixed strategy? Would you ever play a mixed strategy for this game? Why or why not?

4. Zero-sum game

If the payoffs $(a, -a)$ of every outcome of a zero-sum game were changed so that the new payoffs were $(a + 5, -5a)$, the game would no longer be zero sum. But, would the outcome of the game change?

5. **Representation**

   Represent the Pricing game of Example 7.7 in normal form.

6. **Representation**

   Prove that normal and extensive forms are equivalent if information sets are permitted.

7. **Best response**

   What is the best response for the customer in the pricing game (Example 7.7)?

8. **Dominant strategy**

   Suppose that you are not well prepared for a final, and you think you might fail it. If you miss the exam, you will certainly fail it. What is your dominant strategy: attend or miss? Why?

9. **Bayesian game**

   Does the Bayesian game in Example 7.11 have a dominant strategy for the row player? If so, what is it?

10. **Repeated game**

    Suppose that both players in Prisoner's Dilemma (Example 7.16) play their dominant strategy in an infinitely repeated game with a discount factor of 0.6. What is their payoff for the repeated game?

11. **Dominant-strategy equilibrium**

    Interpret the meaning of the dominant-strategy equilibrium of Example 7.15. Look up how the 802.11e enhanced distributed access channel (EDCA) protocol solves this problem.

12. **Iterated deletion**

    Show an example of a pure strategy that is dominated by a mixture of other pure strategies, although none of the strategies in the mixture dominate the pure strategy.

13. **Maximin**

    What are the maximin equilibria in Examples 7.10 and 7.15?

14. Maximin in a zero-sum game

Show that in Example 7.19, if Row uses any value of p other than 0.5, then it may get a payoff lower than 2.5 if Column plays either pure or mixed strategies.

15. Nash equilibrium

Referring to Example 7.20, assume that if Column plays a mixed strategy with probability $qH + (1 - q)T$ instead of its Nash equilibrium strategy. What is Row's mixed-strategy best response?

16. Correlated equilibrium

Does the WiFi game of Example 7.6 have a correlated equilibrium? If so, describe it.

17. Price discrimination

Outline the design of a price-discrimination mechanism with n player types whose valuations are known.

18. VCG mechanism

The CIO of a company wants to decide how much capacity to buy from its ISP. The cost of capacity is \$20/Mbps/month. Three departments in the company value capacity as follows: department 1 (D1) values capacity x Mbps/month at \$20$(*1 - e^{-0.5x})$, D2 values it at \$40$(*1 - e^{-0.5x})$, and D3 values it at \$80$(*1 - e^{-0.5x})$.

 a. Assuming the disutility of ISP payment is linear in the amount of payment, what is the overall function that the CIO should maximize?

 b. What is type of each department?

 c. What is the optimal social choice?

 d. What are the Clarke Pivot payments for each department?

 e. Is this budget balanced?

8

Elements of Control Theory

A computer network is an engineered system designed to meet certain design goals. Two such goals are **responsiveness** and **stability**. Responsiveness allows a system to continue to meet its performance goals despite changes in its operating environment, such as workload fluctuations or component failures. Stability prevents a system from failing or from being sent into uncontrollable oscillations due to certain inputs. Control theory provides powerful tools for building responsive and stable systems. For example, mathematically modeling the behavior of a controlled system demonstrates a fundamental contradiction between responsiveness and stability: The more responsive a system, the greater the chance that it will be unstable.

This chapter presents the elements of control theory. For simplicity, we consider primarily continuous-time linear control systems and classical control strategies. The concepts here, however, should provide a strong foundation for the interested student to delve further into this subject. Note that Chapter 5 is an essential prerequisite for understanding the material in this chapter.

We first describe a generic control system. We then characterize the behavior of generic first- and second-order systems, culminating with the design and analysis of classical control systems. We end with an introduction to "modern" control systems: state space representation and the principles of observability and controllability, and digital control.

8.1 Overview of a Controlled System

A generic feedback control system is shown in Figure 8.1. The system to be controlled is usually referred to as the **plant**. We assume that the plant and all control elements are continuous, linear, and time invariant. Given a control **input signal** u, the plant responds with an **output signal** y that is also additively influenced by an uncontrollable **disturbance signal** w. The control goal is to maintain the output of the plant at some **reference value** or **command** r despite disturbances. This is done using a **controller**, which compares the reference signal value with the **measured output signal** b, where this measurement itself may be subject to error. The controller chooses a **control signal** u such that the future output of the plant eventually matches the reference input, despite disturbances and measurement errors.

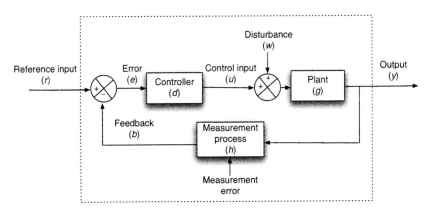

Figure 8.1 General model of a controlled system

EXAMPLE 8.1: A SIMPLE CONTROL SYSTEM

A thermostat-controlled home-heating furnace is an example of a simple control system. A user can use the control interface to specify a desired home temperature r. The controller compares this temperature with the temperature b measured using a sensor. If the difference (error e) is positive, the controller activates a heating furnace by sending it a control signal u, eventually raising the home's air temperature y to the desired reference value. At this point, the error drops to zero and the furnace is turned off.[1] A disturbance w, such as the

---

1. This example is highly simplified. Modern furnaces also have more sophisticated control elements, such as a controller that turns on the furnace slightly before it is needed, so that it heats air instead of accidentally cooling it, and a controller that uses measurements to predict how long a furnace needs to be on to heat the home by a certain amount.

inrush of cold outside air due to opening a door or a window, results in a drop of the measured temperature y. The controller compensates for this disturbance by turning on the furnace and eventually causing the output to return to the reference temperature.

Even this simple example demonstrates three lessons that apply to all control systems. First, immediately after the disturbance, a home's temperature could be far from the reference temperature. The presence of the controller does not guarantee that the home temperature will always be at the reference value, only that, in the absence of disturbances, this reference value will eventually be reached. If a series of disturbances come in quick succession, the system may never reach equilibrium.

Second, given that a system is currently not in equilibrium, it is up to the controller to decide how quickly to restore the system to this state. A system is said to have a high **gain**, or be **responsive**, if the controller tries to restore the system rapidly. Although this is usually desirable, a system with too high a gain can become unstable because in such a system, even a short delay in transferring measurements from the plant to the controller causes the controller to overreact to stale information, causing oscillations. In this example, a controller with too high a gain could result in a home whose temperature persistently oscillates from being too hot to being too cold. Choosing the degree of gain in the controller that balances responsiveness and stability is a critical issue in any control system.

Third, note that the controller simply cannot compensate for measurement errors. For example, if the temperature sensor always reads two degrees higher than the true temperature, the home's temperature will always be two degrees lower than the reference value. Therefore, in any feedback control system, it is important to use the best sensors possible.

EXAMPLE 8.2: CONTROLLING WEB SERVER LOAD

Consider a Web server that responds to GET and POST queries from Web browsers. The server uses a buffer to hold pending requests before they are served so that requests arriving to a busy server are not lost. Figure 8.2(a) shows the times at which requests arrive and depart from the buffer. Requests arrive at discrete time instants (shown on the X-axis) and are served after spending some time in the buffer. For example, request 4 arrives at time 5 and is served at time 7. The system is causal, so the departure curve is always at or below the arrival curve.

Although arrivals and departures are discrete events, it is convenient to model them using a continuous "fluid" approximation as shown in Figure 8.2(b).

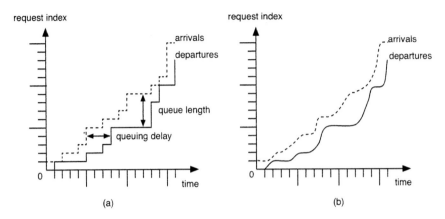

Figure 8.2 (a) Discrete arrivals and departures; (b) fluid approximation

Intuitively, this approximation is obtained by smoothing the arrival and departure curves, which removes abrupt transitions without introducing too much distortion. If queries arrive quickly enough, the fluid approximation has been found in practice to be reasonably accurate and, in any case, greatly simplifies mathematical analysis.

Note that the vertical distance between the arrival and departure curves at any point in time represents the number of queries in the buffer (the queue length) at that time. The control goal is to ensure that this quantity neither exceeds the buffer capacity—causing requests to be lost owing to buffer overflow—nor drops to zero—causing a buffer underflow and idling the Web server, unless, of course, there is no work to be done. Instead, we would like to keep the number of queries in the buffer at some reference value r that is small enough to not greatly impact the server response time but large enough that if the Web server were to suddenly obtain additional capacity, the buffer would not underflow. The greater the value of r, the higher the expected query service rate and the higher the query-processing delay.

The problem is that a client does not know the Web server's service rate, which depends on how many other clients are being served and how long it takes to satisfy a client request. We model this uncertainty by representing the Web server's service rate as a time-varying "disturbance" $w(t)$. The control goal is to manage the client request rate $u(t)$ to prevent buffer underflow and overflow. Specifically, we assume that the controller is given a buffer-occupancy reference value $r(t)$ and that it is instantaneously informed of the current number of bits in the buffer, denoted $y(t)$. The controller uses this feedback information to choose $u(t)$ such that $y(t)$ tracks $r(t)$ despite disturbance $w(t)$.

Note the similarity between this control system and a home thermostat. In both cases, the controller tries to keep output y at the reference level r despite disturbance w by comparing the measured state of the system with the desired reference value.

8.2 Modeling a System

Motivated by Example 8.2, we turn our attention to the process of mathematically modeling a system, which can be viewed either as the plant or as the controlled system shown in the dotted box in Figure 8.1. Both the plant and the controlled system have an input and an output, where the output depends on the input. By using identical approaches to model both the *open* uncontrolled system and the *closed* controlled system, we can recursively control a complex system. That is, we can model and control one aspect of a plant, then represent this controlled system as black box when modeling the remainder of the system. This approach is necessary to control a complex system. We will study some practical problems using this approach in Section 8.7.

Choosing which aspects of a system should be modeled and which aspects can be ignored is an art rather than a science. Developing a system model that is mathematically tractable and yet represents all the relevant aspects of the system will usually require several rounds of refinement. We first outline an approach that has been found to work well in practice and then focus on three mathematically equivalent representations of a system.

8.2.1 Modeling Approach

Start by understanding the working of the system and its component parts. Determine the physical capabilities of each component, its limits of operation, and the operating regimes where it is linear or nonlinear. Components in a control system can usually be described in terms of the concepts of **effort** and **flow**. Effort represents a system input that causes a flow. The product of effort and flow is **power**, and the total power expended over some time duration is called **energy**. For example, in a mechanical system, forces correspond to effort, and velocities correspond to flow. The product of force and velocity is mechanical power, and the integral of power over time is the amount of mechanical energy used. In an electrical system, voltages correspond to effort and currents to flow. Their product is electrical power, whose integral is electrical energy. Similarly, in a computer network, the quantity of data that needs to be sent from a source to a destination represents effort, and the rate at which data is sent corresponds to flow. Although they can be analogously defined, the concepts of power and energy are not commonly used in computer networks.

System components can be either active or passive. Active elements generate power (not energy!) that flows through the system. The dynamic operation of the system is essentially an attempt to redistribute this power over time. In contrast, passive elements store and dissipate energy but do not generate power. In an electrical system, a voltage source, such as a battery, is an active element that drives the system, whereas capacitors and inductors are passive elements that store and dissipate energy. Similarly, a data source is an active component that generates effort that causes a flow on links and into routers. In contrast, a buffer is a passive component that stores and releases energy, like a capacitor.

The next step is to capture the laws, such as conservation, that constrain the operation of the system. For example, in a mechanical system, Newton's laws form the basic equilibrium constraints. In a computer network, the rate at which a buffer stores data is the difference between the data arrival and departure rates. Similarly, during the slow-start phase of a TCP connection, the rate of transmission grows exponentially. These constitute the mathematical laws of operation of the corresponding components.

Finally, state the intended goal of the control system in terms of the ideal equilibrium operating point (which, by convention, is defined to be zero). If possible, quantify the permissible operating error. This makes it possible to determine the degree to which a chosen control law meets requirements.

At the end of the modeling process, it should be possible to capture the operation of the system in a handful of equations. We will see some concrete examples of the modeling process shortly.

8.2.2 Mathematical Representation

Three common ways to mathematically represent a system (i.e., either the plant or the dotted box in Figure 8.1) are by the **state variable**, the **impulse response**, and the **transfer function** representations. Our discussion assumes that the system is **linear** and **time invariant** (**LTI**). Recall that a time-invariant system is one whose parameters do not change with time: If the system has an output $y(t)$ at time t for an input $u(t)$, it has the output $y(t - T)$ for an input $u(t - T)$. That is, if $y(t) = G(u(t))$, then $y(t - T) = G(u(t - T))$. Recall also that a linear system is one that exhibits **superposition**: If the input u_1 leads to output y_1 and input u_2 leads to output y_2, then for all constants k_1 and k_2, the input $(k_1 u_1 + k_2 u_2)$ leads to the output $(k_1 y_1 + k_2 y_2)$. That is, if $y_1 = G(u_1)$ and $y_2 = G(u_2)$, then $k_1 y_1 + k_2 y_2 = G(k_1 u_1 + k_2 u_2)$. For an LTI system, it is always possible to choose the initial time to be $t = 0$. We assume the system to be causal, so the input signal is zero for $t < 0$.

State Variable Representation. In the state variable representation, we first choose a set of state variables that completely characterize the state of the system. Note that by choosing the set of state variables, we are implicitly deciding which aspects of a system to model and which to ignore: a subtle and far-reaching decision.

The number of state variables in the system typically corresponds to the number of energy-storage elements in the system, because each state variable tracks the amount of energy currently in that storage element. In an electrical network with, say, three capacitors and four inductors, we need at least seven state variables. For the Web server in Example 8.2, there is only one energy-storage element, so we need only one state variable: for example, the buffer-occupancy level $y(t)$, which, in this simple example, is also its output variable. In general, the set of state variables is not unique: The system could equally well be characterized by a state variable corresponding to $\dot{y}(t)$, which is the buffer fill or drain rate rather than its occupancy level.

We denote the set of state variables by the column vector $x(t)$, whose dimension is the **order** of the system. The system is represented by the equations that govern the evolution of $x(t)$. We first consider a **single-input single-output system**, with scalar input u and a scalar output r. To model the complete system (i.e., including the disturbance input), we also consider a vector disturbance w. Let

$$x(t) = \begin{bmatrix} x_1(t) \\ x_2(t) \\ \ldots \\ x_n(t) \end{bmatrix}$$

Then, any linear time-invariant system can be represented using the following state-update equations, where the parameter t has been left out for clarity:

$$\dot{x}_1 = a_{11}x_1 + a_{12}x_2 + \ldots + a_{1n}x_n + b_1 u + f_1 w_1$$
$$\dot{x}_2 = a_{21}x_1 + a_{22}x_2 + \ldots + a_{2n}x_n + b_2 u + f_2 w_2$$

(EQ 8.1)

$$\ldots$$

$$\dot{x}_n = a_{n1}x_1 + a_{n2}x_2 + \ldots + a_{nn}x_n + b_n u + f_n w_n$$

Moreover, the output can be written as a function of the state, the disturbances, and the input as

$$y(t) = c_1 x_1 + c_2 x_2 + \ldots + c_n x_n + du + e_1 w_1 + \ldots + e_n w_n$$

where scalar constants are given by a_i, b_i, c_i, e_i, and f_i. Using matrix notation, we can compactly write this as

$$\dot{x} = Ax + bu + Fw$$
$$y = c^T x + du + e^T w$$
(EQ 8.2)

where the matrix A, the diagonal matrix F, and the column vectors b, c, w, and e are appropriately defined.

Note that the a_{ii} terms represent how the state element x_i evolves independent of the other state elements, whereas the a_{ij} terms represent the degree of coupling between the ith and jth state elements. If these coupling terms are zero, the matrix A is diagonal, and the system can be decomposed into a set of n noninteracting systems. It is often possible to transform the basis set of state elements into an alternative set of elements that either diagonalizes A or at least puts it in the Jordan normal form, with elements only on the diagonal and one row above. This maximally decouples the system, making it easier to analyze. This **similarity transformation** is discussed further in Section 3.5.7.

EXAMPLE 8.3: STATE REPRESENTATION OF A WEB SERVER

We use the state space representation to model the Web server of Example 8.2. We wish to model the entire system, so the model incorporates the disturbance input w. We choose the state variable $x(t)$ to be the same as the buffer-occupancy level $y(t)$. Then,

$$\dot{x} = u - w$$

is the state-update equation of the system. Clearly, the output of the system is identical to the buffer-occupancy level $y(t)$.

The state space model can be easily extended in two ways. First, it can be used to represent systems with multiple inputs and outputs. In this case, the input u is replaced by the vector u, the output y is replaced by the vector y, and the disturbance w by the disturbance vector w. The details are straightforward and are left as an exercise to the reader.

Second, the state space model can also be used to represent nonlinear time-invariant systems as follows:

$$\dot{x} = f(x, u, w)$$
$$y = g(x, u, w)$$
(EQ 8.3)

where the vectors x and y represent the state and output vectors of a multiple-input multiple-output system with input vector u and disturbance vector w, and the vector functions f and g represent arbitrary functions. It is often possible to **linearize** such a system around an operating point x_0, u_0, w_0 by approximating the functions f and g, using the multivariable form of the **Taylor expansion**:

$$\dot{x} \approx f(x_0, u_0, w_0) + (x - x_0)^T \nabla xf + (u - u_0)^T \nabla uf + (w - w_0)^T \nabla wf \qquad \text{(EQ 8.4)}$$

where ∇xf, ∇uf, and ∇wf are the gradients of f with respect to the x, u, and w vectors, respectively. The function g can be similarly linearized. Note that this approximate linearization is valid only in the immediate neighborhood of the equilibrium operating point x_0.

Impulse Response Model. Many practical systems of interest have a single scalar input u. In this case, it is possible to represent the system by its **impulse response**. Recall from Section 5.4.3 that if we know the response $g(t)$ of an LTI system to a Dirac delta input, we can compute its response to *any* input $u(t)$ by convolving the input signal $u(t)$ with the impulse response $g(t)$. When using this model, we assume that the system is in equilibrium at time $t=0$, or $x(0) = 0$. Also, if we are modeling the entire system (not just the plant), the input signal should incorporate the disturbance. The output $y(t)$ is given by

$$y(t) = \int_0^t u(\tau)g(t - \tau)d\tau = u(t) \otimes g(t) \qquad \text{(EQ 8.5)}$$

The impulse response model is rarely used in practice: Its main purpose is as a step in the derivation of the *transfer function model*, which we describe next.

Transfer Function Model. Consider a system at equilibrium at time 0 that is described by the impulse response function $g(t)$, so that the output $y(t)$ is given by Equation 8.5. By taking the Laplace transform of both sides we get:

$$Y(s) = U(s)G(s) \qquad \text{(EQ 8.6)}$$

In other words, we obtain the Laplace transform of the output by multiplying the Laplace transform of the input (which, if necessary, incorporates a disturbance input) with the Laplace transform of the impulse response, rather than computing a convolution, as is required with the impulse response function. This simple form of the output makes it convenient to represent a single-input single-output causal system by the Laplace transform of its impulse response, which we call its **transfer function**.

The transfer function of many common systems takes the form $N(s)/D(s)$, where $N(s)$ and $D(s)$ are polynomials in s. The highest power of s in $D(s)$ is called the **order** of the transfer function. Consider a denominator polynomial $D(s)$ of order m. The m roots of $D(s)$, that is, the m values of s for which $D(s)$ is zero, denoted $\alpha_1, \alpha_2, ..., \alpha_m$, are the values of s for which $Y(s)$ is undefined, and these are called the **poles** of the system. It turns out that these poles have a deep significance because, using the technique of partial fraction expansion discussed in Section 8.11, $Y(s)$ can be written as a sum of terms of the form $\dfrac{A}{(s-\alpha)^r}$. Referring to row 6 of Table 5.4 in Section 5.8 and recalling that the Laplace transform is linear, we see that the corresponding term in $y(t)$, obtained by taking the inverse Laplace transform, is $A\dfrac{t^r}{r!}e^{\alpha t}$. Therefore, if the pole is negative, the corresponding term in the output decays with time; if, on the other hand, it is positive, the output grows with time. We like a system to be **stable**, which informally means that for a bounded input, the output also should be bounded. This is possible only if all system poles lie in the left half of the complex s plane. (We discuss this notion in more detail in Section 8.8.) Thus, the nature of $D(s)$ allows us to quickly determine the overall behavior of the system, reinforcing the usefulness of the transfer function system model.

EXAMPLE 8.4: TRANSFER FUNCTION MODEL

We now derive the transfer function model of the Web server system. Recall that the state space representation of the system is

$$\dot{x} = u - w$$

This is a single-input single-output system that is initially at equilibrium, so that $y(0) = 0$. Therefore, we can use a transfer function to model it. The output y is the same as the state variable x. To incorporate the disturbance into the input signal, we write

$$v = u - w$$
$$\dot{x} = v$$

We obtain the transfer function by taking the Laplace transform of both sides:

$$sY(s) - y(0) = V(s)$$
$$Y(s) = V(s)\left(\frac{1}{s}\right) + \frac{y(0)}{s}$$

so that

$$G(s) = \frac{1}{s}$$

is the required transfer function model of the system.

"Modern" versus "Classical" Control. The classical approach to control uses transfer function models. Although the results are intuitive, this approach does not permit the modeling of multiple-input multiple-output and nonlinear systems. The "modern" approach, instead, uses the state variable model, which easily generalizes to these domains and can also draw on linear algebra for compact notation and a deep theoretical basis. In keeping with our goal of presenting intuition rather than formalisms, we will use the classical approach, with a brief treatment of the state variable approach in Section 8.8.

8.3 A First-Order System

One of the simplest systems that can be characterized by a transfer function is a **first-order** system with a transfer function

$$G(s) = \frac{K}{1 + \tau s} \qquad \text{(EQ 8.7)}$$

where K is called the **gain parameter** and τ is called the **system time constant**. The reason for this nomenclature is best understood by considering the response of this system to a step input $u(t)$, that is, an input that is one unit for all $t > 0$. Recall that the Laplace transform of a step input is $1/s$. Therefore, the Laplace transform of the output, $Y(s)$, is given by

$$Y(s) = \frac{K}{s(1 + \tau s)}$$

It is easy to see that the roots of the denominator are $s=0$ and $s = -\frac{1}{\tau}$. We use this fact to compute the partial fraction expansion as

$$Y(s) = K\left[\frac{1}{s} - \frac{\tau}{1 + \tau s}\right]$$

Using Table 5.4 in Section 5.8, we compute

$$y(t) = K\left(1 - e^{\frac{-t}{\tau}}\right) \qquad \text{(EQ 8.8)}$$

which is shown in Figure 8.3 for $K = 2.5$ and $\tau = 2$.

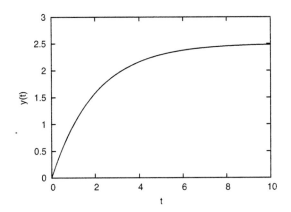

Figure 8.3 Step response of a first-order system with gain 2.5 and time constant 2

A close examination of Equation 8.8 and Figure 8.3 reveals the following.

- In response to a step input, the output rises rapidly, eventually asymptoting to a value that is K times the input value of 1. In other words, in steady state, the system magnifies the input by a factor of K, thus justifying K as the system gain parameter.

- The system reaches $(1 - 1/e)$, or roughly 63% of its final value, when $t = \tau = 2$ and 99.33% of its final value when $t = 5\tau = 10$. For all practical purposes, the system reaches its asymptotic value at time 5τ, justifying τ as the system time constant.

- A step input is like a sharp kick to the system. We can write the system's **step response** to this input as $y(t) = K(1 - e^{-t/\tau}) = K - Ke^{-t/\tau}$. The first term is the **steady state response**, and the second term is the **transient response**. In general, given any sharp change in input, any system will exhibit both forms of response. We are interested in quantifying both. Given the particularly simple form of the Laplace transform of a step function, we often characterize a system by its step response.

- Step inputs are easy to generate. Therefore, if we can model a system as a first-order system, it is possible to numerically obtain the value of K and τ by giving it a step input and plotting its output.

8.4 A Second-Order System

Intuitively, a second-order system arises when the system responds to the input by accumulating and then releasing energy. A classic example is a violin string excited by a bow. As the bow moves over the string, the string distorts, accumulating energy. At some point, the accumulated energy is sufficient to overcome the motion of the bow, and the string returns and then overshoots its neutral position. The process repeats, resulting in an oscillation, powered by the energy of the bow.

Compared to a first-order system, a second-order system is more complex but still relatively easy to analyze. Its transfer function is given by

$$G(s) = \frac{K}{\dfrac{s^2}{\omega_n^2} + \dfrac{2\varsigma s}{\omega_n} + 1} \qquad \text{(EQ 8.9)}$$

A second-order system is characterized by three factors: its **gain** K, its **natural frequency** ω_n (in radians/second), and its **damping ratio** ς (read *zeta*). As before, to understand the physical meanings of these terms, we consider its unit step response. For a step input, we have

$$Y(s) = \frac{K}{s\left(\dfrac{s^2}{\omega_n^2} + \dfrac{2\varsigma s}{\omega_n} + 1\right)}$$

We study four cases corresponding to different values of ς.

8.4.1 Case 1 (Undamped System): $\varsigma = 0$

When $\varsigma = 0$,

$$Y(s) = \frac{K}{s\left(\dfrac{s^2}{\omega_n^2} + 1\right)} = \frac{K\omega_n^2}{s(s^2 + \omega_n^2)} = K\left(\frac{1}{s} - \frac{s}{s^2 + \omega_n^2}\right)$$

Using Table 5.4 in Section 5.8, we compute

$$y(t) = K(1 - \cos\omega_n t) \qquad \text{(EQ 8.10)}$$

which is shown in Figure 8.4 for $K = 2.5$, $\omega_n = 2$.

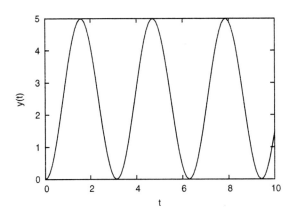

Figure 8.4 Unit step response of an undamped second-order system
with $K = 2.5$, $\omega_n = 2$

The output of an undamped second-order system is oscillatory, with a frequency of ω_n. The gain parameter determines the amplitude of the oscillations. These justify naming K and ω_n as the gain and natural frequency, respectively.

8.4.2 Case 2 (Underdamped System): $0 < \varsigma < 1$

When $0 < \varsigma < 1$, the Laplace transform of the step response is given by:

$$Y(s) = \frac{K}{s\left(\dfrac{s^2}{\omega_n^2} + \dfrac{2\varsigma s}{\omega_n} + 1\right)} = \frac{K\omega_n^2}{s(s^2 + 2\varsigma s + \omega_n^2)} = K\left(\frac{1}{s} - \frac{(s + \varsigma\omega_n)}{(s + \varsigma\omega_n)^2 + \omega_d^2} - \frac{\varsigma\omega_n}{(s + \varsigma\omega_n)^2 + \omega_d^2}\right)$$

where $\omega_d^2 = \omega_n^2(1 - \varsigma^2)$.

Using Table 5.4 in Section 5.8, we compute

$$y(t) = K\left(1 - e^{-\varsigma\omega_n t}\left(\cos\omega_d t + \frac{\varsigma}{\sqrt{1 - \varsigma^2}}\sin\omega_d t\right)\right)$$

$$y(t) = K\left(1 - \frac{e^{-\varsigma\omega_n t}}{\sqrt{1 - \varsigma^2}}\left(\sqrt{1 - \varsigma^2}\cos\omega_d t + \varsigma\sin\omega_d t\right)\right)$$

Let $\varsigma = \cos\theta$ so that $\theta = \cos^{-1}\varsigma$. Then, $\sqrt{1 - \varsigma^2} = \sqrt{1 - (\cos\theta)^2} = \sin\theta$, so that

$$y(t) = K\left(1 - \frac{e^{-\varsigma\omega_n t}}{\sqrt{1 - \varsigma^2}}\left(\sin\theta\cos\omega_d t + \cos\theta\sin\omega_d t\right)\right)$$

From the identity $\sin(A + B) = \sin A \cos B + \cos A \sin B$, we get

$$y(t) = K\left(1 - \frac{e^{-\varsigma\omega_n t}}{\sqrt{1 - \varsigma^2}}\sin(\omega_d t + \cos^{-1}\varsigma)\right); \ t \geq 0 \qquad \text{(EQ 8.11)}$$

From the form of Equation 8.11, we see that the sinusoidal oscillation is modulated by a decaying exponential of the form $e^{-\varsigma\omega_n t}$. For a fixed value of ω_n, as ς increases, the exponent dies down more rapidly, damping the system. This justifies calling ς the damping ratio. We also see that the phase of the sinusoid is shifted (compared to the undamped system) by a phase angle $arc\tan\dfrac{\sqrt{1 - \varsigma^2}}{\varsigma}$, a function of ς.

Figure 8.5 shows $y(t)$ for different values of ς, while keeping the values of K and ω_n the same as in the case of the undamped system: $K = 2.5, \omega_n = 2$. As ς approaches 1, the transient response of system becomes less oscillatory. For example, when $\varsigma = 0.2$, the system continues to oscillate even after five time periods (i.e., t=10). On the other hand, when $\varsigma > 0.8$, the output steadily approaches the asymptotic value of 2.5.

Intuitively, the damping ratio determines the responsiveness of the system. When this ratio is small, the system is "jumpy," responding immediately to a stimulus but taking a long time to reach steady state after receiving a shock. As the ratio increases, the system is more sluggish but reaches its asymptote smoothly.

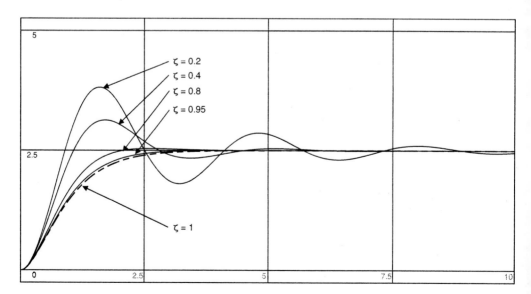

Figure 8.5 Unit step response of an underdamped second-order system with $K = 2.5, \omega_n = 2; \varsigma = 0.2, 0.4, 0.8, 0.95, 1.0$

8.4.3 Case 3 (Critically Damped System): $\varsigma = 1$

When $\varsigma = 1$, we say that the system is **critically damped**. When subjected to a unit step input, this system is neither too responsive nor too sluggish, rising smoothly to its asymptotic value. Of course, choosing parameters to achieve critical damping for any real system can be a challenge!

To mathematically study such a system, we use the partial fraction expansion of $Y(s)$ as before to find

$$Y(s) = \frac{K\omega^2}{s(s^2 + 2\omega s + \omega^2)} = K\left[\frac{1}{s} - \frac{\omega}{(s+\omega)^2} - \frac{1}{s+\omega}\right]$$

$$y(t) = K[1 - e^{-\omega_n t} - \omega_n t e^{-\omega_n t}] \qquad \text{(EQ 8.12)}$$

Note that the output $y(t)$ has no sinusoidal components. The corresponding function is shown in Figure 8.5. Comparing the output of a critically damped system with that of an undamped and underdamped system, it should be clear why a critically damped system is ideal.

8.4.4 Case 4 (Overdamped System): $\varsigma > 1$

When the damping ratio exceeds 1, the output of a second-order system becomes less and less responsive to a step input. Such a system is **overdamped**. We can mathematically study the system as follows. We have

$$Y(s) = \frac{K\omega_n^2}{s(s^2 + 2\varsigma\omega_n s + \omega_n^2)}$$

The roots of the second term in the denominator, from the quadratic formula, are

$$\frac{-2\varsigma\omega_n \pm \sqrt{4\omega_n^2\varsigma^2 - 4\omega_n^2}}{2},$$

so that

$$Y(s) = \frac{K\omega_n^2}{s(s + \varsigma\omega_n + \omega_n\sqrt{\varsigma^2 - 1})(s + \varsigma\omega_n - \omega_n\sqrt{\varsigma^2 - 1})}$$

For convenience, let $\gamma = \sqrt{\varsigma^2 - 1}$. From the inverse Laplace transform of the partial fraction expansion, we find that

$$y(t) = K\left[1 + \frac{e^{-(\varsigma + \gamma)\omega_n t}}{2\gamma(\varsigma + \gamma)} - \frac{e^{-(\varsigma - \gamma)\omega_n t}}{2\gamma(\varsigma - \gamma)}\right] \qquad \text{(EQ 8.13)}$$

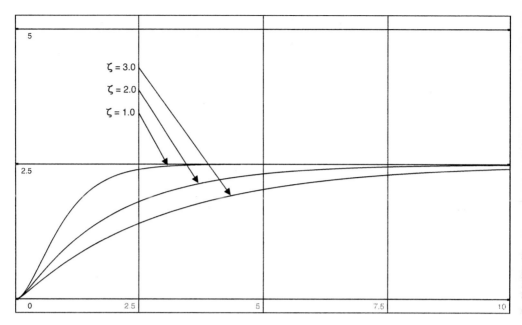

Figure 8.6 Unit step response for an overdamped system with
$K = 2.5, \omega_n = 2, \varsigma = 1.0, 2.0, 3.0$

The step response has no sinusoidal components, being the difference between two exponential curves. The function is plotted in Figure 8.6, with the same values of K and ω_n as before. We see that as the damping ratio increases, the system takes progressively longer to reach its asymptote.

To summarize, the behavior of a second-order system is controlled by its gain, damping ratio, and natural frequency parameters. The gain controls the steady state response to a unit step input. When underdamped, the natural frequency controls the step-response oscillation frequency. Finally, the damping ratio controls the responsiveness of the step response. In designing a control system, it is usually possible to choose arbitrary values for these three parameters. Our goal, therefore, is to tune the system to achieve the desired gain and critical damping.

In practice, no system is truly a second-order system: This is just a convenient approximation. However, the system gives us valuable insights into the behavior of many real systems, as the next example demonstrates.

EXAMPLE 8.5: ROUTE FLAPPING AS A SECOND-ORDER SYSTEM

In a computer network, the dynamic selection of least-delay routes between two nodes can be modeled as a second-order system. Consider two nodes A and B that are connected by two edge-disjoint paths. Suppose that all the traffic from A to B goes over the first path. This load increases the delay on this path, which we can model as the accumulation of energy. At some point, the energy on the path is so large that the routing algorithm running at node A decides to route traffic destined to B on the second path. This reduces the energy on the first path and increases it on the second. As before, this results in an over-accumulation of energy on the second path, resulting in an oscillatory system exhibiting **route flapping**.

To make this concept more precise, consider a network in which both paths from A and B have a capacity of 1 unit/second. As long as the load from A to B is smaller than 1 unit/second, both paths are uncongested, and the system does not exhibit oscillations. However, suppose that A injects load at the rate of 2 units/second into the first path. This will result in the buffer on the path building up at the rate of 1 unit/second. Suppose that the routing protocol running at A switches paths when the path delay exceeds 5 seconds. This will happen at $t = 5$ seconds. At this point, the load switches to the second path, and the queue there will build up at the rate of 1 unit/second until at time $t = 10$ seconds, traffic will revert to the first path. Clearly, the oscillations have a period of 10 seconds.

EXAMPLE 8.6: DAMPING ROUTE FLAPPING

We saw the oscillatory behavior of a naive threshold-based routing protocol in Example 8.5. We can use the insights from second-order systems to reduce oscillations by using damping. The essence of damping is to reduce system responsiveness. We use this insight as follows: Suppose that the routing algorithm, instead of sending *all* data on the shortest path, distributed load inversely proportional to the measured path delay. Then, the load from A to B would be spread on both paths, increasing overall capacity. Moreover, if there were a sudden increase in delay along one path, load would be proportionally redistributed to another path. By reacting less aggressively to an increase in load, this damped routing algorithm would reduce the oscillatory behavior of the network. The open shortest path first (OSPF) routing protocol in the Internet allows multipath routing for equal-cost paths, so this form of damping is feasible even in practice.

8.5 Basics of Feedback Control

We are now in a position, finally, to investigate the basics of feedback control. We use the transfer function model to study a simple feedback system. We also investigate the goals of a control system and learn how these goals can be achieved using feedback control.

Recall the abstract model of a continuous, linear, time-invariant control system in Figure 8.1. Assume that all inputs and outputs are scalar. Then, we can use transfer functions to model the behavior of each of the control blocks. That is, if the input to a control block G is the signal $u(t)$ and its output is the signal $y(t)$, we can model the control block by using the transfer function $G(s)$, so that the Laplace transform of the output, $Y(s)$, is merely the product of the transfer function and the Laplace transfer of the input $U(s)$:

$$Y(s) = G(s)U(s)$$

This allows us to redraw Figure 8.1, replacing each control block by its corresponding transfer function and each signal by its Laplace transform, as shown in Figure 8.7.

The use of the transfer function model allows us to state the system equations as follows (we omit the argument s for clarity):

$$Y = GU + GW \tag{EQ 8.14}$$

$$E = R - B = R - HY \tag{EQ 8.15}$$

$$U = DE = D(R - HY) \tag{EQ 8.16}$$

From Equations 8.14, 8.15, and 8.16, we can write

$$Y = GDR - GDHY + GW$$

$$Y(1 + GDH) = GDR + GW$$

$$Y = \left(\frac{GD}{1 + GDH}\right)R + \left(\frac{G}{1 + GDH}\right)W \tag{EQ 8.17}$$

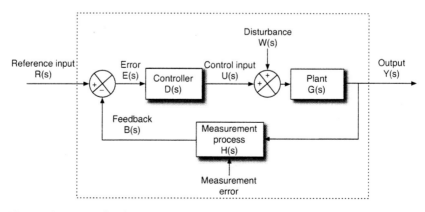

Figure 8.7 Transfer function model of a single-input single-output linear time-invariant feedback control system

Equation 8.17 is the fundamental equation of a feedback control system. It shows that the output is a linear combination of two terms, one arising from the Laplace transform of the reference signal $R(s)$ and the other from the Laplace transform of the disturbance $W(s)$. Note that the only variable that can be modified by a system designer is D, which represents the controller. A common situation is that the measurement process simply feeds the output back to the input, so that $H(s) = 1$: Such a system is called a **unity feedback system**.

We now use this equation to investigate the goals of a control system and how they are achieved by a feedback control system. Essentially, we will compare the controlled system whose output is given by Equation 8.17 with a system with no feedback (i.e., $H = 0$), whose output is given by $Y = G(DR+W)$.

8.5.1 System Goal

The primary goal of any controller is to ensure that $y = r$ despite w. We assume that we can design the controller, and therefore choose D, more or less as we wish, within some limits, to meet this goal.

It is illuminating to consider how this system goal is achieved in the context of three systems: an uncontrolled system, a controlled system with no feedback, and a system with feedback control. The output of an uncontrolled system is affected by disturbances, and so the control goal is achieved only if $w = 0$. In contrast, a controller that lacks feedback can compensate for a disturbance by predicting it. If it can predict disturbances accurately, it can achieve the system goal. For instance, suppose that an oven temperature controller knows that every time the oven door is opened, a certain amount of heat is lost, and so the heating element needs to be turned on for a certain duration. This controller could maintain oven temperature despite a disturbance created by a door opening by sensing the state of the oven door. In contrast, a feedback control system measures the effect of a disturbance on the output (e.g., the effect of a door opening on the oven temperature) and can use the system-transfer function to determine the appropriate input that removes the effect of the disturbance.

In many situations, the command r is held constant for a reasonably long duration of time. In this case, the goal of a controller is to ensure, first, that the output quickly reaches r and second, that the output stays at r despite disturbances. The time taken for the output to get close to r from its initial state is called the **settling time**. The discrepancy between the actual output and the reference input after the settling time is past is called the **steady state error**.

8.5.2 Constraints

In achieving the system goal, a controller must take the following constraints into account. The constraints are *stability, disturbance rejection, transient response, linearity, measurement error,* and *robustness.* We consider each in turn.

Stability. Feedback control systems can become unstable if they are improperly designed. Stability essentially means that the output returns to the desired value chosen by a command input despite small variations in the control input or the disturbance. Two widely used stability criteria are **bounded-input, bounded-output (BIBO) stability** and **zero-input** stability.

- A system is BIBO stable if, given that the system is initially in equilibrium, any input with bounded magnitude results in an output that also is bounded, although the system may potentially oscillate indefinitely within some bound.

- A system is zero-input stable if, given that the input is zero, all initial states result in the system's eventually reaching the zero equilibrium state.

EXAMPLE 8.7: STABILITY

The Web server system of Example 8.2 is BIBO stable if, starting with a zero initial queue size, the request queue size does not exceed some bound for all request arrival streams. The system is zero-input stable if, given that the initial queue length is finite, as long as no more requests are accepted into the queue, the queue size eventually drops to zero.

Feedback control systems typically achieve stability by ensuring that the control does not overreact to a disturbance. We study this in more detail in Section 8.8.

Disturbance Rejection. A control system should reject any changes in the output owing to a disturbance. From Equation 8.17, we see that the noise input W is attenuated by a factor of $\dfrac{G}{1 + GDH}$. In contrast, an uncontrolled system or a system without feedback control is subjected to the entire disturbance. This shows the benefit of feedback in rejecting disturbance.

Transient Response. When a system in its steady state is subjected to a sudden disturbance, it takes a while for the system to return to equilibrium. This is like a jolt to the handlebar of a bicycle: It takes some time for the bicycle to return to its steady path. The behavior of the system during this time is called its **transient**

response. If a control system is not properly designed, a sharp disturbance can result in the system's becoming unstable or collapsing.

A feedback control system gives designers a control "knob" to shape a system's dynamic response. To see this, we write Equation 8.17 as

$$Y = \frac{GDR + GW}{1 + GDH}$$

Note that the behavior of $y(t)$ is given by the inverse Laplace transform of this expression, which in turn depends on the roots of the denominator. For instance, if all the roots of the denominator have a strictly negative real component, then $y(t)$ is the sum of decaying exponentials so that the transient response eventually dies down. A designer, therefore, can choose D so that the denominator polynomial has this behavior. This intuition lies at the heart of **pole placement**.

Linearity.   A control system designed assuming that the system is LTI will not function correctly when the system is driven into a range where it is nonlinear. Therefore, we must be careful to ensure that the system always stays in the linear range and that, if a disturbance pushes it into a nonlinear regime, the control input brings the system back into a linear regime. In a feedback control system, the system is likely to continue to be linear when the feedback error is small. A designer may need to take special measures to deal with the situation when the feedback error is large. For example, in a computer network, when the network is congested, packet losses from overflowing buffers make the system nonlinear. One reasonable control rule is for sources to drastically reduce their data-transmission rates in the presence of packet loss to restore normal operation. (In practice, a TCP source can be viewed as intentionally placing the system into near-congestion to maximize network utilization.)

EXAMPLE 8.8: LINEARITY

Consider the Web server of Example 8.2. This system is linear as long as the request queue is neither overflowing nor underflowing. If the queue is, for example, overflowing, the error term will be large. In this case, a designer could add a special control rule to set the input rate u to 0, so that the queue drains as quickly as possible and the system reenters the linear regime.

Measurement Error.   A feedback system measures the output by using a sensing or measurement device. Importantly, the feedback system *cannot* compensate for an error in this sensor. For instance, if a thermostat sensor is off by 1 degree, the controlled system has a steady state error of 1 degree. Therefore, it is critical that the measurement process be as error-free as possible.

A second form of measurement error arises from delays in the measurement process. Consider a thermostat that takes 5 minutes to measure the room temperature. In such a system, once the setpoint is reached, the furnace would be left on 5 minutes too long, raising the room temperature beyond the setpoint. At this point, the furnace would be turned off, and the room temperature would return to the setpoint, then drop below it for at least 5 minutes before corrective action could be taken. It is clear that the delayed measurement results in a persistent oscillation in the output signal (i.e., the room temperature). In general, feedback delays can cause oscillations or even instability. The general approach to deal with such delays is to be cautious in responding to a measurement, recognizing that it may reflect stale input. This can be achieved by damping the control input. We will consider dealing with feedback delays more fully in Section 8.7.

Robustness. A controller is designed subject to many assumptions: that the system is linear, that the system model is accurate, that the measurement is correct, and that the measurement is not subjected to too much delay. Moreover, we must also assume that the system behavior does not change over time, owing to wear and tear or software upgrades. These are strong assumptions. Therefore, it is necessary to design a controller that does not exhibit poor behavior when one or more of these assumptions are violated. The theory of **robust control** deals with the design of control systems that work well despite bounded variations in the system parameters and is described in more advanced textbooks on control theory.

8.6 PID Control

Proportional-integral-derivative (PID) control, the simplest classical approach to controller design, refers to controllers whose control input is proportional to the error, to the integral of the error, or to the derivative of the error. PID controllers may use two or even three modes simultaneously. We study each type of controller in turn. Note that in all three modes a higher loop gain improves responsiveness.

8.6.1 Proportional-Mode Control

With proportional control, the control signal is a scalar multiple of the feedback error, so that $u = K_p e$ or, in the transform domain, $U = K_p E$, where K_p is called the **loop gain**.[2] The greater the loop gain, the larger the control action corresponding to a disturbance. Therefore, a large loop gain makes the controller more responsive.

---

2. This is not the same as the system gain. The loop gain is the ratio of the command to the error; the system gain is the ratio of the output to the input, which, in the case of a perfectly controlled system, should be 1.

Note that the control input is proportional to the error, so that, if the system in steady state needs a nonzero control input, there needs to be a nonzero steady state error, also called the **droop**. To keep the steady state error small, we need to make the loop gain large. However, this reduces damping and can make the system unstable. (We will return to this topic when we study system stability in Section 8.8.)

EXAMPLE 8.9: PROPORTIONAL-MODE CONTROL

Consider the design of a proportional controller for the Web server in Example 8.2. Recall that its transfer function $G(s)$ is given by $\frac{1}{s}$. Suppose that the command r is the desired setpoint of the request buffer. Then, the error is given by $r - y$. For proportional control, the control input is proportional to this error.[3] Specifically, the controller chooses an input u such that, if there is no further disturbance, the system output y returns to the desired setpoint r after a time τ. That is,

$$u = \frac{r - y}{\tau},$$

so that the loop gain is $\frac{1}{\tau}$. Recall that $Y = \frac{1}{s}(U - W) = \frac{1}{s}\left(\left(\frac{R}{\tau} - \frac{Y}{\tau}\right) - W\right)$, which can be rearranged to get

$$Y = \frac{R}{1 + s\tau} - \frac{W\tau}{s(1 + s\tau)}$$

To study the step response of this controller, set $W = 0$ and $R = 1/s$. Then, $Y = \frac{1}{s(1 + s\tau)}$. Using partial fractions to expand this,

$$Y = \frac{1}{s} - \frac{1}{s + \frac{1}{\tau}},$$

and taking the inverse Laplace transform, we find $y(t) = 1 - e^{-t/\tau}$. That is, when there is no disturbance, if the input command is a step signal, the output is a step signal (i.e., the desired value because $y = r = 1$) along with a transient response that decays exponentially over time. The smaller the value of τ, the larger the loop gain and the faster the decay of the transient response.

---

3. If the error is negative (that is, the buffer occupancy is greater than the setpoint), the controller must send "negative" packets into the buffer. For simplicity, we interpret this to mean that the controller sends special "cancel" requests that have the effect of removing pending requests from the Web server's request buffer.

We investigate the steady state error in the step response (assuming zero disturbance) by using the final value theorem, which states that

$$\lim_{t \to \infty} x(t) = \lim_{s \to 0} sX(s).$$

Thus,

$$\lim_{t \to \infty} e(t) = \lim_{s \to 0} sE = \lim_{s \to 0} s\left(\frac{1}{s} - Y\right) = \lim_{s \to 0} s\left(\frac{1}{s} - \frac{1}{s} + \frac{1}{s + \frac{1}{\tau}}\right) = 0$$

This shows that, independent of the loop gain, the steady state error is zero.

8.6.2 Integral-Mode Control

The motivation for integral control is the intuition that the magnitude of the control input should depend not only on the current value of the error but also the total error built up in the past: The greater this overall accumulated error, the greater the correction. Mathematically, with integral control, $u = K_i \int e$ or $U = K_i \frac{E}{s}$, where K_i is the loop gain. Integral control removes the need for a steady state error term but usually makes the control less stable, as the next example demonstrates.

EXAMPLE 8.10: INTEGRAL-MODE CONTROL

Consider the design of an integral controller for the Web server in Example 8.2 with transfer function $G(s) = \frac{1}{s}$. For integral control, the control input u is proportional to the integral of the error: $e = (r - y)$, so $u = K_i \int (r - y)$ and

$$U = \frac{K_i(R - Y)}{s},$$

where the loop gain is K_i. Now, $Y = \frac{1}{s}(U - W) = \frac{1}{s}\left(\left(\frac{K_i(R - Y)}{s}\right) - W\right)$, which can be rearranged to get

$$Y = \left(\frac{K_i}{s^2 + K_i}\right)R - \left(\frac{s}{s^2 + K_i}\right)W$$

To study the step response of this controller, set $W = 0$ and $R = 1/s$. Then,

$$Y = \frac{K_i}{s(s^2 + K_i)} = \frac{1}{s} - \frac{s}{s^2 + K_i}.$$

Taking the inverse Laplace transform, we find $y(t) = (1 - \cos\sqrt{K_i}t)$. That is, when there is no disturbance, if the input command is a step signal, the output is the step signal along with a persistent sinusoidal oscillation with magnitude 1 and period $\frac{1}{\sqrt{K_i}}$.

The transient response neither grows nor decays with time: We call a system with such a response **marginally stable**. This demonstrates our claim that the introduction of integral-mode control diminishes system stability. Note that the larger the loop gain, the slower the oscillation frequency.

8.6.3 Derivative-Mode Control

Derivative-mode control recognizes the fact that control actions (for the same degree of error) should differ depending on whether the error trend is increasing or decreasing. If the error trend (its derivative) is increasing, the controller needs to take stronger corrective action, but when the error trend is decreasing, the controller must back off the control action to prevent overreaction. Thus, derivative-mode control tends to dampen the actions of a controller.

Derivative-mode control cannot be used in isolation, because a constant steady state error, no matter how large, has a zero derivative. To avoid steady state error, derivative-mode control is combined with either proportional-mode or both integral- and proportional-mode control.

Note also that derivative-mode control is very sensitive to high-frequency noise in the measurement process: Spikes in measurement noise are interpreted as a sharp increase in system error. To avoid this problem in practice, measurements must be filtered using a low-pass filter before using them as the basis of derivative-mode control.

Mathematically, with derivative-mode control, $u = K_d\left(\frac{de}{dt}\right)$ or $U = K_d E s$, where K_d is the loop gain. We demonstrate derivative-mode control through an example.

EXAMPLE 8.11: DERIVATIVE-MODE CONTROL

Consider a derivative controller for the Web server in Example 8.2 with transfer function $G(s) = \frac{1}{s}$. For derivative control, the control input is proportional to the derivative of the error, so that $U = K_d(R - Y)s$, where the loop gain is K_d. Now, $Y = \frac{1}{s}(U - W) = \frac{1}{s}((K_d(R - Y)s) - W)$, which can be rearranged to get

$$Y = \left(\frac{K_d}{1 + K_d}\right)R - \left(\frac{1}{s(1 + K_d)}\right)W$$

To study the step response of this controller, we set $W = 0$ and $R = 1/s$. Then, $Y = \frac{K_d}{s(1 + K_d)}$. Taking the inverse Laplace transform, we find $y(t) = \frac{K_d}{1 + K_d}$. That is, when there is no disturbance, if the input command is a step signal, the output is an attenuated step signal with no transient response. Note that the larger the loop gain, the smaller the attenuation in the input signal.

We can investigate the steady state error in the step response (assuming zero disturbance) by using the final-value theorem. We have $Y = \frac{K_d}{s(1 + K_d)}$, so from the final-value theorem, the asymptotic value of $y(t)$ is $\frac{K_d}{(1 + K_d)} \neq 1$, which demonstrates our earlier claim that derivative-mode control results in a nonzero steady state error. However, note that the steady state error is a decreasing function of the loop gain, so the steady-state error can be reduced by increasing the loop gain.

8.6.4 Combining Modes

Each of the three basic control modes—proportional, integral, and derivative—has its advantages and disadvantages. Therefore, it is common to combine modes in a single so-called **PID controller.** Such a controller has three control parameters that correspond to loop gains in each mode. That is, for an error E, we have

$$U = \left(K_p + \frac{K_i}{s} + K_d s\right)E$$

$$D = \left(\frac{K_d s^2 + K_p s + K_i}{s}\right)$$

(EQ 8.18)

The relative contributions of the three modes can be adjusted using the gain factors. Intuitively, the use of proportional mode corrects for error, the use of integral mode removes steady state error, and the use of derivative mode corrects for instability that may be produced by the integral mode and dampens the control action.

8.7 Advanced Control Concepts

Having studied the basic PID control, we now examine, at an intuitive level, some more advanced control concepts that are applicable to control systems in computer networks.

8.7.1 Cascade Control

When trying to accomplish a complex control objective for a plant or process that exhibits multiple timescales of behavior, it is often useful to layer control. For example, with two layers of control, a lower-layer controller, operating at a faster timescale, controls a portion of the system to achieve a desired setpoint, and the higher-layer controller, operating at a slower timescale, dynamically chooses the setpoint to achieve the top-level control objective. This is called **cascade control**.

EXAMPLE 8.12: CASCADE CONTROL

Consider the use of cascade control to optimize the communication between a Web browser client and a Web server. A Web browser can have multiple connections open to multiple Web servers, where each connection queries for and fetches a set of data objects to be rendered on the screen.[4] Ideally, the connections should make progress at rates proportional to the amount of data being transferred over the connection, so that all the elements of the Web page can be rendered at the same time.

Recall that query-request rate control operates at the tens to hundreds of milliseconds timescale and adjusts the sending rate from a source to ensure that the buffer-occupancy level at the Web server is close to a desired setpoint. Recall from Example 8.2 that the greater this setpoint, the greater the achievable end-to-end throughput. This suggests the use of a higher-layer controller that dynamically modifies the setpoint of the buffer-occupancy level to achieve the overall control objective. Specifically, the higher-layer controller has, as its

---

4. As a simplification, we assume that all queries are of equal size and take equal amounts of time to process, so that we need to control only the number of queries, independent of their size. Generalizing from this simplified case to the true situation is left as an exercise to the reader.

control goal, the desire to have all connections make equal fractional progress on their queries. The error term for this controller is the difference between the actual fractional progress made by a connection and the mean fractional progress made by all the clients. If this error term is negative, the connection is a lagging connection, and its setpoint is increased using proportional-, integral-, or differential-mode control. On the other hand, if this error term is positive, the connection is a leading connection, and its setpoint is similarly decreased.

To make this example concrete, consider a browser that has three connections to three different Web servers, where the first connection fetches three query responses, the second fetches five query responses, and the third fetches ten responses. Therefore, they should make progress at the relative rates of 3:5:10. Suppose that at some point in time, the higher-layer controller finds that the first connection has retrieved two responses, the second has retrieved three responses, and the third has retrieved five responses. The fractional progress made, therefore, is 2/3:3/5:5/10 = 0.66 : 0.6 : 0.5. The mean progress is 0.59. Therefore, the higher-layer controller decreases the setpoint of the first connection, leaves the second connection's setpoint nearly unchanged, and increases the setpoint of the third connection.

8.7.2 Control Delay

Our discussion so far has assumed that the measurement of the plant output is instantaneously available to the controller. This is, of course, almost never the case. Delays in measurement are particularly challenging for controllers developed for computer networks, where measurement delays can be significant. We first describe the mathematical modeling of measurement delay and then describe the effects of delay on control.

Measurement delays are easy to represent mathematically. Recall from Table 5.3 in Section 5.8 that a delay of τ seconds corresponds to multiplying the Laplace transform of a signal by $e^{-s\tau}$. Therefore, with feedback delay, we find that the error E is given by

$$E = R - e^{-s\tau}Y \qquad \text{(EQ 8.19)}$$

We can then use this input as the basis for, say, proportional control, where $U = K_pE = K_p(R - e^{-s\tau}Y)$. The subsequent analysis of this system proceeds as before, except that going from the Laplace domain to the time domain is complicated because we cannot use partial fraction expansion, which applies only to ratios of polynomials. Instead, we can use the **Pade approximations** of the exponential function:

$$e^{-s\tau} \approx \frac{1 + \dfrac{(-s\tau)}{2}}{1 - \dfrac{(-s\tau)}{2}}$$

$$\approx \frac{1 + \dfrac{(-s\tau)}{2} + \dfrac{(-s\tau)^2}{12}}{1 - \dfrac{(-s\tau)}{2} + \dfrac{(-s\tau)^2}{12}}$$

which replace the exponential with increasingly accurate polynomial ratios. More elaborate Pade approximations can be found in the literature.

The general treatment of control systems with delays is complex and beyond the scope of this book. However, two observations are relevant. First, a practical approach to deal with delays is to predict the current system state from past measurements, using an appropriate predictor. Once this is done, the problem reduces to the standard zero-delay control system. Many sophisticated techniques for time-series prediction can be used for this purpose. Second, the general effect of delays is that the controller does not know the response to its prior control action. To prevent oscillations and instability, the controller should choose to be cautious in its actions, delaying its next control action until it has learned the response to its prior action. This leads to a fundamental trade-off between responsiveness and stability. In most practical systems, stability is more important and comes at the cost of decreased responsiveness. For example, in TCP, to dampen the control input, control actions are taken no faster than once per round trip time, and the response to a loss event is artificially delayed by up to half a second. This reduces oscillations, though it also reduces responsiveness.

EXAMPLE 8.13: EFFECT OF CONTROL DELAY

Consider a transport-layer flow-control algorithm that takes control actions in one of two ways (Figure 8.8). If it receives an acknowledgment with the explicit forward congestion notification (EFCN) bit set to zero, indicating that the corresponding data packet did not experience congestion, it increases its sending rate additively; otherwise, it decreases its sending rate multiplicatively. This is a controller with an undamped response. In contrast, consider a flow-control algorithm that collects the EFCN bits set on packets sent during each window of duration one round trip time (measured from the start of the connection), then takes control actions once per round trip time, depending on whether the majority of the bits were set. This controller dampens its response.

Let us do a thought experiment to study the behavior of the two systems. To exaggerate the difference in their behavior, we will assume that the source has

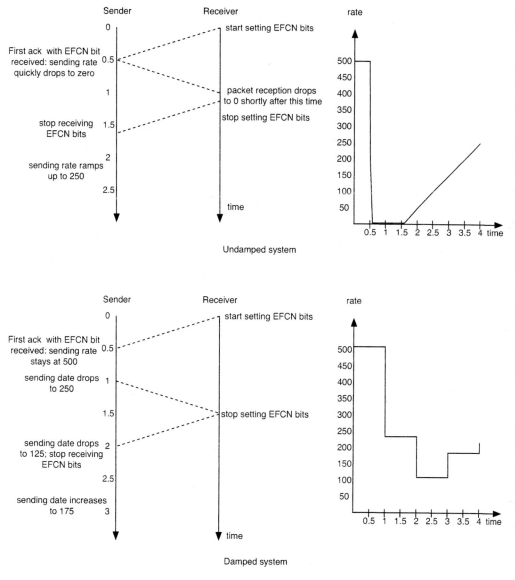

Figure 8.8 Figure for Example 8.13

an infinite number of packets to send and that its fastest sending rate is 1,000 packets per second. Assume also that the delay from the time that an EFCN bit is set to the time that it is received by a sender is 0.5 seconds and that the end-to-end delay is also 0.5 seconds (i.e., the single bottleneck link is next to the receiver), so that the round trip time (RTT) delay is 1 second. Finally, assume that the capacity of the bottleneck link is 500 packets per second, the additive increase factor is 50 packets/RTT, and that the multiplicative decrease factor is 0.5.

We conveniently define the system to be in equilibrium when the source is sending packets at 500 packets/second and the bottleneck link is serving packets at 500 packets/second. Consider the time evolution of control for the damped and undamped controllers when the system is initially at equilibrium and when, at time 0, the bottleneck service rate decreases abruptly to 250 packets/second, owing to the arrival of another flow.

With both the undamped and the damped controllers, packets with EFCN bits arrive to the sender at time 0.5. With the undamped system, on the arrival of the first acknowledgment packet with an EFCN bit set, the source immediately reduces its sending rate to 250 packets/second, further reducing its rate with every additional acknowledgment. Note that in equilibrium, the source has 500 packets outstanding, all with bits set. So the source reduces its rate to nearly 0 by time 1.5, when the last of the EFCN bits is received. Then, no more bits are set, so the source increases its rate by 50 packets/RTT, reaching its new equilibrium value of 250 at time 6.5. The subsequent time evolution is straightforward. Note that the effect of this immediate response is to quickly drain the bottleneck queue of any packets that are buffered there owing to the drop in the link-service rate.

With the damped system, the source continues to send at the rate of 500 packets/second until time 1 because it takes control actions only at times 1, 2, 3, and so on. At time 1, it has received 500 acknowledgments, of which 250 have bits set and 250 do not. Assume that, in this borderline case, the source reduces its rate to 250 packets/second at time 1. In the time interval from 1 to 2 seconds, it sends 250 packets but receives 500 packets with EFCN bits set (left over from the first round trip time). So, it reduces its rate once more to 125 packets/second. No more bits are set subsequently, and the source ramps up its rate to 250 over the next 3 seconds. Note that, owing to the delayed response, the bottleneck queue is drained much more slowly than with the undamped system.

Damping decreases responsiveness, so the effect of a disturbance persists longer, but the magnitude of the impulse response diminishes, and the system returns to equilibrium sooner. This is characteristic of any control system with control delays.

8.8 Stability

Consider a system that is not subject to a disturbance for some length of time. We expect such a system to eventually settle down so that its output y matches the command input r. A system whose output persists at its setpoint is said to be in **equilibrium**, or **relaxed**. By convention, we denote this state—and the corresponding command and output—by a **zero** vector. In many cases, this ideal equilibrium state may never be achieved. Yet it is important because it is the state that a system *strives* to achieve.

Suppose that a system in equilibrium is subjected to a time-limited disturbance. Ideally, if the disturbance is small, the change in the output also should be small. Moreover, the system should rapidly return to equilibrium when the disturbance ceases. We call such an ideal system a **stable** system.

To further grasp the concept of stability, imagine a cone that is lying on its side and another that is balanced on its point. A small disturbance to a cone balanced on its point results in a large change (it falls down); when the disturbance is removed, the cone does not return to its previous balance. In contrast, a small disturbance to a cone lying on its side results in a small change in position, although it may not return to the original equilibrium state when the disturbance is removed.

Besides these two responses to a small disturbance, a third possible response is for the system to oscillate, where the magnitude of the oscillations decays over time. This is akin to a rocking chair or a guitar string subjected to a small impulse disturbance. Depending on the desired output behavior of the system, such a response could be characterized as either stable or unstable.

When designing a controller, it is very desirable that the controlled system be stable. In this section, we study the conditions under which a controlled system can be guaranteed to be stable. Before doing so, it is worth distinguishing between two types of stable responses.

1. A system is said to be **bounded-input, bounded-output** (**BIBO**) stable if the output of the system is bounded in magnitude by some value M as long as the disturbance is bounded in magnitude by m.

2. A system is said to be **zero-input** stable if, for all initial states of the system, including nonequilibrium states, when both the command and the disturbance inputs are zero, the system eventually reaches the equilibrium state.

Both BIBO and zero-input stability are relatively easy to characterize for LTI systems. However, for time-varying or nonlinear systems, a system may be stable for some classes of disturbances but not others, or may be stable for small disturbances but not large ones. Such systems may also have multiple equilibrium states and may move from one equilibrium state to another when subject to small disturbance, much like a round pencil lying on its side when subjected to a small torque. Such multiple equilibria arise naturally in computer networks.

EXAMPLE 8.14: METASTABILITY IN THE TELEPHONE NETWORK

The telephone network core is organized as a clique where traffic from any node to any other node follows a one-hop path. This routing is simple but inefficient, in that the one-hop path does not make use of capacity available on two-hop paths. Consider a clique where all links have unit capacity so that the one-hop path from any node A to any other node B has capacity 1. If the clique has n nodes, there are an additional $n - 2$ two-hop paths between them also with unit capacity. So node A could send traffic to node B at a rate as high as $n - 1$. However, using two-hop paths comes at the cost of using twice the network capacity per traffic flow (i.e., two links instead of one). This has the following effect: If the network has a high traffic load so that most one-hop paths are nearly at capacity, the addition of a small additional load on a one-hop path could cause diversion of the excess load to one of the alternative two-hop paths. If these two-hop paths also are close to capacity, additional traffic on either of these hops would cause the use of additional two-hop paths. At high loads, this process continues until most traffic traverses two-hop paths, reducing network efficiency to 50%. This inefficient state turns out to be persistent: Even if traffic volume decreases, most traffic would still traverse two-hop paths. Thus, the system has more than one equilibrium.[5]

Despite the presence of multiple equilibria, note that the system is both BIBO and zero-input stable. To see this, we define the input to the system to be its traffic load and the output as the carried load. The system is in its relaxed state when traffic load is zero, corresponding to a zero carried load. If a small disturbance adds traffic to the system, it is carried on a one-hop path, and the carried load equals the traffic load. Therefore, as long as the input is bounded, so too is the output, showing BIBO stability.

To prove zero-input stability, consider a network in which the traffic load is nonzero at time zero but there is no additional load after time zero. In this case, once the traffic is delivered to its destination, the network always eventually returns to the zero state, as desired.

The instability, or rather, change in state from one equilibrium state to another, is caused by a disturbance when the system load is *high*. We see, therefore, that BIBO and zero-input stability criteria are rather weak. Perhaps a better way to view them is that a system that fails even these two weak stability criteria is not particularly robust.

---

5. This unstable equilibrium can be avoided by reserving a fraction of each link's capacity for one-hop paths.

EXAMPLE 8.15: COMPUTER NETWORK STABILITY

A proof along the lines of Example 8.14 shows that nearly all computer networks are trivially both BIBO and zero-input stable if we accept the definition that the output of the system is the overall carried load and the zero state is the zero-load state. We could also define the output of the network as the sum of all the router buffer occupancies, so that a congested network would have a large output amplitude. But all buffers, in practice, are bounded in size. So, no matter what the input load, they cannot exceed a predefined constant. From this perspective, again, computer networks are trivially stable. (The most common manifestation of marginal stability is probably the presence of a persistent oscillation, as we saw in Example 8.5.)

8.8.1 BIBO Stability Analysis of a Linear Time-Invariant System

This section presents the conditions under which a continuous single-input, single-output LTI system is BIBO stable. If the system has input $r(t)$, output $y(t)$, and impulse response $g(t)$, then, from Equation 5.28 in Section 5.4:

$$y(t) = \int_{-\infty}^{\infty} g(\tau)r(t-\tau)d\tau = \int_{0}^{\infty} g(\tau)r(t-\tau)d\tau$$

where the second step follows from the fact that for a causal system, the impulse response is zero when $t < 0$. The magnitude of the output is bounded by

$$\left| \int_{0}^{\infty} g(\tau)r(t-\tau)d\tau \right| \leq \int_{0}^{\infty} |g(\tau)||r(t-\tau)|d\tau \leq r_{max} \int_{0}^{\infty} |g(\tau)|d\tau$$

where r_{max} is the maximum value of the input. The output is bounded as long as the quantity

$$\int_{0}^{\infty} |g(\tau)|d\tau,$$

which is the integral of the absolute value of the impulse response $g(t)$, is bounded. To compute this quantity, we first consider the Laplace transform of the impulse response: the transfer function $G(s)$. It can be shown that the transfer function of any LTI system that can be modeled as a set of differential equations can be written as the ratio of two polynomials in s:

$$G(s) = \frac{b_0 s^m + b_1 s^{m-1} + \ldots + b_m}{s^n + a_1 s^{n-1+\ldots+a_n}} \qquad \text{(EQ 8.20)}$$

The impulse response $g(t)$ of any real system is real, that is, it has no complex coefficients. Therefore, by the definition of the Laplace transform, its Laplace transform $G(s)$ also has real coefficients, and the roots of its denominator polynomial $s^n + a_1 s^{n-1+\ldots+a_n}$ must be either real and distinct, real and repeated, or conjugate complex; and it cannot have nonconjugate complex roots. Using partial fraction expansion (see Section 8.11), such a transfer function can be written in the form

$$G(s) = \begin{cases} \dfrac{a_1}{(s-\alpha_1)} + \dfrac{a_2}{(s-\alpha_2)} + \ldots + \begin{array}{c} \text{other distinct} \\ \text{real roots} \end{array} \\[3mm] \dfrac{a_k + jb_k}{(s-(\alpha_k + j\beta_k))} + \dfrac{a_k - jb_k}{(s-(\alpha_k - j\beta_k))} + \ldots + \begin{array}{c} \text{other complex} \\ \text{conjugate roots} \end{array} \\[3mm] \dfrac{a_{m(r)}}{(s-\alpha_m)^r} + \dfrac{a_{m(r-1)}}{(s-\alpha_m)^{r-1}} + \ldots + \dfrac{a_{m(1)}}{(s-\alpha_m)} + \begin{array}{c} \text{other repeated} \\ \text{roots} \end{array} \end{cases} \qquad \text{(EQ 8.21)}$$

What does this look like in the time domain? The Laplace transform is linear, so we can take the inverse transform term by term.

- For a term of the form

$$\frac{a_i}{(s-\alpha_i)},$$

the corresponding time-domain term is $a_i e^{\alpha_i t}$, which decays exponentially to zero whenever $\alpha_i < 0$; that is, the root lies on the X-axis in the left half of the complex s plane. In this case, the integral of the absolute value of the impulse response is bounded, and the system is stable. If $\alpha_i = 0$, the output is constant, the integral is unbounded, and the system in unstable.

- For complex conjugate terms of the form

$$\frac{a_k + jb_k}{(s-(\alpha_k + j\beta_k))} + \frac{a_k - jb_k}{(s-(\alpha_k - j\beta_k))},$$

the corresponding time-domain term is $2e^{\alpha_k t}(a_k \cos\beta t - b_k \sin\beta t)$. Note that the expression in the parentheses is the difference between two sinusoids and therefore is bounded in magnitude. The output corresponding to this pair of terms decays to zero, corresponding to a bounded integral, if and only if α_k, the real part of the complex conjugate root, is negative, so that the pair of roots lie in the left half of the complex s plane. If the real part is zero (i.e., the root lies on the j axis), the system oscillates, and this oscillation does not decay over time. This system is marginally stable.

- A similar but somewhat more complicated analysis shows that if the system has repeated real or complex roots, then the corresponding time-domain output decays to zero, and the integral of the impulse response is bounded if and only if the real part of the root lies strictly in the left half of the complex s plane: Repeated roots on the j axis lead to marginally stable systems, and repeated roots in the right half of the complex s plane lead to unstable systems.

Summarizing, we see that an LTI system is BIBO stable if and only if *all* the roots of the denominator polynomial of its transfer function lie in the left half of the complex s plane. If even one root lies on the right half of the plane, the system is unstable. For the special case of conjugate roots on the j axis: (1) if the pairs of conjugate roots on this axis are distinct, the system is oscillatory but bounded; (2) if the pairs of conjugate roots on this axis are repeated, the system is unstable. This simple characterization allows us to quickly determine whether a single-input, single-output LTI system is BIBO stable simply by finding the roots of its denominator polynomial: These are also called the **poles** of the system. This can be determined using numerical algorithms, such as the Jenkins-Traub algorithm.

EXAMPLE 8.16: BIBO STABILITY OF AN LTI SYSTEM

Determine the stability of an LTI system with denominator polynomial $3s^4 + 5s^3 + 7s^2 + 12s + 1$.

Solution:

Using a numerical solver, we find that the roots of this polynomial are -0.08753, -1.6486, $0.03475 \pm j1.51936$. Since the conjugate roots lie in the right-half plane, the system is unstable.

EXAMPLE 8.17: BIBO STABILITY OF AN LTI SYSTEM

Determine the stability of an LTI system with denominator polynomial $s^4 + 50s^2 + 625$.

Solution:

We factor the polynomial as $(s^2 + 25)^2 = ((s + j5)(s - j5))^2$, so that there are two repeated roots at $\pm j5$. The system has repeated roots on the j axis and is therefore unstable.

EXAMPLE 8.18: STABILITY OF A WEB SERVER CONTROLLER

Determine the stability of the proportional-, integral-, and derivative-mode controllers of Examples 8.9–8.11.

Solution:

For the proportional-mode controller, we have $Y = \dfrac{R}{1+s\tau} - \dfrac{W}{s(1+s\tau)}$. Ignoring the disturbance, the transfer function of the controlled system is given by $G = \dfrac{1}{1+s\tau}$. The root is at $s = -\dfrac{1}{\tau}$. Since $\tau > 0$ (it is a time constant), the system's single pole, which corresponds to this root, is always in the left half of the complex s plane and is therefore always BIBO stable.

For the integral-mode controller, we have $Y = \left(\dfrac{K_i}{s^2 + K_i}\right) R$ so that $G = \left(\dfrac{K_i}{s^2 + K_i}\right)$ and the roots are at $\pm jK_i$. The conjugate poles on the j axis indicate that the system is oscillatory and therefore bounded but BIBO marginally stable.

For the derivative mode-controller, we have $Y = \left(\dfrac{K_d}{1 + K_d}\right) R$, so $G = \left(\dfrac{K_d}{1 + K_d}\right)$, which is a constant that is never 0 (i.e., the system has no pole). The effect of the controller is to act as a constant scalar multiplier to the Laplace transform of the control input. If the input is bounded, so too is the output, which implies that the system is BIBO stable.

There is one corner case that requires special care. Suppose that $G(s)$ has a single set of complex conjugate roots on the j axis, which corresponds to a marginally stable bounded oscillatory system. Suppose that it is excited by an input $R(s)$ that also has complex conjugate roots at the same locations on the j axis. Then, $Y(s) = G(s)R(s)$ has conjugate roots of multiplicity 2 on the j axis, making it both unbounded and unstable. The physical interpretation of this phenomenon is that an input of a sinusoid at a frequency that exactly matches one of the natural frequencies of the system leads to instability owing to **resonance**.

8.8.2 Zero-Input Stability Analysis of a SISO Linear Time-Invariant System

We now turn our attention to zero-input stability of a single-input, single-output (SISO) system. In this context, zero input means that the command given to the system (i.e., r) is 0 and does not change over time. Recall that a system is zero-input stable if, in the absence of any input or disturbance, no matter what the initial state at time zero, the system always eventually returns to its equilibrium state. It is convenient to study zero-input stability by using the state space representation of a system (Equation 8.2):

$$\dot{x} = Ax + bu + Fw$$
$$y = cx + du + ew$$

We have $w = u = 0$, so the state evolution is given by

$$\dot{x} = Ax$$

Taking the Laplace transform of both sides,

$$sX(s) - x(0) = AX(s)$$

$$X(s) = (sI - A)^{-1}x(0)$$

$$= \frac{[C(sI - A)]^T}{|sI - A|}x(0) \qquad \text{(EQ 8.22)}$$

where the second step expands the inverse in terms of the cofactor and the determinant (see Section 3.4.4). The numerator is a matrix whose elements are polynomials in s, and the denominator is polynomial in s. Therefore, $X(s)$ is a vector whose elements are ratios of two polynomials in s. As before, we can expand each element as a partial fraction. For the system to be zero-input stable, we require that every element of the state vector eventually decay to zero. This will be true if and only if the roots of the equation $|sI - A| = 0$, which are the eigenvalues of A, lie in the left half of the complex plane. Because of the importance of this equation, it is also called the **characteristic equation** of the system. Under mild conditions, it can be shown that the roots of the characteristic polynomial are, in fact, identical to the poles of the corresponding transfer function. Therefore, under these conditions, a system is either both BIBO and zero-input stable or neither, and only one of the tests needs to be carried out.

8.8.3 Placing System Roots

The roots of the denominator of the system-transfer function or of the characteristic equation are critical in determining its stability. If a system designer has one or more free parameters, or "control knobs" to control system behavior, these must be chosen such that these roots for the controlled system lie in the left half of the complex plane. This is called **pole placement**, since each root corresponds to a system pole.

Before the advent of digital computers, finding the roots of the characteristic equation was nearly impossible other than for trivial systems. System engineers, therefore, came up with approximation techniques, such as the root-locus method, Bode plots, and Nyquist plots to roughly determine root locations as a function of the system parameters. Today, sophisticated numerical algorithms have simplified the process of finding the roots of any polynomial. Nevertheless, an appreciation of the influence of the system poles on its behavior is critical in designing a robust and stable control system. We will not explore this complex topic in any detail. However, it should be clear that the farther to the left of the j axis that we place a pole, the faster the decay of impulse response transients, which makes the system more responsive. However, this can also lead to instability owing to overcorrection. The goal of the system designer is to balance responsiveness with stability.

8.8.4 Lyapunov Stability

Most real systems, such as computer networks, are neither linear nor time invariant. Yet we would like to understand whether they are stable and to design stable control algorithms for them. Here, we outline Lyapunov stability, an important concept that can be used to study such systems.

Recall from Section 8.2 that we can represent a system using its state variables in the form of a state vector. The system's state space is the set of all values that can be assumed by its state vector. We declare the ideal system state to be its equilibrium, or relaxed, state when all the system state variables are at their nominal zero value: $\mathbf{x} = \mathbf{0}$. The goal of the controller, then, is to move the system from its current state to this ideal state: The path so taken over time is called the system's **trajectory**. The trajectory is much like the path taken by a marble as it rolls down a slope, except that the system's position at any time is described by a state vector rather than a scalar.

A system is said to be **stable in the sense of Lyapunov** if all system trajectories can be confined to a bounded part of the state space as long as the system was initially confined to some other part of the state space. In other words, if we are allowed to choose the initial conditions, a Lyapunov stable system never wanders too far from equilibrium.

More formally, consider a system described by:

$$\dot{x} = f(x(t))$$
$$f(x(t) = 0) = 0$$

(EQ 8.23)

The first equation says that the system-state trajectory can be described in terms of a first-order differential equation. The second equation says that if the system is in equilibrium, then it continues to be in equilibrium (it is a fixed point of $\mathbf{f}$). This, of course, ignores disturbances.

Such a system is said to be **stable in the sense of Lyapunov** at $x = 0$ if, for every real number $\varepsilon > 0$, there exists another real number $\delta > 0$ such that if $\|x(0)\| < \delta$ then for all $t \geq 0$ $\|x(t)\| < \varepsilon$, where $\|x\| = \sqrt{x^T x}$. So, as long as we can choose the initial conditions to be in a hypersphere centered at the origin and with radius δ, the system's trajectories will be confined to a hypersphere centered at the origin and with radius ε.

The system is **asymptotically stable** at $x = 0$ if it is stable in the sense of Lyapunov, and, moreover, $x(t) \to 0$ as $t \to \infty$. That is, we can choose initial conditions so that further evolution is not only bounded but also eventually converges to the equilibrium state.

Our overall goal is to prove that a nonlinear or time-variant system is either stable in the sense of Lyapunov or asymptotically stable. To do so, we define an auxiliary scalar function called the **Lyapunov function** $V(x)$. The Lyapunov function can be nearly arbitrarily defined and corresponds to the amount of energy in the system: The greater the energy, the larger the value of $V(x)$. We can think of a disturbance as adding energy to the system that is dissipated by the actions of the controller, so that the system eventually settles down to equilibrium. It can be shown that a system is stable in the sense of Lyapunov if it is possible to define a Lyapunov function for it such that the Lyapunov function decays over time (owing to the actions of the controller) along all system trajectories.

More formally, the Lyapunov stability theorem states that a system described by Equation 8.23 is stable in the sense of Lyapunov at $x = 0$ if it is possible to define a scalar function $V(x(t))$ such that

- $V(x(t)=0) = 0$

- $V(x(t)) > 0; \; x(t) \neq 0$

- $V(x(t))$ is continuous and has continuous partial derivatives with respect to each component of x

- $\dfrac{dV(x)}{dt} \leq 0$ for all system trajectories

Moreover, if $\dot{V}(x) < 0$ (strictly less than zero) along all system trajectories, the system is asymptotically stable. This is also called **Lyapunov 2-stability**, or stability using the second method of Lyapunov.

The use of a Lyapunov function is both powerful and somewhat open-ended: If such a function can be found, even complex systems can be proved stable. On the other hand, finding such a function is a hit-or-miss process, other than for the simplest cases. In practice, we can use Lyapunov stability as a design tool by defining a plausible energy function and showing that control actions tend to always decrease system energy.

8.9 State Space–Based Modeling and Control

Our discussion thus far has focused on the so-called *classical* approach to control theory. Although intuitive and powerful, this approach assumes a single-input, single-output system and therefore cannot be easily applied to systems with multiple inputs and outputs. Moreover, it focuses only on the stability of the output. In some cases, although the system output may be bounded, internal state variables may oscillate or diverges (For instance, consider a network whose throughput is stable but whose routing oscillates, causing highly variable delays.) Finally, it does not allow for the design of controllers that use vector measurements of the internal system state: They can be based only on the observation of a single output variable. These limitations of classical control led to the development of "modern" state space–based control in the 1950s. This approach relies heavily on techniques from linear algebra, so the reader who wishes to master this section will need to be acquainted with the concepts in Chapter 3. We touch on some elementary techniques in state space–based control in this section, deferring details to more advanced texts on this subject.

8.9.1 State Space–Based Analysis

We begin with the canonical representation of a linear single-input, single-output linear time-invariant system, using the state-space model (Equation 8.2):

$$\dot{x} = Ax + bu + Fw$$
$$y = cx + du$$

(EQ 8.24)

We first study the behavior of the unforced system (i.e., with a zero input) in the absence of disturbances. In this case, the system reduces to

$$\dot{x} = Ax$$

(EQ 8.25)

This looks rather like a first-order homogeneous differential equation, so it is natural to expect that a solution would be of the form

$$x = e^{At}k$$

(EQ 8.26)

where the matrix exponential e^{At} generalizes a standard exponential and can be viewed as a compact representation of the infinite series

$$e^{At} = I + At + \frac{A^2 t^2}{2!} + \frac{A^3 t^3}{3!} + \ldots$$

(EQ 8.27)

and k is a suitably chosen constant vector. Direct substitution shows that this is indeed a solution of the unforced system. Moreover, by setting t to zero in Equation 8.26, it is easy to see that $k = x(0)$, so that the solution of the system is

$$x = e^{At}x(0) \qquad \text{(EQ 8.28)}$$

We view the matrix e^{At} as converting the initial state $x(0)$ to the state at time t, that is, $x(t)$. Therefore, it is also called the **state-transition matrix**.

Computing the matrix exponential can be difficult. There are two ways around it. The first is to transform the A matrix into a form whose powers are easy to evaluate using the similarity transformation discussed in Section 3.5.7. This transformation diagonalizes A so that its powers, and the infinite sum, are easily computed (see Exercise 11). Note that the matrix can be diagonalized only if it has no repeated eigenvalues. Otherwise, the best we can do is to put it in Jordan canonical form, whose powers can also be computed, albeit with some effort. In this case, computing the infinite sum of Equation 8.27 is also somewhat more complex.

To avoid this computation, we can solve the system by using the Laplace transform. Taking the Laplace transform of both sides of Equation 8.25, we get

$$sX(s) - x(0) = AX(s)$$
$$X(s) = (sI - A)^{-1}x(0) \qquad \text{(EQ 8.29)}$$
$$x(t) = \mathcal{L}^{-1}((sI - A)^{-1})x(0)$$

showing that the time evolution of the state of the unforced system is obtained by taking the inverse Laplace transform of the matrix $(sI - A)^{-1}$.

A similar but somewhat more complex analysis allows us to compute state evolution of a SISO system when the input is nonzero as

$$x(t) = e^{At}x(0) + \int_0^t e^{A(t-\tau)}bu(\tau)d\tau \qquad \text{(EQ 8.30)}$$

The first term of this equation describes how the system would evolve in the absence of control, and the second term opens the possibility of setting the system state to any desired setpoint by appropriate choice of the control input u. To study this further, we first describe the conditions under which the system state can be arbitrarily controlled and then discuss how to choose the control input.

8.9.2 Observability and Controllability

The important principles of **observability** and **controllability** describe the conditions that allow a system to be completely controlled: If a system is observable and controllable, it is possible to design a control input that moves the system from any initial state to any desired final state.

A system state $x(0)$ is said to be controllable at time t if there exists a piecewise continuous input u defined over the time period $[0, t]$ such that, with this input, the system moves from state $x(0)$ at time 0 to any desired state $x_d(t)$ at time t. The system is said to be **completely controllable**, or simply **controllable**, if every system initial state is controllable. It can be shown that this is true if and only if the matrix

$$\left[b \ \ Ab \ \ A^2 b \ \ ... \ \ A^{n-1} b \right]$$

has rank n. If A has distinct eigenvalues, this test can be simplified as follows: Let P be a nonsingular matrix that diagonalizes A. Then, the system is controllable if and only if $P^{-1}b$ has no rows that are all zero.

If knowledge of the system-state equations, the output y, and the input u over a finite time interval $[0, t]$ allows us to completely determine the initial state $x(0)$, then that initial state is said to be observable. A system is **completely observable**, or simply **observable**, if all initial states are observable. It can be shown that a system is observable if and only if the matrix

$$\begin{bmatrix} c \\ cA \\ cA^2 \\ ... \\ cA^{n-1} \end{bmatrix}$$

has rank n. If A has distinct eigenvalues, this test can be simplified as follows: Let P be a nonsingular matrix that diagonalizes A. Then, the system is controllable if and only if the matrix cP has no zero columns.

8.9.3 Controller Design

We now discuss how to design a controller for an observable and controllable SISO system. Without loss of generality, we will assume that the desired final state is the system equilibrium state, that is, $x = 0$. We will also focus on a particularly simple form of control input u, of the form

$$u = -kx \qquad\qquad \textbf{(EQ 8.31)}$$

where k is a constant row vector. That is, the scalar control input u is a linear combination of the values assumed by the state elements. First, assume that the disturbance is zero. Then, from Equation 8.24, the state equation is $\dot{x} = Ax + bu$. Substituting Equation 8.31, we get the control equation for the closed-loop control system to be

$$\dot{x} = (A - bk)x$$

By analogy with Equation 8.29, we find

$$x(t) = \mathcal{L}^{-1}((sI - (A - bk))^{-1})x(0)$$

$$= \mathcal{L}^{-1}\left(\frac{[C(sI - (A - bk))]^T}{|sI - (A - bk)|}\right)x(0)$$

where, in the second step, as in Equation 8.22, we have expanded the inverse in terms of its cofactor and determinant. Note that $A - bk$ is a constant matrix. Therefore, as before, it can be shown that the term in the parentheses is a ratio of two polynomials in s. The poles of the system, and hence its stability, are determined by the roots of the characteristic equation of the controlled system $|sI - (A - bk)| = 0$. Our task reduces to choosing k such that the roots of the characteristic equation are suitably placed in the left-hand side of the complex s plane. It can be shown that if a system is controllable, this can always be done. Details can be found in any standard text on modern control (see Section 8.12).

The analysis thus far is for a single-input, single-output system. When dealing with multiple inputs and outputs, the matrix formulation allows us to easily generalize this analysis. Specifically, the vectors b and k are replaced by the B and K matrices, and pole placement involves choosing the elements of K such that the poles of the characteristic equation $|sI - (A - BK)|$ are in the left half of the complex s plane.

In addition to achieving the desired output value y and placing the system poles in the left-half plane, state space–based control can also be used to simultaneously achieve two other objectives: minimizing the magnitude of the deviation of the system from the equilibrium state and minimizing the magnitude of the control input. The first objective bounds the deviation of the system's internal state, not just the output magnitude. The second objective prevents the system from becoming nonlinear owing to an overly large input. These objectives are typically expressed as a minimization of the sum

$$x^T Q x + u^T R u$$

where Q and R are diagonal matrices. A little thought shows that this represents a sum of the form $\sum q_{ii}x_i^2 + \sum r_{ii}u_i^2$, which is the square of the Euclidean distance from the x and u vector from 0, that is, their deviation from equilibrium, which can always be chosen to be at the origin. Such forms are called **quadratic forms**, and the control systems that minimize these quadratic forms are called **linear quadratic controllers**. The rich literature on this topic can be found in any advanced text on control theory.

In designing practical controllers, we often run into the problem that the state is unobservable, so that it is necessary to estimate the state from the output. In this case, the control problem proceeds in two steps. First, we estimate the current system state from observations (the **estimation** problem). This itself can be treated as a control problem: Our goal here is to minimize the error between the predicted output (from the estimated state) and the actual output (from the true state). Second, we control the system by assuming that the estimation is accurate (the **control** problem). The **separation principle** states that the poles of a system designed in this fashion fall into two distinct sets: those that arise from the state-estimation process and those that arise from the control process. Therefore, each can be independently determined.

In building a system with separate estimation and control, it is important to ensure that the estimation errors settle down before being fed into the control system. That is, the system-time constant of the estimation component should be much smaller than the system constant of the control component. A good rule of thumb is to separate the estimation and control system-time constants by one order of magnitude, that is, taking about ten measurements for each control decision. Although with careful design, it is possible to violate this design law, such systems are usually not robust.

8.10 Digital Control

Our discussion so far has focused on continuous-time systems. Here, we briefly discuss systems whose inputs change only at discrete time intervals and whose state, therefore, changes only at these time intervals. These systems are called **discrete-time** control systems or, more commonly, **digital** control systems.

Digital control systems arise in two contexts: from the sampling of inherently continuous systems and in systems that are inherently digital. The first context is typical in process control: for example, in chemical plants, where the pressure or concentration of a reactor vessel is a continuous signal that is sampled by a measurement device. In such cases, the critical problem is to ensure that the sampling process is fast enough to capture the dynamics of the underlying system. (The Nyquist criterion requires that the sampling rate be at least twice the fastest relevant dynamics.)

Computers and computer networks, in contrast, are inherently digital systems because electronic latches prevent the system state from changing other than when a clock "ticks." It would appear, therefore, that such systems are best modeled as digital control systems. This approach, however, turns out to be misleading for two reasons. First, in nearly all modern computers, the clock speeds are in the gigahertz range, corresponding to a clock ticking faster than once per nanosecond. With such high-resolution clocks, system state can change every few nanoseconds, so the use of continuous-time control is a reasonable and much more convenient approximation. Second, in most computer systems, there is not a single systemwide clock but multiple unsynchronized clocks, each with its own clock speed. Standard digital control systems do not adequately model systems with multiple clocks. For these two reasons, a continuous-time model is still the best way to model even inherently digital systems. Nevertheless, for completeness, we outline the basics of digital control.

The analysis of digital control systems is very similar to that of continuous-time systems. Using the state-space representation, we write the state evolution of a single-input, single-output linear time system as

$$x(k+1) = Ax(k) + bu(k) + Fw(k)$$
$$y(k+1) = cx(k) + du(k) + ew(k)$$

(EQ 8.32)

Note that, in general, the matrices that describe the system differ from the ones in a corresponding continuous system.

We analyze the evolution of the system, in the absence of a disturbance, by taking the Z transform of both sides of the first equation to get

$$zX(z) = AX(z) + bU(z)$$
$$X(z) = (zI - A)^{-1}bU(z)$$
$$x(k) = Z^{-1}((zI - A)^{-1}bU(z))$$

Note the similarity between this analysis and that of a continuous-time control system. To first approximation, the same techniques of proportional, derivative, integral, and state space control can be applied to digital control systems. One significant difference is that the stability criterion for BIBO and zero-input stability is that all poles need to be in the unit circle of the complex z plane rather than on the left half of the complex s plane.

EXAMPLE 8.19: PROPORTIONAL-MODE CONTROL OF A DIGITAL SYSTEM

To illustrate digital control, this example studies the design of a discrete-time proportional-mode controller for the Web server in Equation 8.2. We first derive the transfer function in discrete time. Recall that the state space representation of the system in continuous time is

$$\dot{x} = u - w$$

where x is the buffer-occupancy level, normalized so that the zero level corresponds to the desired buffer setpoint r, u is the request rate at time step k, and w is the buffer service rate, modeled as a disturbance. In discrete time, we rewrite this as

$$x(k+1)-x(k) = u(k)-w(k)$$

where we are implicitly assuming that the system-state and input values change only at discrete times. Note that the output y is the same as the state variable x so that

$$y(k+1)-y(k) = u(k)-w(k) \qquad \text{(EQ 8.33)}$$

Suppose that the command r is the desired setpoint of the request buffer. Then, the error is given by $r-y$. For proportional control, we choose the control input to be proportional to this error. Specifically, suppose that the controller chooses an input such that, if there is no further disturbance, the system returns to the desired setpoint after T time steps. That is,

$$u = \frac{r-y}{T}$$

so that the loop gain is $\frac{1}{T}$. Substituting this in Equation 8.33, we get

$$y(k+1)-y(k) = \frac{r(k)-y(k)}{T} - w(k)$$
$$Ty(k+1)-(T-1)y(k) = r(k)-Tw(k)$$

Taking the Z transform of both sides, we get

$$Y(z)(Tz-(T-1)) = R(z)-TW(z)$$
$$Y = \frac{R}{Tz-(T-1)} - \frac{TW}{Tz-(T-1)}$$

To study the stability of this controller, we check the location of the system poles, obtained by solving $Tz-(T-1) = 0$. This has a single solution of

$$z = \frac{T-1}{T}.$$

We see that $|z| < 1$ (the BIBO stability criterion for the Z transform) as long as $T > \frac{1}{2}$. Compare this with the criterion in Equation 8.18.

8.11 Partial Fraction Expansion

Partial fraction expansion allows a complex function $f(s)$ that is the ratio of two polynomials in the complex variable s to be represented in an alternative form to which one can easily apply the inverse Laplace transform. To begin with, let

$$f(s) = \frac{b_0 s^m + b_1 s^{m-1} + \ldots + b_m}{s^n + a_1 s^{n-1} + \ldots + a_n} = \frac{N(s)}{D(s)}$$

We first find the roots of $D(s)$ by solving the equation $D(s) = 0$, usually computed numerically by using such algorithms as the Jenkins-Traub algorithm. Let these roots be $\alpha_1, \alpha_2, \ldots, \alpha_n$. Then, we can write

$$f(s) = \frac{N(s)}{(s - \alpha_1)(s - \alpha_2)\ldots(s - \alpha_n)}$$

The next steps depend on the nature of the roots. There are three cases: distinct roots, complex conjugate roots, and repeated roots.

8.11.1 Distinct Roots

In this case, we write

$$f(s) = \frac{a_1}{(s - \alpha_1)} + \frac{a_2}{(s - \alpha_2)} + \ldots + \frac{a_n}{(s - \alpha_n)}$$

where $a_i \in C$. The coefficient a_i is given by

$$a_i = \lim_{s \to \alpha_i} (s - \alpha_i) f(s)$$

EXAMPLE 8.20: DISTINCT ROOTS

Find the partial fraction expansion of the polynomial fraction $\dfrac{1}{s^2 + 3s + 2}$.

Solution:

We write the fraction as

$$f(s) = \frac{1}{(s + 1)(s + 2)} = \frac{a_1}{s + 1} + \frac{a_2}{s + 2}.$$

Then,

$$a_1 = \lim_{s \to -1} (s+1)\left(\frac{1}{(s+1)(s+2)}\right) = \frac{1}{-1+2} = 1$$

and

$$a_2 = \lim_{s \to -2} (s+2)\left(\frac{1}{(s+1)(s+2)}\right) = \frac{1}{-2+1} = -1,$$

so that

$$f(s) = \frac{1}{s+1} - \frac{1}{s+2}.$$

8.11.2 Complex Conjugate Roots

Suppose $D(s)$ has one pair of complex conjugate roots: They must be conjugate if the coefficients of $D(s)$ are real. Then, we write

$$f(s) = \frac{a_1}{(s-(\alpha_1+j\beta_1))} + \frac{a_2}{(s-(\alpha_1-j\beta_1))} + \ldots + \frac{a_n}{(s-\alpha_n)}$$

It can be shown that a_1 and a_2 are the complex conjugates of each other. Moreover,

$$a_1 = \lim_{s \to (\alpha_1+j\beta_1)} (s-(\alpha_1+j\beta_1))f(s).$$

EXAMPLE 8.21: COMPLEX CONJUGATE ROOTS

Find the partial fraction expansion of the polynomial fraction $\dfrac{1}{s^2-6s+25}$.

Solution:
We write the fraction as

$$f(s) = \frac{1}{(s-(3+j4))(s-(3-j4))} = \frac{a_1}{(s-(3+j4))} + \frac{a_2}{(s-(3-j4))}.$$

Then,

$$a_1 = \lim_{s \to (3+j4)} (s-(3+j4))\left(\frac{1}{(s-(3+j4))(s-(3-j4))}\right) = \frac{1}{(3+j4-(3-j4))} = \frac{1}{j8}$$

and $a_2 = \dfrac{1}{-j8}$, so that $f(s) = \dfrac{1}{j8(s-(3+j4))} - \dfrac{1}{j8(s-(3-j4))}$.

8.11.3 Repeated Roots

If $D(s)$ has repeated roots, the partial fraction expansion is somewhat more complex. Suppose that $D(s)$ has r repeated roots α_1 and that the other roots are distinct. Then,

$$f(s) = \frac{a_{1(r)}}{(s-\alpha_1)^r} + \frac{a_{1(r-1)}}{(s-\alpha_1)^{r-1}} + \ldots + \frac{a_{1(1)}}{(s-\alpha_1)} + \frac{a_2}{(s-\alpha_2)} + \ldots + \frac{a_n}{(s-\alpha_n)}$$

where the ith repeated root, $i = 0, 1, \ldots, r-1$ is given by

$$a_{1(r-i)} = \lim_{s \to \alpha_1} \left(\frac{1}{i!} \frac{d^i}{ds^i} ((s-\alpha_1)^r f(s)) \right)$$

EXAMPLE 8.22: REPEATED ROOTS

Find the partial fraction expansion of the polynomial fraction $\dfrac{1}{s^3 + 7s^2 + 16s + 12}$.

Solution:

We write the fraction as $f(s) = \dfrac{1}{(s+2)^2(s+3)} = \dfrac{a_{1(2)}}{(s+2)^2} + \dfrac{a_{1(1)}}{s+2} + \dfrac{a_2}{s+3}$. Then,

$$a_{1(2-0)} = \lim_{s \to -2} \left(\frac{1}{0!} \frac{d^0}{ds^0} ((s+2)^2 f(s)) \right) = \lim_{s \to -2} \left(\frac{1}{s+3} \right) = 1$$

$$a_{1(2-1)} = \lim_{s \to -2} \left(\frac{1}{1!} \frac{d^1}{ds^1} ((s+2)^2 f(s)) \right) = \lim_{s \to -2} \left(\frac{d}{ds} \left(\frac{1}{(s+3)} \right) \right)$$

$$= \lim_{s \to -2} \left(\frac{s+3 \frac{d}{ds} 1 - 1 \frac{d}{ds} s + 3}{s+3^2} \right) = -1$$

$$a_2 = \lim_{s \to -3} (s+3) f(s) = \lim_{s \to -3} \left(\frac{1}{(s+2)^2} \right) = 1$$

$$f(s) = \frac{1}{(s+2)^2} - \frac{1}{s+2} + \frac{1}{s+3} .$$

8.12 Further Reading

There are many excellent texts on control theory. A standard reference is B. C. Kuo and F. Golnaraghi, *Automatic Control Systems*, Wiley, 2002. Classical control is discussed in detail with numerous examples in M. Gopal, *Control Systems: Principles and Design*, McGraw-Hill, 2008. The standard reference for digital control systems is K. Ogata, *Discrete-Time Control Systems*, 2d ed., Prentice Hall, 1995.

8.13 Exercises

1. **A bandwidth management system**

   Consider the following problem: An ISP wants to ensure that, on a specific congested link, the fraction of P2P traffic is never more than r percent. If this fraction is exceeded, the ISP sends TCP reset packets to P2P connection endpoints, terminating them, and thus reducing their load. For this system, identify the plant, the command, the control input, the disturbance, and the output.

2. **Effort and flow**

   What are the effort and flow variables in the system of Exercise 1?

3. **State space representation**

   Give a state space representation for the system of Exercise 1. Assuming that the control rule is to reduce the number of P2P connections by u connections over a time period T if the current P2P traffic fraction exceeds r percent, represent this in the state-evolution equation. Note that the system is subject to a random disturbance at the instantaneous rate of w.

4. **Transfer function**

   What is the transfer function for the system of Exercise 1 in the regime when the congested link has more than r percent of P2P connections?

5. **First-order system**

   When given a step input, a first-order system reaches 63% of its asymptotic value of 4.25 units at time $3s$. What is its transfer function?

6. **Second-order system**

   Prove that for a critically damped second-order system,

   $$y(t) = K[1 - e^{-\omega_n t} - \omega_n t e^{-\omega_n t}].$$

7. **Proportional-mode control**

   What is the relationship between the loop gain and the system pole for the proportional-mode controller discussed in Example 8.9?

8. **Integral-mode control**

   What is the impulse response of the integral-mode controller in Example 8.10?

9. **Stability**

   Use a numerical solver to determine the stability of an LTI system with denominator polynomial $3s^5 - 4s^3 + 7s^2 + 10s + 1$.

10. **Matrix exponential**

    Prove that $e^{At} = I + At + \dfrac{A^2 t^2}{2!} + \dfrac{A^3 t^3}{3!} + \ldots$ satisfies $\dot{x} = Ax$.

11. **Matrix exponential**

    Show that for a diagonal matrix $e^{At} = \begin{bmatrix} e^{a_{11}t} & 0 & 0 & 0 \\ 0 & e^{a_{22}t} & 0 & 0 \\ \ldots & \ldots & \ldots & \ldots \\ 0 & 0 & 0 & e^{a_{nn}t} \end{bmatrix}$.

    Use this to compute e^{At} for $A = \begin{bmatrix} 3 & 0 & 0 \\ 0 & -4 & 0 \\ 0 & 0 & -1 \end{bmatrix}$.

12. **Partial fraction expansion**

    Find the partial fraction expansion of $\dfrac{s}{(s+3)(s+5)}$.

13. **Partial fraction expansion**

    Find the partial fraction expansion of the polynomial fraction $\dfrac{1}{s^2 - 4s + 29}$.

9

Information Theory

9.1 Introduction

Communication takes many forms, such as e-mail, advertising on billboards, radio, and TV. Despite these different instantiations, every act of communication involves the same four abstract entities: a message **source** sending a **message** to one or more **recipients** over a communication **channel**. For example, when two people correspond by e-mail, a message sender sends an e-mail message to a recipient over the Internet. Similarly, an advertiser communicates to a mass audience by displaying a billboard message to passersby. And, with a radio station, a broadcaster sends audio messages to listeners over a radio communication channel.

This suggests that it may be possible to study all forms of communication by using the same underlying theoretical foundation. This foundation is provided by information theory, which allows us to precisely answer the following questions.

1. How can we mathematically model communication?
2. What is the minimal description of a message?
3. How fast can we send messages over a noise-free channel?
4. What is the effect of channel distortion on this rate?
5. How can we send digital and analog messages over noisy analog channels?

The answer to the first question introduces the fundamental concept of **entropy**, which measures the degree of uncertainty in a system. The second question is answered by the design of optimal **source codes**. The answer to the third and fourth questions is provided by the well-known **Shannon capacity** of a channel. Finally, the fifth question leads to the study of **Gaussian channels**. We study these concepts in this chapter.

9.2 A Mathematical Model for Communication

Communication occurs when a message source sends a message to one or more recipients over a communication channel. For simplicity, let us first focus on a system with a single source, recipient, message, and channel. This system is in one of two states. In the first state, before the receipt of the message, the source knows something that the recipient does not. In the second state, after the receipt of the message and its processing by the recipient, the recipient knows something more than it did before. We attribute this increase in the state of knowledge of the recipient to its receipt of the message. This allows us to quantify the effect of the message, which we will call its **information content**, as its contribution to increasing the state of knowledge of the recipient.

Quantifying the state of knowledge of a recipient is a complex and perhaps impossible task. (If it were easy, we wouldn't need so many examinations!) We must therefore restrict the scope of the problem to a situation in which a recipient's knowledge state can be easily measured. Suppose that the source must choose between one of N equiprobable messages to send to the recipient, and *that the recipient knows this constraint*. Before the reception of the message, the recipient is uncertain about which of the N possible messages it will receive. The receipt of the message removes this uncertainty and therefore is its information content. We see that to quantify the message's information content, we need to somehow quantify the initial degree of uncertainty, or **entropy**, on the part of the recipient.

To fix ideas, suppose that a source could choose from one of 16 equiprobable messages. How much uncertainty does the recipient have? For many good reasons, it turns out that the right way to measure uncertainty is by the base 2 logarithm[1] of the number of possible messages. Denoting the measure of uncertainty or entropy by H, we have

$$H = \log_2 N = \log_2 16 = 4 \qquad \text{(EQ 9.1)}$$

Note that this measure of uncertainty has no relationship to the semantic content of the messages: Information theory regards all messages equally, independent of their semantic content.

---

1. All logarithms in this chapter are base 2 unless otherwise specified.

A consequence of using a logarithmic measure for entropy is that if the number of possible messages doubles, entropy increases by a single unit. We interpret this as follows. When a source can choose to transmit one of 32 possible messages, we can divide these messages into two sets of 16. If the source tells the recipient which of these two sets contains its chosen message, the recipient's subsequent uncertainty reduces to the previous case. Therefore, doubling the number of possible messages adds only a single binary choice, or 1 **bit** of additional uncertainty. This is one reason why a (base 2) logarithmic measure of uncertainty makes good sense. Thus, we can quantify the information content of a message chosen from one of N equiprobable messages as $\log N$ bits.

So far, we have assumed that all messages are equally likely. What if the receiver knows that the source almost always sends message number 13 and rarely any of the other messages? In this situation, the recipient receiving message 13 does not learn very much, but does if it receives an unlikely message: say, message 2. As the saying goes, "A dog biting a man is not news, but a man biting a dog is." We can account for this phenomenon by measuring the entropy of a message x_i whose probability of occurrence is $P(x_i)$ as $\log\dfrac{1}{P(x_i)} = -\log P(x_i)$. This assigns entropy in inverse proportion to message likelihood. Then, given a set of messages, we can compute their average entropy as

$$H = -\sum_i P(x_i)\log P(x_i) \tag{EQ 9.2}$$

More formally, suppose that the random variable X, corresponding to a message chosen for transmission on a channel, assumes discrete values $x_i, x_2, ..., x_N$ according to the probability mass function $P\{X = x_i\} = P(x_i).$[2] Then, the entropy of this random variable is given by

$$H(X) = -\sum_i P(x_i)\log P(x_i) \tag{EQ 9.3}$$

An alternative, more compact, notation is

$$H(X) = -\sum_X P(x)\log P(x) \tag{EQ 9.4}$$

where the notation implicitly indicates that the range of the summation is over all values of $x \in X$.

---

2. To be consistent with the literature, in this chapter we will refer to the probabilty that a random variable x consumes value n_i as $P(x_i)$ rather than $p(x_i)$ as we did in Chapter 1.

We can summarize this discussion as follows. We view the act of communication as the removal of uncertainty on the part of a recipient as to which message x was chosen for transmission by a source on a communication channel. The message is modeled as a random variable X associated with a known probability mass function $P\{X = x_i\} = P(x_i)$. Then, the information content of the message, which corresponds to the uncertainty associated with X, is given by $H(X) = -\sum_i P(x_i)\log P(x_i)$.

EXAMPLE 9.1: ENTROPY OF A SIMPLE MESSAGE SOURCE

Suppose that two generals on the battlefield want to coordinate an attack. This is done by sending a carrier pigeon from one general to another. The message, sent in the evening, says either "Attack at dawn" or "Don't attack at dawn." What is the entropy of this message source, assuming that the two messages are equiprobable?

Solution:

There are two possible equiprobable messages, so the entropy = $\log 2 = 1$ bit.

EXAMPLE 9.2: ENTROPY OF A SOURCE WITH EQUIPROBABLE MESSAGES

Prove that if messages are equiprobable, the definitions in Equation 9.1 and Equation 9.3 agree.

Solution:

We have $P(x_i) = \dfrac{1}{N}$, so $H(X) = -\sum_i \dfrac{1}{N}\log\dfrac{1}{N} = -\dfrac{N}{N}\log\dfrac{1}{N} = -\log\dfrac{1}{N} = \log N$.

EXAMPLE 9.3: ENTROPY OF A RANDOM VARIABLE

Find the entropy of a random variable X whose probability mass function is given by $\left\{\dfrac{1}{2}, \dfrac{1}{4}, \dfrac{1}{8}, \dfrac{1}{8}\right\}$.

Solution:

The entropy is $-(0.5\log 0.5 + 0.25\log 0.25 + 0.125\log 0.125 + 0.125\log 0.125) = 1.75$ bits.

EXAMPLE 9.4: ENTROPY OF A BINARY RANDOM VARIABLE

Suppose that a random variable X takes on the values $\{0,1\}$ with probability $\{p, 1 - p\}$. For what value of p is its entropy maximum? Minimum?

Solution:

$$H(X) = -\sum_i P(x_i)\log P(x_i) = \frac{1}{N}(p\log p + (1-p)\log(1-p)).$$

This function is plotted in Figure 9.1. It is clear that the maximum entropy is 1 when $p = 0.5$ and that the minimum entropy is 0 when $p = 0$ or 1. In general, it can be shown that entropy is maximum when choices are equiprobable and that entropy is zero (there is no uncertainty) when the random variable is no longer random.

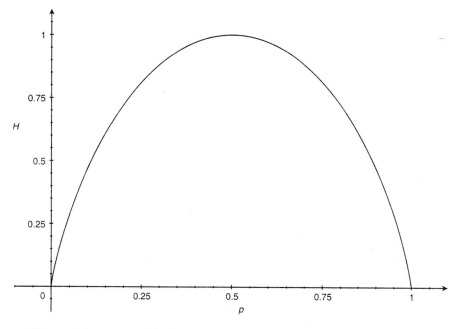

Figure 9.1 Entropy of a binary random variable that takes values $\{0,1\}$ with probability $\{p, 1 - p\}$. The X-axis shows p, and the Y-axis the corresponding entropy.

An important property of entropy is that the entropies of independent random variables are additive. That is, if the entropy of random variable X is $H(X)$, the entropy of random variable Y is $H(Y)$, and X and Y are **independent**, the entropy of their joint distribution, $H(XY)$, is given by

$$H(XY) = H(X) + H(Y)$$ (EQ 9.5)

Intuitively, if a message source were to first send a message described by random variable X and then another message described by the random variable Y, the pair of messages is described by their joint distribution XY. The overall entropy, however, is additive, as long as the two random variables are independent.

9.3 From Messages to Symbols

To compute the entropy of a source, we have assumed that it can send a finite number of messages and that we can determine the probability with which it selects each message for transmission on a channel. This definition of a message source is rather unrealistic. After all, the set of messages transmitted by a radio or TV station or by e-mail is practically infinite. Moreover, there is no obvious way to associate a probability with each message that could potentially be sent on these communication channels.

We address these issues as follows. First, note that, in practice, the infinite set of messages that could be sent on any communication channel is always represented using **symbols** from a finite alphabet. Statistical analysis of large numbers of messages reveals symbol frequencies, which asymptotically tend to symbol probabilities. This allows us to compute entropy at the symbol level, which we call **symbol entropy**.

EXAMPLE 9.5: SYMBOL ENTROPY OF ENGLISH TEXT

Although the set of books in the English language is infinite, they all are written with 26 characters, with some additional punctuation marks. Statistical analyses of many types of English texts show that each character appears with a nearly constant character frequency independent of the text. We can interpret the measured symbol frequencies, therefore, as the corresponding symbol probabilities for typical English text. This allows us to compute the symbol entropy of English text as approximately 1 bit/symbol.

EXAMPLE 9.6: SYMBOL ENTROPY OF DIGITAL IMAGES

Digital images are large matrices of picture elements, or **pixels**. Each pixel in, for example, a red-green-blue (RGB) digital image denotes the intensity of the corresponding portion of the analog image in the red, green, and blue portions of the optical spectrum. Intensities in each part of the spectrum are commonly represented as 1-byte or 8-bit quantities, so that each pixel corresponds to a 24-bit quantity. We can regard these as symbols in the language of images. This gives us an "alphabet" of 2^{24} symbols to represent all possible images. In principle, we can compute the empirical probability of each symbol, to compute the symbol entropy of digital images.

Symbol entropy is not the same as message entropy. For example, studies have shown that the statistical frequency of the letter q in a typical English text is 0.095% and that of u is 2.758%. However, given that the prior letter is q, the probability of sending a u is nearly 100%. So, the entropy of the digram "qu" is smaller than the sum of the entropies of the individual symbols q and u, which shows that they are not independent. We see that increasing the message length by one decreases message source entropy. Intuitively, it should be clear that it is possible to asymptotically approach the true message probabilities, and therefore true message entropy, by considering the statistical frequencies of longer and longer symbol sequences in a representative message corpus. For example, if one were to analyze all English character and punctuations sequences—say, 10,000 symbols long—it would be possible to compute the entropy associated with nearly every English sentence. Of course, the number of such messages would be incredibly large, so this would be a tremendously expensive computation. Nevertheless, at least in principle, it is possible to associate probabilities with nearly all English sentences.

To sum up, given a message source, by identifying the underlying alphabet of symbols and computing the relative frequencies of occurrence of longer and longer symbol sequences in a representative message corpus, we can approximately determine its entropy.

9.4 Source Coding

We now consider the problem of optimally encoding messages from a message source. We assume that the source sends messages by using symbols chosen from some known finite alphabet and that, using the approach outlined earlier, we can compute the probability of selecting each message or, at least, an asymptotic limit by considering increasingly longer symbol sequences. This permits us to compute the entropy of the source. Our task is to rewrite messages by using a *code* such that coded messages are, on average, as short as possible. This allows us to transmit the fewest number of bits on a channel or to store the messages in a file of the smallest possible size. We will demonstrate that by using the optimal *Huffman* code, the average code length is at most 1 bit more than the source entropy.

We model a source as a random variable X that takes on values corresponding to messages x_i, where each message is composed of one or more symbols that are themselves sequences of elementary symbols chosen from an alphabet χ.[3] For example, for the case of a source of messages in English text, the alphabet χ of elementary symbols could consist of the 26 letters in the English alphabet, symbols could be English words, and messages could be sequences of words. Alternatively, each English letter could itself be treated as a separate message.

Coding consists of computing a coded message $c(x_i)$ for each possible message x_i. A coded message is composed from special symbols (**codewords**) chosen from a **code** C. Without loss of generality, we will assume that the codewords are chosen from the alphabet $\{0, 1\}^+$, the set of binary strings of length 1 or more. For example, to code English text, we could assign one of 26 binary sequences to each English character. Alternatively, we could assign suitably chosen binary strings to all English words in a comprehensive dictionary.

In choosing a coding scheme, some rules are obvious. First, it does not make any sense to assign the same codeword to different message symbols: This prevents unambiguous decoding by the recipient of the code. Second, it is desirable that no codeword be the prefix of any other codeword: This allows a codeword to be decoded immediately on reception. A code that satisfies these two properties is said to be an **instantaneous code**.

EXAMPLE 9.7: INSTANTANEOUS CODES

Consider a message source that sends one of four messages a, b, c, or d. Two possible codes for this source follow.

Message Symbol	Code I	Code II
a	00	00
b	001	01
c	1	10
d	11	11

---

3. Formally, a source is modeled as a stationary, ergodic Markov chain (see Section 6.2.7) that may have state-dependent probabilities of message generation but whose message-generation process is determined by its stationary distribution. If message x_j is generated with probability $P(i,j)$ when the chain is in state i, and if the stationary probability that the chain is in state i is π_i, the overall probability of generation of message x_j is given by $P(x_j) = \sum_i \pi_i P(i,j)$.

With Code I, on receiving the coded message 0011, the receiver cannot decide after seeing the first two zeroes whether the source sent symbol a or b. The situation is actually a lot worse: This string cannot be unambiguously decoded, even though each message symbol has a unique code! In contrast, with Code II, no codeword is a prefix of any other codeword, so all received messages can be not only unambiguously decoded but also decoded immediately on receipt of the corresponding codeword. Therefore, Code II is instantaneous and Code I is not.

The previous example demonstrates that it is possible to come up with many possible coding schemes for the same message source. What coding scheme is the best? Clearly, it is advantageous for a code to be instantaneous. But it is trivial to construct many equivalent instantaneous codes for the same message source (see Exercise 4). So, being instantaneous is not a sufficient criterion for optimality. Intuitively, we would like a code to be not only instantaneous but also the shortest possible. That is, given the probability with which messages are sent, we would like to minimize the mean length of a coded message. This allows us to send the fewest bits on a potentially expensive communication channel.

An optimal coding scheme must take two factors into account. First, coding schemes typically become more efficient as message symbols are constructed from longer sequences of elementary symbols. Second, coding schemes become more efficient if shorter codes are assigned to more frequently used symbols. These factors are illustrated by the next two examples.

EXAMPLE 9.8: CODING DIGIT SEQUENCES

Consider coding messages that are sequences of decimal digits. If we assign a codeword to one digit at a time (i.e., a codeword corresponds to 1 elementary symbol), we need 4 bits to encode each of 10 possible symbols. This gives us 16 possible codewords, of which 6 are wasted. The mean coding efficiency is 4 bits/1 elementary symbol = 4 bits/elementary symbol. On the other hand, if we assign a codeword to two digits at a time (i.e., a codeword corresponds to 2 elementary symbols), there are 100 possible symbols, so we need at least 7 bits per codeword, leading to a coding efficiency of 7 bits/2 elementary symbols = 3.5 bits/ elementary symbol. Arguing similarly, we find that when a symbol corresponds to a sequence of 3 elementary symbols, we need 10 bits per codeword, for a coding efficiency of 10 bits/3 elementary symbols = 3.33 bits/elementary symbol. This trend is not monotonic: With each message symbol corresponding to 4 elementary symbols, we need 14 bits per codeword, for a mean of 3.5 bits/elementary symbol. Nevertheless, the coding efficiency declines asymptotically.

EXAMPLE 9.9: CODING ENGLISH LETTERS

Consider coding messages that are sequences of English letters. If we consider coding one letter at a time, we need 5 bits/elementary symbol, because there are 26 English letters (actually, 27, if we consider "space" as a necessary elementary symbol). As before, we can increase coding efficiency by considering more than one letter at a time. For example, if we code five letters at a time, there are 27^5 = 14,348,907 combinations, which can be represented using 24 bits, for a coding efficiency 24/5 = 4.8 bits/elementary symbol. But an even greater increase in coding efficiency is gained by not coding for impossible sequences of characters. For example, we need not assign codewords to sequences such as qx and zx. Even better, we should assign short codewords to commonly occurring sequences and longer codewords to rarely occurring sequences. Doing so would obviously minimize the mean length of a coded message.

A code has an intuitive geometric representation as a binary tree, with each codeword corresponding to a path from the root to a leaf or a nonleaf node. For example, Figure 9.2 shows the binary trees corresponding to Code I and Code II in Example 9.7. In the tree for Code I, the path from the root to the node marked a is labeled 00, which is the codeword representing a. Note that the codeword for a corresponds to a nonleaf node because it is on the path to the codeword for b. This violates the prefix property, making it impossible to decode the string 00 until after seeing the next symbol at least and, actually, not even after that!

Generalizing from this example, for an instantaneous code—one that satisfies the prefix property—every codeword must correspond to a leaf in the binary tree representation. Consider a tree corresponding to an instantaneous code with codewords of length at most L. If we were to expand this to form a complete tree of height L, we would have 2^L leaves. Some of these leaves must correspond to actual

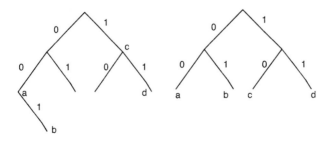

Figure 9.2 Binary trees corresponding to (left) Code I and
(right) Code II in Example 9.7

codewords, others are descendants of codewords obtained by completing the tree, and still others are neither codewords nor descendants of codewords. A codeword i of length l_i corresponds to 2^{L-l_i} leaf nodes. For example, if $L=5$, and $l_3 = 2$, the third codeword will correspond to eight leaves. Each set of descendant leaf nodes is nonoverlapping with any other set. Therefore,

$$\sum_i 2^{L-l_i} \leq 2^L$$

$$\sum_i 2^{-l_i} \leq 1$$

(EQ 9.6)

where the second equation is derived by dividing both sides of the first equation by the quantity 2^L. This **Kraft inequality** constrains the choice of codeword lengths for instantaneous codes.

The Kraft inequality allows us to relate the minimum expected codeword length for an instantaneous code to the message entropy. To see this, note that the expected codeword length is given by

$$E = \sum_i P(i)l_i$$

To minimize this sum subject to the Kraft inequality, we can use the method of Lagrange multipliers (see Section 4.6.1) to minimize

$$G = \sum_i P(i)l_i + \lambda \sum_i 2^{-l_i}$$

For the moment, we ignore the fact that codeword lengths are integral and treat them as reals. Then, we can find the minimal value of G by differentiating it with respect to l_i to find

$$\frac{\partial}{\partial l_i}G = P(i) - \lambda 2^{-l_i}\ln 2$$

Setting this to 0, we get

$$2^{-l_i} = \frac{P(i)}{\lambda \ln 2}$$

(EQ 9.7)

When the constraint arising from the Kraft inequality is binding,

$$\sum 2^{-l_i} = \sum \frac{P(i)}{\lambda \ln 2} = 1 \text{, so } \lambda = \frac{\sum P(i)}{\ln 2} = \frac{1}{\ln 2}.$$

Substituting in Equation 9.7, we get

$$P(i) = 2^{-l_i}$$

or

$$l_i = -\log P(i)$$

so that the expected codeword length

$$E = \sum_i P(i)l_i = -\sum_i P(i)\log P(i) = H(X) \qquad \text{(EQ 9.8)}$$

This is a beautiful and deep result! It shows that the expected length of an instantaneous codeword is lower-bounded by the entropy of the message source. Entropy can therefore be viewed as the intrinsic degree of randomness of the message source.

In deriving this result, we have ignored the integrality constraint; that is, codeword lengths must be integers. It can be shown that the result holds even if this constraint is observed. The consequence of having integer codeword lengths is essentially that real codes are slightly longer than optimal nonintegral codes.

EXAMPLE 9.10: OPTIMAL CODES

Consider the two generals of Example 9.1. Suppose that the probability of sending the message "Attack at dawn" is 0.75 and that the probability of the message "Don't attack at dawn" is 0.25. Then, the entropy of the sending general is $-(0.25*\log 0.25 + 0.75 * \log 0.75) = 0.81$. This means that an optimal code could use as few as 0.81 bits. But, of course, no code can use fewer than 1 bit, so, owing to integrality constraints, the minimum codeword length is 1 bit.

It is possible to use shorter codewords, even in this limited situation, if source messages are allowed to be concatenated to form longer messages. For example, if a general's messages over a hundred days were to be aggregated, it would be possible to represent these hundred messages using fewer than 100 bits on average. However, no matter how clever we are, it is impossible to find an encoding that uses fewer bits on average than the message entropy.

The preceding discussion shows that entropy of a message source is a lower bound on expected codeword length. We now present the **Huffman code**, which is guaranteed to have an average codeword length no longer than $H + 1$, where H is the entropy of a set of messages or symbols. The intuition for this code is straightforward. We would like to have the longest codeword assigned to the least-likely message. We can arrange for this to happen as follows: We pick the two least-likely messages (or symbols) and make them leaf nodes in a binary tree with a common parent. Naturally, the probability associated with their parent is the sum of their probabilities. We can therefore replace the two messages in the set of messages with a virtual message, corresponding to the parent, with this probability. Note that the size of the message set has decreased by one. We now recursively apply this construction to the smaller set of messages, terminating when there are no more messages. It can be shown that this greedy recursive construction leads to an optimal code.

EXAMPLE 9.11: HUFFMAN CODE

Suppose that a message source generates messages with the following probabilities: *a:* 0.125, *b:* 0.125, *c:* 0.5, *d:* 0.10, *e:* 0.15. Construct the Huffman code for these messages. What is the mean code length? What is the message entropy?

Solution:

From Figure 9.3, the optimal code: *a:* 001, *b:* 110, *c:* 1, *d:* 000, *e:* 011. The mean code length is (0.125 * 3 + 0.125 * 3 + 0.5 * 1 + 0.1 * 3 + 0.15 * 3) = 2. The entropy is given by −(0.125 log 0.125 + 0.125 log 0.125 + 0.5 log 0.5 + 0.1 log 0.1 + 0.15 log 0.15) = −(0.375 + 0.375 + 0.5 + 0.33 + 0.41) = 1.99. So, this code is not only optimal but also very close to the entropy limit.

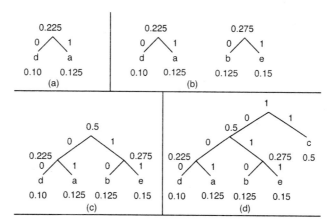

Figure 9.3 Construction of the Huffman code for Example 9.10: (a) *d* and *a* have the lowest probabilities, so they form the first two leaves; (b) the intermediate node from the previous step has greater probability than *b* and *e*, so *b* and *e* form the next two leaves; (c) the two intermediate nodes have the least probability, so they are joined in this step; (d) the final binary tree.

Note that the Huffman code is not unique. In the previous example, for instance, we could have assigned 0 to e and 1 to d in the first step to get a different but also optimal Huffman code. In general, inverting all the bits of a code or swapping two codewords of the same length will preserve optimality.

Note also that to construct a Huffman code, we need to know the probability of occurrence of every message or symbol. Although these can be determined from a corpus of messages, the actual probability of occurrence of a symbol in any message instance will differ somewhat from that of the corpus. Therefore, a Huffman code, though optimal in a broad sense, may not be the optimal encoding for a specific message instance.

9.5 The Capacity of a Communication Channel

A communication channel repeatedly transfers symbols from a message source to one or more recipients. It is modeled as shown in Figure 9.4. Messages from a message source are encoded by a **source coder** that uses techniques such as those discussed in the previous section to eliminate redundancy. Thus, if the entropy of the message source is $H(X)$, the average codeword length at the output of the source coder is at least $H(X)$. These codewords are created from an alphabet of **message symbols**.

We will demonstrate that it is inefficient to transfer message symbols directly on a channel. Instead, message symbols are translated into **channel symbols** by a **channel coder**. Channel symbols are chosen to counteract the effects of a noisy channel. Because they also are a code for source messages, the average codeword length of a channel codeword is also at least $H(X)$.

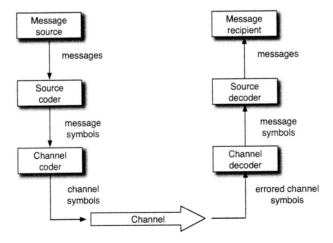

Figure 9.4 Model of a communication channel

The channel transfers channel symbols from a message source to a message recipient. This process may be ideal, in the case of a **noiseless channel**, or may introduce errors, in the case of a **noisy channel**. The output of a noisy channel is a stream of errored channel symbols, which are given to a **channel decoder** that attempts to determine the corresponding message symbols. If the channel code is well chosen, the error rate in determining the message symbols can, in theory, be made vanishingly small. Otherwise, the decoded message symbols may contain a significant degree of errors. Finally, the **source decoder** translates from message symbols back to messages that are given to the message recipient.

Channels that transfer only binary channel symbols (i.e., 0 or 1) are called **binary channels**. If a binary channel can transfer C symbols per second, its bitrate is C bits per second and is also called its **information capacity**. Channels can also transfer more complex symbols. For example, a quadrature phase shift keying (QPSK) channel can transfer one of four distinct symbols, and a 16-quadrature amplitude modulation (QAM16) channel can transfer one of 16 distinct symbols (see Section 5.1.3 for more details). If a channel can transfer one of 2^k distinct symbols, we view it as transferring k bits in parallel. If such a channel can transfer C symbols per second, its information capacity, or bitrate, is kC bits/second.

We will restrict our attention to **discrete memoryless** channels, which transfer discrete symbols. Moreover, the probability of observing a particular output symbol when a particular symbol is input for transmission depends only on the input symbol itself and is independent of prior inputs or outputs.

We first characterize a message source, then study the capacity of an ideal noiseless channel. This sets the foundation to study the capacity of a noisy communication channel.

9.5.1 Modeling a Message Source

Recall that we model a message source as a random variable X that takes on values corresponding to messages x_i, where each message is composed of one or more symbols. From Equation 9.8, each message can be represented by an instantaneous binary code whose expected codeword length (in bits) is at least the message entropy $H(X)$. Therefore, a source that generates M messages per second must be coded at a rate of at least $MH(X)$ bits per second. This is called its **information rate**. We can equivalently view this source as generating entropy at the rate of $MH(X)$ bits per second. Therefore, the information rate is also called the **entropy rate** of the source. Intuitively, this is the rate at which a receiver becomes uncertain about the state of a message source.

Suppose that encoded messages generated by a source are independent of each other: This is a good approximation for codes over sufficiently long message lengths. Then, a source with entropy $H(X)$ that generates M messages per second can generate up to $2^{MH(X)}$ distinct messages per second. In general, if the information rate of a source is R, it can generate up to 2^R distinct messages per second. Conversely, if a source can generate N distinct and independent messages per second, its information rate is no more than $\log N$ bits per second, where equality is reached only if all messages are equiprobable. We summarize this as

$$\text{information rate } \leq$$
$$\log(\text{number of distinct and independent messages/second}) \qquad \textbf{(EQ 9.9)}$$

EXAMPLE 9.12: SOURCE INFORMATION RATE

Consider a source that generates ten independent messages/second. Let the per message entropy be 3.5 bits. Then, the source can be viewed as generating entropy at the rate of 35 bits/second. Moreover, the source can generate up to 2^{35} distinct messages each second. This may sound like a lot, but a little thought reveals that the source is essentially generating 35 independent bits per second. The upper bound on the total number of distinct messages is, therefore, simply the total number of distinct binary strings of length 35 bits, which is 2^{35}.

A message source that selects message symbols independently and with identical distribution (*i.i.d.*) and that has an entropy $H(X)$ exhibits an interesting property: The messages that it generates fall into two distinct sets. One set, called the **typical** set, has $2^{H(X)}$ equiprobable elements; the other set, called the **atypical** set, has the rest. It can be shown that almost all messages generated by such a source fall into the typical set. It is therefore possible to code messages from the source with only $H(X)$ bits yet find only a vanishingly small number of messages from the source to be uncodable. This **asymptotic equipartitioning property** is a consequence of the law of large numbers, which states that the arithmetic average of an ensemble of i.i.d. random variables converges to their mean (see Section 1.7.4). This property implies that Equation 9.8 continues to hold even when an i.i.d. message source is coded using a noninstantaneous code.

EXAMPLE 9.13: TYPICAL MESSAGES

Consider a message source that generates the 0 symbol with probability 0.9 and the 1 symbol with probability 0.1. The probability that this source generates the sequence 111111111 is 10^{-9}. Indeed, if *any* message sequence has k or more 1 symbols, the probability of this message sequence is no greater than 10^{-k}. If we consider all sequences of length m symbols, where $m > k$,

$$\binom{m}{k} + \binom{m}{k+1} + \dots + \binom{m}{m}$$

sequences have a probability no greater than 10^{-k}. For any probability level ε, we can choose an m such that

$$\binom{m}{k} + \binom{m}{k+1} + \dots + \binom{m}{m}$$

messages, of the 2^m possible messages, have a probability less than ε. These are the atypical messages generated by the message source.

Note that the entropy of this source is 0.469 bits/symbol. So, if the source generates independent messages with m symbols, the total entropy of this set of messages is $0.469m$ bits. The size of the typical set is therefore $2^{0.469m}$ elements. For example, if $m = 100$, the size of the typical set is $2^{(100)(0.469)} = 2^{46.9}$. This number is large but still much, much smaller than the total number of messages with 100 symbols, 2^{100} (their ratio is $1.04 \cdot 10^{-16}$).

9.5.2 The Capacity of a Noiseless Channel

The information capacity of a noiseless channel is trivially given by the rate at which it transfers symbols. Assume that there are 2^k distinct channel symbols. Then, a noiseless channel that can transfer C channel symbols per second has an information capacity of C symbols/second, or kC bits/second.

One of the fundamental theorems of information theory, called the **channel capacity theorem**, states that a noiseless channel of capacity kC can carry messages from a source that generates entropy at the rate of $MH(X)$ bits per second if and only if

$$kC > MH(X) \tag{EQ 9.10}$$

EXAMPLE 9.14: CAPACITY OF A NOISELESS CHANNEL

Consider an ideal noiseless channel that can transmit one of four symbols: A, B, C, or D each second. We can view this as carrying the equivalent symbol sequences 00, 01, 10, 11 giving it an information-carrying capacity of 2 bits per second. Recall that the message source in Example 9.10 has an entropy of 1.99 bits/message. Therefore, this channel can carry messages from this source if and only if the message-generation rate is lower than $2/1.99 = 1.005$ messages/second.

9.5.3 A Noisy Channel

All physical channels are **noisy**; they introduce errors so that the received channel symbol may differ from the one that is transmitted. Over a noisy binary channel, this implies that a 0 transmitted symbol is sometimes received as a 1 and vice versa. The presence of noise degrades a channel and reduces its capacity. The degree of capacity reduction depends on the characteristics of all three: the channel, the message source, and the channel coder.

EXAMPLE 9.15: A NOISY CHANNEL

Consider a noisy binary channel that corrupts the channel symbol 0 with probability 0.9 and the channel symbol 1 with probability 0.01 (see Figure 9.5). If message symbols are coded so that channel symbols consist predominantly of 0 symbols, many, perhaps all, of the transmitted messages will be corrupted. In contrast, if message symbols are coded so that the channel symbols consist predominantly of 1 symbols, few transmitted messages will be corrupted.

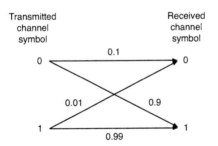

Figure 9.5 Representation of a noisy channel

Let us take a closer look at the effect of a noisy channel on channel symbols sent from a source. We study how a channel decoder, on receiving a channel symbol, can determine which channel symbol was actually transmitted.[4]

Consider the channel shown in Figure 9.5. Suppose that the channel decoder receives the symbol 1. With probability 0.9, it is due to the reception of a corrupted 0 symbol; with probability 0.99, it is due to the reception of an uncorrupted 1 symbol. Similarly, if the channel decoder receives the symbol 0, with probability 0.1, it is due to the reception of an uncorrupted 0; with probability 0.01, it is due to the reception of a corrupted 1. Thus, the probabilities with which the decoder receives a 0 or a 1 depend both on the probability with which the channel coder sends a 0 or a 1 *and* the

---

4. For simplicity, from now on, when we write *symbol*, we mean *channel symbol*.

way in which the channel corrupts a symbol. This is made explicit by considering the **joint probability distribution**[5] of the symbol sent and the symbol received.

Denote the transmitted symbol at the output of the channel coder by the random variable X and the received symbol at the input of the channel decoder by Y. Then, the discrete joint probability distribution $P(XY)$ assigns probabilities to each possible combination of X and Y. To make this concrete, consider a channel coder that sends a 0 symbol with probability p and a 1 symbol with probability $1 - p$ over the channel in Figure 9.5 where symbol probabilities are independent and identically distributed (i.i.d.). Then, the joint probability distribution of X and Y is given by Table 9.1.

Table 9.1 The Joint Probability Distribution of X and Y

$P(XY)$	$X=0$	$X=1$
$Y=0$	$0.1p$	$0.01(1-p)$
$Y=1$	$0.9p$	$0.99(1-p)$

The **marginal** distributions of X and Y, $P(X)$ and $P(Y)$ are given by Table 9.2 and Table 9.3.

Table 9.2 The Marginal Probability Distribution of X

	$P(X)$
$X=0$	p
$X=1$	$1-p$

Table 9.3 The Marginal Probability Distribution of Y

	$P(Y)$
$Y=0$	$0.1p + 0.01(1-p)$
$Y=1$	$0.9p + 0.99(1-p)$

The **conditional** distribution of X given that $Y = 0$ is given by Table 9.4, and the conditional distribution of X given that $Y = 1$ is given by Table 9.5. We similarly compute the conditional distribution of Y for the cases when $X = 0$ and $X = 1$ in Table 9.6.

---

5. Readers unfamiliar with joint distributions should review the material in Section 1.2.1 at this point.

Table 9.4 The Conditional Distribution of X Given That $Y = 0$

	$P(X|Y=0)$
$X=0$	$0.1p/(0.1p + 0.01(1 - p))$
$X=1$	$0.01(1 - p)/(0.1p + 0.01(1 - p))$

Table 9.5 The Conditional Distribution of X Given That $Y = 1$

	$P(X|Y=1)$
$X=0$	$0.9p/(0.9p + 0.99(1 - p))$
$X=1$	$0.99(1 - p)/(0.9p + 0.99(1 - p))$

Table 9.6 The Conditional Distribution of Y Given X

	$P(Y|X=0)$	$P(Y|X=1)$
$Y=0$	0.1	0.01
$Y=1$	0.9	0.99

These discrete probability distributions demonstrate two effects of a noisy channel. First, given a particular distribution of symbol probabilities $P(X)$ at the output of the channel coder, the noisy channel modifies the symbol probability distribution at the input of the channel decoder to $P(Y)$. This is evident when we compare Tables 9.2 and 9.3. Second, a noisy channel makes it necessary for the channel decoder to work backward to determine which symbol had been sent when a particular symbol is received. This is evident from Tables 9.4 and 9.5.

Discrete probability distributions similar to those shown in these six tables can be computed for any channel coder, channel decoder, and channel. These distributions let us compute the corresponding entropies, respectively, $H(XY)$, $H(X)$, $H(Y)$, $H(X|Y=0)$, $H(X|Y=1)$, $H(X|Y)$, and $H(Y|X)$. We interpret these entropies as follows.

- $H(X)$: The uncertainty at the channel decoder as to which symbol was sent by the channel coder.

- $H(Y)$: The uncertainty at the channel coder as to which symbol will be received at the channel decoder. This uncertainty depends on the characteristics of the message source, the message coder, the channel coder, and the channel.

- $H(XY)$: The uncertainty at an outside observer who can observe both the channel coder and the channel decoder of the occurrence of the symbol pair (transmitted symbol, received symbol).

- $H(X|Y=0)$: The uncertainty at the channel decoder as to the transmitted symbol conditional on the fact that a symbol 0 was received. Formally, we define

$$H(X|Y=0) =$$
$$-(P(X=0/Y=0) \log P(X=0/Y=0) + P(X=1/Y=0) \log P(X=1/Y=0))$$

- $H(X|Y=1)$: The uncertainty at the channel decoder as to the transmitted symbol conditional on the fact that a symbol 1 was received. Similarly,

$$H(X|Y=1) =$$
$$-(P(X=0/Y=1) \log P(X=0/Y=1) + P(X=1/Y=1) \log P(X=1/Y=1))$$

- $H(X|Y)$: The uncertainty at the channel decoder as to the transmitted symbol conditional on the fact that a symbol Y was received. This is given by

$$
\begin{aligned}
H(X|Y) &= P(Y=0)H(X|Y=0) + P(Y=1)H(X|Y=1) \\
&= \sum_Y P(y)H(X|y) \\
&= -\sum_Y P(y)\sum_X P(x|y)\log P(x|y) \\
&= -\sum_Y P(y)\sum_X \frac{P(xy)}{P(y)}\log P(x|y) \\
&= -\sum_X \sum_Y P(xy)\log P(x|y)
\end{aligned}
$$

- $H(Y|X)$: The uncertainty at the channel coder as to the received symbol conditional on the fact that a symbol X was transmitted. By symmetry, this is given by

$$
\begin{aligned}
H(Y|X) &= \sum_X P(x)H(Y|x) \\
&= -\sum_X \sum_Y P(xy)\log P(y|x)
\end{aligned}
$$

These entropies allow us to define the information-theoretic meaning of communication over a noisy channel. Recall that this view is that the act of communication as the removal of uncertainty on the part of a recipient as to which symbol X was chosen for transmission by a source on a communication channel.

Let the **mutual information** $I(X;Y)$ corresponding to a particular source, channel coder, and channel and measured in units of bits/symbol be defined as

$$I(X;Y) = \sum_X \sum_Y P(xy) \log \frac{P(xy)}{P(x)P(y)}$$ (EQ 9.11)

It can be shown (see Exercise 14) that

$$I(X;Y) = H(X) - H(X|Y)$$ (EQ 9.12)

$$I(X;Y) = H(Y) - H(Y|X)$$ (EQ 9.13)

That is, the mutual information between a transmitter and a receiver is the reduction in the uncertainty on the part of the receiver about the symbol sent by the transmitter due to the receipt of a particular symbol. Symmetrically, it is also the reduction in the uncertainty on the part of the transmitter about the symbol received at the receiver due to the transmission of a particular symbol. According to information theory, communication over a noisy channel can be precisely defined as the creation of mutual information between the transmitter and the receiver.

EXAMPLE 9.16: MUTUAL INFORMATION

Compute the mutual information for a channel coder that sends a 0 symbol with probability 0.1 and a 1 symbol with probability 0.9 over the channel of Figure 9.5.

Solution:

The probability of each symbol on the channel is given by

	P(X)
X=0	0.1
X=1	0.9

Therefore, $H(X) = -(0.1 \log 0.1 + 0.9 \log 0.9) = 0.469$. To compute $H(X|Y)$, we first need to know the distribution of Y. From Table 9.3, we find this to be

	P(Y)
Y=0	0.019
Y=1	0.981

From Table 9.4, the conditional distribution of X given $Y = 0$ is

	P(X|Y=0)
X=0	0.526
X=1	0.473

which has an entropy of $-(0.526 \log 0.526 + 0.473 \log 0.473) = 0.624$. It is interesting to note that when the received symbol is 0, the receiver is more than 50% sure that the sender sent a 0 even though the corruption rate for 0 is 90%. The reason is that the corruption rate of 1 is very low.

From Table 9.5, the conditional distribution of X given $Y = 1$ is

	P(X|Y=1)
X=0	0.092
X=1	0.908

which has an entropy of $-(0.092 \log 0.092 + 0.908 \log 0.908) = 0.443$. We multiply these conditional entropies by the probability of Y being 0 or 1, respectively, to compute $H(X|Y)$ as $0.019* 0.624 + 0.981*0.443 = 0.446$. Therefore, the mutual information is

$$I(X;Y) = 0.469 - 0.446 = 0.023 \text{ bits/symbol}$$

We interpret this to mean that the information content of each bit sent on the channel is only 0.023 bits. The remainder is wasted channel capacity owing to the presence of channel noise. In contrast, with a binary noiseless channel, each transmitted symbol has an information content of 1 bit.

Note that the first term in Equation 9.12 depends only on the nature of the source but that the second term depends jointly on the nature of the source, the nature of the channel coding scheme, and the nature of the communication channel. This opens the door to control channel symbol probabilities to compensate for the impairments introduced by the channel and maximize mutual information on the channel.

EXAMPLE 9.17: CODING FOR A NOISY CHANNEL

Suppose that a channel can transmit one of four symbols A, B, C, or D and that the probability of corruption of the symbol D is much greater than the probability of corruption of the other three symbols. Consider a source that can generate one of 16 message symbols: say, the English letters a–p. A naive coding for this source would be to code each source symbol with a pair of random channel symbols. For example, we may code the source symbol d as the channel codeword AD and f as BB.

The problem with this approach is that, owing to the nature of the channel, channel codewords that contain a D will be more likely to be corrupted than channel codewords that do not contain D. If commonly occurring source symbols are allocated these error-prone channel codewords, $H(X|Y)$ will be greater, reducing the mutual information. It is more efficient to first determine the probability of generation of each source symbol a–p, and allocate channel codewords containing the channel symbol D only to the least-likely source symbols. Using this scheme, the least-likely source symbol would be allocated the channel codeword DD. This reduces the probability of channel codeword corruption, increasing the mutual information.

Alternatively, depending on the source symbol probabilities, it may be better to avoid using D altogether when forming channel codewords. This would have the effect of making certain source symbols have a longer encoding on the channel—because at least some source symbols will correspond to a channel codeword that uses three rather than two channel symbols—but may still increase the mutual information on the channel.

Generalizing from this example, we see that we can, in principle, given a probability distribution over source message sequences, choose an appropriate channel coding scheme to control the probability distribution over channel symbols. In other words, we can choose the channel coding scheme to control the distribution $P(X)$ such that the mutual information $I(X;Y)$ is maximized.

Shannon's fundamental theorem for a noisy channel proves that this maximum mutual information, given by $\max_{P(X)} I(X;Y)$ is also the greatest rate at which information can be carried over a noisy channel if the probability of decoding errors is to be made vanishingly small. It is not possible to send information faster than the maximum mutual information without introducing a significant number of uncorrectable errors. Moreover, there exists some coding scheme such that a source, when coded with it, achieves a transmission rate arbitrarily close to this upper limit with an arbitrarily small error rate. Shannon's theorem does not, however, state how this coding scheme is to be found. However, both **turbo codes** and **low-density parity codes** come close to this ideal rate even in practice.

The proof of Shannon's theorem is elegant and instructive. It proceeds along the following lines. First, Shannon shows that if a source sends i.i.d. symbols drawn from a distribution $P(X)$, most sufficiently long strings of symbols are *typical* and have an entropy close to the source's intrinsic entropy. Second, he computes the effect of sending a sequence of n i.i.d. symbols over a noisy channel when using a *random* encoding, showing, roughly speaking, that this maps *each* typical n-sequence of symbols to one of $2^{nH(Y|X)}$ distinct and *equiprobable* sequences of symbols, all of which are equally likely. Third, Shannon shows that the maximum number of distinct messages arising from the receipt of typical strings is $2^{nH(Y)}$. Therefore, if a transmitter transmits at most $\dfrac{2^{nH(Y)}}{2^{nH(Y|X)}} = 2^{n(H(Y) - H(Y|X))}$ distinct messages, these messages will be almost surely decodable. Each message has n symbols, so the contribution of each symbol to the total set of messages is bounded by $2^{(H(Y) - H(Y|X))} = 2^{I(X;Y)}$. By analogy with the number of messages sent over a noiseless channel (see Equation 9.9), we conclude that the capacity of a noisy channel is $I(X;Y)$ bits/symbol. The channel capacity is achieved when this is maximized.

EXAMPLE 9.18: CAPACITY OF A NOISELESS CHANNEL

We revisit the capacity theorem for a noiseless channel here. For a noiseless channel, when Y is known, so too is X. Therefore, the uncertainty in X, given Y, is zero; that is, $H(X|Y) = 0$. So, $I(X;Y) = H(X) - H(X|Y) = H(X)$. Shannon's theorem tells us that the greatest rate at which information can be carried over this channel is given by $\max_{P(X)} I(X;Y) = \max_{P(X)} H(X)$. Obviously, such a channel can carry messages from any source with entropy $H(X)$ smaller than this maximum. Thus, the capacity of a noiseless channel presented earlier is a special case of Shannon's theorem.

EXAMPLE 9.19: CAPACITY OF A SYMMETRIC BINARY CHANNEL

A symmetric binary channel carries only two symbols, 0 and 1, and its probability of symbol corruption, e, is the same for both symbols. Suppose that a source sends the 0 symbols with probability p over this channel. Then, it is received as a 0 symbol with probability p and as a 1 symbol with probability pe. Let us compute the mutual information of this channel. For this, we need to compute $H(X)$ and $H(X|Y)$. We have $H(X) = -(p \log p + (1-p) \log (1-p))$.

To compute $H(X|Y)$, we use the equation

$$H(X|Y) = P(Y = 0)H(X|Y = 0) + P(Y = 1)H(X|Y = 1)$$

To begin with, we have

$$P(Y = 0) = P(\text{uncorrupted } 0) + P(\text{corrupted } 1) = p(1-e) + (1-p)e$$

Similarly,

$$P(Y = 1) = P(\text{corrupted } 0) + P(\text{uncorrupted } 1) = pe + (1-p)(1-e)e$$

Now, to find $H(X|Y = 0)$ we need to compute $P(X = 0 | Y = 0)$ and $P(X = 1 | Y = 0)$. These are given by $\dfrac{p(1-e)}{p(1-e) + (1-p)e}$ and $\dfrac{(1-p)e}{p(1-e) + (1-p)e}$ respectively.

Therefore,

$$H(X|Y = 0) = -\left(\frac{p(1-e)}{p(1-e) + (1-p)e} \log\left(\frac{p(1-e)}{p(1-e) + (1-p)e} \right) + \frac{(1-p)e}{p(1-e) + (1-p)e} \log\left(\frac{(1-p)e}{p(1-e) + (1-p)e} \right) \right)$$

Similarly, we compute

$$H(X|Y = 1) = -\left(\frac{pe}{pe + (1-p) + (1-e)} \log\left(\frac{pe}{pe + (1-p)(1-e)} \right) + \frac{(1-p)(1-e)}{pe + (1-p)(1-e)} \log\left(\frac{(1-p)(1-e)}{pe + (1-p)(1-e)} \right) \right)$$

We substitute these back into the expression to obtain the mutual information $H(X|Y)$ as

$$-(p(1-e) + (1-p)e)\left(\frac{p(1-e)}{p(1-e) + (1-p)e} \log\left(\frac{p(1-e)}{p(1-e) + (1-p)e} \right) + \frac{(1-p)e}{p(1-e) + (1-p)e} \log\left(\frac{(1-p)e}{p(1-e) + (1-p)e} \right) \right)$$

$$-(pe + (1-p) + (1-e)e)\left(\frac{pe}{pe + (1-p) + (1-e)}\log\left(\frac{pe}{pe + (1-p)(1-e)}\right) + \frac{(1-p)(1-e)}{pe + (1-p)(1-e)}\log\left(\frac{(1-p)(1-e)}{pe + (1-p)(1-e)}\right)\right)$$

To maximize the mutual information, arguing from symmetry, we should choose $P(X)$ such that $p = 0.5$. This simplifies the expression to $I(X; Y) = 1 + e\log e + (1-e)\log(1-e) = 1 - H(E)$ where E can be thought of as the uncertainty added by the channel.

EXAMPLE 9.20: CAPACITY OF A NOISY TYPEWRITER

Consider a typewriter that can type the lowercase letters a–z but whose output is noisy, so that when a character is depressed, the output is either the character itself or the next character in the alphabet modulo 26 with equal probability. What is the capacity of this channel?

Solution:

We use the relationship $I(X;Y) = H(Y) - H(Y|X)$ to compute the mutual information. By symmetry, mutual information is maximized when the characters are chosen with equal probability; it could not be minimized, because this happens when a single character is chosen with probability 1. In this case, $H(Y|X) = \log 2 = 1$, because on seeing a character in the output, there can be at most two possible inputs. The outputs are equiprobable because the inputs are equiprobable and the probability of corruption is 0.5. So, $H(Y) = \log 26$. Therefore, $I(X;Y) = \log 26 - 1 = \log 26 - \log 2 = \log (26/2) = \log 13$. This information capacity is reached if every alternate character in the input is used.

Computing the capacity of a channel is difficult because it requires a precise characterization of the error probabilities for every transmitted symbol, as well as the inherent entropy of the message source. However, the *Gaussian channel* is a special case in which channel capacity can be determined using a different approach. This is the case we study next.

9.6 The Gaussian Channel

Our discussion so far has focused on message sources that transmit digital information over a digital channel. Of course, in practice, both sources and channels are analog, and a digital channel is an idealization of this reality. In this section, we discuss how to model an analog, or continuous, source and how we can compute the capacity of a noisy continuous channel.

9.6.1 Modeling a Continuous Message Source

Audio and video sources are continuous signal sources. We consider how such continuous signals can be sent over a digital channel. For simplicity, we first consider a specific audio source: human speech.

Human speech is generated as a continuous variation in air pressure produced by a combination of the lungs, diaphragm, vocal chords, throat, mouth, tongue, and lips. This signal is completely represented as a continuous function of pressure over time, such as the one shown in Figure 9.6.

To transmit this signal over a digital channel, we first need to **sample** the signal at evenly spaced points in time. This is equivalent to multiplying the signal with a set of evenly spaced Dirac delta functions or an **impulse train** (see Section 5.9.1). Recall that, the Nyquist criterion states that to prevent aliasing, the sampling function should have a frequency at least twice that of the highest-frequency component of a signal (see Section 5.9.3). We will assume that the highest-frequency component of the signal—that is, the greatest frequency at which the Fourier transform of the signal is nonzero—is W. Then, to prevent aliasing, the sampling function should have a frequency of at least $2W$, so that the continuous function should be represented by at least $2W$ samples per second.

To send these samples on a digital channel, we need to represent each sample as a binary number. We do this by choosing a set of **quantization levels** as shown on the Y-axis of Figure 9.7. At each sample time, we encode the signal by the binary number corresponding to the closest quantization level. If the quantization levels are chosen with care, the errors introduced by quantization are negligible and, in most cases, below the threshold of detection by human receivers. For human speech, it turns out that the quantization levels are not evenly spaced, as one might

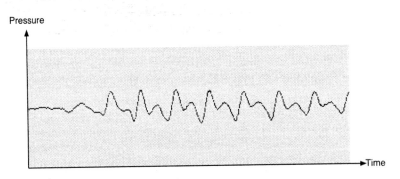

Figure 9.6 A typical speech signal

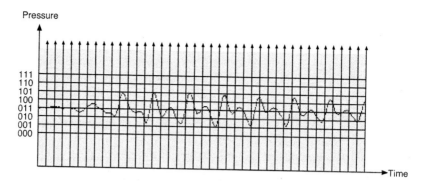

Figure 9.7 A quantized speech signal. The first few sample values are 011,011,011,011,010,011....

expect, but closer spaced near the origin and wider spaced farther away. This models the differential sensitivity of the human ear to sounds of different magnitudes.

As a result of sampling and quantization, a continuous speech signal is translated into a series of digital values. This digital signal is then easily transmitted over a digital communication channel.

A similar approach can be used to digitize other types of continuous signals. To digitize two-dimensional signals, such as movie images, we define a two-dimensional path that covers the entire surface of the image over which the quantized samples are periodically collected. This also results in an output signal consisting of a series of digital values.

The time series of signal values can be represented as $x_1, x_2, \dots$, where the x_i are binary numbers. Any signal with n such values corresponds to a point in n-dimensional space. Each signal value typically represents a voltage. The corresponding *energy* is proportional to the square of the signal voltage, so that, with an appropriate choice of units, we can write

$$\text{signal energy} = \sum_{i=1}^{n} x_i^2 \qquad \textbf{(EQ 9.14)}$$

The expression on the right-hand side is the square of the Euclidean distance of the point from the origin. We interpret this to mean that the energy associated with a signal point in a suitable n-dimensional space is the square of its distance from the origin.

9.6.2 A Gaussian Channel

Unlike ideal digital channels, which carry only 0 and 1 symbols, channels in practice are continuous and analog and can be modeled as transporting real numbers from a transmitter to a receiver. A noiseless continuous channel has infinite information capacity because a single real number with its inherent infinite precision can encode an infinite amount of information. Of course, over a real channel, the presence of noise corrupts the transmitted signal and limits the channel's information capacity.

The noise over many commonly used continuous channels is well modeled as **white Gaussian noise**. The individual values of such an ideal noise signal are uncorrelated and independent and have amplitudes drawn from a Gaussian distribution. The noise value is added to the transmitted signal value, and the received signal is their sum. A continuous channel subject to Gaussian noise is called a **Gaussian channel**.

The use of a continuous channel to carry digital information and the impact of noise is demonstrated in Figure 9.8. Two signal amplitudes are designated as the levels corresponding to the symbol 0 and the symbol 1, respectively. The transmitter periodically places a 0 or 1 symbol for transmission on the channel. This transmission is subject to a random noise, so that the received signal, which is the sum of the channel and noise signals, differs from the transmitted signal. Moreover, owing to channel noise, the received digital information may also differ from what the transmitter intended, as shown.

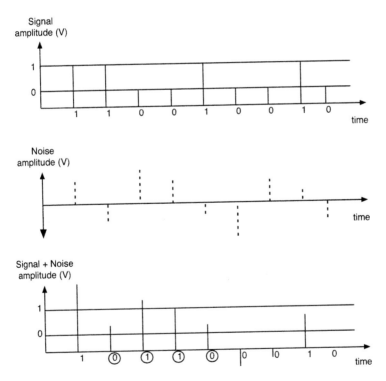

Figure 9.8 Carrying digital data on a continuous channel. The top figure shows the intended digit sequence and the corresponding signal amplitudes. The middle figure shows the random channel noise at each signal transmission time. The resulting corrupted signal is shown in the bottom figure, with errors circled.

It should be clear from Figure 9.8 that, if the noise amplitudes are kept unchanged, increasing signal amplitudes by transmitting signals at a higher power reduces the effect of noise. If signal levels, therefore, could be chosen to be sufficiently high, the effect of noise would be negligible, and the channel would become nearly noiseless. However, each transmission of a signal requires energy. Creating an effectively noiseless channel may require the expenditure of large amounts of energy. If this energy is to come from a limited power source, such as the battery of a mobile phone, using large signal amplitudes would quickly drain the device battery. This is highly undesirable and a good reason to curtail signal levels.

A second reason to constrain signal levels has to do with signal transmission over a noisy wireless channel. In a wireless channel, two transmitters within range of the same receiver **interfere** with each other to their mutual detriment, and both their transmissions are lost because each acts as a noise source to the other. If the signal amplitudes were large, a high-power transmitter would be heard across a wider geographical range and therefore would interfere with more transmitters, actually reducing their overall channel capacity. Indeed, in the limit, if transmitters were to transmit with an arbitrarily large signal strength, only one transmitter anywhere in the universe should be permitted to be active at any given time in any frequency band to avoid interference at its intended receiver!

9.6.3 The Capacity of a Gaussian Channel

We now compute the capacity of a Gaussian channel. We study the transmission and reception of a fixed-length message or block of n signal values, $x_1, x_2, ..., x_n$, where each signal value is a sequence of binary digits. An example of such a block with $n = 8$, corresponding to the signal in Figure 9.7, is 011, 100, 011, 011, 011, 100, 100, 011. Recall that the entire block of signal values can be represented by a single **signal point** in an n-dimensional space with energy

$$\sum_{i=1}^{n} x_i^2 .$$

To satisfy the Nyquist criterion, a source of a continuous signal whose highest-frequency component is W (also called a signal with **band width** W) has to send at least $2W$ samples per second. Let T denote the time taken to transmit one block of signal values. In this time, the receiver receives $2WT$ samples. Therefore,

$$n = 2WT$$

Consider a *typical* block generated by a message source that selects symbols i.i.d. (see Section 9.5.1). It can be shown that the average energy per signal value of a typical block, given by

$$\frac{1}{n}\sum_{i=1}^{n}x_i^2,$$

is almost surely some fixed value P, for a large enough block size n. The total energy of a typical block, therefore, is almost surely $2WPT$ joules. Now, this is the energy associated with a point in n-dimensional space that is at a distance of $\sqrt{2WPT}$ from the origin. This means that the point corresponding to a typical block almost surely lies on the surface of an n-dimensional hypersphere of radius $\sqrt{2WPT}$.

Every transmitted sample is corrupted by noise, so in a time period T, there will also be $2WT$ noise values. Suppose that the average noise energy is given by N. We can show that, for a Gaussian noise source that generates typical noise sequences, the set of $n = 2WT$ noise values will lie almost surely on the surface of a hypersphere of radius $\sqrt{2WNT}$. Geometrically, we view this to mean that each signal point sent by the transmitter gets distorted onto a point that lies on the surface of a hypersphere with radius $\sqrt{2WNT}$ centered at the signal point, as shown in Figure 9.9.

If two signal points are closer together than $2\sqrt{2WNT}$, a receiver will be unable to determine which signal point the transmitter intended. On the other hand, if the source chooses channel codewords so that every pair of signal points is spaced at least $2\sqrt{2WNT}$ units apart, the receiver will almost surely be able to determine the intended signal despite the noise.

How many distinct signals can the transmitter choose to send in time T if they are to be decodable despite noise? This turns out to be a packing problem. We use the mathematical fact that the volume of an n-dimensional hypersphere of radius r is proportional to r^n. Over time period T, the total received energy is $2WT(P+N)$, which corresponds to signals that lie on the surface of an n-dimensional hypersphere of radius $\sqrt{2WT(P+N)}$ and volume $(\sqrt{2WT(P+N)})^n$. Each signal lies in

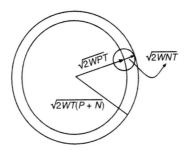

Figure 9.9 Geometric view of a Gaussian channel. Signal points corresponding to message blocks lie on a hypersphere of radius $\sqrt{2WPT}$. Due to noise, each point is distorted onto a point that lies on the surface of a hypersphere centered on the signal point and with radius $\sqrt{2WNT}$. Points corresponding to noisy signal blocks lie within a hypersphere of radius $2WT(P+N)$.

the center of an n-dimensional hypersphere of radius $\sqrt{2WNT}$ and volume $(\sqrt{2WNT})^n$. Therefore, the total possible number of signals that can be sent in time T cannot be more than their ratio, which is

$$\frac{(\sqrt{2WT(P+N)})^n}{(\sqrt{2WNT})^n} = \left(1 + \frac{P}{N}\right)^{n/2} = \left(1 + \frac{P}{N}\right)^{WT}.$$

From Equation 9.9, this corresponds to an information-carrying rate of at most

$$\frac{1}{T}\log\left(1 + \frac{P}{N}\right)^{WT} = W\log\left(1 + \frac{P}{N}\right) \text{ bits per second.}$$

So far, P denotes the average energy per signal value and N the average energy per noise value. Over any time interval T, their ratio P/N is also the ratio of average signal power, given by P/T, to average noise power, N/T. Moreover, we can view the signal's band width W as a measure of the width of the continuous channel over which it is carried, because the channel can carry any signal whose highest-frequency component is W or smaller. With these substitutions, we can state the capacity of a Gaussian channel as

channel capacity = band width * log(1+P/N)   **(EQ 9.15)**

Shannon showed that codes over very long blocks of signal values can asymptotically achieve this capacity.

The ratio of the mean signal power to the mean noise power is often abbreviated as SNR and is measured in decibels (dB), where

$$SNR\ dB = 10\log_{10}\left(\frac{P}{N}\right)$$ **(EQ 9.16)**

A simple way to convert from decibel values to normal values is to divide by 10 and raising 10 to the power of the resulting value. For example, 40 dB corresponds to a ratio of $10^{40/10} = 10{,}000$.

EXAMPLE 9.21: CAPACITY OF A GAUSSIAN CHANNEL

What is the channel capacity of a channel with band width 20 MHz if the SNR is 30 dB?

Solution:

Since $P/N = 10^{30/10} = 1{,}000$, the channel capacity is $20*10^6 * \log(1000+1) = 20*10^6 * 9.96 = 199.2$ Mbps. In other words, this channel has an inherent capacity of nearly 10 (bits/second)/Hz.

We note in passing that most computer networking practitioners refer to the information capacity of a potentially noisy communication channel as its "band width" measured in bits/second. This conflates many concepts. Strictly speaking, a channel of band width W Hz refers to a channel that can carry signals whose highest frequency component is smaller than W Hz. So, band width should be measured in Hz, not bits/second. Second, the information-carrying capacity of a noisy channel depends on the SNR of the carried signal. Without knowing the SNR, the channel's information-carrying capacity (properly measured in bits/second) is unknown. However, for a nearly noiseless channel, such as an optical fiber, measuring information capacity in bits/second is reasonable.

The capacity of a wireless channel is greatly diminished by interference that arises from the simultaneous reception of two transmitted symbols at a receiver. Each transmitter appears as a source of noise to the other, decreasing the SNR. To take this into account, when studying wireless channels, we often refer to the SINR (signal to [interference + noise] ratio). This is demonstrated by the next example.

EXAMPLE 9.22: WIRELESS INTERFERENCE

Consider a WiFi (802.11b) wireless receiver that can receive symbols from transmitter A with an SNR of 30 dB or transmitter B with an SNR of 25 dB or from them both. What is the effective information capacity of the channel from A to the receiver and from B to the receiver when they are individually and simultaneously transmitting?

Solution:

A WiFi channel has a channel band width of 22MHz. When only A is transmitting, $P/N = 10^{30/10} = 1,000$. So, the channel capacity is $22*10^6 * \log(1001) = 22*10^6 * 9.96 = 219.12$ Mbps. Note that when using 802.11g encoding (orthogonal frequency division multiplexing, or OFDM), the best achievable rate in practice is 54 Mbps, which is a factor of 4 below the theoretical limit at this SNR.

When only B is transmitting, $P/N = 10^{25/10} = 316.2$. So, the channel capacity is $22*10^6 * \log(316.2) = 22*10^6 * 8.30 = 182.7$ Mbps.

When both A and B are transmitting, we can compute the SINR as follows. Let the noise power be N. Then, the signal power of transmitter A is $1000N$, and the signal power of transmitter B is $316.2N$. When B's signal is viewed as noise, the SINR is

$$\frac{1000N}{N + 316.2N} = 3.15.$$

So, the channel capacity is reduced to $22*10^6 * \log(4.15) = 45.17$ Mbps. Symmetrically, from B's perspective, the SINR is

$$\frac{316.2N}{N + 1000N} = 0.316.$$

This results in a negative value of $\log(P/N)$, which we interpret as a channel of zero information capacity; indeed, the signal is more than swamped by the noise.

9.7 Further Reading

Information theory was described by its creator in C. Shannon and W. Weaver, *Mathematical Theory of Communication*, University of Illinois Press, 1963. J. Pierce, *An Introduction to Information Theory*, Dover, 1981, is a concise, articulate, and lovely little book that presents the elements of information theory with little math and great insight. The standard text in this area is T. Cover and J. A. Thomas, *Elements of Information Theory*, 2nd ed., Wiley, 2006. A more sophisticated mathematical treatment can be found in R. Gallager, *Information Theory and Reliable Communication*, Wiley, 1968.

9.8 Exercises

1. **Entropy**

   Find the entropy of a random variable X whose probability mass function is given by $\left\{\frac{1}{4}, \frac{1}{4}, \frac{1}{4}, \frac{1}{8}, \frac{1}{8}\right\}$.

2. **Entropy**

   What is the entropy of a source that generates equal-length messages of 100 symbols chosen uniformly randomly from an alphabet of 16 symbols?

3. Instantaneous codes

Consider the following code:

Message Symbol	Code
a	00
b	001
c	1
d	11

What are the possible symbols that correspond to the code string 0011?

4. Instantaneous codes

Is the following code instantaneous? Why or why not?

Message Symbol	Code
a	00
b	01
c	101
d	100

5. Digit coding

What is the asymptotic limit in efficiency, measured in bits/digit, when coding decimal digit sequences with binary strings?

6. Feasibility of a code

Your friend tells you that he has invented an instantaneous binary code for a set of 12 messages where the code lengths are 2, 2, 2, 3, 4, 6, 6, 6, 7, 7, 7, and 7 bits. Should you believe him?

7. **Optimal codes**

Consider a message source that generates message symbols with the following probabilities:

Message Symbol	Probability
a	0.23
b	0.34
c	0.15
d	0.28

What is the expected length of the shortest instantaneous code to represent messages from this source?

8. **Huffman codes**

Give two Huffman codes for the message source of Exercise 7. What is its expected code length?

9. **Huffman codes**

Give an example where the Huffman code of Example 9.11 is not the optimal code for a specific message generated by the source.

10. **Entropy rate**

Suppose that a source of Exercise 7 generates 100 independent symbols/second. What is its entropy rate? How many distinct messages can it generate in 100 seconds?

11. **Typical messages**

Consider a message source that independently generates 0 symbols with probability 0.9 and 1 symbols with probability 0.1. Suppose that we define all messages with a probability of strictly lower than 10^{-10} to be atypical. If all messages generated by the source are 12 symbols long, what fraction of its distinct messages are atypical? How many codes should be assigned to messages of length 50 symbols to ensure that the number of uncoded messages is vanishingly small?

12. A noiseless channel

Consider a noiseless channel of capacity 100 bits/second. How many symbols can it carry from the message source of Exercise 7?

13. Mutual information

Compute the mutual information for a channel coder that sends a 0 symbol with probability 0.2 and a 1 symbol with probability 0.8 over the channel of Figure 9.5.

14. Mutual information

Prove $I(X;Y) = H(X) - H(X|Y) = H(Y) - H(Y|X)$.

15. Capacity of a binary symmetric channel

What is the capacity of a binary symmetric channel with an error probability of 0.001? Compare this to the channel capacity when the error probability is 0.

16. Capacity of a Gaussian channel

What is the channel capacity of a channel with band width 10 MHz if the SNR is 5 dB? What should be the SNR in decibels to achieve a channel capacity of 50 Mbps?

Solutions to Exercises

Chapter 1 Probability

1. **Sample space**

   The sample space for CW is the discrete set {CWMIN, 2 * CWMIN, 4 * CWMIN, ... 2^n * CWMIN}, where n is chosen so that 2^n * CWMIN < CWMAX. The sample space for backoff, given CW, is a subset of the real line defined by [0, CW].

2. **Interpretations of probability**

   An objective interpretation would be that we have a complete weather model that has an inherent source of randomness. Given this model and the current weather conditions, the model predicts that the probability of a snowstorm is 25%.

   A frequentist approach would be to look at all prior days when today's weather conditions also held and look at the number of such days when there was a snowstorm the next morning. Then, 25% of the time, given the current weather, there was a snowstorm the next morning.

   A subjective interpretation would be that an expert, who knew all the variables, would take 4:1 odds (or better) on a bet that it would snow tomorrow.

3. **Conditional probability**

   a. We have P(UDP) = 0.2, and P(UDP AND 100) = 0.1. So, P(100 | UDP) = 0.1/0.2 = 0.5.

b. Here, P(UDP) = 0.5 and P(100 | UDP) = 0.5. So, P(100 AND UDP) = 0.5*0.5 = 0.25.

4. **Conditional probability again**

Before you know the protocol type of a packet, the sample space is all possible packet lengths of all possible protocol types. After you know the protocol type, the sample space includes packet lengths only for that protocol.

5. **Bayes's rule**

$P(UDP | 100) = (P(100 | UDP)P(UDP))/P(100)$. We need $P(100) = x$. Then, $P(UDP | 100) = 0.5 * 0.2/x = 0.1/x$.

6. **Cumulative distribution function**

a. $F_D(i) = \sum\limits_{j=1}^{i} \dfrac{1}{2^j} = 1 - 2^{-i}$.

b. $f_{C(x)} = \dfrac{1}{x_2 - x_1}$, so $F_C(x) = \int\limits_{x_1}^{x} \dfrac{1}{x_2 - x_1} dx = \dfrac{x - x_1}{x_2 - x_1}$.

7. **Expectations**

a. $E[D] = \sum\limits_{j=1}^{i} \dfrac{i}{2^j}$.

b. By geometry, $E[C] = (x_2 + x_1)/2$. (You can also derive this analytically.)

8. **Variance**

$$V[aX] = E[a^2 X^2] - (E[aX])^2 = a^2(E[X^2] - (E[X])^2) = a^2 V[X].$$

9. **Moments**

$$M_\mu^3 = E((X - \mu)^3) = E(X^3 - 3X^2\mu + 3X\mu^2 - \mu^3) = M_0^3 - 3\mu E(X^2)$$
$$+ 3\mu^2 E(X) - \mu^3 = M_0^3 - 3M_0^1 M_0^2 + 3\mu^2 M_0^1 - \mu^3.$$

The result follows from the fact that $M_0^1 = \mu$.

10. MGFs

$$\int_{0}^{1}\left(1 + tx + \frac{(tx)^2}{2!} + \frac{(tx)^3}{3!} + \dots\right)dx = x\Big|_0^1 + \frac{tx^2}{2!}\Big|_0^1 + \frac{t^2x^3}{3!}\Big|_0^1 + \frac{t^3x^4}{4!}\Big|_0^1 + \dots$$

$$= 1 + \frac{t}{2!} + \frac{t^2}{3!} + \frac{t^3}{4!} + \dots$$

$$= \frac{1}{t}\left(t + \frac{t^2}{2!} + \frac{t^3}{3!} + \dots\right)$$

$$= \frac{1}{t}\left(1 + t + \frac{t^2}{2!} + \frac{t^3}{3!} + \dots - 1\right)$$

$$= \frac{1}{t}(e^t - 1)$$

11. MGFs

To find the rth moment, we differentiate the MGF for the uniform distribution:

$$\frac{1}{t}(e^t - 1) \ r \text{ times and then set } t \text{ to zero.}$$

Working directly from the series, we need to differentiate the expression

$$1 + \frac{t}{2!} + \frac{t^2}{3!} + \frac{t^3}{4!} + \dots \ r \text{ times and set } t \text{ to } 0.$$

Note that all terms with powers of t smaller than r disappear when we differentiate this series r times. Moreover, all terms with powers of t greater than r disappear when we set t to zero after differentiation (why?). Therefore, the only term we need to consider is $t^r/(r + 1)!$ It is clear that when we differentiate this r times, we get the term $r!/(r + 1)!$, which reduces to $1/1 + r$ as stated.

12. MGF of a sum of two variables

The MGF of the sum of two independent uniform random variables X_1 and X_2 is

$$\frac{1}{t^2}[e^t - 1]^2,$$

so, the MGF of $(X - \mu)$ is given by

$$\frac{e^{-\mu t}}{t^2}[e^t - 1]^2.$$

To find the variances we need to differentiate this expression twice with respect to t and then set t to 0. Given the t in the denominator, it is convenient to rewrite the expression as

$$\left(1 - \mu t + \frac{\mu^2 t^2}{2!} + \ldots\right)\left(1 + \frac{t}{2!} + \frac{t^2}{3!} + \ldots\right)\left(1 + \frac{t}{2!} + \frac{t^2}{3!} + \ldots\right).$$

(We have divided $e^t - 1$ by t in each of the second and third terms, where the ellipses refer to terms with third and higher powers of t, which will reduce to 0 when t is set to 0.) In this product, we need consider only the coefficient of t^2, which is

$$\frac{\mu^2}{2!} + \frac{1}{3!} + \frac{1}{3!} - \frac{\mu}{2!} - \frac{\mu}{2!} + \frac{1}{2!2!}.$$

Differentiating the expression twice results in multiplying the coefficient by 2. Note that for the sum of two uniform standard random variables, $\mu = 1$, so that when we set t to zero, we obtain

$$E((X - \mu)^2) = V(X) = 2\left(\frac{1}{2} + \frac{1}{6} + \frac{1}{6} - \frac{1}{2} - \frac{1}{2} + \frac{1}{4}\right) = \frac{1}{6}.$$

As a check, note that the variance of each variable is 1/12, so that the variance of the sum is the sum of the variances, as we found.

13. MGF of a normal distribution

The MGF of $a+bX$ is

$$e^{at}M(bt) = e^{at}e^{\mu bt + \frac{1}{2}\sigma^2(bt)^2} = e^{(a + \mu b)t + \frac{1}{2}(\sigma^2 b^2)t^2}.$$

Set $a = \frac{-\mu}{\sigma}$ and $b = \frac{1}{\sigma}$. Then,

$$e^{(a + \mu b)t + \frac{1}{2}(\sigma^2 b^2)t^2} = e^{\left(\frac{-\mu}{\sigma} + \frac{\mu}{\sigma}\right) + \frac{1}{2}\left(\frac{\sigma^2}{\sigma^2}\right)t^2} = e^{\frac{t^2}{2}},$$

which is the MGF of an $N(0,1)$ variable.

14. Bernoulli distribution

Consider the event E defined as "Room X is making an outgoing call during the busy hour." Clearly, $P(E) = p = 1/6$. The probability of 5 simultaneous calls is

$$\binom{20}{5}\left(\frac{1}{6}\right)^5\left(\frac{5}{6}\right)^{15} = 0.129$$

and of 15 simultaneous calls is $\binom{20}{15}\left(\frac{1}{6}\right)^{15}\left(\frac{5}{6}\right)^5 = 1.33*10^{-8}$.

15. Geometric distribution

Packet and ack transmissions are geometrically distributed with parameter $p = 0.9$. So the expected number of packet transmissions is $1/p = 1.11$, and the expected number of ack transmissions is also 1.11. These are independent events, so the expected number of data transmissions for successful packet+ack transfer = 1.11+1.11 = 2.22.

16. Poisson distribution

a. Using the binomial distribution, the value is

$$\binom{10}{8}(0.1^8)(0.9^2) = 0.36*10^{-6}.$$

For the Poisson approximation, $\lambda = 1$, so the value is

$$P(X = 8) = e^{-1}\left(\frac{1^8}{8!}\right) = 9.12*10^{-6}.$$

b. Using the binomial distribution, the value is

$$\binom{100}{8}(0.1^8)(0.9^{92}) = 0.114.$$

For the Poisson approximation, $\lambda = 10$, so the value is

$$P(X = 8) = e^{-10}\left(\frac{10^8}{8!}\right) = 0.112.$$

It is clear that as n increases, the approximation greatly improves.

17. Gaussian distribution

Consider the cumulative distribution of

$$Y = F_Y(y) = P(Y \le y) = P(aX + b \le y) = P\left(X \le \frac{(y-b)}{a}\right) = F_X\left(\frac{(y-b)}{a}\right) \text{ if } a > 0.$$

Then,

$$f_Y(y) = F'_Y(y) = F_X'\left(\frac{(y-b)}{a}\right) = \frac{1}{a}f_X\left(\frac{(y-b)}{a}\right) = \frac{1}{a\sigma\sqrt{2\pi}}e^{-\frac{\left(\left(\frac{y-b}{a}\right)-\mu\right)^2}{2\sigma^2}}$$

$$= \frac{1}{a\sigma\sqrt{2\pi}}e^{-\frac{(y-b-a\mu)^2}{2a^2\sigma^2}} = \frac{1}{a\sigma\sqrt{2\pi}}e^{-\frac{(y-(b+a\mu))^2}{2a^2\sigma^2}}.$$

Comparing with the standard definition of a Gaussian, we see that the parameters of Y are $(a\mu + b, (a\sigma)^2)$. A similar calculation holds if $a < 0$.

18. Exponential distribution

We have $1/\lambda = 5$. We need to compute

$$1 - F(15) = 1 - (1 - e^{-\lambda x}) = e^{\frac{-15}{5}} = e^{-3} = 4.98\%.$$

19. Exponential distribution

Because the exponential distribution is memoryless, the expected waiting time is the same, 200 seconds, no matter how long your break for ice cream. Isn't that nice?

20. Power law

x	$f_{power\_law}(x)$	$f_{exponential}(x)$
1	1	0.27
5	0.04	$9.07*10^{-5}$
10	0.01	$4.1*10^{-9}$
50	$4*10^{-4}$	$7.44*10^{-44}$
100	$1*10^{-4}$	$2.76*10^{-87}$

It should now be obvious why a power-law distribution is called heavy-tailed!

21. Markov's inequality

a. We need $1 - F(10) = e^{-20} = 2.06*10^{-9}$.

b. The mean of this distribution is 1/2. So, $P(X \geq 10) \leq \frac{0.5}{10} = 0.05$. It is clear that the bound is very loose.

22. Joint probability distribution

a. $p_X = \{0.5, 0.5\}$; $p_Y = \{0.2, 0.8\}$; $p_Z = \{0.3, 0.7\}$; $p_{XY} = \{0.1, 0.4, 0.1, 0.4\}$;
$p_{XZ} = \{0.15, 0.35, 0.15, 0.35\}$; $p_{YZ} = \{0.1, 0.1, 0.2, 0.6\}$

b. X and Y are independent because $p_{XY} = p_X p_Y$. X and Z are independent because $p_{XZ} = p_X p_Z$.

c. $P(X = 0 \mid Z = 1) = P(X = 0 \text{ AND } Z = 1)/P(Z = 1) = 0.35/0.7 = 0.5$.

Chapter 2 Statistics

1. Means

To minimize

$$\sum_{i=1}^{n} (x_i - x^*)^2,$$

we differentiate the expression with respect to x^* and set this value to 0. We find that

$$\frac{d}{dx^*} \sum_{i=1}^{n} (x_i - x^*)^2 = \sum_{i=1}^{n} -2(x_i - x^*) = 0,$$

so that $\sum x_i - \sum x^* = 0$. Rewriting $\sum x^*$ as nx^*, we get the desired result.

2. Means

$$\frac{1}{n}\left(\sum_{i=1}^{n} (x_i - \mu)^2 - n(\bar{x} - \mu)^2 \right) = \frac{1}{n}\left(\sum_{i=1}^{n} (x_i^2 + \mu^2 - 2x_i\mu) - n(\bar{x}^2 + \mu^2 - 2\bar{x}\mu) \right)$$

$$= \frac{1}{n}\left(\sum_{i=1}^{n} x_i^2 + \mu^2 - 2x_i\mu - \bar{x}^2 - \mu^2 + 2\bar{x}\mu \right)$$

$$= \frac{1}{n}\left(\sum_{i=1}^{n} x_i^2 - 2x_i\mu - \bar{x}^2 + 2\bar{x}\mu \right)$$

$$= \frac{1}{n}\left(\sum_{i=1}^{n} x_i^2 - \bar{x}^2 + \sum_i 2\bar{x}\mu - 2x_i\mu \right).$$

But $\sum_i (2\bar{x}\mu - 2x_i\mu) = 2n\bar{x}\mu - 2n\bar{x}\mu = 0$, hence the desired result.

3. Confidence intervals (normal distribution)

The sample mean is 61.11. We compute

$$\sum_{i=1}^{n} (x_i - \bar{x})^2$$

as 936647.76. Therefore, the variance of the sampling distribution of the mean is estimated as 936,647.76/(17*16) = 3,443.55, and the standard deviation of this distribution is estimated as its square root: 58.68. Using the value of $\pm 1.96\sigma$ for the 95% confidence interval, the 95% confidence interval is 61.11 $\pm$ 115.02. The very large interval is due to the outlier value.

4. Confidence intervals (*t* distribution)

We substitute the value of $\pm 2.12\sigma$ in Example 2.6 to obtain the confidence interval as 61.11 $\pm$ 124.40.

5. Hypothesis testing: comparing the mean to a constant

The mean is 2.46%. We compute the variance as 0.0076% and the standard deviation as 0.87%. We could use the *t* distribution to test the hypothesis, but it is clear by inspection that 2% lies within one standard deviation of the mean, so we cannot reject the null hypothesis. For the sake of completeness, the confidence interval for the *t* distribution with 9 degrees of freedom (at the 95% level) is 2% $\pm$ 2.262 * 0.87%.

6. Chi-squared test

The critical value of n_1 is when the chi-squared value is $X = (n_1 - 42)^2/42 + (100 - n_1 - 58)^2/58 = 3.84$. Solving, we get $n_1 > 51.67$. So, a value greater than or equal to 52 will result in the hypothesis being rejected.

7. Fitting a distribution and chi-squared test

The total number of time periods is 28 + 56 +...+ 5 = 1,193. The total number of arrivals is (28 * 2)+(56 * 3)+...+(5 * 16) = 8,917. Therefore, the mean number of packets arriving in 1 ms is 8,917/1,203 = 7.47. This is the best estimate of the mean of a Poisson distribution. We use this to generate the probability of a certain number of arrivals in each 1 ms time period, using the Poisson distribution. This probability multiplied by the total number of time periods is the expected count for that number of arrivals, as follows.

Number of Packet Arrivals	2	3	4	5	6	7	8	9	10	11	12	13	14	15	16
Count	28	56	105	126	146	164	165	120	103	73	54	23	16	9	5
Expected Count	19	47	88	132	164	175	164	136	102	69	43	25	13	7	3

The chi-squared value is computed as $(28 - 19)^2/21 + (56 - 47)^2/47.... + (5 - 3)^2/3 = 19.98$. Since we estimated one parameter from the sample, the degrees of freedom $= 15 - 1 - 1 = 13$. From the chi-squared table, with 13 degrees of freedom, at the 95% confidence level, the critical value is 22.36. Therefore, we cannot reject the hypothesis that the sample is well described by a Poisson distribution at this confidence level.

8. **Independence, regression, and correlation**

a. If the number of peers were independent of the uplink capacity, as the uplink capacity changed, the number of peers should remain roughly constant and equal to the population mean, whose best estimate is the sample mean. Therefore, the expected value of the number of peers is 50 + 31 +...+ 49/10 = 40.4.

b. The chi-squared variate is $(50 - 40.4)^2/40.4 + (31 - 40.4)^2/40.4 + ... + (49 - 40.4)^2/40.4 = 27.93$. Because we estimated one parameter from the data set (i.e., the mean), we have $10 - 1 - 1 = 8$ degrees of freedom. We find that at the 95% confidence level, the critical value of the chi-squared distribution with 8 degrees of freedom is 15.51. Therefore, we can reject the hypothesis that the number of peers is independent of the uplink capacity with 95% confidence. The critical value at the 99.9% level is 25.125, so we can reject the hypothesis even at the 99.9% level.

c. We use the equation $b = \dfrac{\sum (x_i - \bar{x})(y_i - \bar{y})}{\sum (x_i - \bar{x})^2}$ to find $b = 0.21$.

d. Using $r = \dfrac{\sum (x_i - \bar{x})(y_i - \bar{y})}{\sqrt{(\sum (x_i - \bar{x})^2)(\sum (y_i - \bar{y})^2)}}$, we find $r = 0.952$, which is close to 1.

Therefore, we can state that the two variables are well represented by a linear relationship, which indicates dependence rather than independence.

e. The portion of variability in the number of peers that can be explained by the uplink capacity is $r^2 = 90.1\%$.

9. Correlation coefficient

For convenience, we use the following notation:

$$X^2 = \sum (x_i - \bar{x})^2,$$
$$Y^2 = \sum (y_i - \bar{y})^2,$$
$$XY = \sum (x_i - \bar{x})(y_i - \bar{y}),$$
$$S^2 = \sum (y_i - a - bx_i)^2$$

Ignoring the summation symbol, we can rewrite the summand $(y_i - a - bx_i)^2$ as

$$\left(y_i - \left(\bar{y} - \bar{x}\frac{XY}{X^2} \right) - x_i\frac{XY}{X^2} \right)^2 = \left((y_i - \bar{y}) - \frac{(x_i - \bar{x})XY}{X^2} \right)^2$$

$$= \left(Y^2 + \frac{(XY)^2 X^2}{X^2 X^2} - 2\frac{(XY)^2}{X^2} \right) = \left(Y^2 - \frac{(XY)^2}{X^2} \right)$$

$$= \left(Y^2 - Y^2 \left(\frac{(XY)^2}{X^2 Y^2} \right) \right) = Y^2(1 - r^2)$$

as desired. To understand the third step, recall the presence of the summation symbol.

10. Single-Factor ANOVA

Here, $I = 3$ and $J = 10$. We compute $\overline{Y_{1.}} = 55.53$, $\overline{Y_{2.}} = 55.94$, $\overline{Y_{3.}} = 55.95$. This allows us to compute $SSW = 3102.29$ and $SSB = 1.15$. The F statistic is therefore $(1.15/2)/(3102.29/27) = 0.0050$. Looking up the F table, we find that with $(3, 27)$ degrees of freedom, the critical F value, even at the 5% confidence level, is 2.96. The computed statistic is far below this value. Therefore, the null hypothesis cannot be rejected.

Chapter 3 Linear Algebra

1. Transpose

$$\begin{bmatrix} 4 & 7 & 3 \\ 0 & 82 & -2 \\ -3 & 12 & 2 \end{bmatrix}$$

2. Matrix multiplications

$$\begin{bmatrix} -44 & 118 & -54 \\ 59 & 14 & -24 \\ -40 & 20 & 40 \end{bmatrix}$$

3. Exponentiation

The proof is by induction. The base case is for $k=2$, where by direct computation, we find that

$$\begin{bmatrix} a_{11} & \cdots & 0 \\ \cdots & a_{ii} & \cdots \\ 0 & \cdots & a_{nn} \end{bmatrix} \begin{bmatrix} a_{11} & \cdots & 0 \\ \cdots & a_{ii} & \cdots \\ 0 & \cdots & a_{nn} \end{bmatrix} = \begin{bmatrix} a_{11}^2 & \cdots & 0 \\ \cdots & a_{ii}^2 & \cdots \\ 0 & \cdots & a_{nn}^2 \end{bmatrix}.$$ The inductive assumption is that

$$A^k = \begin{bmatrix} a_{11} & \cdots & 0 \\ \cdots & a_{ii} & \cdots \\ 0 & \cdots & a_{nn} \end{bmatrix}^k = \begin{bmatrix} a_{11}^k & \cdots & 0 \\ \cdots & a_{ii}^k & \cdots \\ 0 & \cdots & a_{nn}^k \end{bmatrix}.$$ Then, we compute the $k+1$th power of A as

$$A^k A = \begin{bmatrix} a_{11}^k & \cdots & 0 \\ \cdots & a_{ii}^k & \cdots \\ 0 & \cdots & a_{nn}^k \end{bmatrix} \begin{bmatrix} a_{11} & \cdots & 0 \\ \cdots & a_{ii} & \cdots \\ 0 & \cdots & a_{nn} \end{bmatrix} = \begin{bmatrix} a_{11}^{k+1} & \cdots & 0 \\ \cdots & a_{ii}^{k+1} & \cdots \\ 0 & \cdots & a_{nn}^{k+1} \end{bmatrix}.$$

4. Linear combination of scalars

The linear combination is $10 * 0.5 + 5 * 0.4 + 2 * 0.25 + -4 * 0.25 = 5 + 2 + 0.5 - 1 = 6.5$.

5. Linear combination of vectors

The first element of the linear combination is given by $1 * 0.5 + 3 * 0.4 + 7 * 0.25 + 2 * 0.25 = 0.5 + 1.2 + 1.75 + 0.5 = 3.95$. Computing the other elements similarly, we obtain the solution [3.95 5.8 6.2 6.15].

6. Linear independence and rank

The coefficient matrix is given by $\begin{bmatrix} 12 & 2 & -4 \\ 2 & 2 & -24 \\ 2.5 & 0 & 5 \end{bmatrix}$. If the vectors are independent,

the rank of this matrix will be 3, so that Gaussian elimination would result in no equations being reduced to the trivial form 0=0. We proceed with Gaussian elimination as follows: Equation 3.3 does not contain the second variable, so we remove the second variable from the second equation by subtracting the first

row from the second row, to get $\begin{bmatrix} 12 & 2 & -4 \\ -10 & 0 & -20 \\ 2.5 & 0 & 5 \end{bmatrix}$. It is clear that the second row is

the third row multiplied by −4, so that if we add 4 times the third row to the

second row, we get $\begin{bmatrix} 12 & 2 & -4 \\ 0 & 0 & 0 \\ 2.5 & 0 & 5 \end{bmatrix}$. Can we reduce any of the remaining equations

to the form 0=0? It is clear that the first row is not a multiple of the third row, because the second element of the third row is 0, and the second element of the first row is not. Hence, the rank of the coefficient matrix is 2, which is smaller than 3, so that the three vectors are *not* independent.

7. Basis and dimension

Two of the three vectors are linearly independent, so we have two vectors in the basis and a generated vector space of dimension 2. One possible basis is simply the two vectors themselves, that is, {[12 2 −4], [2.5 0   5]}. We can get another basis by multiplying either vector by any scalar. For example, we can multiply the first vector by 0.5 to get another basis as {[6   1   −2], [2.5 0   5]}.

8. Gaussian elimination

Noticing that the third equation has a zero in the second column, we will eliminate the second variable in the first row as well, by subtracting twice the sec-

ond row from the first row, to obtain $\begin{bmatrix} 22 & 0 & -16 & 9 \\ -8 & 2 & 4 & -2 \\ 10 & 0 & 4 & 1 \end{bmatrix}$. We can eliminate the third

variable from the first row by multiplying the third row by 4 and adding it to the first row, to get $\begin{bmatrix} 62 & 0 & 0 & 13 \\ -8 & 2 & 4 & -2 \\ 10 & 0 & 4 & 1 \end{bmatrix}$. We can read off $x_1 = 13/62 = 0.2096$. Substitut-

ing in the third row, we find $2.096 + 4x_3 = 1$, so that $x_3 = (1 - 2.096)/4 = -0.274$. Substituting these in the first row of the original equation, we find $6 * 0.2096 + 4 * x_2 -8 * -0.274 = 5$, so that $x_2 = 0.3876$.

9. Rank

Consider the ith row of a nonzero diagonal matrix. Its diagonal element is a_{ii}, which is not 0, but all other elements in the ith column are 0. Therefore, there is no way to obtain the ith row as a linear combination of the other rows. Since this is true for all i, the rows are all linearly independent, and the rank of the matrix is n. Note that the rows are therefore a basis of the corresponding vector space.

10. Determinant

Expanding by the second column, we find the determinant to be $8 * (4 * 2 - 3 * (-3)) - (-2) * (4 * 12 - 7 * (-3)) = 8 * (8 + 9) + 2 * (48 + 21) = 8 * 17 + 2 * 69 = 274$.

11. Inverse

We already know that the determinant of the matrix is 274 (see Exercise 10). The cofactor C_{11} is given by $(-1)^{1+1}(8 * 2 -(-2) * (12)) = 16 + 24 = 40$. $C_{21} = (-1)^{1+2}(0 * 2 -(-2) * (-3)) = -(-6) = 6$. Computing the other cofactors similarly,

we obtain the inverse as $\dfrac{1}{274}\begin{bmatrix} 40 & 6 & 24 \\ 22 & 17 & -69 \\ -38 & 8 & 32 \end{bmatrix}$.

12. Matrix as a transformation

Let the angle made by the vector from $(0,0)$ to (x, y) be t, and let its length be r. Then, we can write x and y as

$$x = r \cos(t),$$
$$y = r \sin(t).$$

Let the rotated vector join the origin to the point (X,Y). We expand:

$$X = r \cos(t + p) = r (\cos(t)\cos(p) - \sin(t)\sin(p)) = x * \cos(p) - y * \sin(p),$$
$$Y = r \sin (t + p) = r(\sin(t)\cos(p) + \cos(t)\sin(p)) = y * \cos(p) + x * \sin(p).$$

We can write this as

$$\begin{bmatrix} X \\ Y \end{bmatrix} = \begin{bmatrix} \cos(p) & -\sin(p) \\ \sin(p) & \cos(p) \end{bmatrix} \begin{bmatrix} x \\ y \end{bmatrix}$$

so that the rotation matrix is $\begin{bmatrix} \cos(p) & -\sin(p) \\ \sin(p) & \cos(p) \end{bmatrix}$.

13. Composing transformations

We compute the composition as

$$\begin{bmatrix} \cos(p) & -\sin(p) \\ \sin(p) & \cos(p) \end{bmatrix} \begin{bmatrix} \cos(t) & -\sin(t) \\ \sin(t) & \cos(t) \end{bmatrix}$$

$$= \begin{bmatrix} \cos(p)\cos(t) - \sin(p)\sin(t) & -\cos(p)\sin(t) - \sin(p)\cos(t) \\ \sin(p)\cos(t) + \cos(p)\sin(t) & -\sin(p)\sin(t) + \cos(p)\cos(t) \end{bmatrix}$$

$$= \begin{bmatrix} \cos(p+t) & -\sin(p+t) \\ \sin(p+t) & \cos(p+t) \end{bmatrix},$$

which we recognize as a rotation by a total of $t+p$ degrees, as expected.

14. Eigenvalues and eigenvectors

The characteristic equation is $\begin{vmatrix} 1-\lambda & 9 \\ 4 & 1-\lambda \end{vmatrix} = 0$, so that $(1-\lambda)^2 - 36 = 0$,

and we get $\lambda = -5, 7$ as the eigenvalues.

We compute the eigenvector corresponding to the value -5 by solving the equation

$$\begin{bmatrix} 1 & 9 \\ 4 & 1 \end{bmatrix} \begin{bmatrix} x_1 \\ x_2 \end{bmatrix} = (-5) \begin{bmatrix} x_1 \\ x_2 \end{bmatrix}.$$

This gives us the equations $x_1 + 9x_2 = -5x_1$; $4x_1 + x_2 = -5x_2$. Either one can be solved to get $x_2 = -(2x_1)/3$, corresponding to an eigenvector family of scalar multiples of $[1 \ -2/3]^T$.

We compute the eigenvector corresponding to the value 7 by solving the equation

$$\begin{bmatrix} 1 & 9 \\ 4 & 1 \end{bmatrix} \begin{bmatrix} x_1 \\ x_2 \end{bmatrix} = 7 \begin{bmatrix} x_1 \\ x_2 \end{bmatrix}.$$

This gives us the equations $x_1 + 9x_2 = 7x_1$; $4x_1 + x_2 = 7x_2$. Either one can be solved to get $x_2 = 2x_1/3$, corresponding to an eigenvector family of scalar multiples of $[\ 1\ 2/3\ ]^T$.

15. Computing $A^n x$

From Exercise 14, we know that the eigenvectors of $\begin{bmatrix} 1 & 9 \\ 4 & 1 \end{bmatrix}$ are $\begin{bmatrix} 1 \\ \frac{2}{3} \end{bmatrix}$ and $\begin{bmatrix} 1 \\ \frac{-2}{3} \end{bmatrix}$.

We recognize that the vector $\begin{bmatrix} 8 \\ 0 \end{bmatrix}$ can be written as $4\begin{bmatrix} 1 \\ \frac{2}{3} \end{bmatrix} + 4\begin{bmatrix} 1 \\ \frac{-2}{3} \end{bmatrix}$. Hence,

$$\begin{bmatrix} 1 & 9 \\ 4 & 1 \end{bmatrix}^5 \begin{bmatrix} 8 \\ 0 \end{bmatrix} = \begin{bmatrix} 1 & 9 \\ 4 & 1 \end{bmatrix}^5 \left(4\begin{bmatrix} 1 \\ \frac{2}{3} \end{bmatrix} + 4\begin{bmatrix} 1 \\ \frac{-2}{3} \end{bmatrix} \right) = 4\begin{bmatrix} 1 & 9 \\ 4 & 1 \end{bmatrix}^5 \begin{bmatrix} 1 \\ \frac{2}{3} \end{bmatrix} + 4\begin{bmatrix} 1 & 9 \\ 4 & 1 \end{bmatrix}^5 \begin{bmatrix} 1 \\ \frac{-2}{3} \end{bmatrix}$$

$$= 4\left(-5^5 \begin{bmatrix} 1 \\ \frac{-2}{3} \end{bmatrix} + 7^5 \begin{bmatrix} 1 \\ \frac{2}{3} \end{bmatrix} \right) = \begin{bmatrix} 54728 \\ 53152 \end{bmatrix}$$

16. Finding eigenvalues

The matrix is symmetric, so its eigenvalues are real. From the Gerschgorin circle theorem, the eigenvalues lie in the intersection of the real intervals [4–1.5 4+1.5], [6–1.3 6+1.3], [5–0.8 5+0.8] = {[2.5 5.5], [4.7 7.3], [4.2 5.8]} = [2.5 7.3].

17. Power method

We start with the initial vector $x_0 = \begin{bmatrix} 1 \\ 1 \end{bmatrix}$. Applying the matrix once, we get $x_1 = \begin{bmatrix} 10 \\ 5 \end{bmatrix}$.

The Rayleigh ratio evaluates to ([1 1] $*$ $\begin{bmatrix} 10 \\ 5 \end{bmatrix}$)/([1 1] $*$ $\begin{bmatrix} 1 \\ 1 \end{bmatrix}$) = 15/2 = 7.5. Repeating,

we get $x_2 = \begin{bmatrix} 55 \\ 45 \end{bmatrix}$, and the ratio evaluates to 775/125 = 6.2. After one more iteration, we get $x_3 = \begin{bmatrix} 460 \\ 265 \end{bmatrix}$, and the ratio evaluates to 37,225/5,050 = 7.37. For the

fourth iteration, we get $x_4 = \begin{bmatrix} 2845 \\ 2105 \end{bmatrix}$, and the ratio evaluates to 1,866,525/281,825 =

6.622. We see that the series slowly converges to the dominant eigenvalue of 7.

To compute the dominant eigenvalue, we start with $x_1 = \begin{bmatrix} 10 \\ 5 \end{bmatrix}$, which we rescale to $x_1 = \begin{bmatrix} 1 \\ 0.5 \end{bmatrix}$. Then, $x_2 = \begin{bmatrix} 1 & 9 \\ 4 & 1 \end{bmatrix} \begin{bmatrix} 1 \\ 0.5 \end{bmatrix} = \begin{bmatrix} 5.5 \\ 4.5 \end{bmatrix}$, which we rescale to $\begin{bmatrix} 1 \\ 0.818 \end{bmatrix}$.

Thus, $x_3 = \begin{bmatrix} 1 & 9 \\ 4 & 1 \end{bmatrix} \begin{bmatrix} 1 \\ 0.818 \end{bmatrix} = \begin{bmatrix} 8.362 \\ 4.818 \end{bmatrix}$, which we rescale to $\begin{bmatrix} 1 \\ 0.576 \end{bmatrix}$. Finally, $x_4 = \begin{bmatrix} 1 & 9 \\ 4 & 1 \end{bmatrix} \begin{bmatrix} 1 \\ 0.576 \end{bmatrix} = \begin{bmatrix} 6.184 \\ 4.576 \end{bmatrix}$, which we rescale to $\begin{bmatrix} 1 \\ 0.734 \end{bmatrix}$ and is the estimate of the dominant eigenvector. Compare this to the true value of $x = \begin{bmatrix} 1 \\ 0.66 \end{bmatrix}$.

18. Diagonalization

This is the matrix with the same eigenvalues as the given matrix: $\begin{bmatrix} -5 & 0 \\ 0 & 7 \end{bmatrix}$.

19. Stochastic matrix

The matrix is left- (or column-) stochastic but not right- (or row-) stochastic, because its columns add to 1.0, but its rows do not.

20. State transitions

The initial state vector is $[0.5 \ 0.5 \ 0]^T$. After one time step, the state vector is

$\begin{bmatrix} 0.25 & 0.1 & 0 \\ 0.5 & 0.9 & 0 \\ 0.25 & 0 & 1.0 \end{bmatrix} \begin{bmatrix} 0.5 \\ 0.5 \\ 0 \end{bmatrix} = \begin{bmatrix} 0.175 \\ 0.7 \\ 0.125 \end{bmatrix}$. After another time step, the state vector is

$\begin{bmatrix} 0.25 & 0.1 & 0 \\ 0.5 & 0.9 & 0 \\ 0.25 & 0 & 1.0 \end{bmatrix} \begin{bmatrix} 0.175 \\ 0.7 \\ 0.125 \end{bmatrix} = \begin{bmatrix} 0.11375 \\ 0.7175 \\ 0.16875 \end{bmatrix}$. Therefore, the probability of being in state

1 after two time steps is 0.11375 and of being in state 2 after two time steps is 0.7175.

Chapter 4 Optimization

1. Modeling

This problem has many solutions. Here is one possibility.

Control variables (from the statement of the problem):

- x_i : starting point of flight i
- d_i : duration of flight i, $d_i \geq 15$
- The cost of ticket for the ith flight, t_i

Note that the number of passengers in a flight is not a control parameter, because it is related to the cost of a ticket; once the cost of the ticket is determined, the number of passengers cannot be independently controlled.

Fixed parameters:

- The possible take-off locations, V
- The cost of chase vehicle (gas needed, maintenance, etc.) per kilometer of travel.
- Location of the roads, R
- The cost of the natural gas, g, per minute of flight
- Pilot's wages, w, per minute of flight

Input parameters:

- The wind speed and direction for flight i

Transfer functions:

- Where a balloon lands, as a function of starting point, wind speed and direction, and flight duration
- The number of passengers p as a function of the cost of a ticket
- A function that, given the cost of every process in the business, computes the cost of flight i

Output parameters:

- For flight i, the distance of the balloon's landing spot from a road
- Number of passengers for flight i, p_i
- The cost of flight i, denoted f_i

Objective function:

- Maximize $p_i t_i - f_i$

Empirically estimating the transfer functions:

- Empirically determining the landing spot for each starting point, for each wind speed and direction
- Determining the number of passengers for a cost by trial and error or by doing a market study
- Determining empirically, as a linear combination of the fixed parameters, the cost of a flight

2. Optimizing a function of two variables

The following figure shows the plot for the curve $2x_1 - x_2 = 1$ subject to $x_1 \geq 0$ and $x_2 \geq 0$. The system does not impose any constraint on how large x_1 and x_2 can grow, so the maximum value is unbounded. We know that the minimal value is at a vertex; in this case, we have only one (0.5, 0). If we evaluate the function in (0.5, 0) and at a randomly chosen point—say, (3, 5)—we get:

$$O(0.5, 0) = 5$$
$$O(3, 5) = 15$$

Using this information, we know that the minimum value of O, given the constraints, is 5 at (0,5, 0). There is no maximum value, since O is unbounded in the space determined by the constraints.

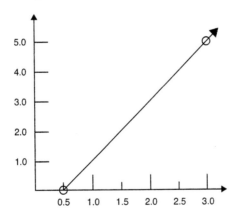

3. Optimizing a function of three variables

The following figure shows the plot for the plane $x_1 + x_2 + x_3 = 1$ for x_1, x_2, x_3 non-negative. The resulting polyhedron serves to find the optimal values of O. The optimal value has to be at a vertex, so we evaluate the value of the objective function at the three vertices:

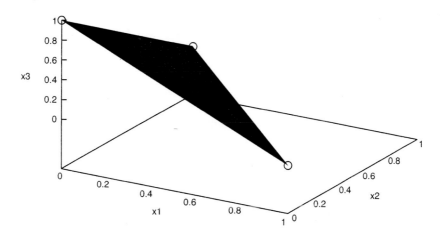

$$O(1, 0, 0) = 5$$
$$O(0, 1, 0) = 2$$
$$O(0, 0, 1) = -1$$

Clearly, the maximum value is reached at point $(1, 0, 0)$ and the minimum value is reached at point $(0, 0, 1)$.

4. Network flow

We will consider the problem when there is only one source node s. (If we have many sources, we can always create a new source with unbounded capacity connected to all the sources, each with limited capacity.) Similarly, we can unify all the sinks to form a single sink t.

Let $G = (V, E)$ be the graph, and let f_{ij} be the flow between nodes v_i and v_j. Let c_{ij} be the capacity of link from v_i to v_j. The classical problem is stated as

$$O = \sum_i f_{si} \quad \text{subject to}$$

$$\sum_i f_{ij} = \sum_k f_{jk} \quad \forall j \notin \{s, t\}$$

$$f_{ij} \leq c_{ij} \quad \forall i, j$$

We can interpret the "capacity of a warehouse" in two ways. One way to interpret it is that no more than cap_j flow can go through warehouse j. To model this, we add the following constraint:

$$\sum_i f_{ij} \leq cap_j \quad \forall j$$

A more complex interpretation of the constraint is that each warehouse has a limited storage capacity. This would allow the ingress flow to exceed the egress flow for a limited duration of time. Specifically, if the storage capacity of warehouse j is B_j, denoting the flow on link $v_i - v_j$ by $f_{ij}(t)$,

$$\sum_i \int_{t_1}^{t_2} f_{ij}(t)dt \le \sum_k \int_{t_1}^{t_2} f_{jk}(t)dt + B_j \quad \forall j \notin \{s,t\}, \forall t_1, \forall t_2 \qquad s.t. \ t_1 < t_2$$

so that the ingress flows to any node j, integrated over all possible time periods, never exceeds the egress flows, integrated over the same time period, taking into account the possibility of storing B_j units in the warehouse.

5. Integer linear programming

Let the variable x_{ijh} indicate whether user i can schedule a job on machine h at time period j. Let the cost and benefit of assigning machine h to user i at time period j be c_{ijh} and g_{ijh}, respectively. Then, the function to optimize is

$$O = \sum_{i=1}^{n} \sum_{j=1}^{m} \sum_{h=1}^{k} (g_{ijh} - c_{ijh})x_{ijh}$$

The obvious constraints are that $x_{ijh} \in \{0,1\}$, which makes the problem an ILP. In addition, we express the constraint that at each time slot, a machine can be assigned to at most one user, using the constraint

$$\sum_{i=1}^{n} x_{ijh} \le 1 \quad \forall j, h$$

6. Weighted bipartite matching

Standard bipartite matching allows us to place only one ball in one urn. We modify the elements of the bipartite graph as follows: given m urns indexed by i, we create a new set M' that contains $2m$ elements, labeled m'_{i1} and m'_{i2}. Now, create links from K to M' where the payoff on the link from placing ball k_j in urn m'_{i1} and m'_{i2} is the same as the payoff from placing ball k_j in urn m_i in the original problem, or p_{ji}. The solution to the weighted bipartite matching problem in M' trivially gives us the solution to the problem in M.

7. Dynamic programming

Let $D(i,j)$ denote the numbers of errors in a match that between the first i characters in S and all possible substrings formed from the first j characters in L.

Suppose that $S(i) = 1(j)$. Then, $D(i, j) = D(i - 1, j - 1)$.

Otherwise, we can compute $D(i, j)$ as the smallest of penalties computed from one of three actions:

a. Substituting $S(i)$ with $L(j)$ with a penalty of 1 added to $D(i - 1, j - 1)$.

b. Deleting the $L(j)$th character, so that we are matching the first i characters of S with the first $j - 1$ characters of L, which costs $D(i, j - 1)$ + a penalty of 1.

c. Deleting the $S(i)$th character, so that we are matching the first $i - 1$ characters of S with the first j characters of L.

We can rewrite this as

> If $S(i) = D(j)$
> > then $D(i, j) = D(i - 1, j - 1)$
> > else $D(i, j) = \min(\ D(i - 1, j - 1) +1, D(i, j - 1) +1, D(i - 1, j) +1)$

Note that in all cases, $D(i, j)$ depends on a smaller index of either i or j or both, which creates an optimal substructure with reusable results.

If we start with $i = 1, j = 1$, we can memoize the $|L||S|$ entries and compute scores in time proportional to $|L||S|$. We set $D(i, 0) = i$ and $D(0, j) = j$ as boundary conditions. The string associated with each memoized position is the best match for that position and is kept track of in the table, depending on which of the three actions was chosen to compute that position.

8. Lagrangian optimization

Both functions are continuous and twice-differentiable. We define the Lagrangian $F(x, y, \lambda) = x^3 + 2y + \lambda(x^2 + y^2 - 1)$. Setting $\nabla F = 0$, we get

$$\frac{\partial F}{\partial x} = 3x^2 + 2\lambda x = 0 \qquad \text{(EQ S.1)}$$

$$\frac{\partial F}{\partial y} = 2 + 2\lambda y = 0 \qquad \text{(EQ S.2)}$$

$$\frac{\partial F}{\partial \lambda} = x^2 + y^2 - 1 = 0 \qquad \text{(EQ S.3)}$$

Solving Equation S.1, we get two solutions for x, denoted x_1 and x_2:

$$x_1 = 0, x_2 = -\frac{2\lambda}{3}$$

Corresponding to x_1 we solve Equation S.3 to find $y_{11} = 1$, $y_{12} = -1$ and put these in Equation S.2 to get $\lambda_{11} = -1$, $\lambda_{12} = 1$. The extermal values of $z = x^3 +$

$2y$ for this solution of x therefore are 2 and -2, achieved at the points $(0,1)$ and $(0,-1)$.

Corresponding to x_2, we find from Equation S.3 that $\frac{4}{9}\lambda^2 + y^2 = 1$. Substituting $\lambda = -\frac{1}{y}$ from Equation S.2 and solving for y, we find that y is complex, so that there

are no real points (x,y) satisfying Equation S.3. Therefore, the only viable extremal points are the two found earlier, which correspond to a constrained maximum and constrained minimum, respectively.

9. Hill climbing

We start with K random points and compute the optimal value reached at each point. If we have K unique results, we return the best point. Otherwise, we eliminate the repeated results—say, r of them—and start again with r points and repeat the process (remembering those results already computed). When we reach K distinct points, the algorithm finishes and returns the global optimum. Note that we could iterate infinitely before finding the K local optima. However, without making any additional assumptions about the space, we cannot guarantee a better method to find the global optimum.

Chapter 5 Signals, Systems, and Transforms

1. Complex arithmetic

$$e^{-j\frac{\pi}{2}} + e^{j\frac{\pi}{2}}$$

$$= \left(\left(\cos\left(-\frac{\pi}{2}\right) + j\sin\left(-\frac{\pi}{2}\right)\right) + \left(\cos\left(\frac{\pi}{2}\right) + j\sin\left(-\frac{\pi}{2}\right)\right)\right)$$

$$= 2\cos\left(\frac{\pi}{2}\right)$$

$$= 0$$

2. Phase angle

This is given by $\operatorname{atan}\left(\frac{1}{1}\right) = \frac{\pi}{4}$.

3. Discrete convolution

$$z(5)= \sum_{\tau = -\infty}^{\infty} x(\tau)y(5-\tau).$$

This reduces to computing products $x(a).y(b)$, where $a + b = 5$. These are the pairs $(1, 9), (3, 5), (5, 4), (2, 7), (5, 1), (8, 3)$, whose products are $9, 15, 20, 14, 5, 24$ and whose sum $= z(5) = 87$.

4. Signals

Temperature readings from a digital thermometer.

5. Complex exponential

The projection is obtained by setting the real value to 0, so that the curve is given by the expression $j5e^t \sin(3t)$. This curve lies entirely in the complex (Im-t) plane. It corresponds to a sinusoid of frequency 3Hz whose amplitude increases exponentially with time. At time 0, it has an amplitude of 5; at time 1/3, an amplitude of $5e$; at time 2/3, an amplitude of $5e^2$; and, in general, at time $3k$, an amplitude of $5e^k$.

6. Linearity

$$H(k_1 x_1 + k_2 x_2) = \left(\frac{5d(k_1 x_1)}{dt} + 1\right) + \left(\frac{5d(k_2 x_2)}{dt} + 1\right)$$

$$= \left(\frac{5k_1 dx_1}{dt} + 1\right) + \left(\frac{5k_2 dx_2}{dt} + 1\right)$$

$$\neq H(k_1 x_1) + H(k_2 x_2),$$

so the system is not linear.

7. LTI system

Any sinusoid can be written as the sum of equal and opposite complex exponentials. A complex exponential input to an LTI system results in a complex exponential output. Since the system is LTI, a sinusoidal input will result in an output that is the sum of equal and opposite complex exponentials, which sum to a real sinusoid that is potentially a scaled and phase-shifted version of the input but with the same frequency.

8. Natural response

The natural response is given by the differential equation $(2D^2 + 11D + 15)y(t) = 0$. This can be factored as $2((D+3)(D+2.5))y(t) = 0$. Thus, the natural response is given by $c_1 e^{-3t} + c_2 e^{-2.5t}$, where the two constants can be determined from the initial conditions $y(0)$ and $\dot{y}(0)$.

9. Natural response

The natural response is given by the differential equation $2D^2 + 1 = 0$, whose factorization is $\left(D - \dfrac{j}{\sqrt{2}}\right)\left(D + \dfrac{j}{\sqrt{2}}\right)$. The system is therefore given by

$$c_1 e^{\frac{-jt}{\sqrt{2}}} + c_2 e^{\frac{jt}{\sqrt{2}}} = y(t).$$

Setting $y(0) = 0$, we get $c_1 + c_2 = 0$. Setting $\dot{y}(0) = 1$, we get

$$\frac{-jc_1}{\sqrt{2}} + \frac{jc_2}{\sqrt{2}} = 1,$$

which we can rewrite as $c_1 - c_2 = j\sqrt{2}$. Solving, we get

$$c_1 = -\frac{j}{\sqrt{2}}, \; c_2 = \frac{j}{\sqrt{2}},$$

so that the natural response is $-\dfrac{j}{\sqrt{2}} e^{\frac{-jt}{\sqrt{2}}} + \dfrac{j}{\sqrt{2}} e^{\frac{jt}{\sqrt{2}}} = y(t)$. The frequency of this signal is $\dfrac{1}{\sqrt{2}}$ Hz.

10. Stability

The signal reduces to the complex sinusoid $j\sqrt{2}\sin\left(\dfrac{t}{\sqrt{2}}\right)$, whose real value is always zero, so that the system is stable.

11. Fourier series

Since the series is infinite, we can choose to center one of the pulses on the origin and compute the Fourier coefficients in the range $-T_0/2$ to $T_0/2$. The kth coefficient of the Fourier series corresponding to this function is given by

$$c_k = \frac{1}{T_0} \int_{-\frac{T_0}{2}}^{\frac{T_0}{2}} x(t) e^{-jk\omega_0 t} dt.$$

In this range, the function is $1+t$ in the range $[-\tau, 0]$, $1 - t$ in the range $[0, \tau]$ and 0 elsewhere. For convenience, let $a = -jk\omega_0$. Then, the integral reduces to

$$c_k = \frac{1}{T_0}\left(\int_{-\tau}^{0}(1+t)e^{at}dt + \int_{0}^{\tau}(1-t)e^{at}dt\right)$$

$$= \frac{1}{T_0}\left(\int_{-\tau}^{0}e^{at}dt + \int_{-\tau}^{0}te^{at}dt + \int_{0}^{\tau}e^{at}dt - \int_{0}^{\tau}te^{at}dt\right)$$

$$= \frac{1}{T_0}\left(\int_{-\tau}^{\tau}e^{at}dt + \int_{-\tau}^{0}te^{at}dt - \int_{0}^{\tau}te^{at}dt\right)$$

We can solve this as $\frac{1}{T_0}\left(\frac{1}{a}e^{at}\Big|_{-\tau}^{\tau} + \frac{ate^{at}-e^{at}}{a^2}\Big|_{-\tau}^{0} - \frac{ate^{at}-e^{at}}{a^2}\Big|_{0}^{\tau}\right)$, which reduces to

$$\frac{1}{aT_0}\left((e^{a\tau}-e^{-a\tau}) + \left(\frac{e^{-a\tau}-1}{a}+\tau e^{-a\tau}\right) - \left(\frac{e^{a\tau}-1}{a}-\tau e^{a\tau}\right)\right)$$

$$= \left(\frac{(a-1)}{a^2T_0}(e^{a\tau}-e^{-a\tau}) + \frac{\tau}{aT_0}(e^{a\tau}+e^{-a\tau})\right)$$

12. Fourier series

The fundamental frequency $\omega_0 = \frac{2\pi}{10}$. The third coefficient is the value of

$$X(\omega) = \frac{\tau\omega_0}{2\pi}\frac{\sin\left(\frac{\omega\tau}{2}\right)}{\frac{\omega\tau}{2}}$$

for the value $\omega = 3\omega_0 = \frac{6\pi}{10} = 0.6\pi$. This is given by $\frac{1}{10}\frac{\sin(0.3\pi)}{0.3\pi} = 0.085$.

13. Fourier transform

Since the function is nonzero only in the range [0,1], the transform is given by

$$X(j\omega) = \int_{0}^{1}(1-t)e^{-j\omega t}dt = \int_{0}^{1}e^{-j\omega t}dt - \int_{0}^{1}te^{-j\omega t}dt.$$

This reduces to $\frac{e^{-j\omega t}}{-j\omega}\Big|_{0}^{1} + \frac{(-j\omega)te^{-j\omega t}-e^{-j\omega t}}{\omega^2}\Big|_{0}^{1} = \frac{e^{-j\omega}-1}{-j\omega} + \frac{(-j\omega)e^{-j\omega}-e^{-j\omega}+1}{\omega^2}$.

14. Inverse Fourier transform

The inverse transform is given by

$$x(t) = \frac{1}{2\pi} \int\limits_{-\infty}^{\infty} \pi(\delta(\omega + \omega_0) + \delta(\omega - \omega_0))e^{j\omega t}d\omega$$

$$= \frac{1}{2} \int\limits_{-\infty}^{\infty} \delta(\omega + \omega_0)e^{j\omega t}d\omega + \frac{1}{2} \int\limits_{-\infty}^{\infty} \delta(\omega - \omega_0)e^{j\omega t}d\omega.$$

Applying Equation 5.15 twice, the integral reduces to $\dfrac{e^{j\omega_0 t} + e^{-j\omega_0 t}}{2}$, which from Equation 5.5 is $\cos(\omega_0 t)$.

15. Computing the Fourier transform

Using the time-shift and linearity properties and the standard transforms, this is given by $(\pi(\delta(\omega + \omega_0) + \delta(\omega - \omega_0)))e^{j\omega t_0} + (j\pi(\delta(\omega - \omega_0) - \delta(\omega + \omega_0)))e^{-j\omega t_0}$.

16. Laplace transform

We use Euler's formula to rewrite the signal as $u(t)\left(\dfrac{e^{j\omega_0 t} - e^{-j\omega_0 t}}{2j}\right)$. By definition,

$$X(s) = \int\limits_{-\infty}^{\infty} u(t)\left(\frac{e^{j\omega_0 t} - e^{-j\omega_0 t}}{2j}\right)e^{-st}dt = \frac{\left(\int\limits_{0}^{\infty} e^{j\omega_0 t}e^{-st}dt - \int\limits_{0}^{\infty} e^{-j\omega_0 t}e^{-st}dt\right)}{2j}$$

$$= \left(\frac{1}{2j}\left(\frac{1}{s - j\omega_0} - \frac{1}{s + j\omega_0}\right) = \frac{\omega_0}{s^2 + \omega_0^2}\right),$$

with the region of convergence is $Re(s) > 0$. The poles are at $s = \pm j\omega_0$, and the transform is either always 0 if ω_0 is zero or never zero, otherwise.

17. Laplace transform

From the previous exercise and the time-shifting property of the Laplace transform, this is given by $\dfrac{e^{st_0}\omega_0}{s^2 + \omega_0^2}$.

18. Using the Laplace transform to solve a system

From Table 5.4 the Laplace transform of the transfer function $H(s)$ is given by $\dfrac{s}{s^2 + \omega_0^2}$, $Re(s) > 0$. Moreover, because $x(t) = e^{-t}u(t)$, from Table 5.4 $X(s) = \dfrac{1}{s+1}$, $Re(s) > 1$. Therefore, the transform of the system response

$$Y(s) = \left(\frac{1}{s+1}\right)\left(\frac{s}{s^2 + \omega_0^2}\right) = \frac{s}{(s+1)(s + j\omega_0)(s - j\omega_0)}, \; Re(s) > 1.$$

Expanding by partial fractions, we get

$$Y(s) = \frac{\left(\dfrac{-1}{1 + \omega_0^2}\right)}{(1+s)} + \frac{\left(\dfrac{1}{2(1 - j\omega_0)}\right)}{(s + j\omega_0)} + \frac{\left(\dfrac{1}{2(1 + j\omega_0)}\right)}{(s - j\omega_0)}.$$

This allows us to write the time evolution of the system as

$$y(t) = \frac{-e^{-t}}{1 + \omega_0^2} + \frac{e^{-j\omega_0 t}}{2(1 - j\omega_0)} + \frac{e^{j\omega_0 t}}{2(1 + j\omega_0)}.$$

19. Discrete-time Fourier transform

The transform is given by $\dfrac{1}{1 - 0.5e^{-j\omega T}}$.

20. Discrete-time-and-frequency Fourier transform

The fourth Fourier value, with $k = 3$, $X\left[j\dfrac{6\pi}{9}\right]$ is given by

$$\frac{1}{9}\sum_{n=0}^{8} x[nT]e^{-\frac{3j2\pi n}{9}} = \frac{1}{9}\left(1e^{-j\frac{6\pi}{9}} + 2e^{-j\frac{12\pi}{9}} + 3e^{-j\frac{18\pi}{9}} + \ldots + 2e^{-j\frac{42\pi}{9}} + 1e^{-j\frac{48\pi}{9}}\right).$$

21. Z transform

The transform is given by

$$\sum_{k=0}^{\infty} kz^{-k}.$$

Assuming that the series converges, denote the sum by S. Clearly,

$$S = \frac{1}{z} + \frac{2}{z^2} + \frac{3}{z^3} + \dots .$$

Therefore,

$$Sz = 1 + \frac{2}{z} + \frac{3}{z^2} + \dots = \left(1 + \frac{1}{z} + \frac{1}{z^2} + \dots\right) + \left(\frac{1}{z} + \frac{2}{z^2} + \frac{3}{z^3} + \dots\right) = \frac{1}{1 - z^{-1}} + S .$$

Thus, $S(z - 1) = \dfrac{1}{(1 - z^{-1})}$, so that $S = \dfrac{1}{(1 - z^{-1})(z - 1)} = \dfrac{z^{-1}}{(1 - z^{-1})^2}$. Now, this

series converges only when $|z^{-1}| < 1$ or $|z| > 1$. In this region of convergence, the operations on the sum are valid.

22. Z transform

From Example 5.27, the Z transform of the function is $\dfrac{1}{1 - e^a z^{-1}}$. Therefore, from

the time-shift rule, the desired transform is $\dfrac{z^{-k_0}}{1 - e^a z^{-1}}$.

Chapter 6 Stochastic Processes and Queueing Theory

1. Little's theorm

a. The mean waiting time is 180 minutes, and the arrival rate is 0.2 patients/minute. Thus, the mean number of patients is their product = 180*0.2 = 36.

b. We do not have enough information to determine the maximum size of the waiting room! We know we need at least 36 spaces, but it's possible that a burst of a hundred patients may arrive, for example, due to an incident of mass food poisoning. But, as a rule of thumb, some small integer multiple of the mean, such as three or four times the mean, ought to be enough. In real life, we are forced to work with such fudge factors because it is often too difficult or too expensive to determine the exact arrival process, which, in any case, may abruptly change over time.

2. A stochastic process

At time 0, $P[X_0 = 10] = 1.0$.

At time 1, $P[X_1 = 9] = 0.2$; $P[X_1 = 10] = 0.6$; $P[X_1 = 11] = 0.2$.

At time 2, $P[X_2 = 8] = 0.2(0.2) = 0.04$; $P[X_2 = 9] = 0.2(0.6) + 0.6(0.2) = 0.24$;
$P[X_2 = 10] = 0.2(0.2) + 0.6(0.6) + 0.2 (0.2) = 0.44$, and, by symmetry,
$P[X_2 = 11] = 0.24$; $P[X_2 = 12] = 0.04$.

3. Discrete- and continous-state time processes

4. Markov process

The process is Markovian because the probability of moving from stair i to stairs $i - 1$, i, and $i + 1$ do not depend on how the person reached stair i.

5. Homogeneity

The transition probabilities are time-independent, and therefore the process is homogeneous.

6. Representation

a.

$$\begin{bmatrix} \cdots & \cdots & \cdots & \cdots & \cdots & \cdots & \cdots \\ 0 & 0.2 & 0.6 & 0.2 & 0 & \cdots & \cdots \\ \cdots & 0 & 0.2 & 0.6 & 0.2 & 0 & \cdots \\ \cdots & \cdots & 0 & 0.2 & 0.6 & 0.2 & 0 \\ \cdots & \cdots & \cdots & \cdots & \cdots & \cdots & \cdots \end{bmatrix}$$

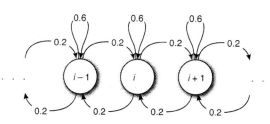

b. The rows need to sum to 1 because at each time step, the process has to move to *some* state. The columns do not need to sum to 1. (Think of a star-shaped state-transition diagram with N states surrounding state 0, where state 0 has $1/N$ probability of going to any other state, and every state returns to state 0 with probability 1.)

c. We need to assume the boundary conditions. Suppose that at stair 1, the probability of staying at the same stair is 0.8 and that at stair 4, the probability of staying at the same stair is also 0.8. Then, the transition matrix and the state-transition diagram are as follows.

$$\begin{bmatrix} 0.8 & 0.2 & 0 & 0 \\ 0.2 & 0.6 & 0.2 & 0 \\ 0 & 0.2 & 0.6 & 0.2 \\ 0 & 0 & 0.2 & 0.8 \end{bmatrix}$$

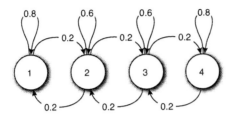

7. Reducibility

The chain is irreducible because every state can be reached from every other state.

8. Recurrence

State 1 is recurrent because the chain is finite and irreducible. $f_1^{\ 1}$ is the probability that the process first returns to state 1 after one time step, and this is 0.8. $f_1^{\ 2}$ is the probability that the process first returns to state 1 after two time steps, and this is 0.2 * 0.2 = 0.04. $f_1^{\ 3}$ is the probability that the process first returns to state 1 after three time steps. This can happen after a transition to state 2, a self-loop in state 2, and then back. Thus, the value is 0.2 * 0.6 * 0.2 = 0.024.

9. Periodicity

The chain is not periodic, because of the self-loop in every state. A trivial chain with period N is a ring with N states, with the transition probability of going from state i to state $(i+1) \bmod N = 1$.

10. Ergodicity

No state in the chain is nonergodic, because the chain is finite aperiodic and irreducible.

11. **Stationary probability**

   From Theorem 6.2, because the chain is ergodic, we obtain

   $$\pi_1^* = 0.8\pi_1^* + 0.2\pi_2^*$$
   $$\pi_2^* = 0.2\pi_1^* + 0.6\pi_2^* + 0.2\pi_3^*$$
   $$\pi_3^* = 0.2\pi_2^* + 0.6\pi_3^* + 0.2\pi_4^*$$
   $$\pi_4^* = 0.2\pi_3^* + 0.8\pi_4^*$$
   $$1 = \pi_1^* + \pi_2^* + \pi_3^* + \pi_4^*$$

   This can be easily solved to obtain $\pi_1^* = \pi_2^* = \pi_3^* = \pi_4^* = 0.25$. (If you choose other assumptions for the boundary states, your computation will differ.)

12. **Residence times**

   Since $p_{11} = p_{44} = 0.8$, the residence times in these states is $1/(1 - 0.8) = 1/0.2 = 5$. $p_{22} = p_{33} = 0.6$, so the residence times in these states is $1/0.4 = 2.5$.

13. **Stationary probability of a birth-death process**

   a. Similarities: Both are graphs, with each node corresponding to a discrete state. Differences: The notation on an edge is the transition rate, not transition probability. The sum of rates leaving a node does not add up to 1, but the total ingress rate matches the total egress rate at each node.

   b. $\begin{bmatrix} -2 & 2 & 0 & 0 \\ 2 & -6 & 4 & 0 \\ 0 & 4 & -6 & 2 \\ 0 & 0 & 2 & -2 \end{bmatrix}$

   c. We have

   $$-2\pi_0^* + 2\pi_1^* = 0$$
   $$2\pi_0^* - 6\pi_1^* + 4\pi_2^* = 0$$
   $$4\pi_1^* - 6\pi_2^* + 2\pi_3^* = 0$$
   $$2\pi_2^* - 2\pi_3^* = 0$$
   $$\pi_0^* + \pi_1^* + \pi_2^* + \pi_3^* = 1$$

   This yields: $\pi_0^* = \pi_1^* = \pi_2^* = \pi_3^* = 0.25$.

14. Poisson process

Consider a pure-death process (i.e., a birth-death process whose birth rates are zero). Clearly, the interdeparture times are nothing more than the residence times in each state. But we know that the residence times in a homogeneous continuous-time Markov chain are exponentially distributed (see 6.3.2). Q.E.D.

15. Stationary probabilities of a birth-death process

We see that in this chain, $\lambda_i = \mu_{i+1}$ so immediately we get $\pi_0^* = \pi_1^* = \pi_2^* = \pi_3^*$. By summing them to 1, we can see that they are all 0.25.

16. M/M/1 queue

It is not M/M/1 because the state-transition rates are state-dependent.

17. M/M/1 queue

a. The packet length is 250 bytes = 2,000 bits, so that the link service rate of 1,000,000 bits/sec = 500 packets/sec. Therefore, the utilization is 450/500 = 0.9. When the link queue has one packet, it is in state $j = 2$ because one packet is being served at that time. Thus, we need $\pi_2^* = 0.9^2 * 0.1 = 0.081$. For the queue having two packets, we compute $\pi_3^* = 0.9^3 * 0.1 = 0.0729$. For ten packets in the queue, we compute $\pi_{11}^* = 0.9^{11} * 0.1 = 0.031$. (Compare these with values in Example 19, where the load is 0.8.)

b. The mean number of packets in the system is $0.9/1 - 0.9 = 9$. Of these, eight are expected to be in the queue.

c. The mean waiting time is $(1/500)/(1 - 0.9) = 0.002/0.1 = 0.02 = 20$ milliseconds.

18. Responsive (M/M/∞) server

The ratio is:

$$\frac{e^{-\rho}\rho^j \frac{1}{j!}}{\rho^j(1-\rho)} = \frac{e^{-\rho}}{j!(1-\rho)} = \frac{1}{j!(1-\rho)e^\rho} = \frac{C}{j!}$$

where C is a constant with respect to j. Therefore, for an M/M/∞ queue, the probability of being in state j diminishes proportional to $j!$ compared to being in state j for an M/M/1 queue. Clearly, this favors much lower queue lengths for the M/M/∞ queue.

19. M/M/1/K server

Packet losses happen when there is an arrival and the system is in state $j=11$. This is upper bounded by P_{11}, which is given by

$$P_{11} = \frac{1-\rho}{1-\rho^{K+1}}\rho^j = \frac{0.1}{1-0.9^{12}}0.9^{11} = 0.0437$$

20. M/D/1 queue

a. The mean number of customers in the system for such a queue is given by

$$\rho + \frac{\rho^2}{2(1-\rho)} = 0.9 + \frac{0.9^2}{2(0.1)} = 4.95,$$

which is roughly half the size of an equivalently loaded M/M/1 queue (from Exercise 17(b)).

b. The ratio is $\dfrac{\rho + \dfrac{\rho^2}{2(1-\rho)}}{\dfrac{\rho}{1-\rho}} = 1 - \dfrac{\rho}{2}$. This tends to 0.5 as the utilization tends to 1.

c. Under heavy loads, the mean waiting time for an M/D/1 queue is half that of a similarly loaded M/M/1 queue.

Chapter 7 Game Theory

1. Preferences

a. Denote apple = A, banana = B, carrot = C, peach = P. We are free to choose utilities as we wish, so let $U(A) = 0$, $U(C) = 1$. Then, $U(B) = 0.7$ and $U(P) = 0.9$, so you prefer peaches to bananas.

b. Let $P(\text{win B}) = p$. Then, $0.7p + 1(1-p) = .9$, so $0.3p = 0.1$, so $p = 0.33$.

2. Utility functions

Your net utility from transferring x GB is $100(1 - e^{-0.25x})$ if $x < 10$ and $100(1 - e^{-0.25x}) - 5(x - 10)$ otherwise. The plot of these two functions is shown in the figure. It is clear that the maximum occurs at $x=10$ for a value of approximately 92. So, your utility is maximized by transferring exactly 10 GB/month.

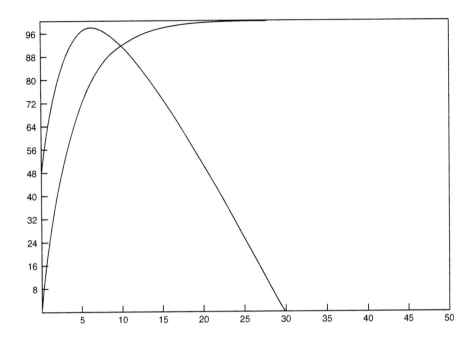

3. Pure and mixed strategies

The only possible first actions are: play corner, play middle, and play center. Depending on which move is played, the second player would have response; depending on that response, the first player would have a response, and so on. A pure strategy for each player is each valid response to the prior move (whether or not it is rational). A mixed strategy would play one of the pure strategies (i.e, the entire sequence) with some probability. It turns out that in tic-tac-toe, with two expert players, a tie is guaranteed with a pure strategy, but a mixed strategy (depending over what you mix) could lose when played against an optimal strategy. So, it never makes sense to mix. In general, every component of a mixed strategy must be a potentially winning strategy. Otherwise, the mixed strategy would improve by discarding a component that can never win.

4. Zero-sum game

No, because utilities are unique only to an affine transformation.

5. Representation

	L	M	H
Y	$(1, a - 1)$	$(2, a - 2)$	$(3, a - 3)$
N	$(0,0)$	$(0,0)$	$(0,0)$

6. Representation

We need to prove two things: (a) if information sets are permitted, every normal-form game can be represented in extensive form; (b) if information sets are permitted, every extensive-form game can be represented in normal form. To prove (a): Given a normal-form game with n players, draw a tree of depth n, where all moves by the first player are associated with a node with an edge leading from the root to that node, and all nodes are in the same information set. Then, from each such node, draw an edge for each possible move for the second player, and place each set of nodes in the same information set. Repeat for each successive player, and label the leaves with the payoff from the corresponding array element. To prove (b): Given the extensive-form game, form paths from the root to each leaf. Decompose the path into moves by each of the players, and find all possible moves by each player each time it is allowed to make a move. Let S_i^t denote the set of moves that player i can move on its t turn. Then, the strategy space for player i is the cross product of these sets. Finally, the normal form is an n-dimensional matrix with the ith dimension indexed by the strategy space of the ith player and the corresponding element having the payoff for these strategies.

7. Best response

The best response depends on the value of a. For each of the strategies of the ISP (i.e., L, M, and H), the best response is Y if $a - price > 0$; otherwise, it is N.

8. Dominant strategy

If you attend, your payoff is your utility for either pass or fail; if you miss, your payoff is your utility for fail. Assuming that utility(pass) > utility(fail), your payoff for attending is as good as or better than the payoff for not attending. So, your dominant strategy is to attend.

9. Bayesian game

It is easy to verify that no matter the type of the column player (strong or weak signal), the best response for Row if Column plays S is D and if Column plays

D, it is S. Therefore, knowing the type of the column player does not help Row, and the game does not have a dominant strategy for Row.

10. Repeated game

The one-shot payoff is −3 for each, so the repeated payoff is

$$-3 * \sum_{i=0}^{\infty} 0.6^i = -3/0.4 = -7.5.$$

11. Dominant-strategy equilibrium

It is dominant for both players to send rather than wait. In equilibrium, they always send right away, so their packets always collide, and in fact, no progress is made, so that delays are actually infinite. This game illustrates the aphorism: Haste makes waste. The EDCA protocol allows higher-priority (delay-sensitive) stations to wait for a shorter time than lower-priority stations before accessing the medium, therefore making it more probable that they would get access to the medium earlier and experience a shorter delay.

12. Iterated deletion

Consider the following game, where we show the payoffs only for Row:

	C1	C2
R1	0	0
R2	1	−1
R3	−2	2

Neither R2 nor R3 dominates R1. However, any mixed strategy of R2 and R3 that plays R3 with a probability greater than 2/3 dominates R1. Therefore, we can delete R1 from the game.

13. Maximin

In Example 7.10, Row can get as low as −1 with S but at least 0 with D, so its maximin strategy is D. Column is assured 1 with S, so its maximin strategy is S, and the equilibrium is DS.

In Example 7.15, Row maximizes its minimum payoff with S. The game is symmetric, so the maximin equilibrium is SS.

14. Maximin in a zero-sum game

In Figure 7.3, note that when p is smaller than 0.5, the column player can play pure strategy C1 to reduce Row's payoff below 2.5. Similarly, if p is greater than 0.5, Column can use a pure strategy C2 to reduce Row's payoff. For any value of p, Column can play a mixture $qC1 + (1 - q) C2$ to give Row a payoff of $q(p + 2) + (1 - q)(4 - 3p)$. To make this smaller than 2.5, we set $q(p + 2) + (1 - q)(4 - 3p) < 2.5$, or $q > (3 - 6p)/(4 - 8p)$. For instance, if $p=0$, $q > 3/4$, and if $p = 1$, $q > 3/4$. (The inequality is not valid when $p = 0.5$.)

15. Nash equilibrium

Let the row player play $pH + (1 - p)T$. Then, its payoff, given Column's mixed strategy, is $p(q - (1 - q)) + (1 - p)(-q + (1 - q)) = 4pq - 2q - 2p + 1 = (1 - 2p)(1 - 2q)$. If $q < 0.5$, p should be 0, otherwise p should be 1. Intuitively, if the column player is more likely to play T, then Row should play T for sure and vice versa.

16. Correlated equilibrium

Consider an external agency that tells the players to play $pDS + (1 - p)SD$. When Row is told to play D, it knows that it will get a payoff of -1 if it deviates. Similarly, when told to play S, Row will get 0 (instead of 1) if it deviates. So, Row will not deviate, independent of the value of p. By symmetry, the same analysis holds for Column, and therefore we have a correlated equilibrium. The external agency can arrange for any desired payoffs to Row and Column by adjusting p.

17. Price discrimination

Assume that the valuations of each player are $v_1,...,v_n$ for minimum quantities of $q_1,...,q_n$. The scheme is essentially to charge v_i for q_i, adjusting for the fact that player i could buy multiples of q_j $j<i$ if that minimizes its total cost.

18. VCG mechanism

a. The overall function is $(20 + 40 + 80)(1 - e^{-0.5x}) - 20x = 140(1 - e^{-0.5x}) - 20x$.

b. The types are the only unknowns in the utility functions (i.e., 20, 40, and 80, respectively).

c. The optimal social choice comes from maximizing the function in (a). Setting $f(x) = 140(1 - e^{-0.5x}) - 20x$, solve for $f'(x^*) = 0$, so that $x^* = 2.5055$.

d. To compute x^{-1}, we maximize $(120(1 - e^{-0.5x}) - 20x)$ to get 2.197. Similarly, $x^{-2} = 1.832$, and $x^{-3} = 0.8109$. Thus, $p_1 = v_2(x^{-1}) + v_3(x^{-1}) - (v_2(x^*) + v_3(x^*)) = (40 + 80)(1 - e^{-0.5*2.197}) - (40 + 80)(1 - e^{-0.5*2.5055}) = 120 * (e^{-1.25275} - e^{-1.0985}) = -5.718$.

Similarly, $p_2 = v_1(x^{-2}) + v_3(x^{-2}) - (v_1(x^*) + v_3(x^*)) = 100(e^{-1.25275} - e^{-0.5*1.832}) = -11.439$,

$p_3 = v_1(x^{-3}) + v_2(x^{-3}) - (v_1(x^*) + v_2(x^*)) = 60(e^{-0.5*0.8109} - e^{-1.25275}) = 60 *$
$(e^{-1.25275} - e^{-0.4055}) = -22.857$.

  e. No, the budget is not balanced: The CIO has to pay each department.

Chapter 8 Elements of Control Theory

1. **A bandwidth management system**

   The plant is the congested link. The command is the desired maximum percentage of P2P traffic on this link. The control input is the number of P2P connections that are reset at a particular time. The disturbance is the intrinsic fluctuations in the number of P2P connections. The output is the percentage of P2P connections on the link.

2. **Effort and flow**

   The effort is the number of connections that need to be reset at a point in time. The flow is the number of connections that are actually reset per unit time.

3. **State space representation**

   The natural state variable for this system is $x(t)$ = the current fraction of P2P traffic. The state evolution is given by

   $$\dot{x} = \left\{ \begin{array}{l} -\dfrac{u}{T} + w \;\; \text{if } (x > r) \\[2mm] w \;\; \text{otherwise} \end{array} \right\}$$

4. **Transfer function**

   The output y is related to the input by

   $$\dot{y} = -\frac{u}{T} + w .$$

   Taking the Laplace transform of both sides, we get

   $$sY(s) = \frac{-U(s)}{T} + W(s) .$$

Ignoring W, we have

$$\frac{Y(s)}{U(s)} = G(s) = -\frac{1}{sT},$$

which is the desired transfer function.

5. First-order system

A first-order system reaches the 63% mark at τ, so $\tau = 3$. The asymptotic value is K, so $K = 4.25$. The transfer function is

$$G(s) = \frac{K}{1 + \tau s} = \frac{4.25}{1 + 3s}.$$

6. Second-order system

We have $Y(s) = \dfrac{K}{s\left(\dfrac{s^2}{\omega_n^2} + \dfrac{2\varsigma s}{\omega_n} + 1\right)} = \dfrac{K}{s\left(\dfrac{s^2}{\omega_n^2} + \dfrac{2s}{\omega_n} + 1\right)} = \dfrac{K}{s\left(\dfrac{s}{\omega_n} + 1\right)^2}.$

We use partial fraction expansion to write this as

$$Y(s) = K\left[\frac{1}{s} - \frac{\omega_n}{(s + \omega_n)^2} - \frac{1}{(s + \omega_n)}\right].$$

The solution is obtained by finding the inverse Laplace transform term by term, using Table 5.4.

7. Proportional-mode control

The system pole is at $-$(loop gain).

8. Integral-mode control

The impulse response is

$$Y = \frac{K_i}{(s^2 + K_i)} = \sqrt{K_i}\left(\frac{\sqrt{K_i}}{s^2 + (\sqrt{K_i})^2}\right).$$

Taking the inverse Laplace transform, this is given by $\sqrt{K_i}\sin\sqrt{K_i}t$.

9. Stability

The roots are -0.10812, $-0.72122 + j0.61911$, $-0.72122 - j0.61911$, $1.44195 + j1.15457$, $1.44195 - j1.15457$. Because two roots have a real component in the right half of the complex s plane, the system is BIBO unstable.

10. Matrix exponential

We have

$$e^{\dot{A}t} = 0 + A + \frac{2A^2t}{2!} + \frac{3A^3t^2}{3!} + \dots = A + A^2t + \frac{A^3t^2}{2!} + \frac{A^4t^3}{3!}$$

and

$$Ae^{At} = A\left(e^{At} = I + At + \frac{A^2t^2}{2!} + \frac{A^3t^3}{3!} + \dots\right) = A + A^2t + \frac{A^3t^2}{2!} + \frac{A^4t^3}{3!} + \dots .$$

Both terms are equal term by term; and therefore, the infinite sums also are equal, proving that

$$e^{At} = I + At + \frac{A^2t^2}{2!} + \frac{A^3t^3}{3!} + \dots \text{ satisfies } \dot{x} = Ax .$$

11. Matrix exponential

Because A is diagonal, $A^r = \begin{bmatrix} a_{11}^r & 0 & 0 & 0 \\ 0 & a_{22}^r & 0 & 0 \\ \dots & \dots & \dots & \dots \\ 0 & 0 & 0 & a_{nn}^r \end{bmatrix}$.

So, $e^{At} = I + At + \frac{A^2t^2}{2!} + \frac{A^3t^3}{3!} + \dots =$

$$\begin{bmatrix} 1 & 0 & 0 & 0 \\ 0 & 1 & 0 & 0 \\ \dots & \dots & \dots & \dots \\ 0 & 0 & 0 & 1^r \end{bmatrix} + \begin{bmatrix} a_{11}t & 0 & 0 & 0 \\ 0 & a_{22}t & 0 & 0 \\ \dots & \dots & \dots & \dots \\ 0 & 0 & 0 & a_{nn}t \end{bmatrix} + \begin{bmatrix} \frac{a_{11}^2}{2}t^2 & 0 & 0 & 0 \\ 0 & \frac{a_{22}^2}{2}t^2 & 0 & 0 \\ \dots & \dots & \dots & \dots \\ 0 & 0 & 0 & \frac{a_{nn}^2}{2}t^2 \end{bmatrix} + \begin{bmatrix} \frac{a_{11}^3}{3!}t^3 & 0 & 0 & 0 \\ 0 & \frac{a_{22}^3}{3!}t^3 & 0 & 0 \\ \dots & \dots & \dots & \dots \\ 0 & 0 & 0 & \frac{a_{nn}^3}{3!}t^3 \end{bmatrix} + \dots$$

$$= \begin{bmatrix} \sum_i \dfrac{(a_{11}t)^i}{i!} & 0 & 0 & 0 \\ 0 & \sum_i \dfrac{(a_{22}t)^i}{i!} & 0 & 0 \\ \cdots & \cdots & \cdots & \cdots \\ 0 & 0 & 0 & \sum_i \dfrac{(a_{nn}t)^i}{i!} \end{bmatrix} = \begin{bmatrix} e^{a_{11}t} & 0 & 0 & 0 \\ 0 & e^{a_{22}t} & 0 & 0 \\ \cdots & \cdots & \cdots & \cdots \\ 0 & 0 & 0 & e^{a_{nn}t} \end{bmatrix}.$$

Therefore, e^{At} for $A = \begin{bmatrix} 3 & 0 & 0 \\ 0 & -4 & 0 \\ 0 & 0 & -1 \end{bmatrix} = \begin{bmatrix} e^{(3t)} & 0 & 0 \\ 0 & e^{(-4t)} & 0 \\ 0 & 0 & e^{-t} \end{bmatrix}.$

12. Partial fraction expansion

Let $\dfrac{s}{(s+3)(s+5)} = \dfrac{a_1}{s+3} + \dfrac{a_2}{s+5}$.

$$a_1 = \lim_{s \to -3} (s+3)\frac{s}{(s+3)(s+5)} = \lim_{s \to -3} \frac{s}{(s+5)} = -1.5.$$

$$a_2 = \lim_{s \to -5} (s+5)\frac{s}{(s+3)(s+5)} = \lim_{s \to -5} \frac{s}{(s+3)} = 2.5.$$

13. Partial fraction expansion

Using the quadratic formula, we find $s = 2 \pm j5$. Therefore, we write the fraction as

$$f(s) = \frac{1}{(s-(2+j5))(s-(2-j5))} = \frac{a_1}{(s-(2+j5))} + \frac{a_2}{(s-(2-j5))}.$$

Then,

$$a_1 = \lim_{s \to (2+j5)} (s-(2+j5))\left(\frac{1}{(s-(2+j5))(s-(2-j5))}\right)$$

$$= \frac{1}{(2+j5-(2-j5))} = \frac{1}{j10}$$

and $a_2 = \dfrac{1}{-j10}$, so that $f(s) = \dfrac{1}{j10(s-(2+j5))} - \dfrac{1}{j10(s-(2-j5))}.$

Chapter 9 Information Theory

1. Entropy

The entropy is $-(0.25\log 0.25 + 0.25\log 0.25 + 0.25\log 0.25 + 0.125\log 0.125 + 0.125\log 0.125) = 2.25$ bits.

2. Entropy

Since all messages are equally likely, the entropy is given by log(number of distinct messages) $= \log(16^{100}) = 100\log 16 = 400$ bits.

3. Instantaneous codes

acc, ad, and bc.

4. Instantaneous codes

The codewords lie at the leaves of a binary tree, so this code is instantaneous.

5. Digit coding

The number of distinct strings represented by n decimal digits is 10^n; which can be represented by a binary string of length no shorter than $\log 10^n$. The mean number of bits per digit is given by

$$\frac{\log 10^n}{n} = \log 10 = 3.32,$$

which is also the asymptotic limit.

6. Feasibility of a code

From the Kraft inequality, $\sum_i 2^{-l_i} \le 1$. Here, we have

$$\sum_i 2^{-l_i} = \frac{1}{4} + \frac{1}{4} + \frac{1}{4} + \frac{1}{8} + \frac{1}{16} + \frac{1}{64} + \frac{1}{64} + \frac{1}{64} + \frac{1}{128} + \frac{1}{128} + \frac{1}{128} + \frac{1}{128}$$
$$= 1.015625 > 1.$$

This violates the Kraft inequality, so you should disbelieve your friend.

7. Optimal codes

The source entropy is 1.94 bits, which is also the expected length of the shortest instantaneous code.

8. Huffman codes

Two possible Huffman codes are a: 00, b: 01, c: 10, d: 11, a: 01, b: 00, c: 10, d: 11. The expected code length 2 bits, which is less than (entropy + 1) bits, because the entropy is 1.94 bits.

9. Huffman codes

Consider the source message $aabbaaabb$. Since there are no c or d symbols in the message, we could use for this message the code a: 0, b: 1, which has a shorter encoding than the Huffman encoding.

10. Entropy rate

Each symbol has an entropy of 1.94 bits. In 1 second, the source generates 100 independent symbols, so its entropy rate is 194 bits/second. In 100 seconds, it generates an entropy of 19,400 bits, which corresponds to $2^{19,400}$ distinct messages.

11. Typical messages

The number of distinct messages with 12 symbols is $2^{12} = 4096$. For a message to be atypical, it must have at least 10 of the 1 symbols. The total number of such messages is

$$\binom{12}{10} + \binom{12}{11} + \binom{12}{12} = 66 + 12 + 1 = 79.$$

So, the fraction of atypical messages is 79/4096 = 0.0192.

The entropy per symbol is 0.469 bits, so the entropy of a set of messages of length 50 symbols is 23.35. The size of the typical set is $2^{23.35} = 10,691,789$ messages, and this is the number of codes that need to be assigned to messages of length 50 symbols to ensure that the number of uncoded messages is vanishingly small.

12. A noiseless channel

Each symbol from this source has an entropy of 1.94 bits. So, the channel can carry 100/1.94 = 51.55 symbols/second.

13. Mutual information

The probability of each symbol on the channel is given by:

	$P(X)$
$X=0$	0.2
$X=1$	0.8

Therefore, $H(X) = -(0.2 \log 0.2 + 0.8 \log 0.8) = 0.72$. To compute $H(X|Y)$, we first need to know the distribution of Y. From Table 9.3, we find this to be

	$P(Y)$
$Y=0$	0.028
$Y=1$	0.972

From Table 9.4, the conditional distribution of X given $Y = 0$ is

	$P(X|Y=0)$
$X=0$	0.7142
$X=1$	0.2857

which has an entropy of 0.863 bits.
From Table 9.5, the conditional distribution of X given $Y = 1$ is

	$P(X|Y=1)$
$X=0$	0.185
$X=1$	0.815

which has an entropy of 0.691. We multiply these conditional entropies by the probability of Y being 0 or 1, respectively, to compute $H(X|Y)$ as $0.028 * 0.863 + 0.972 * 0.691 = 0.695$. Therefore, the mutual information is $I(X;Y) = 0.72 - 0.695 = 0.024$ bits/symbol.

14. Mutual information

$$I(X;Y) = \sum_X \sum_Y P(xy) \log \frac{P(xy)}{P(x)P(y)} \quad \text{(by definition)}$$

$$= \sum_X \sum_Y P(xy) \log \frac{P(x|y)}{P(x)} \quad \text{(by definition of conditional probability } P(x|y) = \frac{P(xy)}{P(y)} \text{)}$$

$$= \sum_X \sum_Y P(xy) \log P(x|y) - \sum_X \sum_Y P(xy) \log P(x) \quad \text{(expanding log } (a/b) \text{ as log } a - \log b)$$

$$= -H(X|Y) - \sum_X \left(\sum_Y P(xy) \log P(x) \right) \quad \text{(from definition of } H(X|Y))$$

$$= -H(X|Y) - \sum_X P(x) \log P(x) \quad \text{(summing } P(xy) \text{ over } Y \text{ gives us } P(x))$$

$$= H(X) - H(X|Y).$$

The symmetric result is obtained by converting $\frac{P(xy)}{P(x)P(y)}$ to $\frac{P(y|x)}{P(x)}$ in step 2 and proceeding along the same lines.

15. Capacity of a binary symmetric channel

$C = 1 + e\log e + (1 - e)\log(1 - e)$ bits/symbol. We have $e = 0.01$, so $C = 1 + 0.001$ log 0.001 + 0.999 log 0.999 = 0.991 bits/symbol. This is 0.009 bits/symbol lower than the channel capacity of the noiseless channel, whose capacity is 1 bit/symbol.

16. Capacity of a Gaussian channel

$P/N = 10^{5/10} = 3.162$. So, the channel capacity is $10 * 10^6 * \log(1 + 3.162) = 10 * 10^6 * 2.06 = 20.6$ Mbps. To achieve a capacity of 50 Mbps, we set $50 * 10^6 = 10 * 10^6 * \log(1 + P/N)$, so that $\log(1 + P/N) = 5$, and $P/N = 31$. This corresponds to a decibel value of $10 * \log_{10}(31) = 14.9$ dB.

Index